Women, the Family, and Divorce Laws in Islamic History

 Contemporary Issues in the Middle East

Women, the Family, and Divorce Laws in Islamic History

Edited by

Amira El Azhary Sonbol

With a Foreword by
Elizabeth Warnock Fernea

Syracuse University Press

Dedicated to
Zahiyya al-Sawi and Soad al-Odeissy

First Edition 1996
02 03 04 05 06 07   8 7 6 5 4 3 2

This book is part of the Mohamed El-Hindi Series on Arab Culture and Islamic Civilization and is published with the assistance of a grant from the M.E.H. Foundation.

The paper used in this publication meets the minimum requirements of American National
Standard for Information Sciences—Permanence of Paper for Printed Library Materials,
ANSI Z39.48-1984. ∞™

Library of Congress Cataloging-in-Publication Data

Women, the family, and divorce laws in Islamic history / edited by
    Amira El Azhary Sonbol ; with a foreword by Elizabeth Warnock
    Fernea.—1st ed.
        p.   cm.—(Contemporary issues in the Middle East)
    Includes bibliographical references (p.   ) and index.
        ISBN 0-8156-2688-6 (alk. paper).—ISBN 0-8156-0383-5 (pbk. :
    alk. paper)
        1. Muslim women—History.   2. Women—Legal status, laws, etc.
    (Islamic law)—Arab countries.   3. Domestic relations (Islamic law)—
    Arab countries.   I. Sonbol, Amira El Azhary.   II. Series.
    HQ1170.W84   1996
    305.48′6971—dc20   95-40354

Manufactured in the United States of America

Contents

Tables

Foreword

Elizabeth Warnock Fernea

The work that follows, *Women, the Family, and Divorce Laws in Islamic History,* challenges the received wisdom about the status of Middle Eastern women. It does so on many levels, putting in question Western perceptions: Middle Eastern women as passive and incapable of acting to improve their position; Middle Eastern women as prisoners of Islamic family law; Middle Eastern women as pathetic figures universally deprived of their inheritance.

Amira El Azhary Sonbol, the editor, and herself a historian, demonstrates the folly of intellectual interpretation based on a single reading of the text or archive, or a single monograph describing women in one Middle Eastern country at a particular time in history. She has done this by gathering together eighteen essays by historians of differing origins and perspectives: men and women who are Middle Easterners, Europeans, and Americans. Fourteen of the articles are based on careful archival research in several languages. The articles also demonstrate that archival documents may not always yield the same answers: what emerges depends on the questions asked, and those questions in turn depend on the preconceptions and interests of the researcher.

Sonbol's contributors are looking at archival materials with fresh eyes and asking new questions of those documents. This approach is important for any history. For example, Sharon Quigley Carpenter, recorder of deeds for the city of St. Louis, Missouri, has noted in a recent article that if one examines the historical materials themselves rather than the generalized indexes of those materials, women in St. Louis had far more equality with men before 1850. She points out that Oscar Collet, in an effort to help historians, produced in the mid-1800's an alphabetical index of all colonial and postcolonial records. In so doing, he made slavery disappear—on paper—because "emancipations" are not in his index. And any economic transactions or property inherited by a woman was indexed under her husband's name, even if he were dead! Only now have women historians begun to bypass the Collet index and search painstakingly through the individual documents. And as they do so, a very different picture of Missouri women emerges—economically independent, capable of divorce and remarriage, enjoying political rights.[1]

This is what Amira Sonbol is doing in her work, looking backward and forward in time at women's legal and economic position. New research methods, new language skills, new scholars, often women like Sonbol herself, are beginning to change the way Middle Eastern history is viewed, to animate and deepen serious women's studies across the globe. This is a hopeful and encouraging trend.

Forty years ago, when I first traveled to the Middle East with my husband, the social anthropologist Robert Fernea, information about the actual lives of Middle Eastern women was almost nonexistent. From what was to be found in the writings of travelers and missionaries, I gained an idea of a group that was oppressed, enslaved, veiled, illiterate, passive, yet at the same time exciting and erotic! My mother urged me to enlighten these poor people. They were exceptions, of course. Lady Mary Wortley Montagu (1688–1762), the wife of the British ambassador to the Sublime Porte, traveled to Istanbul in 1717 and wrote that Turkish women, despite their veils, or *yashmaks,* were "the only free persons in the Ottoman Empire." Why? Because they had the right to own, manage, and inherit property, a right which English women did not gain until the twentieth century. Generally, travelers and missionaries sent home the accounts that the readers expected, accounts that only confirmed Western preconceptions. Even in this century, Gertrude Bell could explain that Middle Eastern women were poor and disorganized housekeepers as they had "no proper cupboards"; and Edith Wharton, on the basis of one afternoon in the company of a Moroccan gentleman's wives, could repeat that, indeed, these women were hardly human, pathetic and passive, without ambition or energy. It is not surprising that early Western feminists decried the state of Middle Eastern women and

---

1. This changed only when Napoleon sold his claims to the Mississippi in the Louisiana Purchase, and the Mississippi territory came under English common law. That law disenfranchised women, and so the Collet index is a historical document of their changed status.

saw their mission as one of bringing these creatures up to the level Western women had achieved. My mother certainly felt that way!

For many years after the first period in the Arab world, I obediently read anthropological accounts of the new paradigm that explained everything about Middle Eastern women: this was the public-private split. Men occupied the public sphere of politics and economics, the important areas of life. Women occupied the private sphere, the world of family, which was seen as peripheral to the center of society. Slowly, I realized that this assessment, like the accounts of early travelers and missionaries, was also a construction, albeit a more sophisticated one, based on preconceived ideas about the role of women and men. Like the new Anglo rulers who came into the Missouri territory convinced that English common law was the basis for male and female roles, the British and American anthropologists constructed Middle Eastern society in their own image. The importance of family relationships in economic and political life, the subject of this book, was completely disregarded.

Thus, one might conclude, as I did, that Western perceptions of Middle Eastern women are based not only on a limited knowledge of the area and the culture and on old preconceptions but also on their perceptions of themselves. Western women from the English-speaking world have struggled for the past century to achieve some economic, legal, and political parity, attempting to overcome a long tradition of inequality. Coming from behind, they sometimes lay upon women in other societies the burdens from which they have only recently been freed. This is particularly problematic in regard to the Middle East, given the early cultural superiority of the Middle East, and the recent shifts in economic and political power between East and West.

The writers of the essays that follow Sonbol's informative introduction are urging the reader to look beyond old paradigms, to reevaluate preconceptions, to consider new evidence and new interpretations. Paul Ricoeur, the anthropologist, once wrote that "hermeneutics is the comprehension of the self by means of the detour of the comprehension of the other." This is good advice, for Westerners have often judged, rather than tried to "comprehend" the other. Amira Sonbol and the contributors to this volume are pulling back the veils of history, providing us with the means to begin to comprehend the status of women in seventeenth-, eighteenth-, and nineteenth-century Middle Eastern society. We are in their debt.

Contributors

Abdal-Rehim Abdal-Rahman Abdal-Rehim is professor, Department of History, Azhar University in Cairo, and is at present on loan to the Department of History of the Emirates. Previously, he taught at Princeton, Tokyo, Qatar, and Riyadh universities and was president of the Egyptian Historical Association. Among his dozens of books and articles, the following works have been the most acclaimed: *al-Rif al-misri fi al-qarn al-thamin ʿashar; al-Maghariba fi misr fi al-ʿasr al-ʿuthmani; Fusul min tarikh misr al-iqtisadi wa al-ijtimaʿi fi al-ʿasr al-ʿuthmani.*

Mohamed Afifi is associate professor of history, Cairo University. Author of a number of articles on Ottoman Egypt, he has published two books on that period: *al-Awqaf fi misr al-ʿuthmaniyya,* and *al-aqbat fi misr.*

Iris Agmon teaches at the University of Haifa. She participates in conferences held in Israel and Europe.

Julia Clancy-Smith is associate professor of modern North African and Middle Eastern history at the University of Arizona. She obtained her Ph.D. in history from the University of California, Los Angeles, in 1988 and is the author of numerous articles on nineteenth-century North African and French imperial history. She recently published a scholarly monograph entitled: *Rebel and Saint: Muslim Notables, Populist Protest, Colonial Encounters (Algeria and Tunisia 1800–1904),* which was awarded the 1995 Alf Heggoy prize by the French Colonial Historical Society. She is currently working on an edited volume with Frances Gouda devoted to women and the gendered rhetoric of the French and Dutch empires.

Mary Ann Fay is assistant professor of history at the Virginia Military Institute, Lexington, Virginia. She has written on various aspects of women's lives in eighteenth-century Egypt, including their property ownership and the institution of the harem. She is conducting research for a book on elite women in Ottoman Egypt sponsored by the Fulbright Scholars Program and a grant from the NEH/American Research Center in Egypt.

Peter Gran is associate professor of Middle East history at Temple University. He is author of *Islamic Roots of Capitalism* and *Beyond Eurocentrism, a New View of Modern World History* (Syracuse University Press, 1996).

Nelly Hanna is assistant professor at the American University of Cairo. She has published widely in Europe and the Middle East. Best known among her numerous books are *Habitait le Caire* and *The History of Bulaq*.

Svetlana Ivanona is an Ottoman historian and expert on Ottoman *sicil*s in the Balkans. Her research focused on "The Mahalle in Bulgarian Towns, 15th-16th c." She is curator at the Oriental Department in the National Library in Sofia. She has published a number of articles and is now writing a book entitled "Marriage and Divorce in the Eighteenth Century According to Local *Sicil*s."

Dina Rizk Khouri is assistant professor of Middle Eastern history at George Washington University. She has published works on the social and economic history of Ottoman Iraq and is currently working on an urban history of Mosul in the Early Modern period.

Dalenda Largueche is assistant professor, Department of History, University of Tunis. Her published works include two books: *Marginales en terre d'islam* and *Watan al-Munastir: Monographie d'histoire régionale 1676–1856*. She has published numerous articles on the history of Muslim women, including: "Crise, femme et violence dans la Tunisie precoloniale" and "Source archivistique et histoire de la femme tunisienne à l'époque moderne: propriété et statut social."

Afaf Lutfi Al-Sayyid Marsot is professor of history at the University of California, Los Angeles. She was president of the Middle East Studies Association in 1977; editor of the *International Journal of Middle East*

Studies, 1980–1985, and president of the American Research Center in Egypt 1990–1993. She has written over thirty articles on the Arab world, women, humor, fundamentalism, and the ʿulamaʾ. She is also the author of *Egypt and Cromer, Egypt's Liberal Experiment,* and *Egypt in the Reign of Muhammad Ali.*

Margaret L. Meriwether is associate professor in the Department of History, Denison University. She is writing a book on family law in Aleppo, 1770–1850. She is the recipient of Fulbright and SSRC fellowships, and is the author of "Women and Economic Change in Nineteenth-Century Syria: The Case of Aleppo," which appeared in the book *Arab Women.*

Najwa al-Qattan is a Ph.D. candidate in history and Middle Eastern studies at Harvard University. Her dissertation is on the socioeconomic history of the Damascene Christian and Jewish communities in the eighteenth and nineteenth centuries. Her publications include "The Damascene Jewish Community in the Latter Decades of the Eighteenth Century: Aspects of Socioeconomic Life Based on the Registers of the Shariʿa Courts," in *The Syrian Land in the 18th and 19th Centuries;* and *"Ahl al-Dhimmah* and the *Shariʿa* Court *Sijills*: A Textual Analysis." Her paper in this volume won the Ibn Khaldun prize for the most outstanding paper submitted by a graduate student in 1994 by the Middle East Studies Association, North America.

Amira Sonbol is assistant professor of Society, History and Law at the Center of Muslim Christian Understanding, School of Foreign Service, Georgetown University. She is the author of *The Creation of a Medical Profession in Egypt* (Syracuse University Press, 1992), "Egyptian Society and Sectarian Strife" in *The Political Economy of Modern Egypt,* and "Egypt" in *The Politics of Islamic Revivalism: Diversity and Unity.* Other contributions include: "Adoption in Islamic Society: A Historical Survey" in *Children of the Modern Arab World* and "Changing Ideals of Feminine Beauty in Islamic Society: A Historical Survey," in *Ideals of Feminine Beauty: Philosophical, Social and Cultural Dimensions.* She is recipient of an NEH/ARCE scholarship.

Barbara Stowasser is chairman of the Center of Arabic Studies and associate professor in the Arabic Department, Georgetown University. She has published numerous articles, including "Women's Issues in Modern Islamic Thought" in *Arab Women: Old Boundaries, New Fron-*

tiers and "The *Hijab:* How a Curtain Became an Institution and a Cultural Symbol." She is also editor of *The Islamic Impulse* and author of *Scripture and Gender: Women in Islam.*

Fariba Zarinebaf-Shahr was born in Iran. She received her Ph.D. from the University of Chicago in Ottoman and Iranian studies in 1991. Her publications include various works on the history of Ottoman and Safavid women, urban history, and Ottoman-Safavid relations. She holds a joint teaching position at Bilkent University in Ankara and at the University of Illinois at Chicago.

Madeleine Zilfi is associate professor of history at the University of Maryland, College Park. She is the author of *The Politics of Piety: The Ottoman Ulema in the Postclassical Age (1600–1800).* She has also published many articles on the Ottoman period. Most notable are "The Diary of a Muderris: A New Source for Ottoman Biography," in *Journal of Turkish Studies* and "Elite Circulation in the Ottoman Empire: Great Mollas of the Eighteenth Century," in *Journal of Economic and Social History of the Orient.*

Women, the Family, and Divorce Laws in Islamic History

Introduction

Amira El Azhary Sonbol

A woman came before the courts demanding to be divorced from her husband, who had broken his word by remarrying his first wife. It seems that, at one point during their marriage, he had divorced the first wife and promised the second never to take back the first. At that time, his second wife made it a condition that she would divorce him if he ever remarried his first wife. After the woman produced the requisite witnesses to his promise and his alleged remarriage, the court granted her a divorce and she received full financial compensation from him (Misr, I'lamat 1274/1857, 34:55–155). In another court case, a woman who had been beaten, abused, and "denied the *shariʿa*'s (Islamic law) guarantee of protection and good treatment" by her husband was refused a divorce by the courts even though she was demanding *khulʿ* (divorce by repudiation), thereby giving up all financial compensation due her from her husband. The husband, who by law had exclusive access to divorce (divorce being exclusively the man's right except in the rare case where it is otherwise declared, which was not the case in this marriage), held out and demanded financial compensation over and above what he would have to pay her in case of divorce. Because the case was complex, it was referred to the *mufti* (on religious legal position) who disregarded the *shariʿa*'s guarantees to the wife yet, using the *shariʿa,* found for the husband and issued a general *fatwa* (juridical opinion) legitimizing a husband's right to exact payment from his wife in return for a divorce (*al-Fatawi al-Islamiya,* 1984, xi).

What makes these two contrasting cases from Egyptian courts interesting is the fact that the first dates from 1274/1857 while the latter dates from 1959. A woman's access to divorce had clearly changed from

1

the middle of the nineteenth to the middle of the twentieth century; yet in both cases, the basis of the law was the *shari*ᶜ*a*. These two cases are not unique but rather illustrate the contrast between the interpretation and application of *shari*ᶜ*a* before and after the legal reforms experienced by the Islamic world since the end of the nineteenth century. Although these findings would not come as a surprise to researchers who are familiar with *shari*ᶜ*a* court records, they contradict a common assumption in Middle Eastern women's studies that modern legal reforms, with the introduction of nationally applied secular and "rational" laws modeled after European ones, brought about positive changes. This "progressive" approach to the history of women and family is part of a wider conceptualization of Middle Eastern history that sees a clear line of demarcation between the modern and the traditional, whereby the latter is characterized as "backward" and the former is seen within the context of a discourse on modernity. Thus, scholars have focused on questions such as: How can Muslim society modernize further? Why do the Muslim masses resist modernization? Who is to blame for the continued backwardness of Muslim society? The blame is usually placed at the door of culture and religion.

Conceptualizing the modern period as diametrically opposite to a "traditional" one has caused numerous misunderstandings in or of the history of Muslim women. Because the modern period has received the greater interest in Middle East women's studies, research on women's distant past has been rare. Feminist historians prefer instead to study the introduction of modernization into Middle Eastern societies. Also, in Western women's scholarship, early emphasis was on serious research in women's history. In Middle East women's studies, theory has proven more popular than empirical historical research. Thus, the most comprehensive study of early Muslim women remains Gertrude Stern's *Marriage in Early Islam* (1939). More recently, a number of scholars have pointed the way toward the need for further historical research. These include Judith Tucker (*Women in Nineteenth Century Egypt*, 1968), Leila Ahmed (*Women and Gender in Islam*, 1992), and Nikki Keddie and Beth Baron, eds., *Women in Middle Eastern History* (1991). Notwithstanding these efforts, scholars continue to search the "past" for explanations for the present subjugation of women, and the role of Islam in this subjugation remains central to Middle East women's studies.

Keddie and Baron (1991, 2) have pointed out how ideologically charged the discourse on Islam in women's studies has become: some scholars are prejudiced against Islam, others deny its responsibility for the subjugation of women, and still others believe that the real role intended for women by Islam has never been implemented because of conditions after the Prophet's death. Another example one could draw from this discourse is that of the veil. It has been a particular favorite among feminist scholars. Numerous books and articles have searched for causes to explain its contemporary reappearance after decades of growing westernization. Some scholars discuss the veil as a weapon of empowerment, while others have identified it with Islam and seen it as an instrument of patriarchal subjugation. Still others try to show its non-Islamic origins (see Zuhur 1992).

The "activist" nature and general acceptance of the modernization paradigm in Middle East women's studies is partly owing to the fact that Middle East women writing about themselves are from social backgrounds that make them receptive to Western discourses and have at the same time been waging a battle for greater equality and rights. Elizabeth Fernea and Basima Bezirgan, eds., *Middle East Muslim Women Speak* (1977), and Margo Badran and Miriam Cook, eds., *Opening the Gates: A Century of Arab Feminist Writing* (1990), show how Muslim women regard their own subjugation and regard the gender relations according to which they are expected to live.

The growing importance of Middle East women's studies is in itself a reflection of the growing importance of women's studies in general and of women scholars in Middle East studies in particular. Thus, it was natural that the first successes in Middle East women's scholarship were works guided by the principles and objectives of the dominant Western feminist paradigm that emphasizes the liberation of women from patriarchal shackles and the achievement of equal access to political and economic power. Therefore, male dominance, or gender relations based on male dominance, is the predominant paradigm in Middle East feminist studies, as it is in Western feminism. Arab feminists like Nawal Saadawi and Salwa al-Khamash have minced no words in their attack on their societies, where women are considered the chattel of husbands, fathers, or brothers. Al-Khamash chose a representative title (here translated) to her book on the subject of enslavement, *The Arab Woman and the Backward Traditional Society* (1973), which focuses on Islamic traditions as the basis for the subjugation of Arab women, notwithstanding the great advancements they have made in education and the professions. To prove the enslavement of women, it is usual to present pertinent Qur'anic verses that refer to men as "keepers" or "protectors" of women because of the physiological differences between them and to *fiqh* (juridical interpretations by the Muslim clergy).

The historical arguments used by Arab feminists focuses on

women's lives in pre-Islamic Arabia: women's participation in battles waged by their tribes, the existence of polygamous and polyandrous marriages, and the wide acceptance of matrilineal practices. Some historians, like Leila Ahmed, have argued convincingly that Islam established a patrilineal, patrilocal system, emphasizing blood-relationships as essential determinants for inheritance of property. To assure legitimate inheritance, a young girl's virginity had to be controlled before marriage; and a wife's sexuality had to be controlled through seclusion, veiling, and a very strict moral code. Thus, according to Ahmed, Islam, with its merchant economy, transformed women who had lived relatively unfettered during the *jahiliyya* period (period preceding the coming of Islam) into the property of their families and husbands (1992, 44). In *Republic of Cousins,* Germaine Tillion takes up the connection between inheritance of property and the subjugation of women. She concludes that the continued practice of cousin marriage among Muslim Mediterranean communities was owing to their wish to keep wealth within the family (1983, 73). "In making inheritance by women obligatory, the Holy Book . . . struck a terrible blow at the tribe . . . even as with more or less good grace they converted to Islam, tribes have bent their energies to evading ever since." The seclusion of women, the use of the veil, cousin marriage, and the domination of women became the answer (1983, 149–50).

Critics of the close association between Middle Eastern women's studies and Western feminism have pointed to the fact that women's studies in the West were born out of a women's movement whose philosophy and direction were based on the concrete experiences and realities of women's lives in Western societies. However, models based on the history of Western women do not reflect the concrete experiences and realities of Middle Eastern women, with the result that cultural and historical specificities have played a minor role in the greater picture presented by Middle Eastern women's studies. According to Fedwa Malti-Douglas, the gender issues represent a "futile dialogue on gender and women [which] has long attracted the West." Referring to Fatima Mernissi's argument in *Beyond the Veil* (1975), Malti-Douglas continues, "[when] women's liberation in the modern Middle East is associated with westernization, the entire subject, willy-nilly, becomes enmeshed in political and civilizational debates" (1991, 3).

Obviously, gender issues unite women around the world, but they manifest themselves differently in different cultures. Thus, one of the most important methodological problems with studies that focus on the question of Islam and the subjugation of women is the acceptance on the part of most scholars of the Qur³an, prophetic *hadiths* (compilations of the traditions of the Prophet), *fiqh* (Muslim jurisprudence), and other religious treatises as representing the *actual* as opposed to the normative condition of women. Different types of research, particularly archival and literary, which are favored by this volume of articles, show that social patterns were in great contrast to the "official" picture presented by these "formal" sources. If anything, the social discourse seems to point to a position quite opposite to what the "formal" discourse presents us. This means that the actual lives women led caused reactionary clergymen to interpret laws more conservatively. The "looser" the women, the stricter the interpretation.

Barbara Stowasser's article, "Women and Citizenship in the Qur³an," is one of four articles placed together at the beginning of this volume that reconsider specific issues of significance to Middle Eastern women's studies: citizenship, modernization, the impact of foreign rule, and the nature of the family. Tackling the discourse on Islam in women's studies, Stowasser questions the essentialism of the widely applied methodology by which *text* is used as proof for the subjugation of women. Rather, as Stowasser shows, notwithstanding the existence of a body of Islamic laws acceptable to the Muslim community at large, there are clear differences between the written word and actual practices during Islamic history beginning with the early formative period. While introducing us to the new subject of citizenship in Islam, she at the same time illustrates the diversity of Islamic scripturalist paradigms regarding women and ties the Qur³an to the historical context of the period of Qur³anic revelations, thereby explaining and comparing Qur³anic laws on citizenship with actual practices. Furthermore, she shows how Muslim communities have adapted laws to their actual practices rather than accepting the "ideals" of exegetic paradigms espoused by either medieval or modernist reformers. By doing so, Stowasser demonstrates why it is dangerous to accept the written "law" as being representative of actual historical conditions relating to social practices.

Similar conclusions are reached by Julia Clancy-Smith in her article *"La femme arabe:* Women and Sexuality in France's North African Empire," and Peter Gran in "Organization of Culture and the Construction of the Family in the Modern Middle East." Using the writings of French travelers, colonial officials, and the famous French feminist suffragists, Clancy-Smith shows how the image of Arab women, and in turn Arab society, was based on "an emerging colonial gaze and discourse fixed upon *la femme arabe,* upon her sexuality, her femininity, her procreative powers." Well-intentioned French feminists tried through their writings to improve the condition of Algerian women; instead, their works emphasized the unique status of Arab women and depicted them as subject to sexual and other abuses rather than as active participants in gender relations pertaining to the historical context in which they found themselves. As Clancy-Smith illustrates, under French rule "visions of empire and collective visions of Muslim sexuality fed into each other." As for Gran, he points out that following the Second World War, modernization theory became the basis of a new twist on Orientalism, by which Middle East society and culture were shown to be backward. Even after modernization theory lost its "prestige" in the 1980s, the study of the Arab family and women's studies continued to provide an area for modernization theory to flourish. Accordingly, research has been focused on the role of the elites of both sexes and, at the same time has given no more than "an impressionistic view of the internal logic of Middle Eastern culture or of the essential adequacy of a way of life of men and women," and of actual gender relations. Addressing the treatment of private versus public spheres in Muslim society, Gran asks whether the scholarly perception of Arab women as occupying a private sphere does not also characterize them as marginal to any public or political life, to history itself. By discussing a generic Arab family in which public and private spheres are clearly delineated, the picture of a submissive wife, sister, or daughter, with no role or voice of her own outside of the house, reinforces the picture of backwardness that modernization theory expounds. Rather than a generic family, Gran argues for a "politically constructed nature of the family" that would show that dividing any society into private and public spheres is an artificial construct at best, that there are a multiplicity of families in various parts of the Arab world, and that the structure of the family and the nature of family and gender relations are specific to time and place.

Recently, scholars have called attention to the importance of drawing connections between gender relations and the historical process by which nation-states evolved in the Islamic world. Deniz Kandiyoti has pointed to the vital connection between gender issues and the efforts of newly established nation-states to forge "new notions of citizenship [by establishing] new legitimizing ideologies and power bases in their respective societies" (1991, 2). To do so, governments attempted to bring about the subordination of the family to the state's will through what Kandiyoti describes as "socialization" designed to free citizens "from the shackles of social customs and practices which are deemed to impede social progress and development" (1991, 9).

This important scholarly effort calls attention to the significance of the political process in the subjugation of women; however, by designating "exclusive control of the family" and "domination of men over women" as "shackles" of society from which secularizing governments tried to "wrest women," (Badran in Kandiyoti 1991, 201) the modern period is again presented in a positivistic way, dichotomously opposed to the traditional period preceding it. According to this view, piecemeal erosion of the religious establishment in the drive toward secularization occurred during the modern period, but personal status laws remained an exception. "For women this created an awkward dichotomy between their role as citizens of the *watan* (nation-state) and as members of the *umma* (religious community). In a division that was never precise, the state increasingly came to influence their public roles, leaving to religion the regulation of their private or family roles" (Badran in Kandiyoti 1991, 203).

There is no question that modernization has changed the situation of Muslim women dramatically and that the status of women has become one of greater openness and less seclusion. However, it should be emphasized that women in premodern Islamic society were quite dynamic and participated in decisions regarding legal and personal status. By looking through *shari^ca* court records, personal status laws, and nineteenth-century legal reforms, a number of articles included in this volume illustrate that women had much to say regarding social and gender relations and that the historical transformations of the last two centuries, although allowing women a greater public role, actually brought about a general deterioration in social maneuverability, especially for women. This deterioration was closely tied to the evolution of new state structures that fit the needs of new hegemonic elite combines, usually formed from alliances between foreign business interests and westernizing national leaders. In the process of nation-state building, the hands of the state extended toward family and personal laws, standardizing, codifying, reforming, and modernizing them. The process had a profound impact on the status of women, creating for them, so to speak, a double jeopardy.

Addressing the question of the impact of modernization on the status of women, Afaf Marsot demonstrates that modernization brought better health services and ultimately modern education to women, but that nevertheless the dynamics of modernization had a regressive effect on women and society at large, at least temporarily. During the decentralized Mamlukid period in Egypt, working-class women played an active part in economic life, and the level of education among men and women did not differ much, with only the *^culama³* (clergy) receiving a superior education. Beginning with Muhammad ʿAli (1805–1848), who as part of his centralization program confiscated most money-making elements and redistributed wealth among his dependents, women lost control over the land they held. As European merchants took control of Egypt's commerce, and cheap European industrial goods flowed into Egypt's markets, participation of Egyptians in economic activity became more localized, and their condition deteriorated as a whole. So did that of women who were previously involved in commercial activities and trade. The trades that remained open to women were either connected with services or with food production. Marsot concludes that modernization should be reappraised because, notwithstanding the benefits of change, women were pushed "down the barrel" in all areas of life, including gender relations.

Two other papers confirm Marsot's findings regarding the activities of women before the modern period. Mary Ann Fay uses eighteenth-century Mamlukid *awqaf* (religious endowment) records to illustrate women's participation in their families' business decisions. While Marsot focuses on urban working-class women, Fay discusses the importance of the roles played by aristocratic women, who enjoyed autonomy over themselves and their property. In short, she shows women as active participants rather than reluctant observers only pushed to participate because of the absence of men owing to the mortality rate resulting from the anarchic political conditions in eighteenth-century Egypt.

Taking on the larger question regarding the continued acceptance of the "oriental despotism" cliché as the dominant image for the Ottoman family, Nelly Hanna tests the paradigm in relation to the Ottoman middle-class household. Her subject is the seventeenth-century family of a Cairene merchant leader, Shahbandar al-Tujjar Ismaʿil Abu Taqiyya. She challenges the widely accepted thesis that women in premodern Islamic society were ruled by the absolute power of a male hierarchy beginning with the husband and ending with the Ottoman sultan, with the result that a wife's physical movement and her ability to control her own life were restricted, making her isolated and at the mercy of her husband. Using *shariʿa* court records dating from the Ottoman period, Hanna illustrates how this model is not born out by fact.

Although researchers should be cautioned against making presumptions regarding the condition of women during the Ottoman period, it is important to emphasize the significance of the connection between the rise of nation-states and gender relations, which Kandiyoti's work outlines. It seems clear that as states in the modern Islamic world began to mobilize work forces and make and arbitrate laws, their legal jurisdiction was extended to social intercourse. In this way, the state became a direct determinant of patriarchal relations, which were molded along the lines of the ruling elites' hegemonic discourses. This new situation, which we can label "state patriarchy," differed from earlier forms of patriarchy where the family head was the arbiter of power relations within the family and in which *'urf* (tradition) determined the extent and nature of the patriarch's powers. In the modern discourse, the state became an actual "creator" of culture as well as the promulgator of laws that were enforced directly from a central government. Because the new states and monarchies were the direct or indirect creations and allies of imperial European powers, they could not depend on "traditional legitimacy" alone for a hegemonic discourse. In regard to women, modernization meant their education and mobilization into the work force where they were needed. However, modernization was not meant to jeopardize traditions regarding gender roles.

Nothing exemplifies more the contradictions of modern state patriarchy than the fact that today Muslim women can aspire to becoming the heads of governments, yet they face often insurmountable difficulties in divorcing their husbands. When asked questions directly related to nation-state building, such as "Who has the right to citizenship?," most Muslim countries deny citizenship to the children of mothers whose husbands are foreigners but bestow citizenship on the children of fathers whether the mother is foreign or not. The situation is described as *"shari'a"* when in fact the question of nationality is itself quite modern. Because in most Muslim countries nationality is tied to property rights, which in turn are closely tied to inheritance, it is clear that the laws are setting up new patriarchal laws that give preference to the male members of society. Significantly, Christian minorities fighting against the application of the Islamic *shari'a* in their communities today have no qualms in accepting Islamic inheritance laws, which demand that a male inherit double the share of a female (Sadiq 1989, 187). In short, questions related to nation-state structures have been used by male-dominated elites to introduce gender inequalities, notwithstanding their endorsement of modernity.

Clearly, the center of the debate regarding the history of women and the family is the question of *shari'a* and the modern division of legal codes and the court system into the secular and religious, whereby the latter was applied to personal status laws and modern secular laws were applied to commerce, property, crime, and politics. This split is generally attributed to nineteenth-century legal reforms, Western penetration, and capitalist growth. One scholar has explained the continued association between Islamic law and Arab nationalism as being a form of nationalist "cultural loyalty" in resisting the cultural colonialism of the West (Hijab 1988, 38–42). As a result, personal status codes continue to be based on the *shari͗a* and are in conflict with modern Western-style constitutions of Muslim states, making it impossible to divide the two, particularly given the wish for independence of Arab states in their fight against imperialism. This has left women in the confusing situation of being guaranteed laws by constitutions that are not reflected in personal status laws.

In such interpretations, therefore, the *shari͗a* has been conceptualized as a static, unchanging system that Muslims believe to be the permanent word of God as delivered through the Prophet Muhammad. According to this view, secular governments tried to change the system but found resistance from the traditional patriarchal order. Thus, the modern reforms that were introduced had to be limited to political and economic spheres while personal and family laws were left to the *shari͗a* courts, which continued to be ruled in accordance with traditional laws that perpetuated gender oppression and the enslavement of women. This approach to the *shari͗a* in women's studies conforms to the findings of general histories of Islamic law as well as to the picture presented by Muslim fundamentalists who claim a "pure" unquestionable authority in the form of a God-given *shari͗a*.

There are a number of problems with this approach to the *shari͗a* that have had an adverse effect on our understanding of gender problems and the role of women in Islamic communities in the past and the present. It is true that *shari͗a* continues as the basis for personal and family laws in the Islamic world, but it is not true that *shari͗a* constitutes an unchanging body of laws or that the laws and their interpretations are the same under nation-state conditions as they had been before the modern period. In fact, as the articles included in this volume show, *shari͗a* is in process, changing from time to time depending on the historical context and the particular moving forces of any given age. If anything, *shari͗a* is the body of acceptable laws of a particular community given legitimacy as the word of God delivered through a Prophet, but which are in actual fact the interpretations of local *qadis* (*shari͗a* court judges) who reflect the *͗urf* (traditions) of the communities in which they serve, using appropriate *fiqh* interpretations that reflect the patterns of actual communal relations. In fact, the term *shari͗a* means acceptable laws, and, as Muhammed Afifi's article shows, the term describes not only an Islamic *shari͗a* but also a Jewish *shari͗a* and a Christian *shari͗a*. Because it has been customary to deal with minorities separately from the Muslim majorities owing to the modern differences between them, most social studies have missed the similarities in legal practices that existed between different *millet*s (non-Muslim religious groups) during the Ottoman period. The contributions in this book of Najwa al-Qattan's study of Syrian Christians and Mohamad Afifi's work on the Egyptian Coptic community demonstrate this point with great clarity. al-Qattan explains why in Ottoman Damascus the case to be made for religious discrimination is much stronger than the case for gender discrimination, while Afifi shows the points at which the Copts resorted to Islamic laws and the courts. Taken together, these two articles (as do most articles in this volume) illustrate the importance of looking at the Ottoman Empire through the specificities of time, place, and cultural conditions.

The *shariʿa* that came into being after the modernization of law and the reform of courts differed from the previous one in that it was designed to favor the new hegemonic order coming to power as part of the nation-state structure. It is a mistake to believe that the *shariʿa* code applied by nation-states in the modern period is simply a vestige of the past and hence to regard traditional laws as the cause for the present subjugation of women, when in fact the causes of subjugation are located in the modern reforms and the handling of personal laws. Therefore, one should avoid seeing modern Muslim states as being consciously involved in socialization to free their populations from the "shackles" of traditional customs because what they are involved in is the institution of new customs labeled as *"shariʿa"* that deny previous freedoms while emphasizing earlier discriminations.

A study of premodern Ottoman courts and family law, as well as the court and legal reforms introduced during the modern period, shows that if modernization was deliberately introduced, it was never meant to be a total system, rather it was intended as an instrument to be used by a new patriarchal order to confirm its powers and not undermine it. To achieve this goal, the state had to hold on to a strict moral code based on particular standardized and codified Islamic principles that suited the new state hegemony. As Madeline Zilfi's article shows, setting new moral standards was nothing new to Islamic society; thus during the early modern "Tulip Era," the Ottoman sultans actually established rules of conduct for women in public places by which they hoped to stem what was being described as "looseness" for that period. As Zilfi shows, however, setting a moral standard for control was one thing, but becoming an instrument of change regarding social customs through the use of *shariʿa* law or enforcing moral discourses was another—one that was to be left to the modern state, as other articles in the book indicate. The modern nation-state encouraged legal reforms that, if anything, increased state control over the family through an amplification of male control over women (wives and daughters) and minor children (girls and boys), and this by establishing state-approved codes of law, standardized education of judges, and restructuring of court systems. These reforms actually limited the social maneuverability that was possible earlier when *qadi*s could pick and choose from all Islamic codes and *ʿurf* precedents.

Reform of the law and the courts has taken different forms in different Islamic countries. But generally speaking, all such reforms included the creation of multiple court systems, the introduction of European legal codes, and the split of law into two codes, a "secular" code to deal with issues of property, crime, and commerce, and a "religious" code for family, personal, and inheritance laws that was even stricter than the religious code that had been applied in *shariʿa* courts before the modern period. In this way, women could be mobilized into the public sphere but would be controlled through social laws. The split in the legal structure has meant that economic and political laws have developed according to logic and structure borrowed from the West. At the same time, "modern" individual rights have not been extended to personal and family law, which has continued to be concerned with communal security. Although the idea of individual rights was kept out of the *shariʿa* courts, the establishment of the Hanafi *madhhab* (creed or school of law) as the main source for *shariʿa* courts and the application of new standardized methods for the selection of *qadi*s in many cases have made juridical decisions less flexible. Under Ottoman rule, the Hanafi code had been an "official" and impirical code; but in *shariʿa* courts, other schools of law (i.e., Maliki, Shafiʿi, and Hanbali *madhahib*) continued to be applied in accordance with a legal philosophy based on *istihsan* and *istihbab* (commendable, well-liked, desirable).

In practical terms this diversity reflects the preference for applying *ʿurf*, or local custom. Thus, in Ottoman courts throughout the empire, the public could chose the *madhhab* to be applied to their cases, and *qadi*s and *muftis* from those *madhahib* continued to administer *fatwas*. The importance of maneuverability in applying different *madhahib* is illustrated in Egypt by lessees' preference for the Hanbali *madhhab* for *waqf* land leases. Unlike other *madhahib*, the Hanbali forbade any increases in the amount of rent over what had been initially agreed upon. It also allowed for the inheritance of leases. These favorable conditions caused even non-Muslim minorities to conclude their leases according to the Hanbali *madhhab* (Afifi 1991, 151). Such advantages to the public would be ended with the establishment of standardized codes of law as part of modern reforms. The precedence given to the relatively inflexible Hanafi *madhhab* in preference to the Maliki and Shafi'i, which were philosophically more attuned to social diversity and the application of *'urf* (Abu Zahra 1980, 1–3), is indicative of the new patriarchal order's elitist and authoritarian nature. Thus, whereas the Maliki and Shafi'i codes were based largely on intent, the Hanafi code applied a disciplinary approach. For example, whereas the Maliki and Shafi'i *madhahib* did not recognize a divorce oath taken by a drunken man unless confirmed by him once sober, the Hanafi *madhhab* allowed the divorce to stand as a punishment to him ('Abdu 1989, 119).

Furthermore, the reforms not only envisioned a unified code but also a "unified" *qadi* system. Where once a *qadi* was nominated to the government by his peers and chosen for his wide-ranging knowledge of Islamic *fiqh*—only the highest levels of the hierarchy being graduates of traditional Ottoman *qadi* schools—the reforms meant that he would be educated in a "designed" program in government-run schools and examined on specific textbooks selected by individuals and committees set up by the government. Their employment would be based on employee laws established by personnel offices and disciplinary boards that deliberate promotions, penalties, dismissal and retirement (Gallad 1895, 1728–30). Thus, *qadi*s became a "product" of the state, trained to institute its will. The state extended its authority further by creating the position of certified notary public *(ma'dhun)* to officiate in marriages and divorces and to ensure that government-issued standardized documents and procedures are followed and transactions are recorded with the state. These responsibilities had earlier been the province of local *shuyukh* who followed the contractual traditions of their various communities, while at the same time assuring that contracts and divorces were legally recorded.

Two papers, my contribution to the volume, deal directly with the changes introduced into Islamic communities as a reflection of legal, court, and *qadi* reforms. The first paper focuses on the question of guardianship and the role it plays in Islamic law. While minor children have always been under the control of a guardian, during the Ottoman period minors (boys and girls) could be married at any age by guardians who had the *wilayat al-ijbar* ("right to force them"). A minimum marriage age of sixteen for women and eighteen for men became a requirement by law in the twentieth century in most Muslim countries. This act was claimed by Muslim feminists and modernizers as a great success, which it would have been had the law ended there. However, the same legal reforms established majority at two-one, while traditionally majority was gauged according to *'aql, rushd* (maturity of mind), and *buluġh* (puberty), which was usually reached by the age of fifteen, and certainly before the age of twenty-one (al-Ghazali 1990, 31). Establishing majority at twenty-one meant that the time during which minors would be under the power of their guardians who controlled their movements and, significantly, their property, was extended for a longer period of time. This extension had a direct bearing on gender relations. Although—as my second paper illustrates—adult women were supposed to have legal authority over their own marriages both before and after the reforms, in fact, legal reforms seemed to have reduced that authority significantly.

The chapters in this volume deal with different countries and subjects, but are all integrated in the sense that they are designed to provide a better understanding of the history of women and the family in Islamic societies. It is only by focusing on historical specificities of societies, studied through documents pertinent to place and time, and by positioning oneself within that context that the realities of social relations can be understood. Applying models based mainly on ideology and on the experiences of other places and ages has only helped obfuscate the realities of gender relations and hence the actual causes of the subjugation of Muslim women today. As a whole, this volume has four main goals.

The first is to focus on the history of women, family law, and divorce, with the purpose of assessing gender relations and the status of women. Women in premodern Islamic societies seemed to take part in determining the conditions for their marriage and hence their financial and legal rights at the time of divorce. Thus, the marriage contract under Ottoman rule was basically a blank piece of paper, which was filled up with particular formulas that repeat themselves from one contract to the other, as well as changeable items depending on the specific marriage and molded by the time and place in which the marriage was contracted. (Ottoman contracts pertinent to gender relations are discussed in detail by Agmon, al-Qattan, Ivanova, Abdal-Rehim, and Hanna). Today, following legal reforms based on the state's desire for standardization and therefore control, the marriage document is a "fill-in-the-blanks" form that allows little if any maneuverability in setting conditions for the marriage and hence limits the woman's ability to define her financial and legal rights during the marriage and later in case of divorce. This practice has caused a lesser accountability for the husband and the deterioration of women's legal rights.

The papers presented in this volume take different approaches and focuses; however, all work together to give a full picture of the history of women before and after the legal reforms based on the documents pertaining to marriage and divorce. Scriptural and literary sources are also used to complement archival research. The Fay and Hanna papers discussed earlier show the inherent role that women of different classes played in Islamic society before the reforms, and Marsot's interpretative essay provides an analysis of the deterioration of women that came about as a result of these reforms and offers a different way for addressing the question of modernization. Dina Rizk Khouri's work on Northern Iraq, an area about which little on this topic is known and whose archival sources are yet to be tapped, takes a different direction but reaches somewhat the same conclusions. Khouri relates how the city of Mosul was transformed by changing patterns of trade and capitalist production during the eighteenth and nineteenth centuries. Using the archival sources of the period, *waqf* and local *shariʿa* court records, as well as biographical dictionaries, poetry, and European records, Khouri discusses the significance of social, political, and economic upheavals to the use of urban and rural space and their impact on women's lives.

A number of papers deal with microlevel cases, adding a dimension of greater specificity to the volume. Thus, Iris Agmon's contribution involves a close study of two particular divorce cases from the *shariʿa* courts of Jaffa and Haifa in early twentieth-century Ottoman Palestine. These archives have rarely been used for the study of women's history. The two cases deal with marital conflicts. By comparing the two cases, Agmon shows the socioeconomic conditions of women, gender and marriage relations, reasons for divorce, custody of minor children, and, importantly, the role played by *shariʿa* courts in constructing the socioeconomic lives of women. She also compares the function of the two courts of Jaffa and Haifa to show the connections between socioeconomic conditions of each town with the legal priorities and decisions of their two courts.

Our second purpose is to raise questions of importance to the history of women and the family that have received little if any attention by scholars. Of particular importance are the issues of violence against women and laws pertaining to children. A number of papers deal with the treatment of children, including my contribution discussed earlier. Margaret L. Meriwether's study, "The Rights of Children and the Responsibilities of Women: Women as *Wasis* in Ottoman Aleppo, 1770–1840," answers a deep need for more studies of family laws in regard to children, an area that has been almost disregarded in histories of Middle Eastern societies past and present. By concentrating on women's guardianship of family property and children, Meriwether takes up the question of the family and its oppression of women, a widely accepted premise in feminist paradigms. Beginning with specific Islamic laws regarding guardianship and comparing them with *shariʿa* court cases from Aleppo, she shows the discrepancy between legal theory and social practices (one of the important theoretical foundations of this volume) regarding women's responsibilities as guardians. Because this was a period of social instability in Aleppo, caused by regional and worldwide economic changes, the appointment of guardians, the execution of inheritance, and the treatment of children gain particular relevance to changes experienced by society during transitional periods. By studying the court cases, Meriwether addresses the issue of patriarchy, raising questions of whether a patriarchal order existed, whether *shariʿa* courts were involved in perpetuating such an order, or whether the reverse is actually true and the courts were the route for affirming and extending the authority of women within the family.

Svetlana Ivanova's essay widens the scope of the book beyond the Ottoman Middle East. For the most part, only the Arab Middle East and Turkey have figured in Ottoman history, and certainly Eastern Europe has never figured in women's studies as part of the larger Ottoman community. Not only does Ivanova bring light to the importance of Eastern European archives for an understanding of Ottoman social history but she also illustrates the particular value of these archives for understanding women's history and family life. Dating from the seventeenth to the nineteenth century, the archives used by Ivanova reach important conclusions regarding the social status of women and their husbands, the nature or divorce and divorce practices particular to that area of the world, married life and the relations between spouses, and the participation of the family and the neighborhood community in settling a family problem. Altogether, the picture presented by Ivanova reconfirms the conclusions of the papers presented in this volume by illustrating the availability of ample sources and evidence for the study of the life of the common people in Islamic society. In her case, it is the importance of the parallel existence and the points of contact between the judicial, highly formalized practice and the traditional customary practices that complete the picture of everyday life. Significantly, this article also documents the extent of women's participation in legal proceedings as plaintiffs, defendants, and witnesses.

Comparing the findings of this paper, whose subject is from an Ottoman European community, with cases from the Arab and Turkish parts of the Ottoman Empire, illustrates the continuities and differences in family practices during the Ottoman period. For example, the Muslim community in Eastern Rumelia had some unique traditions that were probably linked with its status as a minority community among a Christian majority. One tradition involved exchanging gifts between the husband and wife and members of her family at the time of divorce. It was also usual that such an exchange take place in court in front of the *qadi* and was considered an essential part of the proceedings. Such a tradition is not reported for anywhere else in the Ottoman Empire.

Gender violence remains virtually an untouched subject in Middle Eastern studies. Two chapters in this book stress the importance of this subject and point the way to further research. Both begin with the premodern period to illustrate the meaning and patterns of gender violence and how society handled these issues. The papers then address the same questions for the modern period. The results of both are surprising because, under so-called rational modern criminal laws based on human rights and centralized police forces, violence increased significantly within and outside the household and women were victimized and often considered the responsible party. On the social level, however, and outside of court decisions or formal police actions, there is a clear case of continuity in the handling of gender violence.

The chapter contributed by Dalenda Largueche deals with domestic violence in Tunis and focuses on a particular form of punishment for women known as *Dar Juwad,* a house of correction and reeducation for women who are disobedient to marital or parental authority. Using *fatawi* treatises, *shariᶜa* court and police records, and oral history, Largueche studies this central institution, regarded as the most oppressive and psychologically violent to women, in the life of Muslim women and the family. She shows how a simple Islamic institution, intended as a means of reconciliation between a husband and wife with irreconcilable differences turned into a virtual house of imprisonment and punishment for disobedient wives, daughters, and sisters.

My contribution on gender violence raises questions regarding the causes and treatment of rape in Muslim history. Using *shariᶜa* court records, literature, press and police reports, and laws involving rape, I ask why modern Egyptian laws do not recognize *rape* as *ightisab,* preferring to deal with such cases under different titles that make the offense more acceptable in a religious/traditional context, when before modernization of law, *shariᶜa* courts had no qualms about recognizing *ightisab* for what it is and handling it accordingly.

This book also presents chapters dealing with non-Muslim minorities of the Ottoman Empire, as well as areas of the empire where non-Muslims constituted the majority. However, it applies the same methodology and research that is applied to Muslims. The results will prove fascinating because preliminary research has already shown the fallacy of separating the two communities and demonstrates that the idea of separate *millet*s is more a function of state/social relations than it is a function of intersocial or human relations. Minorities have been purposefully left out of studies of Islamic societies, which is a reflection of the application of modern questions and paradigms that focus on the modern differences between Muslim and non-Muslim women. In her article on *dhimmi* (non-Muslim) women in Ottoman Syria, Najwa al-Qattan raises the question about whether the treatment of Christian women according to the *sijills* (records, files) of the *shariʿa* courts was based more on their gender or on their religious affiliation. As she illustrates, the *sijill*s contain data on marriage and divorce, the sale and rental of houses and shops, the various occupations of the population, and the issues that drove them to litigation. Muslim courts were sought after by Jews and Christians in Damascus to the same degree as their Muslim neighbors, in fact, *dhimmi* documents show that the reasons for litigation are identical to Muslim ones in their appearance and formulas used. By showing the different methods of "tagging" and language used in these texts, al-Qattan presents a guide for the use of these texts for understanding the sociolegal and cultural realities of the Damascus court.

Muhammad Afifi writes about Egyptian Copts during the eighteenth century and about cases of gender relations during the twentieth. Like al-Qattan, he illustrates the similarities and differences between the Coptic and Muslim communities, dismissing numerous stereotypes in the process. He focuses in particular on marriage contracts and divorce. Because marriage is a sacrament in Christianity, it is significant that in certain periods of their history, Copts preferred to adopt the Muslim contract so as to avail themselves of the access to divorce. This was particularly so among the wealthy Coptic elite, who wished to enjoy similar benefits to the Muslim elite. Afifi traces in the Coptic community other Muslim traditions, such as polygamy and the buying of women slaves, which the church never approved of and fought strenuously against. He discusses the struggle of the church against these traditions and its final success against elite groups that were undermining its power in determining gender and family relations.

Any historical study of women and the family (indeed, any social history) *must* begin with archival sources, followed closely by literary sources and historical analysis. *Shariʿa* court and *awqaf* records constitute the most important of such archives, and fourteen of the essays presented in this volume are based on such records dating from both the modern and the Ottoman periods. In fact, given the growing body of scholarship in both Ottoman and women's studies, it is surprising that of all periods in the history of Muslim women and the family, it is the Ottoman period that has proven to be the least studied. This is a serious deficiency given the fact that most of the presumptions regarding the modern condition of Muslim women are based on their condition during the Ottoman traditional period preceding it. A number of articles are designed to demonstrate the futility of uninformed arguments regarding the lack of sources for studying the history of Muslim society, to demonstrate the research potential of *shari*ʿa court records, and even to "untangle" these records for scholars who have yet to get a taste of them.

Abdal-Rehim Abdal-Rahman Abdal-Rehim, an acknowledged authority on Egypt's Mahkama Sharʿiyya Archives, discusses how these archives, holding "hundreds of thousands of documents," contain precise and significant details for the study of women and family law during the Ottoman period. By surveying the archives relevant to Cairo and the provinces, he shows their dimension and their potential use for studying such issues as the accessibility of courts to society during the Ottoman period, the practice by women of stipulating marriage and divorce conditions in a marriage contract, alimony, and custody and support of boys and girls. Of particular importance is his use of Egypt's provincial archives, thereby giving us a glimpse of gender relations outside of the capital, Cairo. He also shows what type of documents the archives contain, their dates, and their location.

Fariba Zarinebaf-Shahr does the same for the Ottoman archives in Istanbul and reaches similar conclusions regarding the familiarity of the public with the court system and the common use of their services. Focusing on the Imperial Council, which was considered a supreme court of final appeal for the whole empire, Zarinebaf-Shahr shows the hierarchical nature of *shari*ʿa courts. Women from all over the empire submitted their petitions in person, or via an agent, to the Imperial Council in Istanbul. While introducing a documentary source that is little known to scholars, Zarinebaf-Shahr illustrates its importance and calls attention for the need for further research. Thus, she discusses the contents of seventeenth-century Şikayet Defterleric (grievance petitions) *chekewi,* from Istanbul and illustrates the reasons why women appealed to the court for redress, particularly marital problems and demands for divorce. In contradistinction to generally accepted paradigms regarding the premodern period as an age of isolation and subjugation of women to their husbands and families, Zarinebaf-Shahr's thesis is that Ottoman women were generally aware of their legal rights and took an active role in defending and protecting them whenever they felt they were being violated. They did so through the court system, bringing suits against their husbands, families, legal agents, and estate executives as the case may be.

Finally, the articles included in this volume, separately as well as collectively, propose new methodologies and theories for understanding the history of women and the family. They call for an analysis based on documents specific to time and place, and they ask that historians position themselves within the particular historical context under investigation, that theories be tested rather than applied, and that modern questions regarding social relations not be projected onto the past. They also call for a more careful assessment of the societies being studied; treating the Islamic world as a monolith, whether in the modern or premodern periods, simply obfuscates historical realities. If one of the purposes of women's studies is to discover reasons for the subjugation of women, then obfuscation hides the actual source of this "enslavement" if it existed and continues to persist.

PART ONE

Reevaluating Women's Studies

I

Women and Citizenship in the Qurʾan

Barbara Freyer Stowasser

The Greek scientist Archimedes is reported to have said: "Give me a point outside it, and I will unhinge the world." The study of women's issues in Islam is an enterprise much different from Archimedean physics. For one, cultures are complex webs of interaction of the material, mental and spiritual. Their inner laws, not reducible to those of mechanics, are much more difficult to grasp and describe, let alone predict or manipulate. As each strand is imbedded in the whole, separate consideration remains partial. From the beginning, women's issues were part of Islam's doctrinal message and practical application, a cultural symbol linked with Muslim self-perception(s). Nevertheless, at a time when women's issues, especially women's political rights, have become a token of identity *(symbol)* in the inner-Islamic debates on cultural self-definition in the modern age, such debates occur within a variety of rationally discernible models or patterns *(paradigms)* of integral assertions, theories, and aims *(ideology)*, which are visible to the outsider.

For most Muslims, social, political, and economic issues fall within the parameters of religion and must remain within that context, for only then is morality assured. Religion provides detailed principles and laws of divine origin that Muslim society must follow or find itself in a state of sin. These revealed and transmitted truths are of eternal nature. For most classical theologians and contemporary traditionalist thinkers, doctrine and law are both and equally absolute and immutable. They choose to believe that neither social reality of Muhammad's time nor social developments thereafter influenced the essence of their formulation. Thus, the medieval *shariʿa*—based on revelation, the hallowed precedents of the individually inspired Prophet and his collectively in-

23

spired Companions, and the faultless consensus of the Islamic community—was and is but elaboration and application of God's own legislation. I contend that this worldview is essentially *a-historic*, in that it means to disregard the factors of change and time.

Before proceeding to explore the Qurʾanic text on women's political role in moral Muslim society, it is important to take a closer look at the three constructs mentioned above: symbol, paradigm, and ideology:

Symbol

Of the many approaches of Western social science to the role of religion in culture, classical status has been achieved by Clifford Geertz's definition of religion as "a cultural system of symbols" (1973, 91 ff). Geertz distinguishes between individual symbols and their aggregates, "religious patterns" that, to the religious, are "frames of perception, symbolic screens through which experience is interpreted" as well as "guides for action, blueprints for conduct" (1968, 98). In this definition, the cultural importance of religion consists in "its capacity to serve, for an individual or for a group, as a source of general, yet distinctive, conceptions of the world, the self, and the relations between them. . . . Religious concepts spread beyond their specifically metaphysical contexts to provide a framework of general ideas in terms of which a wide range of experience—intellectual, emotional, moral—can be given meaningful form" (1973, 123). Thus, religious perspective differs from the commonsensical and from the scientific one. Unlike the former, it "moves beyond the realities of everyday life to wider ones which correct and complete them"; and unlike the latter, it "questions the realities of life not out of an institutionalized scepticism . . . but in terms of what it takes to be wider, non-hypothetical truths" (1973, 112).

Paradigm

In its clearest form, the concept of paradigm belongs to science, and it is in works of the philosophy of science that paradigms and paradigmatic changes have best been described. In *The Structure of Scientific Revolutions*, Thomas S. Kuhn defines *paradigms* as "universally recognized scientific achievements that for a time provide model problems and solutions to a community of practitioners" (1970, viii). Kuhn distinguishes "paradigmatic shifts" (e.g., the Copernican, Newtonian, Einsteinian) from "normal science." Paradigm, to Kuhn, is any accepted fundamental scheme, and normal science is what is being done within that scheme until too many observed facts remain anomalous and paradigmatic adjustment, or paradigmatic shift, occurs (1970, 52–65). Social science has borrowed the concept of paradigm but uses it more loosely in the sense of *pattern, framework,* and *model* of general ideas that structure perception and serve as agenda (for those who subscribe to it and share in it). In social science use, then, paradigm is linked to *ideology.* Although separate paradigms may coexist within the same ideology, with time a paradigm may also undergo such changes that the common denominator is weakened and an ideological shift outward ensues, as happens in cases where extremist Islamic modernism crosses over into the realm of secularism.

Ideology

In a felicitous mixture of objective theory and Islamic-history specificity, R. Stephen Humphreys has defined ideology as "a critique of a given sociopolitical system which both describes that system and calls upon its members to sustain, alter, or overthrow it. Ideology is thus both a description and a call to action." Ideologies tend to be utopian, absolute in their claims to represent truth, and centered on a program for action. "The Quran itself proclaims an ideology, a program of social and political action aimed at the creation of a godly society, and Muhammad's career was in large part devoted to carrying out this divinely authorized program of action" (1988, 138–39).

Putting these theoretical constructs now in relation with women's political rights and obligations in the Islamic context, we find that the ideal of the united, unified Islamic community *(umma)* is "a symbol of the faith" in the Geertzian sense, in that the debate of women's issues has remained pan-Islamic in tone and intent. Indeed, the role of women in Islam has itself achieved the status of cultural symbol, seen to have far-reaching implications for the religion as a whole. A number of separate paradigms coexist at present that, on the basis of Qur'an and Sunna, define the woman's "truly Islamic" societal role(s) in quite different terms. Whether the call is to "reform/modernize" women's status (in tune with a perceived inclusive, egalitarian blueprint of the early beginnings) or whether the call is to maintain a threatened "traditional" order (of gender inequality), these voices speak in the language of ideology in that they claim to represent absolute truth and call for action, even when that action consists in the preservation of the traditional system.

The Qur'anic Blueprint of God's Community on Earth: The Islamic *Umma*

The Qur'an speaks of the community of Islam as "the best community produced [or: evolved] for mankind, [whose members] command good and forbid evil and believe in God" (3:110; cf. 3:104); "a median community" (2:143) interpreted as an *umma* of the middle, founded as "a positive, creative mean, an integrative moral organism," sharing the best qualities of both other monotheistic religions (Rahman 1980, 28, 62). The Qur'an aims to establish an egalitarian and just sociomoral order on earth for which the *umma* is both context and vehicle. Individual morality is in part precondition for this society's formation and lasting existence, but individual morality is also, in turn, ensured by the *umma* as long as the latter is free of corruption *(fasad)*. The Qur'an's directives to the *umma* include mandates of distributive justice through welfare spending, strengthening bonds of solidarity between all its members, and struggle in the way of God *(jihad)*.

The Qur'anic *umma* is a theocratic state in that God's will is given language through revelation to His chosen Prophet and spokesman, who thereby also obtains rightful authority to rule. Sovereignty in the *umma* belongs to God, who is the *raison d'état,* the principle of unity, the *umma*'s "Staatsgedanke" which upholds and justifies the continuance of the commonwealth (Von Grunebaum 1962, 142). The *umma,* then, is not and cannot be based on a collective will of citizens who—as Rousseau would have it—contract to live together under laws that they themselves enacted. This may explain why the Qur'an's legal dicta on the rights of political participation are so few in number. In two verses (42:38 and 3:159), the Qur'an recommends consultation *(shura).* A larger number of verses legislate for obedience. The believers are enjoined to "obey God and His Messenger" (4:13–14) and, as the subsequent revelation of 4:59 prescribes, to "obey God, the Messenger, and those with authority among you *(ulu'l-amr minkum)*" (cf. also 4:83). Forbidden are acts of dissension and plotting against the common interest (58:5–10); armed rebellion "against God and His Messenger" and the creation of discord on earth are grave transgressions and punishable with severest penalties (5:36). In cases of infighting, arbitration is recommended before warfare (49:9–10). Those who demoralize the public [by divulging news of a sensitive nature] are censored (4:83). The Qur'an, then, legislates preeminently for the unity and solidarity of God's community. But the Qur'anic paradigm does not envisage civic obedience as obligation imposed regardless of the moral fiber or righteousness of the "holders of authority." Rather, the Qur²an speaks of unjust authority and the morality of rebellion against it in its accounts of the prophets from Noah onward as divinely summoned rebels against the corrupt established order of their day. Corruption is a recurring theme of warning in the Qur²an (e.g., 2:27, 13:25, 7:85, 11:116, 28:77) that calls the righteous to distance themselves lest they be doomed together with the transgressors. No human may take other humans as "lords beyond God" (3:64).

According to the Qur²an, then, membership in the *umma* hinges on righteous submission to the Almighty in faith, worship, and the fulfillment of His law, while the common weal is realized in spiritual and moral well-being, both individual and collective. Are the members of the *umma*, then, "subjects" or "citizens"? Does the Qur²an legislate not only for allegiance owed but political rights shared? An analysis of the Qur²anic prescriptions on women's status in God's polity, outlined in what follows, indicates that Muslims in Qur²anic definition are "subjects" in their relationship to God as their sovereign and lawgiver. The Qur²an also sets up authority to rule citizens; that is, it authorizes rulers from among the best, most pious and virtuous of the community (49:13). Beyond that, all believers, male and female, are called upon to perfect *taqwa* (devoutness, goodness, and virtue) in their individual lives and to ensure it, as social conscience, in the community at large, both by way of personal example and by participation in communal affairs, "commanding what is good and forbidding what is evil" (9:71). Although not involved in the formation of the law—which is divinely ordained—the righteous are thus called upon to participate in the exegetic processes of its application as "citizens" of God's community.

The Qur²an on the Conditions of Women's Citizenship: Female Righteousness as Faith, Devotion, and Godly Conduct

Among the many Qur²anic passages that define human righteousness, frequently revealed in the context of human accounting to God and God's judgment of humankind on the last day, a sizable number of verses are cast in gender-specific language. That is, men and women— whether believers or hypocrites and unbelievers—are addressed specifically and separately. Taken together, these verses define righteous men and women as Muslims (33:35), believers (16:97, 40:40, 57:19, 33:35, 33:73, 9:71–72) who work righteousness (16:97, 40:40) [such as

they who migrated, were driven from their homes, and suffered harm
for the sake of God, fought, and were killed (3:195)]. They are devout
(33:35), they pray (9:71), remember God often (33:35), give alms in
charity (57:18, 33:35, 9:71), fast, are truthful, patient, humble, and
avoid unlawful sexual contact (33:35). In these obligations the righteous
men and the righteous women "belong together" (3:195) as guardians
[or: protectors, friends *(awliya*ᵓ*)*] one of the other, "commanding what is
right and forbidding what is evil" (9:71).

These Qurᵓanic passages place great emphasis on faith, devotion,
worship, and the duties of almsgiving and fasting that represent the
essence of Muslim rituals. In addition, humility, patience, truthfulness,
and chastity outside of marriage—all primarily traits of individual and
private godliness—are included. The Qurᵓanic text leaves no doubt that
male and female believers are equally charged with the fulfillment of
these obligations and that they will reap equal rewards. Individual righteousness is linked to the moral well-being of the community as a whole,
just as individual impiety and immorality work to the detriment of the
collective. Beyond ensuring public morality by way of personal example,
however, God's men and women must also do so through active involvement in communal participation "in obedience to God and His Prophet."
In pursuit of these communal goals, men and women are equal "guardians of each other" (9:71).

The righteousness verses that address men and women separately
are generally dated into the Medinan period, with the exception of 16:97
and 40:40 which are considered late Meccan revelations. The fact that
God spoke specifically to the women of the believers did, of course, not
escape Muslim attention, and this feature of the revelations is generally
"explained" in *hadith* and *tafsir* (Quarᵓanic interpretation) as resulting
from complaints by one, or all, of the Prophet's wives, or by Muslim
women in general, who felt that they were being left out (Ibn Saᶜd 1904,
144). The answer to why such a substantial number of revelations were
specifically addressed to the females of Islam may perhaps best be provided by the Qurᵓanic passages themselves, especially when these are
taken together with the time frame of their revelation. Muslim and
Western Qurᵓanic scholars alike acknowledge that the late Meccan and,
especially, the Medinan *suras* were largely concerned with the structuring of the community of Islam, which included the definition of citizenship in the community as based on individual virtue. Larger concerns
than the Prophet's wives' complaints, then, underlie the Qurᵓan's gender-specific definition of the true believers' obligations and rewards.
To build God's society on earth required women's integration into the

community, and it is for this reason that the Qur'an legislated for equality of the sexes in moral citizenship of the *umma*.

The Qur'an on Women, Communal Affairs and Morality

The Women's Bay'a

A definition of female social morality is found in *sura* 60 (*al-Mumtahana* she who is examined) that furnished the terms by which Muslim women swore fealty (bay'a) to the Prophet in Medina. This *sura* has three interrelated themes: Severing of relations with the infidels (in Mecca), legal and financial stipulations covering cases where the severing of ties involves spouses, and the text of the women's pledge of allegiance to the Prophet. The *sura* first forbids the believers to maintain relations of love and friendship with their enemies—and God's (60:1, 9, 13). The Qur'an then recognizes that the line that separates believer from unbeliever can cut through the core of the family, dividing believing wife from unbelieving husband and believing husband from unbelieving wife. In such cases, the woman's faith is to be tested by way of an examination, and women found to be believers are permitted to remain in Medina as divorced women whose dowers must be restituted to their pagan husbands, just as the dowers of unbelieving wives should be returned to Muslim husbands (60:10–11). The *sura*'s third theme constitutes the women's declaration of faith and pledge of allegiance to the Prophet:

> O Prophet! When believing women come to you to take the oath of allegiance to you: that they will not ascribe partners to God, that they will not utter slander which they have [lyingly] devised between their hands and their feet, that they will not disobey you in what is right *(fi ma'rufin)*, then accept their allegiance, and pray to God to forgive them, for God is forgiving, merciful (60:12).

This oath may have been first applied as, or in relation to, the "examination" that established admission to citizenship status in Medina for the believing female migrants *(muhajirat)*. But Hadith collections, such as the *Tabaqat* of Ibn Sa'd, contain large numbers of traditions that identify by name the Muslim women who pledged allegiance to the Prophet. According to Ibn Sa'd, 129 of these were migrants from Mecca (70 from Quraysh and their confederates and 59 other "Arab women")

(Ibn Sa'd 1904, 161–230), while 349 were Medinan Ansar women (69
Aws) (Ibn Sa'd 1904, 230–39, 251–61) and 280 Khazraj (261–337).
These women did not take the pledge of allegiance together on a single
occasion. For example, according to Ibn Ishaq, the oath was applied to
all of the women of Mecca after the Prophet's conquest of Mecca in A.D.
630. As with the men, female conversion and entering into Islam was an
ongoing process. The large number of women (numbering 478) whose
"pledge of allegiance to the Prophet" Ibn Sa'd has recorded may not all
have sworn fealty in the exact words of 60:12 because the verse was
revealed only in the later Medinan period. But the formula, because of
when and where it *was* revealed, defines the conditions of female citizenship after the full establishment of the *umma*. It is thus an important
political document because (1) it acknowledges women as political actors;
(2) the text enshrines the legal conditions of female membership in the
umma in terms of sins/crimes foresworn that are applicable to all believers regardless of gender and punishment for which, if committed, is the
same for men and women; and (3) the oath's formula to "refrain from
disobedience [to the Prophet] in what is right *(fi ma'rufin)"* enjoins a
general, but not an unconditional, obedience to the community's leader.

Crime and Punishment

According to the revealed text of the women's oath of fealty to the
Prophet, women's admission to citizenship in the Medinan community
hinged on their pledge of responsible individual behavior that would
ensure the community's internal peace and solidarity. The acts foresworn by participants in the women's *bay'a* involved: polytheism, theft,
fornication, infanticide, slander, and disobedience to the leader of the
community in what was equitable. Four, or five, of these transgressions
were later reckoned among the six, or seven, crimes classified by the
jurists of Islam as *hudud* offenses (sing. *hadd)* which are: apostasy, theft,
fornication, slanderous allegation of unchastity (of a woman), wine drink-
ing, armed robbery, and rebellion (which is not always included; Islamic
law does not include murder among the *hudud)*. Jurists grouped these
crimes together because they considered them offenses in which "the
notion of man's obligation toward God predominated" (Coulsen 1964,
124), and they identified them by the name of *hudud* because they
found unalterable punishments for these transgressions as "defined"
(h-d-d) in the Qur'an by God Himself when He laid down the "limits"
or "boundaries" *(hudud)* of His prescriptions (Coulsen 1964, 124). The
common element in these Qur'anic injunctions and prescribed punish-

ments is the equality of male and female believers. In short, if civic equality is measured in terms of equal responsibility under *hudud* law, then Muslim men and women are communal citizens of equal rank.

Issues of Public and Private Modesty

A substantial portion of the Qur'an's social laws deals with issues directly or indirectly related to the control of Muslim sexuality beyond the sexual rights established by marriage and concubinage. Outside of these two areas, the principle of chastity is a governing law of righteous Muslim conduct, implementation of which hinges to a large degree on individual modesty. Here the Qur'an distinguishes between the private and public domains and provides stringent rules on what constitutes righteous comportment in either of these two spheres of life. The issue of privacy looms large in Qur'anic legislation. Access to "inhabited houses" other than one's own must be severely restricted, allowable only when permission to enter has been asked for and granted [by the inhabitants of the house] (24:27–29). Within the private sphere of their domicile, believers must control access to their personal [sleeping] quarters by household slaves and children during times of informal attire (24:58–59). That these regulations are meant to eliminate situations of potential sexual temptation or corruption within the house is quite clear.

If Muslim righteous behavior in the privacy of the home must be marked by modesty of comportment and attire, such behavior is even more imperative in the public arena. Thus, the Qur'an instructs the Prophet: "Tell your wives and daughters and the women of the believers that they should draw their outer garments *(jalabib* [sing. *jilbab])* over themselves, which is more appropriate, so that they are known and not molested" (33:59). This revelation was later followed by the command addressed to Muslim men and women to "lower their eyes and guard their private parts" (24:30–31). To the women, the command adds, "that they draw their scarves *(khumur* [sing. *khimar])* over their bosoms *(juyub* [sing. *jayb])*, and not display their adornment except to their husbands, or their fathers, or their husbands' fathers, or their sons, or their husbands' sons, or their brothers, or their brothers' sons, or their sisters' sons, or their women, or their slaves, or male subordinates who have no natural force *(irba)*, or the children who have no knowledge of women's private parts. And that they not stamp their feet to give kowledge of the adornment which they hide."

By way of hadith-based scripturalist interpretation, medieval traditionalist lawyer-theologians defined a stringent "law of the veil" for

Muslim women based on 33:59 and 24:31; such features as face veils
and face masks were subsumed under this law. Simultaneously, the
interpreters merged Qur'anic definitions of female modesty spelled out
in these *ayas* with the *hijab* (curtain) imposed upon the Prophet's wives
in 33:53 and with Hadiths regarding "strutting about" *(tabarruj)* (33:33)
(Stowasser 1994, 97–99). As elaborated in Muslim law and theology,
these revelations and Hadiths became referents for legal categories of
women's segregation and exclusion from public life. The Qur'an-
ordained modesty of the Muslim woman was interpreted to mean both
her physical and her political invisibility. In contradistinction to these
medieval interpretations that continue to permeate contemporary traditionalist thought, the Qur'anic text of the women's *bay'a* (60:12), revealed *after* the "clothing verse" of *sura* 33 and the "modesty verse" of
sura 24, acknowledged for the Muslim woman her legal competence to
participate in the public act of pledging her moral and political allegiance
and stipulated women's admission to citizenship in the *umma* on conditions exclusive of clothing restrictions, as outlined above.

The Qur'an on Female Righteousness as
Custodianship of Family Solidarity: The Issue of
the Husband's *Qiwama* over His Wife

When the Qur'an defines the believers' social rights and obligations, it establishes parameters of individual Muslim ethical behavior;
its primary purpose, however, lies with the moral well-being of the community as a whole. The extensive family laws of the Qur'an specify
for the Muslim female some basic rights of social status and economic
competence, but the law's intent lies largely with the preservation of the
family order, not the promulgation of male or female individual rights.

Among the many directives concerning the institutions of marriage
and parenthood, one Qur'anic revelation succinctly stipulates that the
godly Muslim family order rests on the husband's authority over his wife
as occasioned by his responsibility for her economic support and on the
wife's obedience to her husband's authority; that is, his *qiwama* (being
in charge). The particular revelation (4:34) that has played important
roles both in classical legal-theological reasoning and also in modern
Islamic thought on women's issues reads:

> Men are in charge of women *(al-rijalu qawwamuna 'ala'l-nisa')* be-
> cause God has endowed the one with more, and because they spend
> of their property for their support. Therefore, the righteous women

are the obedient, guarding in secret that which God has guarded. As to those from whom you fear rebellion, admonish them and banish them to separate beds, and scourge them. Then if they obey you, seek not a way against them. For God is high, ever exalted, great.

The wording of 4:34 parallels verse 4:32, which precedes it. "Do not covet that with which God has endowed the one of you more than the other. To men is allotted a share of what they earned and to women is allotted a share of what they earned. And ask God of His bounty, verily God is omniscient." These two Qur'anic texts, taken together, stipulate a patriarchal family structure based on the husband's economic power and obligation and advise the Muslim wife to obedience without coveting the "gifts unequally bestowed" that underlie this order. This revealed decree of an essential difference in family roles of male and female forms part of the Qur'anic purposes to strengthen the family. Woman's righteousness is realized when she accepts her place and obligations in this divinely legislated system.

Muslim scholastic interpretation, however, extended the applicability of men's *qiwama* to areas beyond the family until it became a fundamental legal principle of male social and political preeminence in the Islamic *umma*.

The Question of Legal Civil "Equality" in the Qur'an

The Qur'an establishes that all humans were and are created equal: "God created you from one soul, then of it He made its mate, and from them twain scattered many men and women" (39:6, 4:1, cf. 49:13). The Qur'an also asserts that "the noblest of you in the sight of God is the one most possessed of *taqwa*" (49:13); that is, the only valid ranking of humans in the eyes of God is one based on godliness and virtue, regardless of lineage, wealth, and power. Ranking is equally independent of gender because believing men and women are equals in obligation to be "guardians" of each other (9:71).

As mentioned earlier, however, the Qur'an does not associate its principle of equal human dignity and worthiness with notions such as absolute and individual social, political, or economic equality. That is, the Qur'an legislates equality in terms not comparable to the natural law concept of "human rights" that Western political theory derived from various ideological and political platforms first formulated and applied in eighteenth-century Europe and America. Indeed, the Qur'an sanctions unequal distribution of economic and sociopolitical power and, especially in its family laws, establishes a link between economic power and social control. For example, 4:34's injunction that "men are in charge of women," quoted above, links men's *qiwama* with male economic power and responsibility (for dower and maintenance expenses for the wife) in the family context. Likewise, the stipulations of the male's right to polygamy, heavily conditional though that right may be (4:3, 129); of his right—not shared by the Muslim female—to marry from among the People of the Book (5:6); and of extensive male powers in initiating and controlling the divorce process (2:226–32, 4:20, 65:1–7) are legislated in reference to the patriarchal family structure and involve some considerations of male economic responsibility. The Qur'anic laws of inheritance where the female's share is half of that of the male in a number of cases (4:11, 12, 176) also fit a patriarchal family framework.

In sum, then, the Qur'anic definition of *equality* consists of several components compatible within the context of the Islamic *umma* as "republic of virtue" but which differ from Western late eighteenth-century sociopolitical theories and legal concepts. These components are, first, that equality is a function of morality and goodness, and second, that it means equal service toward the collective well-being of the community. The task to serve the common weal falls in equal measure to men and women. Their obligations are identical in some categories and not in others, but in all cases the obligations' purpose is to ensure unity and solidarity of the collective.

The Question of "Interpretation"

The foregoing Qur'anic paradigm underwent a paradigmatic shift when the Arab wars of conquest in the seventh and eighth centuries set the stage both for the assimilation of Arabian society into the larger society of the Middle East and reciprocally, for the integration of the conquered peoples into a new political and religious identity. Arabian tribal structure weakened in favor of an empire-wide, urban Islamic society stratified on the basis of class and power (Lapidus 1982, 68–72). These developments had profound consequences for the civil status of women in Islam.

From an early date, the newly emerging sociopolitical order was "brought into harmony" with the Qur'an's sociopolitical laws by the *'ulama'* (religious scholars): Hadith-collectors and compilers, exegetes, jurists, preachers, and the like. *'Ulama'* emergence as a cohesive class of prestige and influence occurred at the end of the eighth century during the period of the early Abbasid caliphs. The latter, in their pursuit of legitimacy in religious terms, favored the religious scholars and provided for them a more secure place and role in the empire by creating a judiciary system that furnished career opportunities concomitant with social status and influence. Consequently, the *ulama'* in a new *esprit de corps* endeavored to "create a new religious synthesis just as their Abbasid masters were attempting to create a new political one" (Khalidi 1985, 42) and in the process acquired recognition as determiners of doctrine and law through the consensus of their group *(ijma^c)* in every generation. Furthermore, being mainly of middle-class background, the *ulama'* had by nature strong communal links as well as staying power that endowed their authority with permanence while the Abbbasid empire from the middle of the tenth century onwards suffered decentralization and fragmentation into small semiautonomous feudal states of limited life spans. These developments contributed to increasing *ulama'* conservatism, reflected in their majority option for imitation of established legal doctrines *(taqlid)* over personal scripture-based reasoning or interpretation *(ijtihad)*. Their conservatism was largely rooted in their desire to preserve the unity of the *umma* at all costs.

Neither during the period of early Abbasid strength nor the following centuries of political decentralization were the *ulama'* by class background or political role motivated to develop principles of Muslim civil rights. On the contrary, by emphasizing and extending the Qur'anic maxim of preeminence of the common weal over individual rights, they largely disregarded notions such as the Qur'anic recommendation of *shura* (political consultation) in favor of the Qur'anic injunction of obedience to "God, His Messenger, and the possessors of authority," under which they subsumed both obedience to God's law [in their custodianship] and also obedience to the governments that upheld it and made its application possible.

In traditional *ulama'* political theory, Muslims were assigned the status of "subjects" of worldly rulers, the latter considered legitimate if supported by *ulama'* approval. Unquestioning obedience was owed these rulers because the religious establishment reckoned preservation of order and prevention of anarchy the community's highest political priority. The process of ideological "disenfranchisement" from Qur'anic legislation to medieval *ulama'* political theory affected, of course, all members of the community. Its targets of least resistance, however, were the women of Islam. Their Qur'anic status as moral citizens of the early Arabian *umma*, enjoined to obedience to their husbands for the sake of family solidarity, was interpreted in the highly stratified urban societies of medieval Islam to mean their legal social dependency and political exclusion.

The definition of Muslim fundamental freedoms, or rights, involves: the right to life, the right to religion, the right to earning and owning property, and the right to personal honor and dignity (Rahman 1980, 46). In continuation of classical *ʿulamaʾ* doctrine, contemporary traditionalist thinkers, emphasizing the male's preeminence over the female, still also disregard, or negate, notions of equal individual political and other rights even of male Muslims. Their paradigm is delineated and continually reinforced in the books and pamphlets, sermons and lectures of traditionalist establishment theologians, who usually speak in their clearest idiom when dealing with questions of women's political rights. For this reason, the debate on women's franchise can provide rich insights into the traditionalist political paradigm as a whole. Examples can be found, for instance, in traditionalist argumentation formulated in Egypt during the early fifties, shortly before Egyptian women got the right to vote and stand for election. Papers presented at a conference on "Women's Political Rights in Islam," convened in Cairo by conservative Muslim thinkers in 1952, were published twenty-six years later, in 1978, (Khamis 1978) to voice the traditionalist point of view. In his paper "The Shariʿa's Position on Women's Rights," the Azharite Muhammad Yusuf Musa sums up the old conservative paradigm:

> We believe that it is . . . not necessary to speak further about the rights which Islam has provided women, this is a clear matter . . . nor about our good Eastern traditions which do not grant women the right to stand for election . . . in accordance with religion and its ordinances. Rather, we want to discuss the defects of the supporters of women's right to political candidacy—i.e. "democracy," "equality," and "freedom"—which allegedly should belong to everybody. There is a fine line between freedom and anarchy which we must strive to preserve, otherwise disaster will follow. "Democracy" and "equality" do not mean that everybody obtains what he wants at the expense of religion and the common interest; rather, they consist in general rights and duties . . . which prevent that people oppress each other, and through which each citizen can confidently obtain the wages of his labor for which he is qualified in terms of nature, abilities, and talents. . . . If equality were absolute, it would turn into oppression . . . and pervert sound practices, since God did not create men as equals in nature, talent, ability, and qualification. . . . Concerning men and women, He said: "Women shall have rights similar to the rights against them, according to what is equitable;

but men have a degree over them" (2:228). The Qur'an confirms this, in these and other verses, which to us is a confirmation of how things really are, besides being God's ordinance (Khamis 1978, 48–50).

Three main points are made here: (1) The (modern/Western) political concepts and institutions of *democracy, freedom,* and *equality* are incompatible with religion and the moral well-being of the community of Islam; equality of all in terms of absolute equal rights would mean that all would strive to realize their ambitions licentiously, that is, at the expense of religion and the common weal, and anarchy and disaster would follow. (2) Men are by nature not equal because God created them different in nature, talent, and ability. Human ambition to assume powers beyond one's God-assigned station in life results in oppression and the perversion of the sociopolitical order. (3) Males are by their nature and also by divine decree the superiors of females, and so women's quest for political participation is an aberration of society's natural order and a sin against the ordinance of God.

In the 1990s, more than a generation later, this old traditionalist paradigm has been affected by fast-paced economic and social change and the resulting, now widely held, notion that *equality* and also some form of *political participation* (as legislated in the Qur'anic principle of *shura*) are part and parcel of the True Islamic System. This shift owes as much to Islamic Modernism as it does to Islamism (Integrism, or "Fundamentalism"). Even though they differ in approaches to the scripture and their understanding of its true meaning, modernists and Islamists share the desire to achieve both an authentic modernity and an authentic, Qur'an-centered, Islam. It is in their differences that gender issues continue to hold center stage. For the modernists, the Qur'an's eternally valid system of values lies behind its "literal," situation-specific laws that were historically and culturally contextualized to fit the Prophet's time, while gender equality (including women's equal political rights) form part of the Qur'an's essential and universal message. For the Islamists, the sexes are also equal, but they are created and fashioned for different tasks, the man to provide for and protect his family, the woman to support him in his struggle and bear and raise their children, so that his natural domain is society at large while hers is the home.

The three scripturalist paradigms on women's citizenship in a truly Islamic society—traditionalist, modernist, and Islamist—presently coexist and have done so for quite some time. As stated at the beginning of this chapter, *paradigms* are *patterns, frameworks* of general ideas that structure perception and also serve as an agenda for the future, so that they function both as *"models for."* The actual situation of Muslim women and throughout history, their societal roles and rights, some of which are explored in this book, form part of such models in that they were, and are, the reality on which the paradigm rests. The model, however, is not one of science but ideology, therefore centered on a program for action that seeks to overcome perceived imperfection in order to create perfection, justice, a godly society.

As shown in this chapter, the Qur'anic laws on women as political actors provide principles of women's welfare within the context of communal welfare. Both of these notions underwent drastic reinterpretation after the Prophet's time. The present debate with its clashing of paradigms may be even fiercer than it was in the early centuries of Islamic history. Yet then as now, paradigms were influential only as long as their proponents were politically powerful, be it in alliance with the state or in opposition to it.

2

Women and Modernization

A Reevaluation

Afaf Lutfi al-Sayyid Marsot

Studies of Muslim women have proliferated in the past decade, although nothing definitive about them has yet come to light. The debate about women largely falls within two opposing arguments: that Muslim women are downtrodden and oppressed as the result of their religion or that Islam liberated women and gave them rights that protected them from oppression. Under either of these arguments are a number of sub-arguments finessing the main arguments. Let us for the time being set aside the religious argument and take the overarching theory regarding women in general, that is assuming that there is an overarching theory that applies to all women and is not one that is strictly guided by Euro-centrism, as is much of social science research.

Anthropologists explain that in societies that sustained themselves through hunting, men were the dominant partners because they did the hunting. When such societies evolved into agricultural societies, the earliest of which lay in the Nile Valley, the valley of the Tigris Euphrates, and China, those societies where the hoe was used treated men and women equally because either gender could handle a hoe; but in societies where the plough was in use, men became the dominant partner. Because the plough needed strength and was predominantly used by males, they became regarded as the breadwinners, although women participated in all other chores (Goody 1976, 19). In nomadic societies, such as those of the Arabian Peninsula where transhumance was a way of life, men were dominant because they had to resort to violence to stave off attacks from rival tribes. In any society that came under occa-

39

sional attack, the military, hence men, became dominant, which implied a built-in dominance for males in all societies unless women also became enrolled in the military. Yet, in the Arabian Peninsula we note that some tribes were matriarchal, where the man joined his wife's tribe; others were patriarchal, where the woman joined her spouse's tribe. When it came to urban communities where men were long-distance traders, a patriarchal system developed because the caravans needed military protection and were subjected to hardships along the way; yet, capital for such ventures could come from either gender, assuming women had access to capital, mostly through inheritance. Capital could be real estate or even camels and caravans. Although we are not sure why some tribes differed from others, even when both followed transhumance, we can at least assume that the status of individuals in society depended on the mode of production within the society, an economic determinant. Because tribal societies held property in common for the tribe, they were egalitarian. The economic determinant is sustained by a political determinant where, in all societies, men undertook the function of protecting their society from outside aggression and as warriors enjoyed a superior status. Consequently, they also developed control of the political functions of society. The third determinant within society is a moral cum legal determinant, for which we can read ethics, religion, etcetera.

Within a male-female relationship, there are further determinants that set the framework for that relationship. The first is the age differential between the couple; the closer they are in age, the more equal they are. On the other hand if there is a large age differential, then the male will have an edge because age casts an aura of wisdom and of greater knowledge of life in general, so that the wife is then expected to defer to the husband in all matters because of his greater age. Second is the degree of wealth that each possesses; whoever possesses greater wealth will have an edge over the partner because that wealth may be used to defray either the necessities or the luxuries. One needs to remember here that access to wealth for women is more restricted than for men. Third is the degree of education; if one partner is more educated than the other, that partner has the edge by virtue of greater knowledge of book learning. Thus, in primitive societies where the spouses have the same age, the same degree of wealth, and the same degree of education, one can expect to find greater equality among spouses. That at least is the general rule, but of course there will be exceptions and other determinants. For example, the male is physically stronger and can abuse the female and force her obedience; or in a warlike society, warriors have an edge as defenders of hearth and home.

Islam and the Prophet Muhammad came to forge a new society that was to heal the breaches of the old one, in disarray from a changing mode of production from the nomadic to the urban/mercantile one; for whereas the former accentuated community, the latter accentuated individual acumen (Ibrahim 1992). Nevertheless, the new society retained elements of that old society; thus it is that we have contradictory pictures of the position of women. We know that some tribes did not value females and indeed exposed them at birth, although how widespread that practice was is unknown; it could hardly have been the dominant practice, for then the tribes would have disappeared from existence. Other tribes valued females and had a sense of equality. Urban areas contained powerful women such as Khadija, the Prophet's wife, and Hind, the wife of the Prophet's major opponent, Abu Sufyan, who were free to behave as they pleased, who therefore had power. Neither wealth nor power implied superiority, but they certainly did not imply an inevitably downtrodden position for women. We must also note that although elite groups set the pace for the rest of the polity, all other social strata do not necessarily abide by the same conditions as the elites.

The Prophet Muhammad clearly did not look upon women as a liability or a sex worthy of subjugation. The Qur'an is full of verses specifying the equality of men and women in religious duty and in rights and obligations. Nonetheless, the Qur'an allowed men four wives, on condition they treated them with equity but also categorically stated that they could not do that, thus it was better to marry only one. The Qur'an allowed men twice the inheritance of women, thus placing women in a different position from that of men.

When the Qur'an specified the right of women to inherit property in much the same fashion as men, albeit in different proportions, the men of Mecca were outraged at having to support women materially as well as having them share in inheritance. It may have been that the lesser share granted women was a means of placating. On the other hand, Medinan women were treated differently by the males, probably because they were an agricultural society, where women shared the labor in the fields with the men. Medinan women displeased Meccan men because of their degree of freedom, which the Meccan men believed set a bad example for Meccan women. The bottom line is that, within a small society such as early Islamic Arabia, there were different gender attitudes amongst different groupings, which should come as no surprise. What should surprise us is not that women were second-class citizens in some communities but that they should have been granted legal rights heretofore unspecified. To date, no society, save some obscure tribes in the Himalayas or elsewhere, treats men and women equally, and so it is not the norm of different gender treatments that we need to examine but the degree to which such different treatment exists. Religion sets out guidelines for society to follow. How society applies and interprets these guidelines is a function not only of religion but of economics, politics, social behavior and circumstances, demographics, and culture; for these elements determined the interpretations derived from the Qur'an. Thus, religion is only one determinant among many that guide a society. It is true that it is perhaps the most important determinant, although I would challenge that in the twentieth century, unlike its importance in past centuries; but it is still only one among many others. To explain further.

When a society lacks sufficient food, males get the lion's share; in times of recession, women are incited to give up their jobs in favor of men; yet, when the men go to war, women are encouraged to fill in the blanks left by the men. Men who lead the army also lead the polity and the judicial power; and although at times women have led the polity, they have not, with the exception of such cases as Amazons, Boadicea, and certain Arab women, led armies yet, nor, save in Indonesia and Sudan have they had judicial powers. Yet, it is women who control and nurture society at large. Psychologists tell us that the one who teaches the child from birth and for the first few years is the one who will have the greatest influence on that child. It is women who teach children social, religious, and ethical values, thus it is women who help perpetuate any discriminatory practices a society might have. Feminists tell us it is because they have plugged into the patriarchal system and derive their status from it. True enough, but why not teach their offspring to break away from such a system? The important point to note is that different circumstances created different social attitudes within the Muslim world and among other societies over different centuries.

When we take the case of Egypt, we note that during the pharaonic period women could marry and divorce at will; they could inherit and deed property at will; they could set up endowments or leave their property to whomever they wished. Women were on a par with men, so that some women were even high-level administrators. Male gods were *either* good or bad, but women goddesses were *both* good and bad; that is, they had a dual nature. Good or bad is here used in the sense that the god benefited humans or harmed them, so that the god Osiris was benevolent and Seth was malevolent. On the other hand, Isis was benevolent in one manifestation but malevolent in another. That dual nature for females seems to have been a very ancient concept that has persisted to the present day and may indeed be part of the ur-memory of mankind: that of the nurturer/destroyer, for example, the goddess Sekhmet, or the mother/whore syndrome. Why that is so is best explained by psychologists who talk of the vagina dentata, the male fear of impotence, of being subjected to voracious female desires. From that fear, in self-defense, the idea developed that it is best to keep females uninitiated, ignorant of their sexuality, virgin before marriage. This was ramified by the importance of property within society leading to accentuating virginity in order to make sure that inherited property went to the right heirs, that is, the children of the legal father, the linchpin of a patriarchal system. If in such societies women inherited property, it was an added reason for keeping them cloistered so that the family could dispose of the heiress in a manner that was advantageous to the family or the tribe.

That may be the reason why the free-wheeling attitude toward women in the Ancient Kingdom became eroded with time and women became more subjugated in the New Kingdom. The ancient Greeks who conquered Egypt were warriors more than peasants. Their society prized military valor, hence strength and men above women. Because of their harsher means of livelihood, only men inherited property and women were property as well to be masked from the public eye by veiling and seclusion to guarantee purity and their disposal at the will of the males in the family. The same attitude reigned in Roman days.

Christianity sent mixed signals regarding women. Jesus made women equal to men, but St. Paul exhorted women to obey men and to abide by their decisions. Women were meant to be biological machines as mothers and wives or else to become chaste and inviolate as nuns worshipping God. In either case, women paid a dowry on marriage, whether it be as brides to a human or brides of Christ. Judaism, which had taken many of its moral codes from the Ancient Egyptians, failed to take the Egyptian attitude toward women as a man's equal but rather made them subservient to the male, even in worshipping God, where a *minyan* (religious quorum) existed with the presence of males only, and females were isolated from males during worship.

Islam brought a different attitude because of different circumstances. Although some women had been accustomed to going into battle with men, others were not. Although some women had been accustomed to inheriting property and to managing that property, others were not. The new Muslim community fell in line with what was customary among a small group among them. Men, however, had been made financially responsible for the upkeep of the family. Women inherited property but disposed of that property as they pleased and were not enjoined to participate in the upkeep of the family. Thus, in one sense women were theoretically freer in their property rights than men, even when they inherited in a lesser proportion. We need also note that women inherited a minimum of half the male portion, but there was nothing that prevented anyone from leaving women heirs even more property through a gift. It was probably that discrepancy in responsibilities that exercised men rather than the principle of women inheriting wealth, which had existed in some communities, especially the Meccan. Muslim society also changed attitudes toward women with differing circumstances, just like all other societies.

The bottom line is that throughout the ages in whatever society, women have been second-class citizens dominated by males. That domination was expressed in religious interpretations, in social injunctions, in legal ones, and in educational ones. Let us examine Egypt as an example of a Muslim society, noting that not all Muslim societies share the same attitudes because much of what passes for Muslim behavior is dependent on different interpretations arising from different customs and habits at different chronological periods.

Bourgeois Women

If we are to expect different attitudes toward women at different times, then there is little sense in going back several centuries to understand the present; but it behooves us to go back as far as a critical period and trace the status of women from that period rather than for millenia. The mid-eighteenth century in Egypt revealed a decentralized government with elite men busied in internecine squabbles that left elite women free to indulge in commercial and economic activities and the acquisition of wealth. Both elite men and elite women who were alien to Egypt had been former slaves, the *mamluks*. Both had to be taught a common language, Turkish, for they came from different ethnicities; and both had to be converted to Islam. There may have been a difference in age, but that seemed to matter little because the men were seldom around and left their property in the keeping of their wives. Also, they feared confiscation of property by the authorities (a commonplace practice then) and assumed that the authorities would be less likely to confiscate property owned by females. There was also little discrepancy in the degree of education among spouses. Thus, both sexes seemed to be on a par as far as age, education, and wealth were concerned, which situation allowed women to become deeply involved in the economic life of the country. What elite women succeeded in doing was also done by bourgeois women. Women of the lower strata, that is working-class women, had little options and deserve a different treatment to which we shall return later (Marsot 1995).

In the nineteenth century, Muhammad ʿAli (1805–1848) brought in a centralized form of government. To keep the ruling elites from fighting each other over land or dues from land, the ruler therefore had to increase the sources of revenue and also to control his elites and make them dependent upon him for bounty. This was done through irrigation schemes, which increased the area of cultivable land and also allowed for several crops a year, which led to commercial agriculture. This is not to say that commercial agriculture had not already existed before Muhammad ʿAli, but it had done so on a limited scale that was greatly expanded under Muhammad ʿAli. What helped the expansion of commercial agriculture was the attraction of European markets for industrially necessary crops, such as cotton, flax, and indigo, and the Peninsular War, which created a demand for grain to feed armies. Thus, a dependable market for such goods became available and encouraged the ruler and his cohorts to change their previous base of financial resources from that of taxing the peasant to that of expropriating the harvest and selling it at preferential rates to the foreign market. The next step was for the elites to displace the peasant, make him a landless wage earner, and turn land into private property on a large scale (land had been used as private property earlier but in a limited fashion). The ruler distributed that land to whomever he wished to reward. This meant that all those on whom the ruler did not depend were cut out of landowning, that is, women. Women had formerly invested in land, as tax farmers, but now they were set aside in favor of government officials and bureaucrats, or native notables who helped the government collect taxes from the population. Thus, one major source of income for women was removed from circulation.

The second source of income was trade and commerce, which were monopolized by the ruler so that no one else could become involved. Women therefore found themselves in consequence of a new patriarchal, centralized system, devoid of participation in any wealth-generating activities. They could eventually inherit land according to Muslim laws, especially after 1858, when the Ottomans passed the land law that simply ratified what had already existed for decades, but then they turned the land over to their male relatives. Which begs the question. The new centralized system also introduced new institutions derived from Europe that militated against women. Banks, stock exchanges, insurance companies, etcetera, in Europe did not recognize the legal existence of women;

and so they followed the same strategies in Egypt. Women were not allowed to open bank acounts in their names or to play the stock market or to indulge in other activities in their own right. Once the male relative became the active partner, even though it may be the woman directing him, he nonetheless became the wielder of power and the detainer of income. Furthermore, with the new centralized system of government, men were perforce delaying marriage. Unlike the Mamluk system, where young *mamluks* were found positions as soon as they had been manumitted and encouraged to wed by their patrons, they were now expected to rise in the ranks through skill and personal endeavor; thus, the age differential grew. Also, in the new bureaucracy, men were expected to be educated; and an education differential operated on top of the age and wealth differentials. Women were therefore inexorably pushed into a subservient position. With few exceptions, women simply turned over their wealth to male relatives. The males in turn encouraged women to become economically passive, and following elite Ottoman custom, segregated them even more strictly in the harem. Native Egyptians followed that custom as a means of aping their Ottoman fellow elites and aspiring to become part of the new ruling elites (Marsot 1984).

As the apex of a pyramidal hierarchy derived from European forms of government, the ruler regarded himself and was looked upon by his subjects as the "father" of the country, the one from whom all blessings flowed *(waliyy al-niᶜam)*. The family followed the same setup, with the father now considered the prime breadwinner, the head of the hierarchy, and the mother coming in second place. This is not to say that at any time before women had been superior to men in any but a few unusual societies, but it did mean that women were now being peripheralized in terms of the accumulation of wealth and made dependent on the male breadwinner, which naturally put women in a lesser position vis-à-vis the male, the disburser of largesse. The attempts to peripheralize women were sustained by religious interpretations that accentuated women's duties as limited to hearth and home and family and that played up her biological functions as opposed to any educational or commercial ones to which she might aspire. As the century went on and British influence dominated in Egypt, the peripheral role of the elite woman was exacerbated and the nineteenth-century British notion of womanhood as "silly," "emotional," and "illogical" (Nicholson 1986) predominated in the country. Egyptian men, aping their British superiors, found it convenient to look upon women in the same fashion, insisting on a spurious *hadith* attributed to the Prophet that said that women "lacked brains and religion." In time, when the British masters needed

larger markets that the female population could supply, they were quick
to point out that Egyptian elite women were uneducated and needed to
become educated, not in religious lore, as education had been identified
in the past, but in Western-style education (Mitchell 1988). Thus, a
generation of young women arose who spoke better European languages
than they did their own, and who were more at ease in European customs and clothing than in native ones. Thus was seen in the last quarter
of the nineteenth century a change in architecture, in clothing, in furniture, even in musical instruments, all now derived from Europe. The
ruling family, Isma῾il and his successors, led the way to the Europeaniza-
tion of Egypt, which the British ocupation exacerbated. This is not to
imply that Egypt became European, but to state that many elements in
Egypt in terms of consumer goods did become Europeanized. Such a
situation militated against local production and encouraged the influx of
foreigners who, benefiting from the preferential terms of the capitula-
tions, set up new department stores, and encouraged the push toward
European imports.

Once secular education became the norm, women chafed at the
limits set upon their movement through the harem system and demanded a change in circumstances. The opportunity arose with the nationalist movement in 1919; for when the men were imprisoned because
of their anti-British activities, the women took over and demonstrated
in favor of independence. Their participation in the nationalist cause
allowed them to leave the harem and remove the veil. Having done that
in the name of nationalism, it was impossible to force them back into the
harem, especially when they made it clear that, unlike European
women, they were not asking for a role in politics but were content to
take over the social services of the country. Political participation was to
come later. In brief, because of the new form of a centralized government that monopolized all sources of wealth and was sustained by foreign ideas of the frivolous nature of women, women were peripheralized
in the nineteenth century and only recovered some of the economic
activities they had had in the eighteenth century in the twentieth
century.

Working-Class Women

What about strata of women other than elites? Working-class
women had always worked and in one sense because they too were
breadwinners had a relatively equal position with males. It is true they
did double duty as both housewives and breadwinners—but that is a

role that most working women all over the world today recognize. Where in the eighteenth century women were part and parcel of the economy as producers of goods, that role was minimized in the nineteenth century. When "value" is defined in monetary terms alone, women's work is not considered as economically productive. Furthermore, through the importation of substitute goods, some women who worked in commodity manufacture lost out. For example, the demand for Ottoman-style headgear worn by harem women was replaced by European-style headgear. Ottoman-style clothing was replaced by European imports, and so on, thus putting certain groups of women out of work. Other women who worked as retailers going from harem to harem to sell their wares now were recycling their goods into European-style goods that they took from harem to harem, but here they found themselves displaced by minority women, who through knowledge of foreign languages could negotiate with owners of department stores for goods to sell on commission. Women who used to teach dance and music were now displaced by European or minority teachers who taught Western music or European instruments instead of traditional music played on the ʿud.

Though some women lost their breadwinning activities, new demands arose supplying them with jobs. One of the new demands came after slavery was outlawed and induced the need for domestic servants of both sexes. Instead of donkey boys, society demanded coach drivers; and instead of bathhouse keepers of both sexes, society preferred to have its own bathrooms (which some of the elite had had in the past) and continued the demand for females who visited houses on a regular basis to bathe the women and carry out other tasks such as hennaing hair and depilation. These *ballanas* were in demand in most households until well into the middle of the twentieth century. Once society had peripheralized elite women, however, all other women suffered the same fate in different degrees; but those who had a profession were the most equal to males, for once the female earned her own living, she was less likely to put up with abuse by her spouse because she was not dependent on him for her livelihood.

Peasant Women

The last group of women were those belonging to the peasant population. In earlier days, for example, the eighteenth century, the family was the productive unit, each member playing a role within that unit. Subsistence economy was the norm, with peasants producing a little extra in order to pay off their taxes, but they were free to plant as they wished and what they wished with no supervision from the tax farmers. With the advent of an export-induced economy that came in the late eighteenth century, some peasants had turned to an export economy in such commodities as rice, indigo, sugar cane, and cotton. Peasants sometimes went into partnerships with merchants to produce such commodities. More usually, such money-making crops were produced by affluent peasants, a kind of *kulak* (rich peasant), later known as a'yan (notables), which included village *shuyukh* and *umdas*. Because agriculture depended on the Nile waters, the norm in the last quarter of the eighteenth century was cycles of good and bad harvests with intervals of plagues and famines that devastated the population. Nonetheless, so long as peasants paid their taxes, they could not be dispossessed from their plots of land, unless the Nile flood was so low in one year that their land could not benefit from the waters (Abdal-Rehim 1974).

With the new regime in the nineteenth century and the new systems of land tenure introduced, only affluent peasants and members of the new elite could benefit from the commercialization of agriculture produce, for the peasant was now turned into a wage laborer hired to work on the property of the landholder. This meant that women, who continued to work in the fields with men but were not paid a wage became dependents of the males. If and when they were hired, such as during harvesting, they were paid much less than males for doing the same piece of work. Cottage industries, such as spinning and weaving, that had supplemented the family income, were forbidden because Muhammad Ali had monopolized these activities and limited them to his new factories—some of which employed women. The only wealth-inducing tasks left to peasant women were raising chickens, breeding livestock, and turning their milk into ghee and cheese, which they then bartered in the weekly markets. Such activities depended on an initial capital outlay to buy the chicks or the cow/*gamoosa* and raise it. In the interim, women worked in the fields with men, raised the children, and nurtured the family, which might include aged parents/in-law. Nonetheless, the main breadwinner was the wage laborer and women's work, even when it added substantially to the family's budget, was regarded as secondary and women as dependents on their males. In case of a divorce, it was difficult for the woman to prove that the cow was hers, unless she had inherited wealth, so that she left the conjugal household with little more than the clothes and goods she had brought into it. Thus, the situation of the peasant woman was the most dependent, even though she worked harder than any other woman but with less to show. She was the most dependent, for her choices were limited. Unless she had a family willing to take her back, which was seldom the case, she had to put up with whatever abuse her husband dished out because she had no other option.

The situation of the peasant woman could only worsen in the twentieth century, when more peasants became landless. It only improved during the Sadat regime (1970–1981), when men were encouraged to emigrate to oil-rich countries and work as laborers. This left a vacuum that created a need for agricultural workers, which women filled. They could, for once, name their own terms because their labor met with little competition. Furthermore, those who had emigrant husbands benefited from the funds remitted by the men, and thus improved their situation (Kerr and Yassin 1982). One must remember that within a village not all women are agricultural laborers. There are women who earn their living as seamstresses or as producers of certain commodities, such as mats, baskets, or as midwives and healers, tellers of fortunes, and entertainers. These are similar to working-class women in the towns, though their markets are smaller; but then the competition is smaller also.

In conclusion, one can see that although religion plays a role in determining attitudes toward women, there are other, perhaps more powerful considerations. Economic realities and the system of government in place plays a great role in determining the status of women. The need for man/womanpower also contributes to that determinant; for when countries seek to industrialize, they need women's labor and so encourage women to participate in these activities. Bear in mind that when a new technology is introduced, women go to the bottom of the line until all the positions have been filled by males and there is need for more hands, whereupon a demand is made on women. Frequently, that demand is couched in nationalistic terms, such as the need to help the nation rise to its potential, that educated mothers bring up educated children, bolstered by an economic situation that necessitates a two-salary family. Religion then is brought in as a clincher to induce women to go out and work by accentuating those interpretations that praise the work of women and the equality of the sexes. Once the need for women's labor is gone, such as during a recession or when unemployment is rising, women are told to stay at home, raise children, and serve their males; and then religion brings out those passages that accentuate the role of women as nurturers and housekeepers. Thus, the basic determinant for the role of women in a society is not religion, which can be interpreted to support whatever is necessary in society, but the economic and political situation. The other determinants come after the fact as a support system. This observation is applicable to all women in all societies and is not limited to Muslim or Egyptian women. Rosy the riveter was a heroine during wartime; but once the army was demobilized, she was told to go back home and not take a job away from a deserving male. The problem with women's being pushed to stay at home is that they tend to reproduce rapidly with disastrous effects on the population problem. Women's reproductive role, when accentuated at the expense of their productive role, creates problems in countries with limited resources, such as most of those in the Third World. Society cannot tell women that their primary function is reproductive and then expect them to limit themselves to one or two children, especially if they are financially dependent on a male and have a limited education. Such women will reproduce rapidly in order to prevent the male from having any extra money to spend outside the household—on another woman perhaps— and to make sure that one of the male offspring will succeed and so become the support of his aging parents. Especially is that important in societies that have no old-age pensions, social security, or medical health for its population.

Middle-strata women who have some education supplement their reproductive roles by acting as educators for their children. In overcrowded, ill-taught schools, the role of the mother becomes important as her children's private tutor. Elite women devise their own roles, for they have the wealth and the leisure time to do as they please. They can acquire a higher degree of education, they can compete with males, and they can design their own roles. That explains why women in Egypt today tend to control a large share of the unofficial market. Elite women set up businesses, sometimes even using their bureaucrat husbands to help eke out the family income; bourgeois women do the same, and working class women; often heads of single households, have to support the family.

3

La Femme Arabe

Women and Sexuality in
France's North African Empire

Julia Clancy-Smith

Shortly before her death in 1904, Isabelle Eberhardt wrote a haunting vignette entitled *Achoura,* which was inspired by the appearance in colonial Algiers of a novel popular art form—the photographer's studio (Clancy-Smith 1992). Achoura was a young woman from the Algerian countryside who, as was true of so many rural Arab or Berber females at the end of the nineteenth century, took up the metier of prostitution as the only escape from village misery or the threat of an undesirable spouse. Seeing Achoura's portrait displayed in a shop window in the capital, Eberhardt observed that:

> In the showcases that stand in front of photographers' shops, exposed to the stares of curious outsiders, you will find a picture showing a woman of the south. She is wearing bizarre garments, and her impressive face, which reminds one of an ancient oriental idol, perhaps, has something spectral about it. A predatory bird with eyes full of mystery. What singular daydreams, one wonders, and in the case of a few rare souls, what glimpse of foreknowledge of the stark, shining south have been evoked by this photograph of an "Ouled Nail" girl in the minds of the passers-by who have stared at it and been troubled by it? (Eberhardt 1978, 31).

Nearly a century after Eberhardt devoted her short piece to Achoura, the libertine "daughters of the Ouled Nail" tribe appear once again, though in a quite different context. In the 1986 edition of Web-ster's *Third New International Dictionary of the English Language,* there is an entry under "Ouled Naïl": "An Arab prostitute and dancing girl of the North African cities usually dressed in brightly colored, be-spangled costumes and ornamental often feathered headdress" (Web-ster's, 1519). Never mind that Achoura bint Said, the heroine of Eberhardt's story, was neither from the Sahara nor a member of the tribe of the Ouled Nail, whose nubile girls supposedly sold their favors to amass a dowry, but rather a Berber woman from the Aurés mountains to the southeast of Algiers. Achoura's photograph had been arranged, contrived, and constructed so as to reflect as well as feed into an emerg-ing colonial gaze and discourse fixed upon *la femme arabe,* upon her sexuality, her femininity, her procreative powers. In Eberhardt's short story, Achoura becomes not only emblematic of an entire class of Alge-rian women in France's African *département* during the Third Republic but also of how visions of empire and collective visions of Muslim sexual-ity fed into each other.

Nevertheless, questions of sex and gender had not always been part of the French imperial project in the Maghreb. From 1830, when General de Bourmont's army landed at Sidi Ferruch to the west of Algiers, until late in that century, the dominant colonial discourse re-volved obsessively around Islam—an active, masculine, seditious Islam seen as posing the most insuperable obstacles to France's civilizing mis-sion. After 1871, military rule was replaced by a civilian administration intent less upon pacification than upon the moral and cultural subjuga-tion of both Algerian men and Algerian women. With this transforma-tion, female status—female Muslim status—increasingly became a key measurement for judging the culturally alien, politically passive "other." Although the discourse regarding Islam as the religion of revolt *par excellence* was never entirely eclipsed in French Algeria, still between 1830 and 1900 another related discourse emerged about Islam as under-girding all indigenous family structure, expressions of sexuality, and all relations between male and female. In the hands of hundreds of Euro-pean writers, travelers, and officials, Islam had been moved from the battlefield into the bedroom.

The visions, imaginations, and representations of empire owed much to the gaze of European men and women directed toward colo-nized women, whether in *Algérie Française,* in the rest of the Maghreb, or in French Africa south of the Sahara. Indeed, in France's overseas possession at the turn of the century, both societies, European and indig-enous, came to view the other through the shifting lens of gender. More-

over, although male colonial authorities in Algeria were the first to raise
the issue of women's place in Islamic society in bureaucratic or semiofficial writings, as the nineteenth century wore on, nonofficial writers, or
Europeans outside of the colonial hierarchy, entered the debate. The
enlarged literary and discursive space afforded to the polemic on the
Muslim woman permitted Western female writers a voice in the nonofficial world of French colonialism. And by 1900, that nonofficial world
played an ever greater part in shaping and even forging imperial designs
and strategies.

In this paper, I examine the writings of two critical participants in
the unfolding discourse on the condition of the "Arab woman," which in
the hands of colonial publicists became a code word for all North African
females, both Arab and Berber, as well as eventually for all "Muslim
women." The first is General Melchior-Joseph-Eugéne Daumas (1803–
1871), who represented the masculine voice of the official military hierarchy and whose numerous studies of mainly Algerian pastoral-nomadic
peoples exerted a tremendous influence on European views of Arab
culture and society. The second voice is feminine and nonofficial—that
of the Parisian feminist writer and activist, Hubertine Auclert (1848–
1914). In 1900, Auclert published a study entitled *Les Femmes arabes
en Algérie,* which had a great impact on public opinion in the metropole
as well as in Algeria (Auclert 1900). What is significant about both Daumas and Auclert is that, although they began from very different ideological positions—Daumas was a high-ranking military officer in the
French army and Auclert was a militant suffragist—they arrived at
nearly the same conclusions regarding the worthiness or suitability of
the Algerians for cultural and political assimilation to France. And this
was the fundamental issue underlying all political contestations, whether
in Paris among the members of the *Assemblée Nationale* or in the *com-
munes mixtes* in the Algerian countryside: Could an Arab-Berber Muslim people become French? (Prochaska 1990).

La Femme Arabe: Women in the
Discourse of the Official Colonial World

One of the earliest official writers to claim to speak about—if not
for—Algerian women, and thus to offer them up to European view, was
General Daumas. Arriving in Algeria in 1835 as a young lieutenant to
fight with the African army, Daumas headed the newly created Bureaux
Arabes in 1841, an institution that was to prove so critical not only for
controlling the indigenous population but also in the elaboration of a

corpus of knowledge and information on native society (Clancy-Smith 1990). Daumas, a flawless speaker of Arabic, drew upon years of close contact with rural or pastoral communities in his numerous publications, for example, *Le Sahara algérien* (1845). In a sense, Daumas was an amateur or proto-ethnographer; his later works, such as *La vie arabe et la société Musulmane* (1869), display many of the chief elements of the emerging disciplines of ethnology and ethnography. Indeed, it could be argued that he was instrumental in forging the methodological and theoretical outlines of what would eventually become the French colonial ethnographer's craft (Vatin 1984).

Sometime toward the end of his life, Daumas wrote an unpublished study, comprised of fourteen chapters and 154 pages of ostensibly documentary material, devoted solely to what he called *la femme arabe* (Daumas 1912). Although the exact date of the text's redaction remains unsure, its composition just before 1871 is important for two reasons. The issue of women's political rights in France was just then becoming a matter of public debate (Moses 1984), and across the Mediterranean the peculiar *pied-noir* society of Algeria was beginning to develop an acute sense of identity, a political and cultural identity distinct from both the metropole and, above all, from the "native" population. In the introduction of his work on the "Arab woman," Daumas makes the following prefatory remarks:

> It seemed to me that if, in all the countries of the world the condition of woman was one of the signs that permitted forming the soundest evaluation of the social state of a people, their *moeurs* and level of civilization, it was extremely important, particularly for our domination of Algeria, to know where we stand on such a controversial subject, one so differently viewed (Daumas 1912, 1).

Daumas was by no means the first European writer to delve into such matters as polygamy, divorce, repudiation, and others, in Muslim society—that tradition had its roots in the medieval period; nor was he the first to denounce what was seen as the universally abject moral, sexual, and social condition of Arab women (Gallup 1973, 81–151). Yet, he appears to have been the first colonial official to establish woman as a distinct object of inquiry, worthy of systematic, scientific scrutiny. Daumas's study raises two related issues. First, what rhetorical and discursive (and thus political) uses does he make of Algerian women; and, second, why was his manuscript published over forty years after his death?

Of primary significance is the fact that the author entitled his treatise *The Arab Woman,* which reduced the cultural complexities of Algerian women to a single, textual monologue by framing the female
question within the regard of a solitary telephoto lens and a single hegemonic discourse. Moreover, Daumas's expository strategies for laying
bare the moral condition of the Arab woman, and thus of Arab society
as a whole, were fundamental to the emerging ethnographic gaze. He
traces her life cycle from birth or *l'enfance,* through adolescence to
marriage and finally to the tomb; this strategy—which might be termed
"womb to tomb"—was subsequently imitated by numerous French writers (e.g., Gaudry 1929, Goichon 1927).

Sex and Assimilation

Daumas begins by noting that there were two schools of thought
regarding the status of Muslim women (Muslim and Arab are employed
interchangeably). According to the first, woman is nothing but an *objet
de luxe,* a sensual, indolent, bored creature, caged like a bird in the
harem. The second view was of woman as a servant or slave condemned
to forced labor, and implicitly forced sex, by her husband. Daumas then
addresses the debate raging on the question of the assimilation of the
Arabs to France, which also had produced two opposing positions. The
first held that sociocultural and thus political fusion between Christians
and Muslims in Algeria was an idle dream or fancy. The second, that
the union of *la fille du vaincu* ("the daughter of the defeated," that is,
Algerian woman) with the son of the conqueror in marriage would result
in an inevitable assimilation by uplifting the Arab family and subsequently the entire Arab people (Daumas 1912, 1). Daumas clearly views
the second position as an impossibility.

Daumas's proclaimed purpose in undertaking his study of women
is "to tear off the veil which still hides the mores, customs, and ideas" of
Arab society. Is there not a suggestion of rape here (Daumas 1912, 2)?
Only then can remedies be found for the *maladies morales* which the
colonizer has perceived in that society. And he warns the reader, if
somewhat obliquely, that he will also be obliged to speak about sex,
although the word itself is not used. At the same time, Daumas maintains
that his scientifically impartial work will be of use not only to the
statesmen and administrators but also to artists and scholars (Daumas
1912, 3).

The ethnographer as voyeur traces the informal education of the
young girl which, from early on, imparts to her *des attitudes voluptu-*

euses and *des habitudes de coquetterie* which, he notes, are contradictory to the extreme social value placed upon female purity. His cultural reference points are the savage American Indians, who are not as civilized as the Arabs, and of course European civilization, although with scant references to Western women. Ethnographic yet prurient, the gaze follows in purportedly objective, narrative fashion the social and sexual biography of the Algerian female. And the reader is invited to peer through a keyhole of an urban Arab home or to lift up the tent flap of a Bedouin dwelling to behold the uneasy intimacy of the Muslim family —undetected.

According to the general, marriage constitutes the fundamental unit of the society and culture under scrutiny. Because "the Arabs do not conceive of love in the same manner as we [Europeans] do," it was in marriage ceremonies that Daumas finds the most formidable barriers to assimilation between French and Muslim. Here Daumas once again feels compelled to warn the reader in advance about salacious material: "As the reader prepares to penetrate into the most intimate of matters in Muslim society, may his curiosity show indulgence for customs which can be revolting to European sensibilities" (Daumas 1912, 34). Yet, Daumas disarms any potential critics by maintaining that the documentary nature of keyhole viewing renders it suitable for consideration, for contemplation. The objective "truthfulness" of Daumas's study rests upon its supporting evidence: his long acquaintance with native society; passages taken directly from the Qurʾan; and anecdotal material, including popular Arab proverbs and sayings. Nevertheless, it is important to note that most of his illustrations and examples are taken from pastoral-nomadic communities, largely in the Sahara, the only place where a French male could enjoy some contact, however limited, with indigenous females. Despite the fact that he introduces information indicating that social rank, region, and ethnicity made significant differences in status and condition, the Arab woman becomes totemic or formulaic in Daumas's hands. "There is no realm in the Arab existence—religion, honor, pleasure, danger, fatigue—from which the idea of woman is absent" (Daumas 1912, 74).

Daumas's work on women, significantly, was not published until well after his death in 1871. But, he must have intended it for a general French audience, one targeted through publication, otherwise his warnings about indelicate material (i.e., sex) would not have been imperative. As mentioned above, it is uncertain exactly when his manuscript was completed, though its completion came at the end of his career. Yet, only in 1912 did the *Revue Africaine,* the paramount, quasi-scientific colonial journal devoted to things Algerian, publish his work posthumously. (Interestingly, this particular volume of the *Revue,* published in Algiers by Jourdan, contains no other pieces on women). Nevertheless, the manuscript must have been available to certain colonial officials and writers before its appearance. A number of authors, including perhaps Adrien Leclerc and Louis Milliot, both of whom published legal studies of Muslim women's status in 1901 and 1910 respectively, appear to cite Daumas, without, however, acknowledging their source (Leclerc 1901, 109–14, and Milliot 1910). Although Daumas's treatise is, in one sense, atypical owing to its early composition, it anticipates later official and nonofficial writing on the female question.

For Daumas, Milliot, Leclerc, and countless other authors, the Arab woman as trope for North Africa Islam and culture represents the insurmountable obstacle to assimilation. As French rule in the Maghreb entered its second century, *la femme arabe* became, somewhat paradoxically, another way of talking about Islam—about the procreation of the Muslim family and sexuality, and, therefore, of a social order so utterly different from European society as to make fusion improbable. Thus, by the century's close, debates about Muslim women take their place along side of the colonial fixation on Marabouts and rebellious Sufi orders (Clancy-Smith 1994). Both the Sufi order and the Arab woman were partially or fully concealed from European view; and the discourse used for both, not surprisingly, employs similar metaphors of penetration, disrobing, and unveiling.

Regarding the crucial question of the timing of the publication of Daumas's study, one hypothesis can be advanced. The appearance in Paris of Hubertine Auclert's provocative *Les femmes arabes,* and her campaign waged from 1888 on to improve the condition, legal and otherwise, of Algerian women, may have been a factor. For Auclert's work supports some of what Daumas was saying, although it conversely argues for assimilation in an area when colonial publicists were beginning to renounce openly that objective for French Algeria. But given the general fixation among the settlers and officialdom with gender boundaries and Muslim sexuality in the period, Daumas's manuscript would probably have been published anyway (Stoler 1989, 1991). Ironically, Auclert may have inadvertently provided yet more ammunition for influential turn-of-the-century antiassimilationists and the *colon* lobby, which argued that attempts to improve the condition of Arab women would prove dangerous politically.

Hubertine Auclert: A Militant French Suffragist

One of the first women writers to claim to speak about as well as for Algerian women and thus to represent them to Europeans was Hubertine Auclert, the founder of the militant wing of the French feminist movement. She is representative of a general trend in European intellectual production whereby women forged a literary niche for themselves through travel narratives, treatises on colonized women, and harem literature. In some cases, this literature also served as a polemical device to argue for various social programs or suffragist causes back in Europe (Clancy-Smith and Gray-Ware Metcalf 1993). Moreover, it could be argued that Auclert's proposals for Algerian women were extensions of the "familial feminism" ideology that she had articulated for women in France.

Auclert was born into a family of provincial bourgeoisie from the Bourbonnais (or Allier) *département,* not far from the city of Montluçon. At the age of sixteen, she entered a convent, the Sisters of Charity of Saint Vincent de Paul, but was asked to leave the order because the nuns characterized her as a bit demented. In reality, Hubertine was not crazy but merely rebellious. Her father, Jean-Batiste Auclert, was a dedicated Republican who adhered to unpopular political principles and openly disagreed with established power. Hubertine was truly her father's offspring, for throughout her life she espoused unpopular causes, the most unpopular of all being the enfranchisement of women in *fin-de-siècle* France (Hause 1987 and Moses 1984).

Her militant public career to win the vote for Frenchwomen began in the mid-1870s, when she left her native region for Paris. She almost single-handedly organized the women's rights campaign through her organizations Droit des Femmes and Suffrage des Femmes. She also founded and edited the first suffragist newspaper in France, *La Citoyenne,* providing most of its financing and writing many of the articles herself.

Hubertine Auclert came to North Africa somewhat accidently. Antonin Lévrier, Auclert's longtime lover, received a post as *juge de paix* in Frenda (Oran), while at the same time learning that his health was in jeopardy, probably from tuberculosis. The dry climate of Algeria was to restore Lévrier's vitality. In 1888, Auclert arrived in Algeria expressly to marry her lover; they were wed in Algiers that year. She spent four years in the country, residing first in western Algeria, then in the oasis of Laghouat, and finally in the capital after her husband took an editorial position on the staff of *Le Radical Algérien*. During the four-year "Algerian interlude," Auclert began her study of Arab women, perhaps as early as 1888 while in Frenda. According to Hause, she had this intention before going to North Africa (Hause 1987, 132–48). In 1892, she returned to Paris a widow. Algeria's climate had not saved her husband. Eight years later, her first full-length treatise, *Les femmes arabes,* was published by Editions Littéraires in Paris.

What sort of Algeria did the leader of French suffragists encounter? Before going to the Maghreb, Auclert had anticipated finding an "earthly paradise"; she found quite the opposite. Racism and bigotry directed against the Algerians, particularly women, were rife and undisguised; questions of assimilation and *pied-noir* cultural and political identity were hotly contested. As she states in the first pages of her impassioned treatise: "In Algeria, there is only a small elite of Frenchmen who would place the Arab race in the category of human beings" (Auclert 1900, 3).

La Mère Patrie: A Cruel Political Mother

For Auclert, the degraded status of the Arab woman symbolized all that was politically amiss in France's domination of North Africa. Her condition had been debased, not ameliorated by seventy years of French rule. Moreover, Auclert accused male colonial officials of complicity with Arab males in respecting Islamic laws and customary practices, such as child marriage, the sale of women, and polygamy—which rendered native females "little victims of Muslim debauchery" (Auclert 1900, 50). Further evidence of some sort of poisonous collusion between conservative Muslim elites and French authorities was furnished by the lamentable state of education for indigenous girls. Although some effort had been made to provide formal education for Algerian Muslim girls before 1861, schools were gradually suppressed after that because it was argued that educational institutions were costly and created a *déclasée* group of educated women accepted by neither society (Auclert 1900, 138–44 and Hause 1987, 142–43). According to Auclert, if the natives were barbarous, France—French men—were at least partially to blame.

Many of the suffragist arguments that Auclert advocated for France were introduced into her arguments regarding the moral and political obligation to uplift Arab women—to turn harem inmates into voters. If Arab men desire access to the ballot box, so do Arab females, who aspire to be assimilated—to become Frenchwomen, set free from their cages, walled homes, and cloisters. If Arab males are backward, it

is partially owing to racism on the part of both the European settlers
and the administrators. But the least advanced socially, morally, and
culturally were indeed the women, subject to masculine whim and tyr-
anny, subject to a double patriarchy, French and Arab. *La mère-patrie*
was really a cruel *marâtre* (stepmother) (Auclert 1900, 37–38). Auclert
also employed the discourse of international or universal sisterhood in
her writings. Yet, as was true of British feminists, who used an identical
discourse to express outrage about the oppression of the Indian women,
that sisterhood was imperial and hierarchical. Unlike many other writers, however, Auclert perceived the nefarious influence of French colonialism upon indigenous society and culture.

It is hardly surprising that in Auclert's passionate polemic, French
suffragist agenda found their way into the Algerian context; yet, the
reverse was also true—the colonial encounter as played out between
men and women in North Africa furnished additional evidence for the
need for women's rights in France. The disenfranchisement of French
women had a deleterious influence not only upon French colonial policies in Algeria generally but also upon French treatment of native
women. True assimilation would be realized when European women
were enrolled into the colonial state as cultural mediators and house-to-
house activists; only they could bring France into the domestic space of
secluded Arab women (Auclert 1900, 14–17, 23–27). The ideology of
European women as moral beacons and guardians, as agents of civilization in the colonies, was a view widely shared and promoted by many
British feminists and nonfeminists. Yet, this does not seem to have been
as fully developed or articulated in French feminism-or at least not with
regard to Algeria (Chaudhuri and Strobel 1992). But for Auclert, the
Arab woman was more than a mere foil to measure progress in feminist
causes back in France. "If women in France enjoyed their share of
power, they would not allow the existence of a law permitting the rape
of children in a French territory" (Auclert 1900, 49).

Arab Marriage Is Child Rape

The most provocative section of Auclert's 250-page work is entitled: "Arab marriage is child rape" (Auclert 1900, 42–52). Here, Auclert
cites unsettling examples of small girls, even infants, given through marriage contracts to men, often much older, in exchange for the bride price.
Noting that the bride price fluctuated in market value with the beauty,
class, age, and productive capacity of the girl, Auclert also suggests that
the impoverishment of the indigenous population had much to do with

these practices, which also deviated in most respects from Islamic law. Although consummation of the marriage was theoretically regulated and postponed until puberty, in actual fact this rule was not always respected, with tragic consequences for the young girl (Christelow 1985 and Charnay 1965). In the decades when the closely intertwined issues of naturalization for Europeans and assimilation for Muslims in Algeria were endlessly debated, charges of unnatural sexual practices provided compelling evidence for those arguing that an insurmountable cultural chasm separated Arab from French.

Auclert's work expands upon (and in much more candid fashion than the general had ever dared) what Daumas had merely hinted at —the morally perverse sexual customs of the natives, above all child marriage. Yet, at strategic moments in her treatise, she asks different questions of the ethnographic material presented so fervently to the reader. French law as applied, or as not applied in Algeria, and colonial courts were as much to blame for these lamentable sexual crimes (Auclert 1900, 47). The fundamental question posed so frequently by Auclert—should not the Third Republic protect and assume a legal and moral guardianship over Arab women, if indeed it was a republic?—was raised in respect to the vote for women in France. The Third Republic could not claim to be such until women's rights and concerns were legally redressed on both sides of the Mediterranean.

A sincere, if self-appointed, advocate for Arab women, Auclert returned to Paris in 1892 without having achieved any concrete results. While still in Algeria, she had submitted some five petitions on behalf of indigenous females to Paris; all of them met with indifference. Back in France, she continued until the end of her life to submit petitions demanding education, the abolition of polygamy, and legal changes in the status of Algerian women—all to no avail. Auclert left Algeria a "lonely pioneer," but she did have her imitators, although not until several decades later. Her arguments were taken up by the Algerian novelist and writer Marie Bugéja in *Nos soeurs musulmanes* (1921) and in other works published after World War I; Bugéja's numerous publications in the interwar period met with official hostility and even censorship (Bowlan 1993).

The one endeavor where Auclert succeeded—in spite of herself —was precisely where she may have failed. By bringing to bear her considerable "skills as a publicist to the education of French opinion about Algeria, much as she had done for the woman question in the previous decade," Auclert may have paradoxically convinced many in both Algeria and France that the Arabs were undeserving of political or civil rights (Hause 1987, 143). Not only did she publicize the condition of Arab girls and women under Islamic and customary law in the colonial press, such as *Le Radical Algérien,* but she also used the Parisian feminist paper *La Citoyenne* as a vehicle for her campaign. In the eyes of settler colonial society, *Les femmes arabes* demonstrated the immutable otherness of the indigenous population, especially when it came to matters of sexuality. Moreover, it was both against and upon this constructed otherness, engendered by the Arab woman, that a distinct European-Algerian identity came in part to be fashioned.

By the eve of the Great War, women—North African women—represented the measure of things—hidden and concealed, yet on display like Achoura's portrait in the photographer's studio window. *La femme arabe* symbolized Arab Muslim culture writ large—its illicit reproduction and regeneration, its unfitness for assimilation. In the developing ethnographic gaze, woman was not only the signifier of sexuality but also of the indigenous culture of sexuality. And why not survey the North African woman from birth to death, from womb to tomb? An exact replica of the interiors on Arab home and a Kabyle house had already been displayed at the 1889 Exposition Universelle in Paris (Celik 1992). In his numerous, influential works of an Arab history and society, Emile-Félix Gautier, a professor at the University of Algiers, wrote on the Muslim family for the lavish 1930 celebration of the Centenary. In *Moeurs et coutumes des musulmans* (1931) are several key codewords that constitute cognitive boxes within boxes devoted to gender and sexuality. Family is a code for harem and harem is a code for (deviant) Arab Muslim sexuality. According to Gautier, there was no home or hearth in the Arab North African household owing to the position and status allotted its women by unchanging law and custom. "Among the differences which oppose our Western society to Muslim society, if one searches to uncover that which is primordial, is the family" (Gautier 1931, 37). The French Empire could never be truly "at home" in Algeria because the requisite domestic foyer did not and could not exist among the natives, although France could continue eternally to rule the country (Gautier 1931, 36–47).

4

Organization of Culture and the Construction of the Family in the Modern Middle East

Peter Gran

For historians and political econo- mists who study the Middle East, the opportunity to experiment to find appropriate theories has been a limited one. They have not had the luxury of an opportunity to figure out what terrain they want to occupy or how to occupy it. In the years following the Second World War, historians came to embrace modern- ization theory. Leading scholars of the period competed with each other to show how backward the Middle East was. In the 1970s–1980s, mod- ernization theory lost prestige except for the one domain within the field that really expanded during that period, the domain of women's studies. In women's studies, modernization theory continued to flourish at least through the 1980s. Given this state of affairs, scholars now have a highly developed view of the role of the West in the Middle East and of elites, male and female, but only an impressionistic view of the internal logic of Middle Eastern culture. How do men and women actually relate? Does life in a family mean what Max Weber took it to mean? Does life in a family equal private, does life outside a family equal public? Is this actually the case either in the Middle East or the West?

In very recent years, modernization theory has weakened a bit —even in women's studies; one now finds some interest in religious revivalism, postmodernism, and new forms of Marxism, trends that seem interesting but that do not yet serve to give a rational understanding of the world, which many of us want, eschewing as they do an empirically- grounded approach to theory in favor of an apriori certainty or scepticism. Handicapped by the narrowness of their epistemologies, these new forms of reflection easily become simply reactions to the dominant modernization discourse or at least very heavily dependent on it.

The essays in this volume stand in contrast to most of what exists in Middle East scholarship. Either as archival studies or as essays of interpretation, they collectively attempt to break this mold of West and non-West and to free their subject matter. In this essay, I seek to encourage this project of emancipation and to this end take up two issues, one a general issue, a part of the residue of modernization theory, the other more specifically a problem of the study of women's history in the Middle East. The general problem to be addressed is the scholarly perception of women as habitually a part of the "private" and hence as marginal to the "public," or to the "political" or to the "historical." The second issue and the one more specific to the study of the Middle East has to do with the Arab family, the "private" within which women are supposed to be situated. Here I wish to argue that despite the acknowledged diversity of Islam, the Arab world, and the Middle East, there is little or no perceived diversity when it comes to "the" Arab or Mediterranean family. It is one area to which the critique of Orientalism has yet to reach. Yet, seemingly if one wishes to challenge positivism and modernization theory and argue for the politically constructed nature of the family or for the historicity of the houswife, then the contingent nature of the family has to be identified.

An inquiry combining the broader and the narrower issues might have the following as its premise: the exclusion of the housewife from the study of history on the face of it seems so illogical that it should go away by itself. Why has this not happened? Why is the issue even scarcely discussed? There must be a somewhat universal acquiescence to the idea of the dichotomy of public and private and how could this be—given the diversity of human thought—unless it was something constantly being manufactured by state ideologies.

In this article, I adopt the presumption of state involvement as a working hypothesis and seek to show that there is in fact an ideology—more precisely ideologies—of the family, which hold public and private in place. Can one show that the logic of a particular type of hegemony would call for a particular version of the ideal family?

In the pages which follow, I try this hypothesis out on four Middle Eastern countries taken to represent the different variants of modern capitalist hegemony. What I imagine is that a ruling class of a predominantly capitalist sort forms alliances with various institutions and individuals so as legitimately to embody the society. In some instances, the state may want to mold an institution such as the family, while in others it simply wants to appear to be the upholder of tradition. Whatever the case, it wants an ideal and it does not want to sanction too much diversity. As a result, one can to a certain extent correlate type of hegemony with type of ideal family. This ideal family once in place serves as a model for that society; it thereby reinforces acceptance of that specific hierarchy.[1] Initial support for the hypothesis appears to come from the fact that governmental records provide evidence about policies toward families; there is, for example, a commentary literature written by social workers. It could of course be objected that social work policy about families is to a great extent a matter of bureaucratic practice and to speak of it as politics means to infer politics from it.

Although this line of observation is fair enough, social workers indeed are fairly far down the hierarchy; still, they do not exist in a vacuum. They stand for much more than themselves, arguably they stand for the hegemony as a whole, often led in this particular by its religious hierarchy, a hierarchy well known for its concern for the promotion of the idea of the family. Has this been a particular concern of scholars? In the past, I think not with one exception, the exception being Antonio Gramsci. The concept of the ideal family experimented with here might well be looked at as a contribution to Gramsci's concept of the "traditional intellectual," that is, a contribution to the religious hierarchy (Gran 1991).

Following Gramsci, one observes that the traditional intellectual upholds the family and the dominant morality and does so in a manner supportive of the interests of the dominant elements of the hegemony (Barclay 1971). Its control of this part of the official worldview gives it leverage throughout the entire state apparatus. This I believe explains how minor government agencies that work with families, such as social worker agencies, groups that are not directly associated with religion, appear often enough to do the bidding of religion. Relatedly, if a power structure abandons its relation with the traditional intellectual for a period, as the Soviets did in the 1920s and later as the Iraqi Ba'th Party

---

1. The beginning of a new trend is emerging in Mervat Hatem's (1992, 231–51) use of the concept of "state feminism," and more diffusely in Kandiyoti 1991. See especially the valuable article by Suad Joseph, "Elite Strategies for State-Building: Women, Family, Religion, and the State in Iraq and Lebanon," 176–200. My model is drawn from *Beyond Eurocentrism: A New View of Modern World History* (Syracuse Univ. Press, 1996).

did, this abandonment seems predictably to open the door to official experimentation with family structure. These periods of course have been the exception; but is it not interesting that when a hegemony is weak, as was often the case in Lebanon from the 1960s to the 1980s, ideologies, such as ideologies of the family, would be among those contested?

To develop these hypotheses, I postulate that Iraq is a "Russian Road" regime, where the state has as its ideal the cross-generational family; that Lebanon is a tribal-ethnic state, where its rulers promote the clannic family as their ideal; that Israel is a "bourgeois democracy," where its rulers emphasize the nuclear family as its norm for the Jewish population; and that Egypt is an "Italian Road" state, where its rulers emphasize the Mediteranean bilateral family.

Iraq as a "Russian Road" Regime

Russian Road regimes are regimes that disguise class conflict through caste ideology. In a typical Russian Road state, one finds a polarized system composed of a "nomenklatura" in a capital city and of a vast population mass kept at a distance in rural areas and provincial towns. There are a number of Russian Road regimes in the modern world. They include not just Middle Eastern countries, such as Iraq, Turkey, Syria after 1970, and Iran but Latin American ones as well, such as Nicaragua, Guatemala, and Peru, as well as Asian ones, for example China and Japan, and East European ones, Russia/The Soviet Union being the one best-studied by scholars to this point.

The hypothesis that Russian Road regimes share a particular approach to family organization, notably the cross-generational family, is put forth as an alternative to the overgeneralized idea of the Arab or Mediterranean family.[2]

From works on women in Iraq, from Iraqi works of literary criticism, and from general works on Iraqi culture, one finds that the overall situation in that hegemony is reflected in the struggle over the ideology

---

2. For the view that there is an Arab family, see the Kuwaiti social scientist Fahed al-Thakeb (1983, 171–78); this view is criticized by implication by a student of Lebanese and Bahraini culture, Fuad I. Khuri (1983, 347–66); it is also criticized by the Egyptian social scientist Hasan el-Shamy (1983, 313–26), who shows that when one assumes the existence of the universal nuclear family with its universal oedipus complex one misreads Arabic culture and the actual problems arising from the differing forms of the Arab family.

of the family. The state wants the married couple of today to be as in the past, clearly urban or clearly rural. But the parents and other relatives—in the case of an urban couple—might well live in the countryside, and there are thus ties between the two. Examples that come to mind are of Iraqi and Russian grandparents, for example, the Babushka, and of the fond recollection of children whose summers were spent in the countryside with these grandparents. The role of the grandparents in this kind of family is thus a key one where elsewhere it might be the role of cousins. The grandparents represent not only a part of each child's life but they are a symbol of wisdom and of power in the adult world as well. The Iraqi man in popular stereotyping looks to his father before anyone else.

Readers familiar with the scholarship on the Iraqi family will no doubt observe that this line of thought is a bit revisionist. A commoner view is that the current government promotes, as its predecessors have since the 1920s, an attack on the traditional tribal family. The government advocates a nuclear-type family, but it does not control the cost of living nor supply an adequate level of daycare, so that in effect married couples are thrown back onto their parents. Resentments abound. Hence, the observation that the Iraqi husband is an "outsider" to the wife, who for her part is closer to her brother, to her own family, and to her son than to him and to the point that in some instances she does not share information with him. And hence, the claim that even the modern social parties and clubs where husband and wife attend together do not work to solidify the married couple. Evidence for this is that in Iraqi as in Turkish families, men given the option, prefer to spend their leisure time out of the home and with other men or with their father (Khayyat 1990, 112).[3] Thus, even with the tendencies of recent years toward a nuclear-family household, one is still justified in categorizing the Iraqi family as a cross-generational family.

Conflicts in Iraqi families reported in scholarly literature appear to reflect the structural features of the family just alluded to. Conflicts frequently occur when wives turn to their families for help against their husbands and against their husband's family. Stereotypically at least, husbands tend not to respect their wife's family and do not establish good communication with them, the reason being there is not the level of

---

3. According to an Iraqi literary critic, the prestige of the older man also leads to marriages of older men and younger women, leading women to lesbianism and to prostitution, these being asides to Shuja' al-'Ani (1986, 87, 108).

"family merger" as one finds, for example, in the Italian Road. Typical husbands would not consider living with their wife's family. Stereotypically as well, women prefer to go outside the system and arrange cousin marriages in order that they might overcome some of these barriers and have leverage on their husbands through the family.

From the perspective of the regime, the cross-generational family is an acceptable one because it is a narrowly constructed one, one bridging the urban-rural divide without undermining that divide. For the family to uphold these divisions, cousins would be irrelevant even burdensome as they might claim entry to the urban caste life where a grandfather would not, a grandfather being in all probability too advanced in years. From the perspective of the regime, too small a family might be dangerous as well. Husband and wife completely might be too individualistic, too much resembling the nuclear family of the democracies and thus too hard for the state to control. The ideal is somewhere between; a small family looking to the father's father.

Change in the Iraqi family as in other families appears to date from the mass education of women. Here, one might insert the point that, as with other regimes around the world, the Iraqi regime became aware that they needed educated women in the work force. In Iraq, mass education of women started with the Ba'thist regime in the 1970s; from that period, commentary literature suggests that the family became increasingly a battleground. Divorce rates skyrocketed (Al-Janabi 1983, 208). It is from that date that large numbers of feminist writings emerge and from that date as well that the state found itself trying to counteract and coopt the growing discontent among women by building up the Iraqi Women's Union. Can there thus really be any question about the interplay between the supposed "public" and "private"? Should not historians in the future try to evaluate what the impact of a rising divorce rate and of increasing domestic tension might mean in the public sphere, if they continue to use a term? Could an increase in strife at home arising from these unresolved problems contribute to a drift toward a war policy?

Another example of the intersection of family and politics. Iraq had an ambitious domestic policy dating back at least to the formation of the Ministry of Labor and Social Affairs, a ministry founded in 1939. Over the years, its main programs were in the urban area; rural initiatives began in 1953. The hallmarks of the ministry's program were the creation of institutions for orphans, the handicapped, and the elderly. Given, however, the reverential social attitudes toward elderly parents, old people's homes have gone "sharply undersubscribed" despite all the problems that home care imposed on the younger generation (Geiger 1968, 311).[4]

One final example. Over the years, as the government came to depend on a female work force, it has had to make concessions to women. Thus, the government has permitted the Code of Personal Status gradually to separate the nuclear family from the authority of the father's family and gradually to eradicate some of the overt inequalities between the sexes; it did not, however—here to note areas of continuing tension—adequately facilitate divorce for women nor eliminate polygamy.

Lebanon as a "Tribal-Ethnic" State

Tribal-ethnic states are a second form of modern capitalist hegemony. They are found in Europe in the Balkans and Scandinavia, in the Middle East, in Africa, in South East Asia, and in the Pacific. In these states, the strategy of the ruling class is to disguise class conflict in two complexly interrelated ways. First, ruling-class culture promulgates the idea of the absolute difference between men and women in terms of biological function as its political idea—as opposed to race, caste, or region—and then second, it promulgates the absolute importance of kinship and blood-based institutions, institutions accentuating the biological basis of society resulting in a society composed of these tribal and ethnic units. Where such regimes are successful, women believe they are protected and free from the burdens of history that men bear. In this type of hegemony, the ideal family is the clannic family. Parallel households, that is, households held together from above by blood ties, are tied together under a single patriarch *(zaʿim);* all the households are composed of members said to be of the same tribe or ethnicity.

Although in Iraqi society people may know their cousins, the actual social role of a cousin is limited. For example, cousins may visit during the forty days of mourning following the death of a family member. By way of contrast, the role of the cousin is appreciably larger and more important in countries such as Lebanon. In many instances, cousins even form a business unit. Commonly, cousins protect each other in their dealings smoothing the way through *wasita,* that is, through serving as

4. For a study of Iraqi state policies, see Sulaiman al-Dulaimi (1990, 383, 385, 451–52). Al-Dulaimi notes that Kuwaitis do more fostering than do Iraqi's, they are more concerned with the overall emotional well-being of children, more committed to mainstreaming while the Iraqi's adopt an institutionalizing, problem-solving approach to children's needs (420–22).

an intermediary. Remittances from cousins living around the world help hold families together back in Lebanon.

As also noted above, the logic of the tribal-ethnic state is that class exploitation is disguised by sexual segregation. Men and women are defined as absolutely different in the Lebanese ʿaʾila or in the neighboring case of the Palestinian *hamula,* there even despite the long history of national struggle.

For gender segregation to work, men need to find remunerated work and to seek their status through it; women need to be kept in roles, whether in or out of the home, that do not compete with those of men. As the crises of modern Lebanon and Palestine have unfolded, the maintenance of this system has not been an easy matter for the ruling classes, even when they have had control, which of course has not always been the case. In both Lebanon and the Palestinian community, economic crises resulted in the high unemployment of men while affording economic opportunities to women, a number of whom were becoming increasingly better educated. To turn now to the theme of counterhegemonic struggle in Lebanon, one must ask oneself that if such conditions persist over a long period of time, would the bonds linking brother, male cousin, and father survive? Put another way, was a dying system of sexual segregation in the years up to and through the Civil War the condition for important Lebanese female writers to emerge?[5] Or, alternatively, was the education and employment of women in this period something ephemoral, something simply related to the service and education-based economy of a city such as Beirut, something that historical analysis would show was not challenging the system?

Different interpretations of the meaning of this period and of the role played by women naturally abound. Based purely on the apparent outcome in the early 1990s, it would seem that the era of the Lebanese Civil War performed a conservative function. This apparent function was one of recentering the society back around male dominance. Recent state policy has played a big role in this. With a Shiʿi fundamentalist predominance—not Shʿism per se—gradually asserting itself, the old clan families of all the groups appear assured in their position; male hegemony in the public sphere is likely to be resserted with a vengance no matter how many educated women there are.

In the other tribal-ethnic case being considered here, the Palestin-

---

5. Sexual segregation is actually a very broad subject. Sudanese, East African, and the more tribal Upper Egyptians pursue another approach to maintaining the woman's loyalty to her natal family by undermining the sexual pleasure of her marriage through clitoridectomy. When women leave, they lose their power be it sexual or economic.

ian case, one need only read the autobiographical account written by the poet Fadwa Tuqan of her youth to see the clan, or *hamula,* structure at work through the years of the British Mandate. Thus, for example, Tuqan wrote that she lived in a world of women, that she could not start composing nationalist poetry because she had little contact with the world outside of her house. All this, however, was ultimately totally modern, as the book makes clear. When she grew up, being upper class, she was sent to England to complete her education and then to return as a part, even a spokesperson, of the system.

Although Tuqan's account may fit with common preconceptions about the *hamula,* other writers on Palestinian family life suggest that such a static tableau is quite misleading; change is taking place allowing for women's organizations to grow out of groups of women. The question is—here to introduce an aside—how much and what kind of change is taking place? Until now, no move is being made by important political groups to eliminate Jordanian Personal Status Law nor to introduce a new race-based system of the sort one would associate with democracy. Still, there is change. Female cousins mobilize each other and in doing so have played a large role in the Intifada. This being the case, perhaps the support—or at least the silent acquiescence—for Hamas among the wealthier Palestinians, those one presumes, who would fear change, can be seen as somewhat analogous to the latent support among wealthy Lebanese, who are in general Amal supporters, for the Shiʿi fundamentalists, that the image of the Hamas sympathizer on the street should not then be allowed to obscure the cross-class character of a movement in part at least aimed at supporting the old status quo in gender (Tuqan 1990; Nazzal 1986; Cooke 1988; Accad 1990).

In looking at the challenge to the clannic family, one might do well to consider its critics, not just among feminist writers, but among doctors. Drs. Myriam Klat and Adele Khudr, medical statisticians, have published works on the problem of inbreeding in Lebanon. It is after all in the clannic family structure that one finds the largest number of available marriage partners, who are also family members. And, as these authors insist, inbreeding from a medical perspective or a developmentalist perspective is unfortunate, as it correlates with many health problems (Klat and Khudr 1986, 138–45).[6]

---

6. It is not surprising to find this concern replicated in other tribal-ethnic states. See e.g., S. A. Khoury and D. Massad (1992, 769–75). Finally in Iraq, where the dominant caste distances itself from the larger mass society, along various lines including that of family structure, the residual consanguinity of the masses comes under attack (Hamamy, al-Hakkak and Taha 1990, 24–29).

Israel as a Bourgeois Democracy

Bourgeois democracy is another one of the forms of modern hegemony. Examples can be found not only in Western Europe and North America but among the settler states of the British Commonwealth. Bourgeois democracies share in common a ruling class strategy of disguising class conflict by accentuating race conflict between the dominant race working class and a minority racial undercaste. Governments in democracies extol the freedom and capacity for individual expression of the dominant race, thereby drawing it close to them. The family structure most congruent with this proposed freedom and individualism is the nuclear family, which is the ideal in these regimes.

As with other family structures supported by contemporary hegemonies, the nuclear family is put to the test when women seek an expanded role outside the home or even the guarantee of the right of divorce or remarriage or of other such mundane achievements, all of which become necessary with the development of capitalism. Divorce for the woman is difficult. During divorce, a woman's prior wealth is at high risk. After a divorce, a woman's support in a democracy comes from alimony, alimony being determined by the earning capacity and willingness to pay of the former husband. Alimony is not maintenance, nor is it the remaining amount of the bride price that the divorced woman could count on in the other hegemonies. It is an insecure form of insurance. Even marriage in a democracy is fairly difficult if the partners are not of the same race, that is, not both Jewish. But even assuming same race, in the case of Israel, a widow needs special permissions to remarry and a twice-married woman is automatically barred from a third marriage (Swirski and Safir 1991, 11–12). Paradoxically, even in a legal marriage in Israel, the wife appears isolated. She cannot claim clan rights, but her husband's family can. Thus, for example, in the Levirate marriage, if the man dies before the woman has produced a child, his brother has claims to make her his wife. To escape this marriage, the widow must sometimes resort to bribery (Riskin 1989).

The severity of Israeli family law relative to that of other democracies is often explained, wrongly I believe, as a part of Judaism. Most Jews living in Western Europe and the United States would not consider submitting to the strictures that Israelis put up with. How then could it have come to be that the government of Israel began to insist that their law was the only true Jewish law? A historian might surmise that much of the actual explanation derives from the Israeli struggle for Palestine. Confrontation with the Palestinians pushed the Israelis to be more "tribal," as confrontation with the Amerindians pushed the American Puritans and Western settlers to be more tribal, trends in both cases accentuating gender inequality, especially at the moment of state formation. Thus, it was that, when in the 1948 parliamentary elections, the dominant secular party Mapai needed additional votes to sustain itself, it chose to turn to the National Religious Party, forging a historic alliance, an alliance more or less codifying Israeli law and politics. Mapai could rule if it agreed to integrate Jewish law to cover not only a wide range of practices in public institutions but the totality of personal status and domestic law as well. Jewish women in this arangement were integrated into the state at a legal disadvantage not unlike what happened to their counterparts, Puritan and Palestinian women, who also were in one way or another entrapped by a democracy.

For the Israeli ruling class to impose a tribal-democracy form of social control, it had to allow Orthodox Jews to dominate law and religion. Orthodox Jews, it appears, were the main group available capable of confronting the several challenges to the hegemony at least until recent years with the rise of Jewish fundamentalism. It was the Orthodox who had the ability of drawing the large Sephardic population from its Arabic cultural roots to its Jewish ones; it was the Orthodox who had the ability in doing so to withstand the financial and cultural pressures exerted by Reform Jews and Conservative Jews in Israel and internationally who called for a greater liberalization in Jewish law.

For the underclasses in all the hegemonies, the ideology of the family is a formidable device of social control. For example, among the Sephardic Jews referred to above, a fear always exists that their parenting will not be deemed adequate and that their children will be snatched and put in the group homes of the Youth Aliyah by Israeli social workers (Jaffe 1983, app.). There has been in fact a considerable incidence of this. Among Palestinians, fear also exists; no family's integrity is safe. And again, it is Israeli social workers, whom one finds entering homes and making major decisions concerning these families. Indeed, among the first acts of the Israeli state vis-à-vis its subjects, Jew and Arab alike, was the creation of specialized institutions for the retarded and the blind, institutions in line with democratic thinking about segregating the defective members of families from the community of the Chosen People, institutions that at least for the Palestinians served psychologically to undermine feelings about the adequacy of their *hamula*s (Blessing and Caspi 1991; Najjar 1992; Jaffe 1982).

Egypt as "Italian Road"

A fourth form of modern hegemony in the modern world can be termed Italian Road in recognition of Gramsci's analysis of the politics and history of his country. In this form of hegemony, the ruling class disguises class conflict by promoting ideas of regionalism and regional culture. Typically, the state tries to play the "Northern" worker off against the "Southern" peasant. Examples of Italian Road regimes other than Italy include Spain, Mexico, India, Brazil, Egypt, and several older cases, for example, late nineteenth-century France and Germany and twentieth-century Syria until 1970, when Ba'thism underwent its profound reformulation in that country. In Italian Road regimes, the ideal family has been termed the bilateral or cousin-based family, in that the relevant individuals are mostly from the same generation; grandparents and patriarchs have no special role; individual rights exist, but within certain boundaries (Levi 1990, 567–78; Censer 1991, 528–38).

In the novel and popular culture of Italian Road states, the tension between the individual and the group seems to mirror the broader struggle between the more feudal "South" and the more capitalist "North." Even today in the case of a country such as Egypt, Cairene families may live for generations as "Southern" or "Northern" families, as the case may be; their ties to the village remain unbroken. Cairo, thus, has an urban culture but it is not as cut off from rural culture as is that of, for example, Baghdad. In the Egyptian case, urban and rural are more fused.

The Egyptian family may be distinguished in the following way:

> If Saudi genealogies could be graphically represented as tall, branching trees emphasizing patrilineal relatives, then Egyptian genealogies in the same idiom would be seen as fat, squat bushes. A Saudi ignores many of the collateral relatives to focus on his long line of descent. The Egyptian places himself somewhere near the center of his genealogical bush with, if he is middle age, considerably more young shoots overhead than stems underneath. The Saudi knows the overall tribal group to which he belongs. The Egyptian with the exception of the well-to-do or the foreign-inspired, has no overarching name to refer to his larger family or even to his own specific family group (Rugh 1984, 56–57).

This means, to expand this contrast, where a Saudi or an African from a comparable tribal state may know his roots backward hundreds of years, one thinks here of the Griots or oral historians, in Egypt a similar person may know dozens of cousins of his fathers and mother's immediate family.

In *Family in Contemporary Egypt,* Andrea B. Rugh shows that the question of whether there is endogamy in Egypt depends on one's definition because the descent group is so large and so "disorganized," so subdivided into affines that reflect class and prestige as much as lineage. In considering the question of a family patriarch, she records that, in her study of one of Egypt's most prominent families, she found that a theoretical patriarch did exist, although more typically there are simply elders. Another insight is that, when Egyptians marry foreigners or even people outside the extended family, the outsider usually assumes the role of an actual family member (Rugh 1984, 56–57). And although the descent group is thus diffuse, it nonetheless comes together for weddings and funerals, occasions that serve to reinforce the idea of the group as a family with family honor. In addition, most young Egyptian couples depend on their parents for financial help and help with day care. In the most elite Egyptian families, economic issues bear on how the ideology is construed. For some, there is a utility in inventing or perpetuating linkages to other parts of the Middle East outside of Egypt. For others, especially for the large landlords, the family is conceived to be a managerial unit. Still, few families—even among the wealthy classes—depend on their land; most make their living individually. Yet at least on a general level, they and indeed many others, think of people from their province or certainly from their village as their relatives. Thus, even when a family lives in Cairo as noted above, it is tied to a rural wing (Springborg 1982).

With regard to choosing a marriage partner, in the Palestinian case, the male cousin has the right to block the female cousin's marriage up to the last moment if he wants her. At least this is sometimes true. This is not true in Egypt. Elders, indeed, may make an attempt to encourage or discourage a marriage in Egypt, but they do not do so with the plan of marrying the woman in question themselves (Abdo-Zubi 1987, 8–9). In sum, two different pragmatisms appear to be at work rooted in the logic of daily family life.

If one were to explain this in terms of family logic, one might note that, in Egypt, the mother-daughter relationship is likely to be a close one; for, even after the marriage, the daughter depends on the tie. It is the mother who could help her daughter mobilize support in the family should disputes arise with the new husband. This tie would contrast with the mother-daughter tie in a democracy, where the daughter would try to flee from what might be the rather depressed situation of her mother seeking support instead from her husband. Hope lies in the future and not in the past. Love, the Egyptian philosopher Zaki Najib Mahmud argues, taking the contrary position, is not a sufficient basis for marriage as is claimed by the proponents of the nuclear family. A similar kind of pragmatism underlies the rationale in Egypt for polygamy. This contrasts with the American style pragmatism, which by way of contrast is more in evidence in the divorce court (Rugh 1984, 133).

One could also examine literary studies and collect examples of how one kind of common sense understands another, how a literary critic's view of family life appears conditioned by his or her own direct experience of family life. The case at hand involves Lebanese reflection on the Egyptian family. In a recent work by a Lebanese literary critic on the writings of the Egyptian novelist Naguib Mahfouz, two points stand out: first, the critic's fascination with the patriarchal or za^{c}im-like figure of Ahmad ʿAbd al-Jawwad from the *Trilogy;* second, the critic's neglect of Mahfouz's female characters and of their evolution. To Egyptians, Mahfouz is the great depicter of Old Cairo, the home of many Upper Egyptian families, families who, in the Egyptian context, are the most tribal-ethnic and who might indeed have a patriarch. What Egyptians find in the *Trilogy*, however, is movement and change, as the values of the Delta, or the "North," impose themselves in the novels even on a Saʿidi or Upper Egyptian family (Barakat 1984, 31; Abou-Zeid 1985). Perhaps one thus could speak of a Lebanese versus an Egyptian reading of Mahfouz. There is much to support the Egyptians' self-perception in this instance. Recall, for example, the orientation of Egyptian social work, a profession that takes the Delta family as its model (Walton and Abo El Nasr 1988, 142–43).

The main argument of this essay has been that the family ought to be studied as a part of politics, if for no other reason than the fact that the state invests a great deal of its resources in upholding its conceptions of an ideal family. Applied to a specifically Middle Eastern context, this project became in the first instance a critique of the dominant paradigm for interpreting families, a paradigm commonly known in Middle Eastern studies as Orientalism. The existence of differing forms of hegemony, each with their preferred form of family, makes the alternative to Orientalism clear. Connecting the two points together, one must conclude that families and households with the issues surrounding them relating to gender, domestic work, health, and so on, are a part of politics and history and ought to be conceived as such by scholars. There remains of course a "private." It lies not in the family per se but in the particularities and specificities of different families (see e.g., Fox-Geno-vese 1993, 234–54).

In drawing this paper to a conclusion, the evidence presented seems to make clear the constructed and historically contingent nature of the public and private in modern times. Rather than go back over this ground, let us take a brief look at where the private and public distinction appears to be going in this the age of state crisis.

What seems clear is that, as the hegemony weakens as in Lebanon, the public and private distinction weakens as well. Likewise, in Israel, there is the problem of maintaining the public and private caused by the banning of divorces; and in Egypt, informal relationships, such as ʿurfi marriage, are starting to appear to separate the love instinct from that which can no longer be afforded, the formal institution of marriage, the traditional mainstay of the private.

What also seems clear is that, as women gain more education and access to jobs outside the home in any of these hegemonies, the logic of public-private is further challenged. States and religions have to contend with the dynamics, which are the result of a rising global unemployment, a situation in which the chances of an uneducated woman finding a job may easily exceed those of any man educated or not. This brings us to today's real economic issues.

How will states of differing hegemonies respond to the new world of no paid jobs. Will they still try to maintain a feminized private and a masculinized public? Will religious officials recognize that the survival of 80 percent of humanity must come from barter, not cash jobs, and that the home and whoever is in it is the center of this economy? If the idea of the public becomes meaningless as a result, does that not mean that not just public and private but the whole bilateral construction of gender will have to change? Where will that leave patriarchy and its apparatniks?

PART TWO

Muslim Women and the Shari^ca *Courts*

5

Women, Law, and Imperial Justice in Ottoman Istanbul in the Late Seventeenth Century

Fariba Zarinebaf-Shahr

*R*esearch on the history of Muslim women has been limited until very recently. This limitation has been mainly caused by the paucity of historical sources on women; but it is also the result of Western and native modernist (and Orientalist) biases regarding the history of the Middle East in general that has affected the nature of scholarship on women in the Islamic world. Although the Western feminist discourse has contributed to a general awareness of the contemporary plight of Muslim women, it has reduced the nature of scholarship to a cultural discourse, according to which only the fusion of Western culture through intellectual borrowing, colonialism, and modernization after the rise of nation-states brought about an improvement in the conditions of Muslim women.[1]

The positive impact of modern Western culture on the legal status of Middle Eastern women is undeniable. The modernization paradigm however, casts a dark shadow on the history of Muslim women before the nineteenth century, based on which this period is treated in general and often stereotypical terms.[2] An improvement on this type of approach is the so-called rise and decline paradigm, according to which the position of Muslim women improved during the early Islamic period (Espo-

---

1. For a critique of this paradigm see, 1982, 521–24. For a general bibliography, see Fariba Zarinebaf-Shahr 1993, pp. 256–66.
2. Keddie and Baron 1991 is an exception.

sito 1975, 99–106), declined after the rise of the Abbasid state (with the exception of the Seljuk and the Mongol periods) until the nineteenth century, and improved again under the influence of Western culture.[3] With the deconstruction of Orientalism, a revisionist approach to the history of Muslim women is badly needed because the old paradigms have failed to explain the revival of Islamic movements in the Middle East and North Africa and the active participation of Muslim women in these movements. Caution must be taken, however, not to engage in a defensive/apologetic debate that can ultimately be misunderstood as a call for the reimposition of the *şeriat* and the promotion of religious values to "rectify the dignity of Muslim women," according to the fundamentalist Muslim view.

Perhaps a more balanced approach would be to set aside momentarily ideological and political issues and instead focus on the social and economic aspects of women's lives in light of recent archival research based on *şeriat* court and petitionary records *(Şikayet Defterleri)* contained in the Turkish Başbakanlik Archives that are the subject of this essay. But first, a brief statement on the development of Western historiography is in order.

According to popular view, Muslim women did not play any role in the social and economic life of their community until very recently owing to their seclusion and segregation.

Origins of this view that has permeated feminist discourse date back to the eighteenth and nineteenth centuries, when European missionaries, colonialists, artists, and merchants started traveling to the Muslim world with a clear perception of Western superiority and a conviction of the decaying Muslim culture. European painters (example, Delacroix, Renoir, and Matisse) depicted Muslim women in erotic scenes of the harem, the slave market, and the bath. According to Mary Anne Stevens, these paintings reflected more the state of mind of the painter than the actual status of the subject matter: "The degree of eroticism would have been unthinkable in images of life in contemporary Europe. But with the Near East, there was an excuse since the work of a painture-ethnographe such as Gerome was ostensibly a matter of scientific observation. It was the stuff of sexual fantasy with the appearance of documentary record" (Stevens 1984, 37).

Among the Christian missionaries, Rev. S. Wilson, who lived in Iran during the second half of the nineteenth century, described the

---

3. For a critique of early scholarship in women's studies, see Tucker 1983.

position of Iranian women as follows: "A wife is in subjection to her husband, a subjection so abject that she does not even dream of the possession of those rights which have been and are being granted to women in Christian lands. She occupies the position of slave to man's pleasure and comfort, and aspires to nothing more" (Wilson 1895, 257).

Although these reports have a ring of truth to them, certainly as far as the general conditions of the lives of women are concerned, they fail to account for the changing position of women long before the advent of the modern state. Moreover, in contrast to this image of Iranian women, it must be noted that they had been very active in the Tobacco Rebellion of 1890, the Constitutional Revolution (1904–1905), and recently in the 1978 revolution (Nashat 1983). The role of these "traditional" women in social uprisings has not received due scholarly attention.

Instead, historical scholarship has focused on the legal status of women contained in the Qur'an, the *hadith,* and the *şeriat.* This approach exposes the ideology of the *ulema* toward women that has influenced the development of Islamic law. Nevertheless, it fails to examine the relationship between law and its perception by women and the dynamic process of its use and application. In other words, owing to the limitation of published and available source material, the actual lives of women, their role in production, and their interaction with the rest of the society and the state are not being studied adequately.

The questions I wish to raise here are the following: Within the constraints of Islamic ideological and legal boundaries, what strategies did Muslim women across different social settings follow to gain a bargaining position in the society in both domestic and public spheres? Did women actively participate in the process of manipulating the existing legal limitations to win a better socioeconomic position? Their actual initiative and their selection of available legal channels is one subject of this paper. In addition, I examine the historical social and economic position of women in the Ottoman Empire by using the rich Ottoman archival source material, the Şikayet Defterleri. It will be argued that, in the Ottoman urban setting, women's sphere of action was by no means restricted by the boundaries set up through religioideological norms such as segregation and public-domestic division based on gender. Although at the ideological level these norms were invoked whenever women transgressed their limits, considerable leverage was given to women that, combined with certain socioeconomic factors, left many in control of their lives. The *şeriat* provided a set of options for women, such as property rights, inheritance shares (although secondary to that of men), and a limited right to initiate divorce that were certainly more available to women with a degree of socioeconomic standing. Women wielded power and exercised initiative in the context of their immediate kin and extended households. For this reason, as I will demonstrate, widowed women and those who lost their fathers were often exposed to abuse by authorities and other heirs, especially when it came to controlling and protecting their economic well-being. The support and protection a woman received from her own immediate kin, especially the male members, strengthened her position vis-à-vis her husband and in-laws. It is important to emphasize a woman's role in the context of both her kin and her marital household. This also explains the emphasis placed on marriage among relatives, not only to protect family property but also to provide a close watch on the behavior of the husband and in-laws. Appealing to the *şeriat* and the Imperial Council was really a last resort for a woman who felt defenseless at the loss of her father and her husband. Women who petitioned the court were careful to make a point of their vulnerability and defenselessness.

Another purpose of this essay is to complement the works of Jennings and Gerber on the women of Kayseri and Bursa during the seventeenth century. Jennings's study focused on the *kadi* court records of Kayseri from 1590 to 1630 and he concludes that (1) women came freely, openly, and regularly to the *şeriat* court; (2) 25 percent of the cases heard by the court involved women as litigants; (3) their suits and defenses against suits were treated in the same manner as those of Muslim men; and (4) because the court upheld their legal rights, the women of Kayseri had an opportunity to participate in the social and economic life of the community (Jennings 1972, 246–47). Haim Gerber's 1980 study of the women of Bursa in the seventeenth century also confirms most of Jennings's conclusions.

I have also made use of another category of Ottoman archival documents, namely, the Şikayet Defterleri located in the Başbakanlik Archives in Istanbul to test the findings of Jennings from a different perspective. The seventeenth century is a period least studied and understood by scholars. Before appreciating the impact of Western economic penetration, integration into world economy, and the rise of reforming states on the status of women, we must have a clear picture of women's life before the nineteenth century. This study is a preliminary step in that direction but first, a few words on the nature of the source material used for the first time to study the history of Ottoman women are in order.

Şikayet Defterleri

The importance of the Şikayet Defterleri as source material for the history of the Ottoman Empire was first brought up by Halil Inalcik (1988). The structure of the Ottoman state was based on the pre-Islamic, Iranian bureaucratic principle of the Circle of Justice. According to this view, a strong state depended on a strong army that was supported by a rich treasury, itself dependent on taxes that were collected from the *reaya,* (tax-paying subjects) the well-being of whom depended on a "just king." The justice of the king or sultan, extended to all subjects, male and female, Muslim and non-Muslim. The sultan was the supreme dispenser of justice (*adalet*), and his role was carried out in the Imperial Council (*divan-i humayun*), where he or his deputy, the grand vizier, sat in person to hear petitions brought by his subjects and to decree imperial orders, copies of which were registered in the *Şikayet Defterleri.* It must be noted that legal cases were first taken to the *kadi*'s court in provincial centers or to his deputies in smaller towns. But because the *kadi* lacked the executive power to enforce legal decisions, it was left up to the governor, his retinue, and the power and authority of the people involved to follow up on legal enforcement. In the process, the rights of many claimants were abused even after the law took their side. The *kadi* in some cases sided unjustly with the defendants and took bribes. As will be demonstrated, many petitions were directed against corrupt *kadi*s. As Jennings has demonstrated, however, women enjoyed open access to the *kadi*'s court, probably because of its informal setting and a dynamic relationship between women and religious authorities, an issue that should be explored further. Obviously, the norms of segregation did not apply too strictly to these settings, and women enjoyed the right of direct appeal. At any rate, when the *kadi* failed to resolve the cases, the right of appeal to the Imperial Council was invoked. Sometimes, the *kadi* himself represented the petitioners and wrote to the Imperial Council, which referred most of the cases back to the *kadi*'s court and only in very urgent cases issued legal decrees. Thus, there was an open line of communication between the tax-paying subjects (in this case women), the Imperial Council that functioned as a kind of supreme court, and the *shari*ᶜa courts in the provinces.

These petitions were presented from all over the empire, from urban centers, villages, and tribes. The copies of imperial decrees (*hüküm*) were bound in a single register, containing two hundred to three hundred folios, each of which had eight to fourteen entries, or cases.

Usually, every register or two corresponded to a single year. The *şikayet* registers in the Başbakanlik Archives cover a period from the second half of the seventeenth century to the beginning of the nineteenth century. Taking Majer's published register dating from 1675 as the focus of this paper, the period under consideration extends from the third quarter of the seventeenth to the beginning of the eighteenth centuries.

Women as Petitioners

The petitions were presented by women directly, through a representative (usually male kin), or by the local *kadi*. Some petitioners presented their cases in writing, and others traveled from such places as Cairo to Istanbul to present their petitions in person. Obviously, the cost and time involved in the process had to make it a worthwhile undertaking for those women who did not reside in Istanbul. In many instances, they came as a group, accompanied by their male and female relatives. Nevertheless, the great majority of the petitions were from the greater Istanbul area. From 1680 to 1706, approximately 8 percent of the total number of petitions were presented from Istanbul. In 1675, although more than 763 petitions involved the residents of Istanbul, Galata, and Üsküdar, the residents of other Ottoman cities also petitioned. Aleppo presented 57 petitions, Izmir 38, Bursa 58, Sivas 64, and Selanik 50 (Majer 1984). The majority of plaintiffs and petitioners were Muslims. Undoubtedly, variation in population and distance were important factors in determining the number of petitions. In addition, for the same period (1680–1706) on the average, the petitions of women counted for 8.24 percent of total petitions from Istanbul (Başbakanlik Archives, Şikayet Defterleri). This average was probably close to the figure from the provinces. For example, in 1675, the percentage of petitions by women from Bursa equaled 8.5 percent (that is 5 out of 58). According to Faroqhi, in the *kadi* courts of Kayseri and Ankara, women plaintiffs and defendants made up 10–20 percent of the cases (Faroqhi 1984, 252–53). This figure is very close to Jennings's findings. And so, women preferred to submit their cases first to the *kadi*'s court and turned to the Imperial Council when they felt they had not been given just treatment by *şeriat* authorities.

This low percentage as compared to 25 percent of the total lawsuits brought in by women to the court of Kayseri can be explained by the fact that women petitioned the Imperial Council in Istanbul after having exhausted regular *şeriat* channels. Because the *kadi* lacked the executive power to enforce the legal decisions, it was a common occurrence to seek redress from a higher, central organ of power. These petitions generally involved such problems as abuse by local officials, inheritance, divorce, and collection of debts. These women were members of different socioeconomic strata in Istanbul, but the majority came from the middle class. Although women who belonged to powerful households were seldom exposed to abuse by local officials, the loss of their male protector (husband, father) left them in a vulnerable position. Moreover, inheritance disagreements occurred among members of all economic strata, but mostly among members of the middle class, where women were left dependent on male relatives for the protection of their property rights. The precarious economic position of women that depended on inheritance, bride price, and dowry made them more aware of their rights and sensitive to any encroachment into this domain. Their fear and resentment of potential cowives and unwed concubines whose offspring were also entitled to a portion of the inheritance from their husband made life a constant scene of intrigue and tension. Fortunately for Muslim women, polygamy was not a common phenomenon but rather remained a limited practice among the economically able members of the society. Women of powerful households, however, made sure that they would not end up in a polygamous marriage and sought the aid, support, and sympathy of their immediate kin to negotiate their marital status before the marriage contract was drawn up. When these family networks failed, women turned to legal channels where the *şeriat* maintained some measure of equity in these matters. Because the *şeriat* upheld the nuclear family and only in rare instances prescribed divorce and polygamy, women enjoyed the right of appeal and were encouraged to bring lawsuits to the court. *Kadi* court records provide detailed information about the kind of lawsuits women brought in, although they lack information on the final outcome of the legal procedure because the *kadi* did not possess executive power. It was for this reason that women petitioned the Imperial Council, although at this stage cases were referred back to the *kadi* in the provincial centers and seldom did the Imperial Council issue a final directive unless the issues had fiscal, administrative, and political implications. In these cases, *kanun* (secular law) offered more detailed and specific solutions. However, in personal matters, the *şeriat* remained indisputable, and the *kadi*'s court the sole legitimate legal channel. For example, the number of petitions dealing with marital problems such as bride price and divorce remained extremely limited owing to the personal nature of this problem and the specific provisions laid out by the *şeriat*. The majority of these cases were taken to the *kadi*'s court, where women were given due treatment;

Table 5.1

Petitions Presented by Women in Istanbul in 1675

Category	Number	Percentage
Inheritance	24	39.0
Property Dispute	21	34.0
Loans	10	16.0
Divorce	3	4.9
Bride Price	3	4.9
Other	1	1.6
Total	62	100.0

and as a result, few cases ended up in the Imperial Council. Still, a few petitions concerning the payment of bride price (*mehr*) were submitted to the Council (Şikayet *Defterleri* 1114/1702, 35:1483).[4] Petitions presented by women in Istanbul in 1675 can be broken down as indicated in Table 5.1.

As demonstrated by table 5.1, most of the petitions presented by women involved problems of an economic nature, although very few cases demonstrate independent economic activity among women. Moreover, these petitions seldom represented those women (lower classes) who earned wages as domestic servants, weavers, agricultural workers, etcetera. Were these women prevented from submitting petitions because they lacked wide and powerful networks? A few petitions submitted by former slaves and by peasant women point to the openness of both the *mehkeme* (Islamic court) and the Imperial Council to members of all classes (Faroqhi 1984, 253). Only more extensive research can answer this question, although we know that peasant women also appealed to the Porte and received due hearing. Who did women petition against? In most cases, as shown in table 5.2, women complained about corrupt *kadi*s, *mütevelli*s (trustees of religious endowments), and other local officials.

The number of petitions against officials (31%) far exceeded those against relatives and husband (23%). The *kadi*'s court received more lawsuits against relatives and husbands involving marital problems. Inheritance disputes were the greatest source of conflict among relatives,

---

4. See doc. 1 at the end of the article.

Table 5.2

Those Whom Women Petitioned Against in 1675

Against	Number	Percentage
*Kadi*s and *Mütevelli*s	15	24.5
Relatives	9	14.7
Debtors	5	8.0
Husband	5	8.0
Local Officials	4	6.5
Creditors	2	3.2
Cowives	1	1.6
Other	20	32.7
Total	61	100.0

and illegal encroachment on their property (landed and urban real estate) by the directors of *vaquf*s (*mütevelli*s) and corrupt *kadi*s who usually conspired with the former made up the second largest number of cases. Each category of petitions is briefly discussed below.

Inheritance and Property Disputes

Muslim women inherited from all their relatives according to the degree of closeness. They inherited fewer shares than their male counterparts, though their shares were protected and upheld by the *şeriat*. Nevertheless, inheritance disputes among heirs—brothers, sisters, cowives, husbands, and corrupt officials (*kadi*s, *mütevelli*s)—made up the largest number of petitions (39%). According to Faroqhi, in seventeenth-century Ankara and Kayseri, inheritance conflicts over *mülk* (private property) and *miri* (state land) counted for 15–24 percent of litigations (Faroqhi 1984, 332). Inheritance was an important source of economic power for women, and in cases of abuse, women were particularly vocal in defending their rights. If a girl was still a minor when she lost her parents, however, chances were high that her guardian (*vesi*), usually an uncle or the *kadi*, would swallow up most of the inheritance before the child came of age. Sometimes, at a later point the heir would file a lawsuit (Faroqhi 1984, 255). The women of Istanbul inherited shares (*hisses*) in residential houses, orchards, shops, household items, jewelry from their mother, and textiles (Seng 1991, 240–41). Inheritance dis-

putes involved landed estates in the form of an orchard or shares in
residential units. Because their inheritance was usually a share rather
than a whole unit, women were under pressure to sell off their portion
to the male heirs. Disputes arose when their portions were sold off without their consent, or when their right to possess the inherited property
was denied. In such cases, other heirs were responsible by bribing the
kadi or his deputies. Inheritance conflicts were also widespread among
male heirs, and usually a whole family would be split up with women
taking sides according to their own interests. These disputes sometimes
would get so prolonged that the landed estate would suffer from neglect
and fall into ruin, thus putting further pressure on women to sell off their
portions. According to Faroqhi, seventeenth-century Kayseri records
show that women sold much more than they bought, and as sellers they
were not the only proprietors but merely held shares in land of deceased
relatives (1984, 254).

The following examples illustrate the challenges women faced in
protecting their property rights against their relatives, state, and religious officials. In an imperial order issued to the *kadi* of Istanbul in mid-
Rebiᵓl-Awwal 1086/April 1675, it was stated that two sisters named
Emine and Hakime presented the following petition in person: they
complained that the *mütevelli* was to sell the house they had inherited
from their deceased father claiming its courtyard as *vakf* property. They
had already obtained a *fetva* from the *kadi* in favor of their claim (Majer,
fol. 117 a:5). Obviously, the *fetva* had failed to generate a positive
response from the *mütevelli,* and these two sisters had to take the next
step in seeking justice. The Imperial Council referred the case back to
the *kadi* to reconsider the matter and to act according to the *şeriat*. In
another order issued to the *kadi* of Uskudar in the end of Zilkade 1085/
May 1675, it was stated that a woman named Amhan, daughter of
Mehmet, had presented a petition claiming that the *kadi* and superintendent of the *beytulmal* (treasury) had illegally taken possession of her
inherited goods worth 8,000 akçes (Majer 1984, fol. 33a, no. 8). Finally,
in a petition submitted by Banafse in Rebiᵓl-Awwal 1085/April 1675,
she complained that her son-in-law, Halil the Janissary had illegally
taken the house and *çiftlik* (agricultural estate) of her deceased husband,
which were inherited by her daughter Fatma, Halil's wife (Majer 1984,
fol. 25a, no. 4). The last two cases illustrate the precarious position of
women in the process of property transfer, for which the *şeriat* had laid
down specific provisions. The very officials in charge of the *şeriat* took
advantage of their positions and confiscated the goods of defenseless
women whenever they could get away with it. The last case demon-

strates the inviolability of a woman's property rights vis-à-vis her husband and the event to which a woman's immediate kin, in this case her mother, was willing to go to protect her daughter's rights against her son-in-law, who happened to be a man of some social standing.

Women and Moneylending

The women of Istanbul participated in the economic life of the community by giving and taking loans. Based on the information that appears in the registers, it is not clear whether they lent money through an intermediary (moneylender) or directly. They probably tried both alternatives, depending on the amount of cash to which they had access. Shrewd businesswomen invested their cash in a variety of ways and did not shy away from charging high interest rates (10–20%). Because cash was not readily available even in a seventeenth-century urban setting, these women undoubtedly were members of higher-income social groups. They acquired cash through selling their inherited shares and the amount involved in moneylending usually did not exceed 1,000 *kuruş*. Women petitioned about their debtors refusal to repay their debts in full. In many cases, women had registered these loans at the court and had obtained a *fetva* proving their claims. Women also took loans from each other, probably to cover their everyday needs. These were women in dire need because they had lost their husbands and had to provide for themselves and their children. They often defaulted because they lacked the ability to repay their loans. For example, in a petition filed by Ayse dated March 1675, she claimed that she had lent 800 kuruş to another woman, who had failed to pay it back upon her request (Majer 1984, fol. 112a, no. 1). It was easier for women to lend to each other than to seek out male creditors; however, in this case the risks of default also increased. At the same time, the creditors and officials might have been more lenient toward women, even though there were many occasions in which women lost the possessions they had placed as surety for loans.

Divorce and Mehr

The last category of petitions presented by Istanbul women involved problems related to marriage and divorce. Because this was a specific domain of the *şeriat* fewer complaints (10%) were reported to the Imperial Council. These complaints concerned the payment of the bride price after the divorce was completed. According to the Hanafi school of law, the marriage contract had to be drawn according to the voluntary consent of both partners, and its violation led to the annulment of marriage by the *mehkeme*. Divorce, however, had to be initiated by the husband; and only in exceptional circumstances (impotence, mental illness, financial reasons, etc.) could a wife sue for divorce and in such cases she had to give up her *mehr* or make payment in return for her freedom (*khul*) (Walther 1993, 66). Usually, it was agreed that a part of the bride price called *mehr-i muaccel* be paid in advance, and the remainder was to be paid in the event of divorce or any time the woman demanded it. It is important to note that *mehr* legally belonged to the wife, even if her husband retained most of it; he could not sell, transfer, or lend it without the consent of his wife. Often in order to retain the *mehr,* men forced their wives to initiate divorce. The following two petitions presented by a certain Halime Hatun, dated Rebi'l-Awwal 1114/July 1702, vividly illustrate these points:

> A *Hüküm* to the Kaimmakam and Kadi of my threshold (read Istanbul): A lady named Halime has come complaining that her husband, Ahmet a resident of Istanbul has illegally taken from her goods worth 399 kus via certain [. . .], another time has taken 100-cash, and again has taken 40 akches to purchase a shop. She has unwillingly reached an agreement (*sulh*) with him, however, since a forced agreement is against the şeriat according to the *fetva* of the şeyhulislam, she has demanded via her deputy (*vekil*) the payment of all her due rights (*hakk,* read cash). This order is issued to you to act according to the *fetva* and the şeriat (Şikayet Defterleri 35:1483).

> To the *kadi* and *Kaimmakam* of my threshold: A lady named Halime has come claiming that her husband, Ahmet, a resident of Istanbul had forced her to sue for divorce and give up her mehr in the year [11 . . .]. However, since the divorce is *khul,* that is, it has been forced upon her and therefore is against the şeriat, she is demanding her legally established *mehr* but he has refused to pay it to her deputy according to a *fetva*. This order is written to you to act according to the şeriat (Şikayet Defterleri 35:1485).

Halime Hatun was obviously a well-to-do lady of some social distinction. In the first petition, Halime complained about her husband's illegal extortion of her goods and cash that amounted to a total of 540 kuruş, by no means a negligible sum according to eighteenth-century standards. She claimed that she had unwillingly reached an agreement with her husband, probably to give up her rights in return for her freedom which is legally termed *khul.* In this petition, it is not specified whether this sum was part of Halime's *mehr,* but the second document is more informative. In the second document, Halime Hatun claimed her husband, Ahmet had divorced her in [. . .]. And so, we learn that the dispute arose after Halime had been divorced, which was also the case when the first petition was filed. Here, she specifically complains that the divorce was *khul;* that is, it had been forced upon her to give up probably the 540 akçes in return for her freedom.

In the second petition, Halime demands the return of her *mehr* (which is specifically stated). The second petition clarifies the vague points in the first complaint; it is thus correct to assume that both petitions were filed by Halime Hatun after divorce and involved the payment of a disputed *mehr.* Therefore, certain points emerge from these cases. First of all, it is obvious that the exact terms of the payment and possession of *mehr* were left deliberately vague so that, in the event of marital discord and divorce, the husband, who most of the time retained most of the *mehr,* could take full possession of it. The only legal recourse left for women was to claim that they had initiated divorce *khul* under duress, which according to the *şeriat* was illegal. It is also clear that women had a hard time in obtaining their *mehr* after divorce, even after filing several lawsuits against their former husbands. Further research on actual marriage contracts is needed to ascertain whether the amount and conditions of *mehr* were specifically stated or were left deliberately vague. In most cases, the amount of disputed *mehr* is seldom mentioned, although it is certain that it was not entirely in cash. The well-to-do men provided their wives with title deeds to landed estates and shares in the ownership of residential property, jewelry, and cash. The bride's family, in turn, provided a dowry that they matched with the *mehr.* The value of dowry was not specified and was left up entirely to the bride's family, but it played an important symbolic role in the determination of *mehr.* A family's status was reflected in the size and value of a dowry they provided for their daughter. Here again, the bargaining position of a woman depended much on her status and her own support networks. Even if she had stipulated certain provisions in her marriage contract, the support of her own family was very important in protecting her rights. The *mehr* was a potential source of economic power for women, and as such they could not really count on its actual remission by their husbands. On the other hand, the dowry, which was given to a woman as a marriage gift by her own family usually in the form of household furnishings, textiles, and jewelry, made up a real asset and belonged legally to her. This was in addition to inheritance from her own relatives, to which she was fully entitled. This takes us back to a point made earlier; namely, that in the absence of an independent source of income, women's socioeconomic position must be studied in the context of their households, especially their paternal kin networks used even after marriage. As their petitions demonstrate, Ottoman women of the late seventeenth century were well conscious of their legal rights and the advantage of their own networks in protecting them, even if they were not in parity with those of Muslim men.

To conclude, compared to their European sisters, Ottoman women in late seventeenth-century Istanbul enjoyed a certain degree of involvement in the social and economic life of their community. Before reaching concrete conclusions on the comparative status of Middle Eastern and European women, further research based on documentation and comparative studies must be carried out. Available studies based on *kadi* court records and this article have demonstrated that Islamic law upheld women's inheritance rights and provided for the legal control and full possession of the bride price and dowry. Inheritance, dowry, and *mehr* made up the primary source of economic income for women; some women invested their cash in trade and moneylending enterprises, and others acquired real estate and actively engaged in buying and selling property. When their rights were transgressed, women across all social classes took advantage of available legal mechanisms to protect their rights and to acquire a position in the public sphere though limited and precarious. This article has demonstrated that proximity to the seat of government provided the women of Istanbul better access to the Imperial Council (high court of appeal). Nevertheless, women from all over the empire petitioned the Imperial Council in person, through the local *kadi,* or a male representative. The content of their petitions varied from those of male subjects, dealing mostly with inheritance and property disputes. Most of these women petitioners belonged to middle-income households, whose livelihood after the loss of a husband, father, or a divorce in certain circumstances depended greatly on inherited shares and the bride price. The *şikayet* registers demonstrate the active participation of Ottoman women in a dynamic process of legal procedure whether through the normal *kadi* court channels or the Imperial Council.

The late seventeenth and the eighteenth centuries were a period of transition from decentralized rule to strong state formation, especially after the Tanzimat reforms in the Ottoman Empire. Although Istanbul, as the capital, did not experience the full impact of decentralization, the rise of non-*askeri* (non-military) households certainly had a positive impact on the position of women. The *şikayet* registers contain a great deal of information on women who belonged to middle-income groups and were outside the ruling class. Unfortunately, the available registers do not cover the entire nineteenth century, but they reflect a strong sense of continuity in the lives of Ottoman women between the seventeenth and the eighteenth centuries.

6

The Family and Gender Laws in Egypt During the Ottoman Period

Abdal-Rehim Abdal-Rahman Abdal-Rehim

*R*esearchers can grasp through their study of *shariᶜa* court documents the nature of the family system and the role of women in this system during the Ottoman era. An examination of these records gives a clear picture of the shape of the Egyptian family during the Ottoman era: the relationship between family members; different marriage patterns that were followed in various parts of the country; the nature of the marriage contract and divorce settlements; and the status of women during that period and the reality of gender relations. Two particular points form the objectives of this essay: first, to illustrate the significance of *shariᶜa* court records for the study of the history of the common people in Islamic society; and second, by using Egypt's *shariᶜa* court archives, to discuss marriage, divorce, and family traditions prevailing in Egypt during the Ottoman period.

In Egypt, such documents are held in several archives, namely: Dar al-Mahfuzat al-ᶜUmumiyya, in which are found most of the documents of the provincial *shariᶜa* courts; Dar al-Wathaiq al-Qawmiyya, in which are held documents of a number of registries of the provincial *shariᶜa* courts; and the Cairo Shahr al-ᶜAqari, in which are found real estate archival records for Cairo and documents of the Cairo *shariᶜa* courts dating from the Ottoman era. Moreover, some provincial *shariᶜa* court documents are still held at those courts' archives or the Shahr al-ᶜAqari of the particular province's capital city. Thus, the Ottoman *shariᶜa* court records are housed in the Alexandria Shahr al-ᶜAqari, and those of Rashid are held at the Damanhur Court of First Instance.

The Egyptian Family and Marriage

The Muslim Egyptian family during the Ottoman period was formed according to the provisions of the Islamic *shari'a* and its principles as set by the Qur'an and Sunna, the latter being interpreted in accordance to four legal schools, or *madhahib:* namely, the Hanafi *madhhab,* which was the official school adopted by the Ottomans, and the Shafi'i, Maliki, and Hanbali *madhahib.* Because the principles of each *madhhab* were different, preferences between *madhahib* also determined the marriage contract. Generally speaking, the Shafi'i *madhhab* predominated in the Nile Delta, the Maliki was predominant in Upper Egypt, and the Hanafi was the most used in Cairo and other important commercial cities. Many reasons existed for these preferences, most of which can be attributed to historical continuity and preference of local traditions (*'urf*).

The Muslim husband or his *wakil* (deputy, proxy), and the wife or her *wakil* used to go to the judge of the particular *madhhab* according to which they wished to be married. Non-Muslim (i.e., Christian or Jewish) marriages were concluded according to the particular *shari'a;* that is, the Christian *shari'a* or the Jewish *shari'a* that were normally officiated by priests or rabbis. The marriage contracts of non-Muslims were usually recorded in *shari'a* court records the same as Muslim marriages.

Marriage almost always took place after an engagement period, which usually depended on the age of the bride; the younger she was, the longer would be the engagement period. Sometimes, it was the age of the groom that delayed the marriage because quite often young boys were betrothed by their guardians, but the marriage could only be concluded when the bridegroom was considered ready. In certain cases, the marriage of minors was concluded and the contract signed by the guardians, but the bride and groom continued to live with their own families until the time when the marriage was consummated and, hence, the contract fulfilled. It was also expected that the financial agreements set out in the marriage, particularly the dowry, be fulfilled before the marriage was consummated. Until such time as the dowry was paid or the minor bride or bridegroom reached *bulugh* (puberty), they continued to live with their respective families.

The procedure was: The two parties to the marriage contract (or their *wakil*s) registered the conditions upon which they were entering into the contract. One of the important stipulations in any marriage contract had to do with the judge's determination of compatibility or social parity *(kafaʾa)* between bride and groom, which observation he recorded in the contract. This condition was in accordance to marriage stipulations established by the Islamic *shariʿa*. It was also required by law that there be at least two trustworthy witnesses to any contract and that it be registered by the judge, who noted all the conditions agreed upon. Included in the contract are the names of the parents, guardians, or *wakil*s (or all of them) of both the bride and groom. The names of the witnesses to the marriage contract were always included. The place of residence and town of origin (in cases where the marriage took place in larger towns with mixed populations from different geographical origins) of each person mentioned in the contract was also recorded. This means that we have data on urbanization and population movements through court records of marriages, divorces, and other contracts.

Among the conditions for marriage that are always included in the marriage contract are the amounts of the *mahr* (dowry), that are paid by the bridegroom to the bride in an advanced *(muqaddam)* and delayed *(muʾakhkhar)* form. The amounts are very clearly spelled out, as well as the conditions according to which the dowry was to be payed, when payments were to be made, how much was to be advanced to the bride at the time of betrothal, how much she was to receive at the time the contract was concluded, and lastly how much was to be paid to the bride during the marriage in the shape of installments (if that was agreed upon). For example, Zaynab bint ʿAbdullah married her betrothed, Ahmad ibn Muhammad ibn ʿUmar, before the Hanafi *qadi*. The *muqaddam* was 4 gold Maghribi dinars, and the *muʾakhkhar* was set at 3 dinars due her upon his death or on their separation. Other conditions of Zaynab and Ahmad's contract included that she receive an allowance of half a silver Sulaymani dinar every month. Furthermore, the husband pledged that if he were to take a second wife, mistreated Zaynab, or changed her residence against her will, (that upon her presenting proof of such allegations) and was willing to cut her *muʾakhkhar* by one dinar, then she would be *taliqa* (divorced) one *talqa* "with which she would own herself" (Jamiʿ al-Hakim 966/1559, 540:200–898).

The conditions often included the place of residence where the wife expected to live. For example, the marriage between Sharaf al-din Mussa ibn Muhammed and ʿAisha bint ʿAli ibn ʿIsa (identified as an adult virgin [*bikr baligh*]) stipulated that the "said husband consented to live with his wife's mother Hajja Mansura bint ʿIsa al-Bishari." The dowry in this case amounted to 33 new gold Sultani dinars, of which 18 were paid in advance. Both the amount of the dowry and the payment arrangements indicate that ʿAisha was a bride of some wealth. It should be noted that the bride's father represented his daughter in this contract, which was typical for Alexandria (957/1550 1:134–641).

Compare this last case to an example from the same Alexandria shariʿa court records that involved a previously married woman (usually referred to as a hurma in Ottoman records). Whereas the contracts are similar, the difference comes in the amount of the dowry, which in this case was 40 silver nisfs, of which Farhana, the bride, declared she had received half, the other half determined as a delayed dowry (Jamiʿ al-Hakim 957/1551, 1:183–824). The difference seems to indicate that virgins received a higher dowry than previously married women; however, the issue is not that simple, as this essay shows.

Another typical marriage was that of Abuʾl-Hassan ibn Ibrahim ibn ʿAbdullah, who married the virgin Ghajariyya bint Khalid ibn Muhammed al-Maghrabi. The contracted mahr was 30 new gold Sultani dinars, of which 8 dinars were received by her mother Ward, and 22 dinars were designated as muʾakhkhar. Abuʾl-Hassan also committed to pay her 6 silver ansaf as a monthly clothing allowance and agreed on her following conditions: if he were to take a second wife "in any manner"; if he were to travel more than once a year or move to a far away place for good; or if he were to beat her violently leaving marks; then he would be entitled to withhold no more than a quarter dinar of the remaining dowry, which would be indisputably hers if she chose to divorce him. In this particular contract, because the bride's father had been absent for over six years, it was her uncle who represented her in the marriage (al-Barmashiyya 994/1589, 707: 113–711; Mahjub 1993, 34).

Sometimes, the dowry was rated partly in gold and partly in silver, the advance being in gold and the delayed in silver. For example, Salim ibn Khidr ibn Shihhata al-Damanhuri married his betrothed, Salima, an adult virgin, daughter of ʿAli ibn Yahya. The dowry was set at 7 new gold Sultani dinars and 200 new silver Sulaymani dinars to be paid in equal installments over twenty years, payment to be made at the end of each year. Furthermore, he agreed to provide her with "winter and summer wardrobes" (al-Barmashiyya 994/1587, 707: 113–711; Mahjub 1993, 34).

From the above we see that the amount of the dowry depended to a certain extent on whether the wife had been previously married. Thus, even though the dowry does not necessarily have to be paid in the form of gold coins, silver was usually the case when the wife was previously married and could have children in her custody from that marriage. Typical amounts paid to previously married women range from 200 to

600 silver nisfs. Previously married women, like virgins, were also usually granted a monthly personal/clothing allowance, which they could
spend on a child from a previous marriage (al-Zahid 1010/1601, 667:16–
58).

When the bride brought with her children from a previous marriage, she often included conditions in the marriage contract pertaining
to the security and support of these children, for which she was the
waliyya. A typical example is that of Mas'uda bint Muhammad, who
made it a condition upon her marriage to 'Umar ibn Muhammad ibn
Abi Bakr that he accept her children from a previous marriage. The
typical entry in the marriage contract in such a case reads: "The said
husband confirmed he knew that his said wife [has] a son born from
another [man]. He (i.e., the husband) accepts that he (i.e. the son) will
eat from his (i.e. the husband's) food and drink from his drink and sleep
on his bed without compensation" (al-Zahid 957/1551, 1:183–824).

It is interesting to note that, in this particular case, the wife must
have been of some wealth because she owned the house the couple was
to reside in: "The husband accepted to dwell with his wife in her house
of residence and that neither she or her son would demand any rent
from him as long as they live together" (Ibid).

Furthermore, the dowry was substantial, amounting to 12 new gold
dinars, 6 of which she received "by her own hands," indicating the social
independence of the wife. Still, even though it is clear that the wife
contracted her own marriage, she was represented by a *wakil* in her
marriage, a *wakil* whose relationship to her is not made clear in the
contract. This should make us pause and ask whether using a *wakil* may,
in many situations, have been no more than a formality related to social
traditions.

Another example supports these findings. The bride, 'Aisha bint
'Ali ibn Sulayman al-Maghribiyya, added a condition to the contract
that required her bridegroom, Mu'allim Shihab al-Din al-Tahhan, to
accept that her children from a previous marriage would live with them
and that he be responsible for their support in return for his lodging in
her home. A proxy was used to marry her, even though she received the
muqaddam of 6 gold dinars (of a total of ten) "by her own hands." Both
the husband and the wife's *wakil* are referred to as "mu'allim" (title of a
skilled head craftsman), the *wakil* being further described as a tailor.
This tells us of the social background of the parties to the contract, and
hence of the family traditions and the prerogatives possessed by adult
women within this class. Additionally, because it is another *mu'allim*
rather than a member of the wife's family who is "giving the bride

away," this is further indication of the freedom to "dispense of herself" that women with relative financial independence enjoyed (al-Zahid 957/ 1551, 1:183–824).

Even though the general rule was the inclusion of preconditions, not all marriage contracts stipulated conditions nor mentioned the amount of the clothing allowance promised by the husband to the wife. An example of this type of contract is that of Fatima bint ʿAmir ibn ʿAli, who married Yusif ibn Sulaiman ibn ʿAbdul-Karim, which is really a very abbreviated form including only the dowry amount, without which the marriage is invalid. "According to God's Qurʾan and his generous Prophet's Sunna . . . The dowry being 16 gold ʿAcrubi (Maghribi) dinars, of which 8 were delayed and 6 dinars received." There were no other stipulations included in the contract and no reference was made to a clothing allowance for the wife. Whether no such allowance was promised, or that the couple preferred not to mention the amount in the contract, is not clear. Both parties to the marriage are recorded as having declared their acceptance and affirmation of the legitimacy of the contract, a condition required to legitimize it (Alexandria, sijillat 957/1550, 1:96–454).

Another twist in regard to the clothing allowance is exemplified by the case of Musa ibn Muhammad, who is recorded as having married the *hurma* Mushbiya bint ʿAbdullah ibn Muhammad. He agreed to a dowry of 4 new gold Sultani dinars, of which 2 had already been received by her, according to her declaration, and 2 were delayed to become rightfully hers in the case of separation from or death of her husband. In this case, no conditions were included regarding a clothing allowance, but being a generous husband, he assumed that duty by adding a stipulation to the contract indicating that he would provide his wife with a yearly clothing allowance (Alexandria, sijillat 957/1550, 1:124–592). In the case of the *mulla*'s marriage mentioned earlier, the bride freed her husband from a clothing allowance (Alexandria, sijillat 1154/1742, 9:137–436).

As in the case of the Turkish *mulla*, marriages were often concluded between non-Egyptians, as well as Egyptians and non-Egyptians. The Syrian and North African communities are particularly well-represented in the records, showing us the size, wealth, and importance of these communities in various parts of Egypt. Thus, whereas they figure prominantly in Lower Egypt's port towns, they are mentioned rarely in the records of Upper Egyptian towns. Marriage contracts of non-Egyptian communities did not differ much from Egyptian contracts. A typical such marriage is between two families originating from Ladhiqiyya in

Syria. Al-Sharif (a title of nobility denoting descent from the Prophet Muhammad) Muhammad ibn al-Sharif ʿAbd al-Qadir al-Ladhiqi married Manals, the adult virgin daughter of Shihab-Aldin ʿAli ibn ʿUmar al-Ladhiqi, for a dowry of 30 gold Sultani dinars, 25 of which were paid in advance, the rest to be paid to the bride in installments over 20 years. The husband was also to pay her 1 dinar yearly as clothing support as long as she remained his wife (Dumyat, sijillat 1005/1597, 28:n.p.-28). The substantial dowry, including the large ratio paid in advance, was typical of the elite of the wealthy city of Dumyat during that period.

As this last contract from Dumyat indicates, marriage contracts from provincial towns did not differ greatly from contracts of cities such as Cairo or Alexandria. Some specifics, however, are clearly different, given the particular social context and the situation in which the couple find themselves. For example, whereas there did not seem to be over-concern with the question of a husband's travel in Cairo (except among the merchant elite), a husband's travel seemed to be of particular concern to women in portstowns. In a typical case from Dumyat, the husband agreed: "If I [travel and] leave my said wife for a period exceeding six months . . . or if I move her from the port (i.e., Dumyat) against her will and [she] can prove this legitimately, and if my said wife releases me of 1/4 dinar of her *muʾakhkhar,* [then] she can be divorced 'one divorce' with which she would own herself" (Dumyat, sijillat 1005/1597, 28:n.p.-28).

From these marriage contracts a number of conclusions can be arrived at.

1. Family relations, including marriage and divorce, during the Ottoman period were theoretically based on conditions laid down by the Qurʾan and the Sunna. Thus, the Qurʾan's admonition for compatibility between the husband and wife seemed to provide a basis for marriage. The usual selection of a particular *madhhab* by both parties was one indication of such compatibility, and the *qadi*'s recording of the marriages indicates that the compatibility factor was met with.

At the same time, if *shariʿa* court archives demonstrate anything, it would be the great diversity of the transactions that were enacted, depending on the time, place, and social conditions of the parties involved. This means that, even though the basic laws followed were *shariʿa* laws, their administration and execution differed not only from place to place but also from case to case. Suiting specific conditions was no problem as long as the main outlines of the *shariʿa* were followed, particularly those pertaining to the "rights" due to either party to the contract. Thus, even though the *shariʿa* guaranteed a wife support, including food, housing, and clothing, such conditions could be waived or amended in the contract when the wife agreed. Similarly, the *shariᶜa* may allow the husband to take four wives, but that right was often waived as a wife's condition for marriage.

2. Local *ᶜurf* played an important role in the marriage process. Different Muslim countries (as well as areas of the same country) had various customs regarding marriage. In Egypt, it was a generally applied custom to precede the marriage by a betrothal period, which followed the signing of the marriage contract and ended with the consummation of the marriage. This allowed the families to note the compatibility of the parties while at the same time protecting the bride and the family's reputation because the fiancée would be entering the home in an official capacity.

3. The marriage contract involved financial transactions of particular importance to the wife; in fact, the payment of a dowry was a requirement of the *shariᶜa*. Thus, the dowry (*muqaddam* and *muʾakhkhar*) was spelled out in great detail, was always calculated in monetary value, and was commonly paid in gold, silver, or a combination of the two. The *muʾakhkhar* usually consituted about half of the *muqaddam,* however in certain cases, particularly when the bride was independently wealthy or had been previously married, a larger portion was paid in advance. Because the *muʾakhkhar* was almost always contested when the wife demanded separation, it was usual for "experienced" wives to demand a larger share of the dowry (or all of it) in advance.

4. It was usual that marriage contracts, particularly in larger towns, include conditions safeguarding the wife's interests. These included: the husband's nonabsence from the marital home for a long or specific period of time; his pledge not to take another wife (or in certain cases, a concubine); his acceptance that his wife's children from previous marriages would reside with them and his pledge to support these children; and a pledge to allocate funds specifically designed for her clothing allowance. It was understood that if either party did not abide by the conditions detailed in the contract, then the other member of the party was free to seek divorce without fulfilling the rest of the obligations demanded by the contract. Thus, a wife could demand and receive a divorce without forfeiting any part of the dowry, unless otherwise specified by the marriage contract.

5. It was usual that the dowry of a virgin be higher than that of a divorced woman. Class played an important role in determining the amount of the dowry, however, as did the wealth, independence, and "desirability" of the bride. Thus, a previously married woman of some wealth actually often received a higher dowry than most virgins of the same town or class.

Women and Divorce

As is the case elsewhere and during other periods, marriages often failed as a result of circumstances related to the husband or wife or other reasons. In such circumstances, the Islamic *shariᶜa* allows for the separation of the husband from the wife. *Shariᶜa* court documents constitute the most important register of divorce cases because it is there that individual cases of divorce are detailed and outlined. Even though it is not clear whether all divorces that took place were recorded in court or whether only disputed divorces were recorded, the registration of large numbers of divorces points to two possibilities: either that such registration was required or that people were careful to receive documentary proof of divorce. This was particularly important for women who could not remarry without presenting proof that they were free to remarry; and as often happened, they found themselves faced with their former husbands' denials that divorce had taken place. In such situations, it was normal for a wife to demand a *fatwa* from the court confirming the divorce. The existence in the records of a large number of such cases is in itself an indication that divorces were normally registered in court.

Usual reasons for divorce or separation included disagreements owing to incompatibility or the existence of "defects" in either husband or wife. The divorce was often final; but in other cases, the separation was temporary and the wife returned to her husband. In such cases, it was usual for the husband to set upon himself certain conditions for the wife to agree to return to him (to be dealt with later).

When the husband initiated the divorce, it was expected that the full conditions of the marriage contract were to be met, particularly the payment of the *muᵓakhkhar,* as well as any portion of the *muqaddam* designated for payment in installments. Divorced wives often sued for alimony and divorce compensation. When a woman proved her case, the court always found for her, and the husband was required to pay. The question of proof, however, was often a complicated matter, particularly when the husband declared this divorce privately or if it was not recorded in court. In such cases, the wife had to provide witnesses to the husband's act. If she could not, then the usual recourse was to claim abandonment and lack of support, which usually lead to divorce. The important point to note is that divorce was the preferred form of separation for a wife because it assured her of the husband's legal obligations due her as detailed by the marriage contract. Besides, there were other compensations made possible by the *shariᶜa:* a one-year alimony, a possible *mut'a* (enjoyment) compensation for a divorce not of her doing, *'idda* (three-month waiting period following divorce before a woman can be remarried) support, and so forth. The amount formed a substantial burden relative to the class the couple originated from, hence the preference of divorce by the wife.

When it was the wife who wished for a divorce and the husband refused, then she was required to appear before the chief *qadi* to explain her reasons for demanding divorce. If she proved that such reasons were "legal" then the *qadi* found for her. Legal reasons included a husband's impotence (interpreted differently according to the particular *madhhab*), a husband's lack of piety, and his nonperformance of Islamic duties, which lent proof to her case against him. A usual cause for a wife's demand of divorce was the husband's nonfulfillment of the marriage contract. If the wife proved this to be so, normally through "acceptable" witnesses, the *qadi* found for her and granted her the divorce without compromising her financial rights.

A large portion of the cases that wives brought before the *qadi*, however, involved husbands who were unwilling to divorce and who had not broken any of the conditions in the marriage contract. In such cases, the wife demanded *khul'* (repudiation), by which the *qadi* allowed for a legal separation, but on condition that the wife forfeit any alimony. In most cases where there was an installment-alimony, the wife was expected to give up that as well. Frequently, the wife was also required to pay back all or part of the dowry paid to her by her husband at the time of marriage. Although in almost all cases of *khul'* the *qadi* granted the wife's wish, in *talaq* (divorce) the wife had to prove *darar* (harm) before *talaq* was granted. The difference had to do with financial rights.

In many court cases where a wife demanded *khul'*, the husband refused the separation and demanded that the wife compensate him over and above her repayment of the dowry and forefeiture of alimony. The payment demanded was often in the form of a sum of money that would be debated in court to reach a compromise. Examples of this type of situation include that of Dalal bint Muhammed al-Si'udi, who asked her husband, 'Ali Bakr ibn Baraka al-Dallal, to divorce her in return for 5 silver dirhams compensation. He agreed to that request and divorced her (Dumyat, sijillat 1005/1597 35:65–204). In such a case, the husband could not take his wife back within the three months that the *shari'a* allowed him, and any conciliation between them had to be on the basis of a brand new marriage contract with new conditions and dowry. For example, Kulthum bint Ahmad ibn Muhammed asked her husband to divorce her in return for a compensation of 1 silver nisf of her delayed dowry. Because she was pregnant and therefore had the right for alimony until she gave birth, she also gave up her right to such support as part of the bargain for her husband to divorce her (Mahfaza Dasht, sijillat 1005/1597, 110:n.p.-371). Generally speaking, the wealthier the wife, the higher the compensation expected from her for the husband to divorce her. The amount of compensation paid by the wife to the husband (or the amount determined by the court as a *mut'a* compensation for the wife when a divorce was not her fault) tells much about the social conditions of the particular society in which the divorce was taking place, the various social levels and classes, and how commercially active these societies were. A normal compensation amount expected of wealthier women was about 5 new gold Sultani dinars over and above relinquishing all the *mu'akhkhar* and alimony due from the husband (Mahfaza Dasht, sijillat 1006/1597, 37:45–124).

Similar cases were reported in smaller towns, such as that of Fatima from Miniyat al-Shuyukh (probably reference to a small village from which a large number of clergymen originated), located in the district of Faraskur. The divorce was recorded in the court of the town of Dumyat, where the husband was working as a porter. Fatima asked her husband, Shihab ibn 'Ali al-Haddad (blacksmith) to divorce her in return for a compensation of 5 silver dirhams. The employment, residence, and amount of the compensation indicate the working-class background of the couple. The same can be said of another case from Dumyat, in which Tawhida requested divorce from her husband, Higazi ibn Ahmad al-Maghribi al-Hayik, indicating that he was probably of North African origin and his profession (or that of his father) was that of weaver. As compensation, she paid him 5 silver dirhams (Mahfaza Dasht, sijillat 1009/1600, 4:57–150). Five Dirhams seemed to be the acceptable compensation for *khul'* among the working classes in Dumyat at the turn of the seventeenth century.

In most cases in which the wife asked for *khul'*, with or without paying her husband compensation, she appeared in front of the *qadi* with her husband, who indicated his agreement to the judge, who then divorced them and recorded the divorce. We do not see cases in which the *qadi* denied the wife's request for divorce or for *khul'*, even when the husband was not willing to go through with it.

Reconciliation and Remarriage

There are literally hundreds of thousands of marriage, divorce, reconciliation, and remarriage contracts recorded in *shari'a* court records in Egypt. In most remarriage contracts, the wife included conditions that took into consideration her new situation and her previous experience with the man she was remarrying. Examples include Halima bint Abdullah ibn Abuʾl-Qasim al-Maghrabi, who "returned to the custody" of her husband, ʿAbd al-ʿAziz ibn Shaʿban, who had divorced her two times. A brand new dowry of 5 gold Maghribi dinars was agreed upon and paid in advance. The remarriage took place in front of the Maliki judge (as was usual with Maghribis) (Alexandria, sijillat 957/1550, 1:144–680). Fatima bint Salim ibn Muhammad, also "returned to the custody" of her divorcé, Muhammad ibn Khidr ibn ʿAbdullah, who paid her a new dowry of 6 new gold Sultani dinars, all paid in advance. The husband also pledged a monthly clothing allowance of 5 silver nisfs and agreed to have her son from a previous marriage "live at his place, eat from his food, drink from his drink, and sleep on his bed." He also accepted the condition that if he were to take another wife or if "another woman was to prevail upon him" then Fatima would be divorced from him and would own herself (al-Hakim, sijillat 966/1559, 540:23–103).

When Latifa bint ʿAli ibn Musa agreed to remarry Yahya ibn ʿUbayd ibn ʿAli, she received, in advance, a new dowry of 4 gold dinars, as well as a committment that he would pay her 5 silver nisfs monthly clothing support. In return, she released him from a 14-gold-dinar debt to which she had been entitled from their first marriage. As condition for remarrying him, Latifa required that, if he were to take back his other divorced wife at any time, then Latifa would be automatically divorced from him three times, whereby she could never become his wife again, unless she first married and lived with another man (Misr al-Qadima, sijillat 1037/1627, 95:223–1010). Polygamy was clearly a source of problems to marriage, and the profusion of cases in which conditions related to second wives were added to remarriage contracts shows that it was both an issue of concern among wives, and at the same time, notwithstanding the complete acceptance that polygamy was legitimated by the *shariʿa,* not really acceptable in Egyptian society. Polygamy constituted one of the principle reasons for divorce as evidenced by court records.

In remarriage contracts in which conditions were added to "tie a husband's hands," we can assume that the husband was at fault in the first divorce. A large percentage of the contracts, however, do not include any conditions but do include a new dowry, whereas there are still others that do not allow for a *muqaddam,* rather than delaying the whole new dowry. Regardless, a dowry, in whatever form, had to be included as required by the *shariʿa.* Examples of conditionless marriages include that of Fatima bint Muhammad, who returned to the custody of her divorcé, ʿAbdullah ibn Ahmad al-Qabbani (weigher of goods) for a dowry of 7 new gold dinars, 2 of which were paid in advance and 5 to be paid in installments of 20 years (Dumyat, sijillat 1037/1627, 38:33–62). Another example is that of Shams bint Yusif ibn ʿAli al-Maghrabi al-Andalusiyya, who accepted to return to the custody of her divorcé, ʿAli ibn Ahmad al-Maghrabi al-Andalusi (both were of North African/Andalusian origins) for a *muʾakhkhar* of 9 new gold Sultani dinars. The husband also pledged to pay for winter and summer wardrobes of a quality equal to that of her peers (al-Salihiyyia al-Nijmiya, sijillat 964/1557, 445:13–35). Similarly, Fattuh bint ʿAbdullah agreed to remarry Muhammad ibn ʿAli for a *muʾakhkhar* of 3 1/2 new gold Sultani dinars. Fattuh also declared that she held in her trust the sum of 10 dinars owed to her husband in the form of a legitimate debt preceding the date of the remarriage. Both husband and wife agreed that neither would owe the other anything except for the delayed dowry agreed upon by their marriage. Hence, we can conclude that the advanced dowry in this case was forfeited against the 10 dinars the wife owed the husband. The husband still pledged her winter and summer wardrobes similar to that of her peers as well as her other matrimonial rights (al-Salihiyyia al-Nijmiyya, sijillat 1004/1596, 317:251–956).

Child Custody

Divorced women were usually given custody of their children, the husband being responsible to pay child support during a legitimate period determined by the *shariʿa,* after which the child was expected to go to live with his or her father. Court records, however, show that children usually remained with the mother even after that age was reached. The amount of alimony and child support was very often decided in court, and wives were known to go to court demanding that such support be increased or that the court force the husband to pay the amount of support stipulated at the time of divorce. The following examples should illustrate how that worked: the Hanafi *qadi* gave Amna bint Ibrahim custody of her son, Abu Zayd, following her divorce and estimated a nursing fee of 1/2 fidda to be paid by her divorcé, the boy's father. Because the latter refused to pay, the judge gave Amna permission to borrow against the money owed her and made the divorcé legally bound to repay it. Amna's custody of Abu Zayd was assumed to last for two years whether she remarried or remained single, lived in town, or moved elsewhere. She was expected back in court after the expiration of the two years, when her custody would be extended, as was usual in such cases (Tobon, sijillat 1008/1600, 188:57–201).

Most *madhahib* agreed that, when a husband died, the wife was entitled to become the guardian of her minor children, with powers over their interest and property. Thus, Muʾmina bint Zayn al-Din ʿAbdul-Rahman, the Shaykh of Suq al-Rubaʿiyya al-Zahari (i.e., a man of some consequence) was made guardian of her minor daughter, Salha, from her deceased husband, Shihab, the merchant "to look into her [daughter's] affairs and interests and dispose of them by selling, buying, taking and giving, receiving funds or spending, in all legitimate dispositions; and to do what guardians are entitled to do legitimately until the said minor reaches maturity, understands her religious duties, and the legitimate handling of money" (al-Qisma al-ʿArabiya, sijillat 1035/1626, 57:27–394).

Similarly, the *qadi* assigned Tajat bint Zayn ibn Karim al-Din as guardian for her two sons, Ahmad and Khatun, after the death of her husband, Muhammad ibn Muhammad ibn Muhiyy-al-Din, the merchant at Suq al-Shuhub. As guardian, she was expected to control their subsantial fortune, which they inherited from their father, including buying, selling, trading and all other kinds of dispositions until they were capable of handling their own money (same formula used as previous case) (al-Qisma al-ʿArabiyya, sijillat 1035/1625, 267:n.p.-322). In yet another case, the *qadi* assigned the woman Rukaya bint Sulayman ibn Muhammad as guardian for her minor son, Muhammed, from her husband, al-Sharafi Yahya ibn ʿAli al-Shami (i.e a Syrian), the goldsmith at Khatt al-Ghuriyya Khan. Accordingly, she became the controller of her minor son's inheritance, with the right to dispose of his share of his father's inheritance, including selling or buying property, and spending any cash income in whatever way she considered to be in his interest. In short, she acted as his legal and legitimate *wakil* until he reached maturity (al-Qisma al-ʿArabiyya, sijillat 1035/1626, 267:470–572).

We can reach a number of conclusions from the above cases reported in Egypt's various *shariʿa* court archives.

In regard to the dowry, it is important to note that the dowry for a second marriage was normally paid in full in advance, showing that it was the husband who had wronged the wife or that he wanted her back. She would not take any future guarantees, perhaps having been bitten once, and hence expected payment in advance. Furthermore, the dowry paid to the wife being remarried was quite substantial, showing that not only did there seem to be no problem for previously married wives to get remarried, and this was the case, even if the dowry seemed to be less for a previously married woman than a virgin, as social status seemed to play a more important role. Thus, a wealthy wife, previously married or not, expected a substantial dowry.

There was a general acceptance of children from previous marriages, who were normally left with their mother and did not seem to be an obstruction to her remarriage, even when she was being remarried to a man other than the father of her child. The evidence thus suggests that the idea that remarriage was difficult for women in Muslim society during the Ottoman period is in fact false.

A wife expected to be paid an allowance for her clothing. In certain cases, she was willing to forego such a pledge on the part of the husband. Whether this means that the *shari'a*'s admonition to support the wife was carried out unless otherwise stipulated is not clear, particularly because of contracts that do not mention a clothing allowance at all and no such question is raised. Most probably, it was a matter of *'urf* than of *shari'a*.

Financial dealings involved in marriage were complicated in Ottoman Egypt, and it is clear that, notwithstanding the role played by the family at the start of the marriage in determining the dowry, it is really the wife who controlled the financial relationship with the husband from then on. In second marriages, it is clear that the wife played a central role in determining the basis upon which the marriage was to take place.

As for conditions, the wife and husband had equal opportunity to lay out the conditions for their marriage or their remarriage. The conditions laid down at the time of marriage usually had to do with: (1) Where they would live: a wife's wish not to move far away from the location of her family home is an indication of the need for support from the extended family. This applied equally to adult and minor brides. (2) The treatment she expected from her husband, that he not abuse her, and if he were to do so then she would have the right to divorce him without giving up any of her financial benefits. (3) The husband's not taking another wife and if he were to do so then she would have the right to divorce him. (4) The husband's not traveling away from home for a long period of time, the period often being stipulated in the contract. Less common demands involved such matters as the wife's wish that the couple live with her family or have a member of her family live with them, that they not live with his family, that she be given the right to visit particular locations (usually her family) whenever she wished or on specific days.

The picture of family life and women's role presented by archival records is clearly a much different one than is usually assumed for women during the Ottoman period. Far from being the "slaves" of men by whom they were ruled, the picture is one of shared responsibilities in which the wife is given custody of her children and becomes the preferred guardian for her minor orphan children and their inheritance. Women had a direct hand in determining their marriage contracts and had access to divorce when the marriage did not work for them. Furthermore, mature previously married women are shown by the archival record to be far from destitute outcasts with no hope of remarriage. Rather, remarriage constitutes a large portion of the marriage entries in the *shari*ᶜ*a* court records. Not only did women marry frequently but maturity and experience played an important role in gender relations.

7

The Divorce Between Zubaida Hatun and Esseid Osman Ağa

Women in the Eighteenth-Century Sharica Court of Rumelia

Svetlana Ivanova

*I*n a Silistra town magistrate *sicil* (archival record) dating from 1206/1791/1792, I came across two *hücet*s (court decisions) concerning the divorce settlement of Zubaida Hatun and her husband, Esseid Osman Ağa (National Library "St. Cyril and Methodius," Oriental Department, R51, fol. 29-B and R51, fol. 30-A, doc. 1). These *hücet*s allow a glimpse of Muslim family life and the legal status of women as determined by *şeriat* courts in Ottoman Bulgaria.[1]

The town of Silistra was one of the large towns on the northwest border of the Ottoman Empire. Situated on the Danube River across from the principalities of Wallachia and Moldavia, it played an important role in the empire's relations with Russia, the Tartars, and the Northern Black Sea region. An old town with remnants of a Roman fortress, Silistra was once part of an ancient Orthodox diocese; under Ottoman rule, it retained its nucleus of Orthodox inhabitants, mainly Bulgarians, a few Greeks, and Wallachians. It also had a population of Armenians, as well as quite a few Muslims. As an economic, military, and transportation center, Silistra was a dynamic provincial town, a fact

1. I mean generally the Ottoman Empire's Central Balkan Provinces, which I provisionally call Rumelia.

which influenced its social life (Dimitrov, Jechev, and Tonev 1988, 8–145).

It was here in Silistra at the end of the eighteenth century that our family drama took place. Neither of the characters in this drama was born in Silistra. As the *hücet*s inform us, Osman Ağa, chief of body-guards to the late Abdi Pasha,[2] was born in the *kasaba* (small town) of Kiangeri in Anatolia but had long since settled in Silistra; according to the norms existing in the Ottoman Empire, he was therefore a perma-nent resident in town, whereas his wife, Zubaida Hatun, who evidently had moved more recently to Silistra from her home town of Hotin, was designated as a guest *(misafira)*. Nowhere were any children mentioned, which may suggest that the marriage was recent.

The divorce proceedings were initiated by Zubaida Hatun's *vekil* (proxy), Esseid Hafiz Musa Efendi, who informed the court that, while married, Zubaida Hatun and Osman Ağa "did not get along" and that, sword in hand, Osman Ağa had threatened to kill his wife and had assaulted her many times. Moreover, he had used blasphemous lan-guage to curse her "faith and religion." The *wekil* then presented the court with a *fetva* (legal decision) from the *müfti* (authorized religious person in town) indicating that blasphemous cursing constituted an abuse that required a renewal of faith and marriage among Muslims *(tecdid iman ve tecdid nikah):* "If Zaid cursed profusely the faith and religion of his wife Hind, then it is necessary to renew the marriage and faith. If it becomes clear that Hind does not agree to this, they should be divorced."

According to the *vekil*, Zubaida Hatun, who was not present in court, was unwilling to renew her marriage and wanted to be divorced *(talak)* from Osman. But Esseid Osman Ağa, who was present in court, denied the curses; and so the court asked the *vekil* to provide legally acceptable, corroborating evidence. Such evidence was given by the "virtuous" Muslim neighbors of Osman and Zubaida who were present in court: "each [of whom] gave *şeriat* a testimony that indeed Osman Ağa cursed profusely the religion and faith of his wife." The court then sent two official court witnesses *(umena-i şerġ)* to Zubaida. She recon-firmed her decision: "I do not agree to marriage renewal." This was recorded on the spot and was communicated to the court. The conclud-ing formula is a short one, as is the case in all *hücet*s. Based on the *fetva*, the court ruled that Zubaida Hatun was divorced from Usman. Upon the

---

2. This is most probably a reference to Elhaj Abdi Pasha, *vali* of Silistra, who died in A.D. 1204 (Dimitrov 1981, 392; Sureyya, 1893–94, 411–12).

parties' request, a record was made of the events that took place. The case witnesses—Muslims, mostly Janissaries—were also registered.

A few days later, on Rajab 15, 1205/October 3, 1792, another case was recorded in the *sicil* involving the same characters. This time, the initiator was Osman Ağa. Present in court were Zubaida's father, Çebeci Başi[3] Mustafa Ağa, and Zubaida's *vekil*. Osman first handed to the *vekil* the 250 kuruş *mehr-i myeccel* (delayed dowry to be paid at the termination of marriage or death of husband) and 60 gold coins minted in Istanbul covering the *mehr-i muaccel* (advance portion of dowry), plus 10 gold coins minted in Egypt. After which, Osman presented the following gifts fixed by the court: 4 packs of broadcoth to his father-in-law Mustafa Ağa; 2 rolls of flower-printed calico from Halab to his mother-in-law and her mother, both of whom "were absent from the courtroom"; and finally, a pair of silver-plated pistols to Zubaida's brother. This completed, Osman declared that he released them from further responsibilities with respect to the gifts and his marital rights. In return, Mustafa Ağa gave Esseid Osman a silver watch as a present; and, on behalf of Zubaida Hatun, her *vekil* presented him with a watch pouch, two tobacco pouches, lined underwear, and other articles, wrapped up in two bundles. After the exchange of the "true *şeriat* gifts," Mustafa Ağa and the *vekil* "released Osman Ağa from any obligations." The record ends with the standard formula: "after *şeriat* confirmation, the fact has been recorded."

The dry and formalized language of the record of these proceedings limits one's ability to gain deeper insight into the family drama. Comparing these documents with those of similar cases, however, allows a more accurate and reliable understanding of official practices, particularly as they pertain to the legal status of women. The following three sections of this essay dealing with marriage, divorce, and separation, provide a textual analysis of the documents pertaining to Zubaida and Osman and other *sicil* records pertaining to gender and legal practices dating from the eighteenth century.[4] One of the important questions raised involves how far Muslim marriages in Rumelia conformed to the

3. Chief of the corps of *çebeçi;* i.e., an Ottoman military corps that is engaged in the fabrication and maintenance of weapons and ammunition for the army.
4. Oriental Department, Collection of Sicils: Vidin, S38/1702–1713; S8/1720–1921; S40 1737–1739; S49/1779–1782. Rousse, R5/1709–1721; R51/1715; R52/1734–1735; R6/1736–1737; R39/1790–1791. Silistra, R50/1792–1792. Sofia, S23/1791–1794. Hadjioglu Pazardjik (now Dobrich), S42/1798–1803. Those cited are part of 107 *şicils*, dating from the eighteenth century and preserved in the archives. I have also taken into consideration *şicils* of the sixteenth and seventeenth centuries from the same collection.

şeriat and how well they illustrate historical conditions unique to the area and the social history of common people.

Marriage

Generally speaking, Muslim marriages are usually performed by the local *imam* (religious personnel) or *kadi* (Turkish: judge) and are expected to follow *şeriat* requirements. The marriage ceremony, however, follows the customs of the particular Muslim country. There are abundant implications that, since the sixteenth century, an effort has been made to model Muslim marriage contracts in central Rumelia in accordance with the *şeriat*. This trend increased during the seventeenth and eighteenth centuries, at the same time that the relative number of Muslim marriage registrations also increased. Still, even in the eighteenth century, most recorded marriage contracts were simple marriage registrations rather than the contractual documents typical of *şeriat* marriages. The entries were concise and not always dated and included little beyond the name of husband and wife, their proxies, the language of "proposal and acceptance," the witnesses' names, and the *mehr* (bride price, dowry) amount (S8, pp. 92–93, S19, pp. 1 and 2; title page, doc. 3; S38, p. 91, doc. 1). Similarly, in the two documents related to Zubaida Hatun and Osman Ağaba no mention is made of the original contract legalizing the marriage between them, except for the "contracted" *mehr*. The *mehr*, required by the *şeriat*, seemed to be the only contractual obligation that consistently appeared in the registrations. A typical marriage contract entry from a Rousse town *sicil*, written in Arabic and dated 1715 reads: "in the name of Allah and in compliance with the *şeriat*, the Rousse town *kadı* Abdullah, son of Alhaj Ibrahim, performed a marriage between Abdalhata and Hava, at a *mehr* of 100,000 akçes, in the presence of two witnesses" (R51, fol. 34-A; doc. 1).[5] The *mehr* was clearly central to Muslim marriages in Rumelia.

Whereas before the eighteenth century the dowry was usually mentioned as a lump sum, documents dating from later in the century evidence the division of the *mehr* into *muaccel* and *müeccel*. The records also show that the bride did indeed receive the *muaccel* at the time of her marriage, and except for cases of *khul*, they remained in actual possession of their *mehr* because it regularly appeared in inheritance records of deceased married women. From the latter part of the

---

5. I wish to express my thankful acknowledgment to A. Stoylova for her assistance in the translation of the document. See a similar document in Akif 1984.

eighteenth century, marriages also included the exchange of gifts. These gifts usually consisted of clothing, bedlinen, and covers. When Aishe divorced Elhacc Omar by *khul,* besides her *müeccel* of 70 kuruş she relinquished 1 mattress, 1 quilt, 2 pillows, 5 copper dishes, 1 basin, 1 ablution pitcher, and 1 chest of *muaccel* (R52, fol. 2-B, doc. 2). Similarly, Kurduman Hatun from a village near Rousse obtained a *khul* divorce from the courts against a *müeccel* of 10 kuruş and a *muaccel* of 4 kuruş, 4 kilos of wheat, and 2 black calves (R51, fol. 35A, doc. 1); and Emrekelsun from Rousse obtained *khul* against 24 kuruş *müeccel,* 1 black calf and 1 *dünüm* of vineyards (R51, fol. 34-B, doc. 7). These *khul* divorce cases are in contrast to that of Zubaida Hatun's, whose divorce settlement included both portions of her *mehr,* which were handed over by Osman to her proxy. These examples illustrate the great diversity in the handling of divorce and contractual settlements, which depended to a great extent on previous agreements and conditions leading to the separation. Marriage conditions were not always recorded, nor was the recording of marriage explicitly stated as a *şeriat* requirement. Here we can mention a customary allowance due any wife by her husband, which numerous documents refer to as having been paid off even though such an allowance was not fixed in the registration of marriage (Mergon, 99–100).

Even though the *şeriat* allowed for polygamy, Muslims in Rumelia tended to remain monogamous in the overwhelming majority of the cases (S8, p. 49, doc. 1; R50, fol. 62-A, doc. 2; R53, fol. 3A, doc 5; R5, fol. 3-A, doc. 2). But it was quite common for both Muslim men and women to marry many times, as shown by the requirement that in the new marriage contracts of previously married women it had to be explicitly stated that they were no longer married (S8, p. 95, doc. 5). This marriage contract was made in the form of a *hücet* indicating the bride's right to remarry, as well as the names of witnesses to the dissolution of her first marriage (S8, p. 47, docs. 1 and 3). Divorce was the most common reason for a woman's having the right to remarry, but there seemed to have been other reasons that were perhaps particular to the situation of Muslims in Rumelia. For example, two witnesses testified that Emine's husband had adopted Christianity (a *şeriat* reason for divorce) and she wanted to marry another man (S8, p. 47, doc. 1). Another divorce entry contained testimony that the departure of a husband was a preset condition for divorce (S8, p. 41, doc. 5; S8, p. 47, doc. 2). From a formal point of view, it was the wife on whose initiative the court session was held; her words were stated in the record in the first person singular: "I want to marry another man."

All marriages had to be concluded in court in accordance to Ottoman regulations. A 1700 *firman* (executive law) reprimanding Vedin's *kadı* for certain actions, included among them his habit of traveling from village to village without any claim applications, putting up in the houses of the *reaya* (citizens), carrying out patrimonial partition by giving excessively high property valuations, and performing conclusions of marriage in order to collect fees (S14, p. 8, doc. 1). Given the contractual nature of Muslim marriages, concluding a marriage in court was probably preferable to women who had little other means available to them to ensure their rights in case of future conflicts with their husbands. For example, to claim her 800 akçes *mehr*, the widow Hava, daughter of Ahmed Beşe, produced witnesses who had been present in court at the time her marriage was concluded and registered (S8, p. 69, doc 2).

But conditions in Rumelia often necessitated a compromise between the official requirement that marriage be performed by the *kadıs* in court and the impossibility of having this requirement implemented in practice. An eighteenth-century document illustrates this compromise. The document is addressed to the *imam* of the *mahalle* (town quarter) where the bride lived, authorizing him to bind in marriage "the virtuous maiden wishing to be married" and the respective bridegroom before witnesses and at an agreed *mehr* "if there were no *şeriat* impediments" (R51, fol. 1-A, doc. 3).[6]

This example illustrates the *mahalle imam*'s important official role. Various sources confirm that the conclusion of marriage in the presence of *mahalle* imams was a widespread practice (S14, doc. 2). It was he who made sure that a religious ceremony did take place, that *şeriat* requirements were met, and that a valid and legally binding marriage was contracted. Furthermore, because he lived among the people, the imam usually had first-hand knowledge of anyone's marital status, which constituted crucial information in establishing a previously married woman's "freedom to remarry"; that is, she was divorced and was past the three-month waiting period (*'idda*). Being competent in religious matters and involved in the administration of the population, the imam was regarded as the person most capable of giving a true estimate to specific situations. But there were clear limits to his functions. An eloquent case from 1704 is registered in a Vidin *sicil*. Mariam Hatun declared that her husband, Ahmed, who lived in Istanbul, had divorced her two years earlier. Now she wanted to marry another man, but her

6. For bans and impediments to the conclusion of Muslim marriages, see J. Anderson 1950, 2, 359.

mahalle Imam Bayram Efendi, whom Mariam Hatun had summoned in court, prevented her marriage by saying that there were şeriat impediments. After hearing the testimony of two witnesses to the divorce, the court ruled that a divorce was indeed in effect, and the *kadı* authorized the conclusions and registration of Mariam Hatun's new marriage (S14, fol. 17-B, doc. 1).

Divorce

The divorce between Zubaida Hatun and Esseid Osman was of the *tefrik* type, that is, divorce through court intervention, which was obligatory when the wife initiated the divorce (Schacht 1970, 161–65). To receive a divorce judgment from court, she had to prove some justification for divorce. Unfortunately, *sicil* documents do not show whether şeriat sanctioned grounds entitling Muslim women to get divorced were used, which include impotence, insanity, incurable disease or, as accepted in certain *madhahib,* the husband's failure to support his wife (el-Nahal 1979, 47). The situations described in the *sicil*s could have been considered equal to şeriat transgression providing grounds for divorce, but there is no clear indication of the fact. A much greater variety of situations are revealed by *fetva*s including a few *illet* (sickness, defects) and *zihar* cases (Fyzee 1974, 162–63). The most usual form of separation was that of *khul,* in which general complaints included: "we did not have a good life together," "there was no understanding between us" or "there were quarrels and dissention between us." A less frequently used addition to this formula was the statement that the husband had physically maltreated his wife. These arguments were sufficient for *khul,* but not for a more favorable divorce from a wife's point of view. *Sicil*s dating from the seventeenth and eighteenth century show the predominance of *khul* divorces, mostly because it was obligatory that they be handled in court. In *khul,* it was usual for a wife to give up any material compensation due her from her husband, including the delayed dowry, and the usual *nafaka* (allowance, support) for herself and her children. Thus, when Hava Hatun from Vidin divorced her husband in 1783 by *khul,* she had to abandon both the *nafaka* and the 1,000 akçes remaining from the 4,000 akçes dowry that was her contracted right owed her, which her husband had committed to pay at the time of marriage. Relinquishing the debt, however, was a condition set by her husband, the tanner Hussein Beşe, to agree to a divorce that was not of his choosing (S40, fol. 46-B, doc. 1). Another Hava from Rousse originally received only 8 *kuruş* from the total of 18 *kuruş* of her dowry at the time of her marriage. To be divorced by *khul,* she abandoned the remaining 10 *kuruş* that had been due her as part of her advance dowry (R6, fol. 34-A, doc. 1). Sometimes, a mother undertook to provide for her children herself, liberating the man she was divorcing from the responsibility. In such cases, the divorce *hücet* included a separate paragraph indicating who the child[ren]'s father was, but that their mother would undertake all their expenses during the usual *hadana* (custody) period of nine years for girls and seven for boys (R6, fol. 28-B, doc. 1: allowance for a boy; R27, fol. 34-A, doc. 3: allowance for a girl). The period for providing child support to an expectant mother was fixed until the age of nine, that is, as for a girl (Dimitrov 1893–94 134 and 136).

For a Muslim woman to obtain *talâk* divorce (allowing her to retain her full financial rights) was far more favorable for her financially. The procedure, however, was more complicated and demanded that a woman provide a substantial reason, such as physical or mental abuse, which could include blasphemy as in Zubaida's *talâk* from Osman, in which physical maltreatment of a wife was accompanied by witnessed blasphemy, thereby providing stronger grounds for *tefrik.*

The existence of grounds for divorce had to be proven by witnesses, (and often their validity was justified by *fetva*), whereas the arguments for *khul* divorce were not at all subject to such requirements of proof. An example of a case of divorce based on blasphemy is registered in the Sofia *sicil* for 1728. In this case, the *kadı* quoted a *fetva* that had been obtained in advance by the petitioning party from a *müfti.*[7] Zaynab's father, Mustafa Ağaba, in his capacity as proxy of his daughter, stated in court in the presence of the husband, Ibrahim Beşe: "The said Ibrahim has cursed the faith and religion of my daughter, therefore I request that she should be divorced." Following the respondent's denial, the court asked for proof of this statement. The statement was confirmed by two Muslim witnesses.

> Based on that testimony and on the Sheriat *fetva* presented by the said proxy and considered by the court, according to which *fetva,* cursing the faith and religion of a faithful Muslim is a reason for divorce, the court issues a decision for the divorce of the said authorizer, as well as a strict order for the said Ibrahim Beşe to pay off and deliver to the said authorizer the amount of ten thousand akçes *mehr* (S309, p. 90, doc. 3).

7. For *fetva*s regarding the necessity of faith and marriage renewal after blasphemy, see *Ottoman Sources on the Islamization Processes in the Balkans* 16–19:293–97 c. (Sofia: 1990).

It is remarkable how great an emphasis is placed by Islam on spoken statements and verbal formulae. This lends credibility to the hypothesis that wives could have taken advantage of a momentary rudeness, lack of self-control, or juridical incompetence of their husbands in order to obtain a divorce with favorable material compensation (Imber 1991).

"Conditional" *talak* or *talak-i bain* (irrevocable divorce) divorce was among legal practices in seventeenth-and eighteenth-century Rumelia. It was usual in such cases for a wife to sue for divorce based on certain conditions included in the marriage contract or fixed by a husband before undertaking a trip, indicating that, if he failed to return within a certain period, his wife was to be considered divorced: *"bain boş olsun; azadik olsun."* (R51, fol. 20-B, doc. 1; R6, fol. 2-A, doc. 2; S8, p. 41, doc. 5). In 1775, the husband of Fatima from Vidin fixed a period of three months, and the husband of Aishe from Rousse, six months. Sometimes, the divorce registration took place at the insistence of the wife's father, who had undertaken her financial support while her husband was away (R51, fol. 20-B, doc. 1). Obviously, the wife's family was not always prepared or able to support her, showing that marriage was an important institution for the material support of women.

Sometimes, complications occurred in regard to these "conditional" divorces. For example, a "conditionally" divorced wife could wish to remarry. To prove her first marriage was dissolved, witnesses were necessary. In a 1773 case from Rousse, Bosnak Kücük Ahmed Beşe complained to the court that his wife, Fatma, had married another man while he was away on business. The wife, however, insisted that her husband had divorced her before his departure by means of a *talak-i bain* (R6, p. 26, doc. 2). When she wished to remarry, her proxy proved, through the help of witnesses, that, upon his departure three months earlier, Kücük Ahmed had said: "If I should not come back within one year, let her be free" (S8, p. 47, doc. 3). The court accepted the testimony of the witnesses and allowed the new marriage. This did not mean, however, that a husband's departure was in itself a valid reason for divorce. There were cases when a wife demanded that she receive financial support from the property of a husband who was traveling, but there was no mention of divorce. But generally speaking, a husband's departure was usually accompanied by some statement regarding divorce, and often his departure was followed by a divorce notification to the wife. A typical case from the Vidin *sicil* is that of Ali Odabaşi, Ariza Hatun's husband, who was missing from home for eight months before sending his wife a letter of divorce *(itlak mektubu)*. Because the letter was undated, the *sicil* entry was fixed as the beginning of the ʿida period (S38, fol. 1-A, doc. 5).

Registering *talak* divorces did not seem to be a usual part of legal procedures. Rather, we learn of them indirectly from Ottoman documents treating the consequences of such divorces like fixing an allowance for the wife or children or settling the delayed dowry. For example, we learn of Mustafa's divorcing Rukie from legal proceedings that she initiated to force him to pay her 67 kuruş he owed from her advanced and delayed *mehr*. In answer, Mahmud produced two witnesses who testified that he had already paid Rukie the 67 kuruş (1195/1781, S49, fol. 9-B, doc. 1). In another interesting case from 1805, even though Nefissa (from the village of Taban, Rousse district) was divorced by her husband, she renounced any financial rights due her from him (R51, fol. 1-B, doc. 5).

In less frequent cases, we learn about an actually enforced *talak* from the legal proceedings instituted by husbands who, faced with their former wives' impending marriage, wished to get back their wives by denying the divorce that had already taken place (as in a previously mentioned case) or by openly repenting it (R1, fol. 2-A, doc. 1; R6, p. 26, doc. 2). A 1669 Vidin *sicil* contains a copy of a *firman*, issued in Edirne and addressed to the *kadi* of Vidin, informing him that a petition was filed with the palace by Saime, resident of Lom Palanka, advising the authorities that her husband, Shaban, had left her. After waiting the period legally required by the *şeriat*, she had taken another husband, the janissary Mahmud. Subsequently, however, her husband had repented the divorce, and, claiming that he had left her against his will, insisted that she should come back to him and procured a *fetva* from the *seyhülislam* backing him up. In her petition to the palace in the capital, Saime asked that her previous husband stop harassing her. In answer to her petition, the authorities issued the *firman* to the *kadi,* ordering him to settle the dispute in accordance with the *şeriat* and to investigate the matter. If the petitioner's allegations proved to be correct, then he was to forbid Shaban from harassing her (S13, fol. 28-B, doc. 2.).

As mentioned earlier, financial consequences constituted the most important aspect of divorce. *Khul* meant that a wife lost some or all her financial rights; in *talak,* however, the wife was often compensated over and above her delayed dowry and alimony, particularly when the divorce was against her wishes and for no fault of hers. In Rumelia, unlike the norm among Muslims, there did not seem to be a special support allowance paid to the wife during the *'ida* period, but it was usual to pay alimony to the wife and children.

Another tradition peculiar to Rumelia, has to do with the exchange of gifts at the time of divorce. It is possible that this tradition concealed the waiving of claims for the return of marriage gifts that may have been recently presented. Narrative literature describes gifts exchanged at the time of marriage within the class of middle townsmen: the bride was presented with a silver jewelry box, a hand mirror, and other toilet articles. On her part, she gave as presents a jeweler-made snuff box and a cashmere shawl. The mother-in-law presented the bride with several yards of red silk fabric and a basket of candies, which were strewn on the floor and on which the bride walked when she kissed the hand of her mother-in-law. The parents of the bridegroom gave money, and those of the bride gave wraps and blankets, utensils, carpets, and a brazier (Garnett 1982, 269). It is therefore possible that the exchange of gifts upon the divorce of Zubaida and Usman may have been a kind of material compensation for the marriage gifts.

Desertion

Divorce was not the only form of legal settlement of marriage problems. As already mentioned, the *sicil*s provide evidence of a number of cases in which, without any formal divorce, a husband deserted his wife or left her without an allowance. Soon after that, the deserted wife directed her claim to the *kadi*, asking for the right to obtain an allowance at her husband's expense, either from property he was known to own or through borrowing. Thus, Emhani Hatun, daughter of Ali from Rousse, declared in court that five days earlier her husband, Hussein, had gone to the village of Chernovi. An allowance of 2 para per day was allocated to her as support money, and a document certifying this was issued to her (R6, fol. 33-B, doc. 3; see also: R51, fol. 14-A, doc. 1; R6, fol. 39-A, doc. 1). Similarly, in her efforts to obtain her due allowance, Aishe Hatun from Vidin, who had been deserted by her husband, the janissary Ahmed, sent an *arzuhal* to the sultan's court. In reply, a *firman* was sent back to the Vidin *kadi*, instructing him that the problem was to be treated in a manner consistent with the *şeriat* which, as interpreted in this case, meant bringing the husband to court and, provided that fifteen years had not yet elapsed, action was to be taken in accordance with law and custom (S38, fol. 44-B, doc. 3; S38, fol. 44-A, doc. 2).

Evidently, in all these cases, wives availed themselves of their *şeriat* right to be supported by their husbands. Support money was not fixed as a lump sum, but as a daily allowance, without specifying the length of time over which it would be payable. It was usually pointed out that an appropriate amount/rate was to be allocated, which possibly reflected the *şeriat* rule that the commitments of a Muslim husband to his family were as large as his financial status could afford.

In other cases, deserted wives also sought allowance for their children. Because it was understood that such an allowance was a father's religious obligation, the court fixed an appropriate allowance and gave an *izin* (permission) to the mother, authorizing her to take loans in the father's name. The period of time over which this allowance was payable by the father was not specified, although such a period was specified for mothers who undertook to provide for their children in case of *khul* divorce (R51, fol. 1-B, doc. 5).

It is particularly important to note the *şeriat* court's mediation in divorce proceedings. The fact that family and marriage problems were settled through the mediation of the *kadı,* who embodied the basic administrative and legal institution in the Ottoman Empire, is an extremely important indication for the legal status of women in society.

Legal Proceedings

In connection with the formalization of the marriage institution in the Ottoman Empire and the role played by the official court authorities in regulating family and marriage relations, it is worthwhile noting the legal procedures themselves to emphasize their direct bearing on the legal system and the position of women in society.

In reference to Zubaida Hatun and Usman's marriage, she was not present in court but had instituted and undertook all legal proceedings through a *vekil.* Following normal legal procedures as practiced in Ottoman courts, the act of nominating her proxy was witnessed by two persons. The proxy was usually a close relative,[8] but women often appointed nonfamily members as their *vekil*s. Men were also often represented by their *vekil*s.

As the divorce of Zubaida and Usman shows, *fetva*s provided the important juridical grounds for determining a legal case. A *fetva* did not have binding force in issuing judgments, but it marked the course of the court hearings. The witnessed evidence of creditable corroborating witnesses was usually required in order to produce legal consequences compatible with *fetva*s. In Ottoman courts, witness testimony represented the strongest substantiating argument and, during the period under consideration, was not superseded by any official or legal documents.

---

8. Father for *khul* divorce R52, fol. 2-B, doc. 2; son for R1, fol. 4-A, doc. 6; brother for *khul* divorce R51, fol. 33-A, doc. 1; mother for receiving *mehr* from the father of a deceased husband R51, fol. 10-B, doc. 2; husband in dispute with his mother-in-law over real estate property R51, fol. 17-A, doc. 3; aunt/sister of the wife's mother about *khul* S40, fol. 20-B, doc. 1.

Witnesses were usually defined in the *hücets* as knowledgeable and trustworthy Muslims, or it was pointed out that a given act had taken place in their presence. Thus, it was the "knowledgeable" neighbors, residents of Kaik Mahalle in Rousse, who gave witness evidence to Ibrahim, by testifying in 1731 that his former wife, Hava, had requested *khul* against her waiver of all financial rights for herself and her son. Hence, the court found against her (R6, fol. 34-A, doc. 2). The witnesses in Zubaida's case were three of her neighbors, two of whom were women. From a formal juridical point of view, there was nothing to prevent a woman from being summoned in court as a witness; when they did, however, the witness of two women was considered equal to that of one man, and the testimony of women alone was not considered sufficient, thus one of the witnesses had to be a man (el-Nahal 1979, 49). The documents show, however, that women appeared rarely in court as witnesses, even though it was common for them to appear as litigants. In most cases for which women gave testimony, they were considered to be well-informed. When investigating a missing person case, for example, fellow villagers/*mahalle* neighbors and close relatives were usually interrogated, among whom were women, who could, in certain cases, be the sole witnesses. In a seventeenth-century case from Rousse, one of the two wives of the late Danubian *kapudan* Ali Pasha wanted to obtain her son's share of the inheritance. The child had died upon birth, but the petitioner tried to prove that he had been born alive two and a half months after his father's death. For this purpose she summoned in court two Muslim women who had been present during the childbirth and therefore could testify that the child had been born alive, had been named Hussein, and had moved his limbs (R2, fol. 4-B, doc. 1).

Finally, it can be stated that a unified procedure, enabling women to obtain a divorce, was observed in the central parts of Rumelia. The *sicil* shows that the predominant number of registered divorces were initiated by the wife, who had to submit reasonable evidence in support of the divorce request, particularly if she expected material compensation from her husband. At the same time, the documents show that former husbands sought every possible way to reduce the material compensation they had to pay their former wives. In a "compromise" case registered in a Rousse town *sicil* of 1737, Ali Beşe divorced his wife but refused to pay her the 40 groş *mehr* remaining from her advance dowry, and she was compelled to institute legal proceedings. Through conciliation, she agreed to an amount of 20 kuruş (R6, fol. 41-A, doc. 1). This example indicates the limitations of a legal system that found difficulty in enforcing court decisions, particularly in places where there was great mobility among the population.

Furthermore, women were often forced to redeem their freedom from undesired family ties. Indicative of this fact are the multitude of cases in which women undertook to bring up their children on their own. In 1737, Hama obtained *khul* by abandoning 1,000 kuruş *mehr* and an allowance (R51, fol. 33-A, doc. 1). In 1716, Rukie, daughter of Osman from Vidin, accepted *khul* against her waiver of 1,000 akçes *mehr* and of support money for the child she was expecting until the child's age of nine (S40, fol. 38-A, doc. 1). Aishe, daughter of Hussein from Rousse, obtained *khul* by abandoning 28 kuruş *mehr* plus her allowance and undertaking to support her two daughters (R6, fol. 25-B, doc. 1).

This courage, which was evidently based on well-estimated future opportunities, becomes even more significant against the background of the other documented cases, in which the husband was obliged to provide support for his children. In 1736, the Rousse court awarded the minor Ali 4 akçes per day support, to be paid by his father to his mother (who sued) (R6, fol. 40-A, doc. 2; R6, fol. 41-A, doc. 2). In 1704, Kadrie from Vidin was divorced by her husband, Elhaj Ali, by *talak*. She requested and received a court award of 2 akçes per day, allocated to the underage Mustafa who was in her custody.[9]

The source material offered here confirms the established fact that the marital status of Muslim men was far stronger than that of Muslim women. For one thing, Muslim men could solve most marriage problems without institutional intervention. Not so the situation for women. Yet, the very fact that women were given some official opportunities was quite an advantage, although it is not clear how far women could and did actually avail themselves of these opportunities. It is difficult for a contemporary person to interpret source material that does not offer the wealth of details found in travelers' accounts and narrative tales. Still *kadi sicil*s, however heavily formalized are the juridical practices recorded in them, provide a unique opportunity for exploring gender relations and the traditional customary practice of the common people in Ottoman society.

---

9. S38, fol. 6-A, doc. 1. See also R4, fol. 121-B, doc. 6: allowance for a child born after divorce; R4, fol. 8-B, doc. 1: Christian wife divorced of her Muslim husband, with receipt of *mehr*.

8

Muslim Women in Court According to the
Sijill of Late Ottoman Jaffa and Haifa

Some Methodological Notes

Iris Agmon

*U*ntil recently, sociohistorical research on women and the family in Muslim society had to rely primarily on two sources, Islamic legal literature and the impressions of observers—mostly foreigners. Each of these has its inherent shortcomings. The first offers the historian no opportunity to trace social changes in different places and periods, and because it lacks the aspect of customary law, even as a legal source the picture it reveals remains incomplete. The second source suffers from the burden of the observer's point of view: his or her preconceptions, fantasies, and prejudices; the always limited ability to enter the sphere of private and family life; and the sporadic nature of such observations.

In more recent years, historians have increasingly turned to a third source for historical reconstruction: the *sijill,* that is, the records of the *shariᶜa* courts, which in different places of the Ottoman Empire have been preserved either fully or partially, and which include documentation of trials and other legal procedures that took place in those courts. In combination with other local sources (*fatwas,* Ottoman archival demographic sources: population registrations, provincial yearbooks, and others), the *sijill* enables the historian to draw a more accurate and

This is a revised version of a paper originally submitted to the 6th International Conference of the Social and Economic History of the Ottoman Empire and Turkey, Aix-en-Provence, July 1992.

detailed picture of the social history of Muslim women. While the resulting picture sometimes confirms existing knowledge, in several cases it has challenged a number of commonly accepted concepts and has helped to highlight the development over time of a variety of social patterns.

In the late Ottoman period, Jaffa and Haifa were going through a rapid process of urban and demographic development and soon became the most important port cities of Palestine, attracting many immigrants from all over the empire, as well as foreigners, who in turn contributed to the dynamic and cosmopolitan character of these cities.

This is the background of the two court cases taken from the *sijill* that form the subject of this paper.[1] The purpose of this essay is twofold: to illustrate some of the methodological problems that come up when using the *sijill* as a historical source and to present some of the issues that are typical of the appearance of women in the *shariʿa* court. The approach, admittedly, is somewhat exceptional. Most often studies based on *sijill* analysis deal with quantification, while a few fully detailed cases are used as illustrations for the phenomena being discussed. The method used here is rather the reverse. The story of the two legal cases, as fully told, stands at the center of the discussion and approximate quantitative aspects are used only to emphasize certain points. The aim is to derive as much information as possible from the story, as it was told in court, by working out its specific circumstances and principal characteristics. It is my contention that the *sijill* as a data source for statistical calculations contains certain limitations, that the *sijill* story in isolation has some advantages that thus far have been overlooked.

The Court Cases

In A. H. Muharram 1332/December 1913, on almost the exact same day, two couples appeared in the *shariʿa* courts, one in Jaffa and the other in Haifa, each presenting their dispute to the judge.

---

1. *Sijill* records of Jaffa and Haifa are incomplete. The Jaffa *sijill* covers most of the period from the early nineteenth century onward and for Haifa they do so intermittently from 1870 onward. The discussion here is based on *sijill* records for the years 1900–1914. It was written during the time I was working on my Ph.D. dissertation, and it is based on its preliminary findings. The dissertation, supervised by Professor Amnon Cohen, to whom I am deeply indebted, has been completed recently. The issues dealt with in this article, as well as those that are only pointed out but need further clarification, are discussed in detail in the dissertation: Iris Agmon, "Women and Society: Muslim Women, the *Sharʾi* Court, and the Society of Jaffa and Haifa under Late Ottoman Rule (1900–

In Jaffa, Jamila bint ʿAli ibn Ahmad Abu Basha sued her husband, al-Sayyid Ibn ʿId Abu Basha, claiming he still owed 17 of her 20 lira faransawi dowry *(mahr),*[2] the "immediate dowry" *(mahr muʿajjal)* he had committed himself to when he married her six years earlier. He also owed her 10 lira faransawi, the value of furniture and other items of property that he had in his possession but that actually belonged to her.[3] When he refused to pay this debt seven months previously, she left the house, and now requested that the court order him to pay this sum, plus alimony and child support *(nafaqa)* for their two-year-old son, Ahmad.

Her husband, al-Sayyid, had a different version of the events. He claimed that he and his wife, Jamila, had divorced seven months earlier, at her request. In return, she had given up all her financial rights, including alimony and child support, the child being indeed al-Sayyid's son, "conceived in his bed," but three years old and not two. Furthermore, the agreement had been fully documented in writing in front of witnesses. The divorce was the result of a dispute that had arisen after he had come back from a trip to Tiberias. During his absence, he had left the store under his wife's supervision; when he returned, he found that various articles were missing, and he believed his wife had something to do with their disappearance.

Four witnesses for the husband were summoned who all testified that they had witnessed the divorce agreement. They identified Jamila and verified her husband's version as to the content of the agreement. Thereupon, the document itself was presented. The judge summoned two additional witnesses concerning the child's age, and these witnesses also confirmed the husband's version. The judge then asked Jamila if she was menstruating regularly (to make sure she had not meanwhile become pregnant and that the divorce agreement was being adhered to).

1914)," Ph.D. diss., Hebrew Univ., 1994. See also a discussion of the methodology of the *sijill* as a source for women's history in an article that was published recently: Dror Zeʾevi, "Women in 17th Century Jerusalem: Western and Indigenous Perspectives," *IJMES* 27 (1995): 157–73.

    2. Lira faransawi, i.e. golden Napoleon (= 20 Fr.), the value of which in Haifa and Jaffa at that time was approximately 109 qurush (less than 1 English pound and less than 1 Ottoman pound, which was 124 qurush). The other financial values in these are either in qurush or in bishlik. The last one means literally "5 qurush," but owing to the gradual devaluation of Ottoman coins, its value at the time of these trials was 3–3.5 qurush.

    3. She probably refers to the *jihaz*—furniture and household items that the husband was obliged to supply his wife upon their marriage. According to *shariʿa* law, these items were meant to be used in the family household, but in case of separation of the couple, go to the wife (J. N. D. Anderson 1970, 366–67).

After all this testimony was given, the judge decided to ask the opinion of the *mufti* concerning the validity of the divorce agreement. The *mufti* concluded that the agreement contained a flaw in that it should have stated the amount of alimony and child support Jamila was relinquishing. Thereupon, Jamila hurried to claim three bishlik per day child support (this time noting that Ahmad was two-and-a-half years old), plus an additional bishlik per day for child care *(hadana)*. Her husband claimed he was unable to pay such a large sum, but Jamila reported that her husband owned a house that he was renting out in the Manshiyya quarter (in the northern end of Jaffa).

At this point, the husband objected that his wife should not receive payment because she was irresponsible as far as caring for the child was concerned, as had been shown by the incident that brought on the divorce. The judge rejected this argument because it was brought up too late. He summoned two witnesses to testify about the husband's financial status; they testified that he was able to pay one bishlik per day, and this was the judge's verdict (Jaffa, A.H. 1331–1332/1913–1914, vol. 152, case 50, 105–8, 112–14, 119–20).

In Haifa, Ibrahim ibn Khalil al-Skandrani presented a request to the *shariᶜa* judge to cancel a previous decision of the court, which had ordered him to increase the daily alimony paid to his wife, Fatima bint Shaykh Khalil Shaqwara, and child support to their twin sons, Hasan and Husayn, from one to one-and-a-half bishlik per day (half a bishlik for each of the three). Ibrahim claimed that the witnesses who had testified earlier that he was able to pay this larger sum had been unaware of his present financial status because they had moved away from Acre, where he was living and served as *muᵓadhdhin* (who calls for prayer), and suggested verifying his story with his colleagues. He also claimed to be supporting a family of twelve and asked permission to bring other witnesses. Furthermore, Ibrahim claimed that the twins were now over eight years old and no longer entitled to child support. He mentioned that they had been born in the rumiyya year 1321, and that if necessary, he could prove this.[4]

Fatima replied that the twins were barely six years old, having been born just as al-Qudsi was appointed judge in Haifa. She added that the latter was the same judge who originally had ordered Ibrahim to pay her alimony and child support. The current judge asked to see the chil-

---

4. That is, *maliyya*, the calendar of the Ottoman administration, which lags two years behind the Muslim calendar *(hijriyya)*. The *mali* year 1321 is almost parallel to 1905.

dren, and decided that they were not yet seven. He ordered Fatima to bring the witnesses who had testified about her husband's financial status. These witnesses, Haifa residents originally from Acre, confirmed that Ibrahim was able to pay the larger amount because he had other income stemming from Qur᾽an reading, trade, and guard work. After checking the witnesses' credibility, the judge ordered Ibrahim to pay the amount determined, thus ignoring Ibrahim's repeated claims that the witnesses could not know of his present financial status.

When his claims were rejected, Ibrahim divorced his wife on the spot by making the three *talaq* (divorce) calls. He requested that Fatima's share of the alimony be paid only until the end of the *ʿidda* period (three months waiting period after divorce during which the wife cannot remarry), and that, when the twins turned seven, they be put in his custody. Fatima reacted by suing for payment of the advanced *(muʿajjal)* dowry of 1,500 qurush and of the postponed *(muᵓajjal)* dowry of 500 qurush. Owing to lack of time, the judge postponed the continuation of the proceedings. At the next session, after checking the twins' birth certificates and establishing that they would be seven years old in six months, he ruled that until that time, Fatima would receive child support for them; she was also to receive half a bishlik per day for herself for the duration of the *ʿidda*. In addition, "Ibrahim was to pay her both dowry sums, thus fully carrying out the divorce agreement" (Haifa, Jaridat al-Zabt, vol. 32 [1331–1332/1913–1914], case 72, 60, 68–69, 72–75).

Methodological Problems

The issues dealt with in these two claims are not unusual in the *sijill* of the Jaffa and Haifa *shariʿa* courts. Many similar marital disputes took a comparable amount of time and were resolved in much the same manner. What is somewhat unusual about these two protocols is their richness of detail and the hints they contain concerning the litigants and the witnesses, their way of life, the circumstances that brought them to court, and the events that took place in the court itself. By carefully examining the information that was recorded and, no less important, the information that was not recorded in these two particular protocols, it becomes possible to illustrate some of the methodological problems and social issues facing the historian using the *sijill* as a source.

The intrinsic advantages of the *sijill* are almost self-evident: as a daily legal register, it forms a record of the lives of the local people, as written down by the local clerks, covering tens and even hundreds of years. For the historian seeking to reconstruct various aspects of ordinary everyday life, the *sijill* offers a perspective unlikely to be found elsewhere. Yet, there are various stumbling blocks, which can be divided into three levels: the events that occurred in court, the domestic events that led to the court case, and the overall social milieu in which all these events took place.

Which of the events that occurred in the court were actually recorded? The court clerk undoubtedly did not record each and every verbal exchange that took place. Thus, for example, the reader only senses that Ibrahim's three *talaq* calls were made out of rage rather than after careful consideration. There are some aspects of the situation that suggest such an interpretation: Ibrahim's use of the three nonretractable calls, as opposed to one reversible call at first, and the timing of the calls. Ibrahim acted following completion of the legal proceedings and the failure of all of his arguments when no time remained for further discussion. Moreover, he had been married more than seven years, and the boys were approaching the age of seven, which meant that they could be transferred from their mother's custody to his, and he would then be exempt from paying child support to his wife. Finally, Ibrahim made his calls following the increase in the alimony he was to pay. In other words, after Ibrahim had been paying alimony to his wife and children for years,[5] he now brought it upon himself to have to pay the dowry as well. Yet, if indeed Ibrahim was in a rage at this stage, we find no sign of it in the documentation.

It is also not clear to what degree the records reflect how the matters were actually presented by the litigants. The impression from many *sijill* protocols is that women in general were very well aware of their *sharicah* rights in regard to personal status and also knew how to

5. Ibrahim and Fatima disagreed on their sons' age, but they both hinted that their separation occurred at the time they were born. Ibrahim insisted that the twins were born in the *rumiyya* year 1321, and that he had been paying his wife alimony and child support since then. Fatima mentioned the name of the judge who was in charge at the time the twins' birth and the legal procedure by which she became entitled to alimony and child support. Going by this information and by the fact that the judge concluded that they were six and a half years old after examining their birth certificates, I was fortunate to find the record of the couple's first trial (Haifa, ʾam 7, 1325–1326/1907–1908, case 70, 129). It took place in Safar 21, 1326 (Mar. 1908), and it corroborated Fatima's version of the twins' age. In it, Fatima mentioned that she had been married to Ibrahim for approximately a year and a half, that she had already given birth to the twins, and that these were not yet weaned at the time of the trial. A simple calculation shows that the twins could not have been born before June 1907, i.e., exactly six and a half years before the trial of late 1913. The record of the first trial also shows that Ibrahim had indeed been paying alimony and child support for almost six years at the time he declared the divorce. See also below.

manipulate these rights in order to win various benefits, as illustrated by the two cases described here. But were women really so knowledgeable and resourceful, or did they appear in court with a jumbled array of grievances and arguments that the judge then organized in order to extract logical *shariᶜa* claims, thus performing something of a legal service for them? And was this not so in the case of Jamila versus al-Sayyid Abu Basha in Jaffa?

The *sijill* does not provide answers to such questions. From the point of view of historical research, either of the alternatives described above—that women knew their rights and had the ability to realize them in court, or that the judge was the one who promoted their rights for them (or any combination)—is feasible. Each leads to a different reconstruction and to different conclusions. Thus, where courtroom events within the court are concerned, the *sijill* serves as a sieve, but provides no tools to enable the reader-historian to determine what was sifted from the whole, and how. This is even more true in regard to the second level, that of the domestic events that led to the court episode. Here perhaps we come up against two shortcomings of the *sijill* as historical source: first, the reader is left uncertain about whether the causes recorded are the actual causes of the dispute; and second, many significant social details are simply not recorded because they lack legal importance.

The first shortcoming stems from the fact that, in *shariᶜa* jurisdiction, the real causes of a dispute have only limited interest: the judge is concerned solely with those causes that fall within *shariᶜa* categories and enable him to make legal decisions. As a result, the circumstances recorded in the *sijill* are not necessarily the true ones, nor do they cover the whole story; they might form a bridge, so to speak, between the dispute and the *shariᶜa*. In effect, it is only by chance that the reader learns of the dispute between Jamila and her husband over the missing articles in the store. Because it did not form the subject of the trial and was brought up only to back up the husband's version, we can be fairly sure here that this was indeed at the root of the divorce, but usually the reader is not so fortunate.

Even the few details of the dispute that do surface in this case highlight the second shortcoming of the *sijill:* Just how much more does a protocol conceal than it reveals? An interesting economic relationship between Jamila and her husband is hinted at—both dealt in some kind of trade—but the substance of this relationship remains obscure. Cases like this, needless to say, prompt many interesting questions regarding women's economic activities and how they are related to various aspects of marriage, questions which remain tantalizingly unanswered.

The Haifa trial illustrates this second shortcoming even better. There are relatively numerous details about Ibrahim (e.g., that he was living in Acre, where he was employed as a *mu'adhdhin* for 70 qurush a month, had additional sources of income, and supported a family of twelve people). But the more interesting character is Fatima. There are indirect hints that either she or her father, who was a *shaykh* according to her pedigree *(nasab),* had some connection to the court. Her father was also present at least during the first session in court, as it was he who legally identified her. There are several other curious details: the judge's demand not only that she present witnesses for her arguments but also that she bring *tazkiya* (supporting witnesses) to vouch for the integrity of her witnesses, which is usually the responsibility of the court; her signing her name in her own handwriting on some of the protocols (the only example of a woman's signature I have found in the *sijill* so far); her reference to the judge who was serving when her twin boys were born; and also the fact that she was able to recall that it was the same judge who originally set the alimony Ibrahim was to pay. If this already suggests that Fatima enjoyed special consideration in the court, that impression becomes even stronger when we consider the treatment Ibrahim received.

With the help of a detailed analysis of the *sijill* of Haifa and other sources, it was possible to find out one crucial piece of information regarding Fatima's background that may explain why she received special attention in court. The leader of the Rifa'i order in Haifa, the most prominent Sufi order of the city, was Muhammad *afandi* ibn *shaykh* Ibrahim ibn *shaykh* Qasim Shaqwara, probably a relative and maybe even a brother of *shaykh* Khalil ibn Ibrahim Shaqwara, Fatima's father. Thus, he had much influence on some of the leading Muslim religious families in the town, especially on the most established, among these the al-Khatib family, whose members held many important positions in Haifa's religious and judicial institutions (Yazbak 1992, forthcoming.). For example, the judge who was appointed in Haifa close to the time of the twins' birth (according to the data found in Fatima and Ibrahim's first trial) was a member of the al-Khatib family, Yunas ibn 'Abd al-Wahid al-Khatib (Haifa, 'am 7 [1325–1326/1907–1908], 74). The name of the judge mentioned by Fatima, al-Qudsi, probably referred to another person who was then one of the court's officials, namely 'Abd al-Raziq al-Qudsi or al-Maqdisi, who on occasion replaced the judge when he was absent (Haifa, 'am 7 [1325–1326/1907–1908], cases 124, 132).

The third methodological level concerns social conditions as a whole. Obviously, allusions to this do arise in court proceedings and thus find their way into the *sijill*. As already mentioned, the two cases presented here are unusually rich in descriptions of socioeconomical circumstances. But transforming such details into data for the wider field of research analysis is far from easy. In addition, using the *sijill* raises quantitative statistical questions regarding, for example, the ratio between the number of people that appeal to the courts and the size of the population, or the representation of different social strata of the population in court. Another set of questions relates to the role of the *shariᶜa* court within a particular society; that is, what can one learn about issues not brought before the *shariᶜa* court from those that *are* brought before it. For example, family and marriage issues were usually discussed in court only when a crisis developed. To what extent can we learn about the full nature of these social institutions from these crisis situations? Or, how can we explore other aspects of the relationship among family members, if the most common aspect raised in court during disputes is the economic one (by itself an interesting fact).

Although with only the two cases discussed here it may be difficult to exemplify questions that come up concerning the overall social conditions, anyone attempting a historical analysis with the help of the *sijill* cannot but be concerned with just such matters. In the following pages, some general social insights are illustrated that introduce some aspects of women's status in marriage and in the *shariᶜa* court system.

Women's Status and Shariᶜa Courts

As mentioned earlier, issues from the sphere of marital relations that are brought up for legal discussion are mainly economic ones. For example, alimony and child support, payments for nursing children (which depend on their age) and dowry payments. The discussion itself is similarly "economic" in character, and is not unlike bargaining: both sides negotiate as though trying to reach a compromise by stating an opening bid obviously much higher or much lower than will be agreed upon in the end. Even matters supposedly based on plain facts, such as children's ages, are negotiated in a similar way.[6] In the Abu Basha case,

---

6. According to Rosen 1989, 11, "The central analogy, the key metaphor . . . about social life . . . is concerned with notions of contract and negotiation." An anthropologist who spent months in the *shariᶜa* court of Sephru in Morocco (during the 1970s and 1980s), Rosen analyzed the work of the *shariᶜa* judge and became convinced that "the aim of the qadi is to put people back in the position of being able to negotiate their own permissible relationships without predetermining just what the outcome of those negotiations ought to be" (17).

the gap between the different versions of the son's age was only a year at the beginning of the discussion, perhaps because the couple was already divorced and the children's age was not expected to become an important economic factor. In the argument between Fatima and Ibrahim, the gap between the versions was two years, and it seems that Ibrahim was trying to mislead the judge by giving the year of birth according to the administrative Ottoman calendar *(maliyya)*, which he referred to as *rumiyya* that lags a couple of years behind the Muslim calendar *(hijriyya)*. It was the only case I have found so far in the *sijill* in which the date of an occurrence was given by a Muslim according to a calendar other than the Muslim one. In other disputes of this nature, such discrepancies were even greater and judges would end up determining an individual's age as they saw fit or according to birth certificates (but not by compromise between the two sides. The nature of this ritual of age bargaining is discussed elsewhere. See n.1.)

The dowry is a socioeconomic element of great importance in legal discussions. The dowry is divided in the marital agreement into two unequal parts: a larger "immediate" or "advanced" part given to the woman upon marriage as a basic condition for its consummation, and a smaller "postponed" part, which serves as an obligation on the part of the husband, to be paid in the event of a divorce, or his death (Schacht 1964, 177). In both cases before us (as in many others) the actual amounts paid "immediately" were only a small part of the amount stated in the agreement, and in the case of Fatima and Ibrahim (and in many others) nothing at all was paid until the divorce. This raises the question about what extent the dowry sums quoted in the *sijill* testify to the financial (or other) status of those involved, and furthermore, which of the dowry sums, if any, do we consider in that case. To use the data of dowry sums correctly, one has to consider both the sums stated in the marital agreement (divided into immediate and postponed dowry) and the sum of the immediate dowry that was actually paid out upon marriage. The latter, including the *jihaz* (trousseau), can serve, it would seem, as an indicator of a couple's economic situation, especially the husband's, whereas the sums appearing in the agreement as immediate and postponed dowry point to the socioeconomic status of the families involved, especially the wife's (the dowry should be in keeping with the standing of the latter's family). Differences between stated and actual sums then testify to the respective bargaining positions of the two families at the time of the agreement, or to the positive or negative personal qualities of prospective husband or wife. In this way, the historian may find many indications in the *sijill* of the socioeconomic situation of those who appear before the *shariᶜa* court. Fatima, for example, had an agreement with her husband in which he had committed himself to pay her a dowry of 2,000 qurush, of which 1,500 qurush would be paid immediately and the rest postponed. Although these sums were relatively low,[7] Ibrahim did not pay the immediate dowry upon marriage. This fact seems to reflect his financial difficulties, which probably also form the background to the litigation he had submitted to the court seven years after the marriage had taken place (in their first trial, of 1908, he declared that he was unable to pay the immediate dowry or even part of it). That he held only a minor position in the religious administration (as *muᵓadhdhin*) with a salary lower than the amount he had been ordered to pay Fatima and the twins, and was involved in a number of other small jobs, seems to reinforce this impression.

Another issue with direct bearing on the financial relationships between husband and wife is the initiation of the divorce. A woman who initiated a divorce usually waived most or even all of her financial rights *(khulᶜ)* (Schacht 1964, 164; J. N. D. Anderson 1970, 367), including the dowry (in case she had not received her immediate dowry upon marriage, she forfeited her right to it in such a divorce), as did Jamila. Her story and those of other women show that while women did indeed initiate divorce proceedings, they usually paid a heavy price for doing so. Many marital disputes, however, give us the impression that women sometimes found ways to provoke their husbands into making the *talaq* call, thus obtaining the divorce without forfeiting their dowry and alimony. In the case of Fatima and Ibrahim, there is no evidence that Fatima initially was interested in causing Ibrahim to make the three *talaq* calls, but he did so nonetheless, much to Fatima's advantage. Still, Ibrahim's initiation of the divorce, in spite of the financial implications involved, seems, as already mentioned, to show that he was in a furious state of mind when he declared the divorce and had not seriously considered the step. His anger could have been instigated by Fatima, even though that is not indicated in the *sijill*.

The trial of Fatima and Ibrahim illustrates a relatively long marriage during most of which the couple were in fact living separately. According to the *shariᶜa*, a wife was entitled to demand her rights as defined in the marital agreement; as long as she did not receive them,

---

7. Though they are not the lowest recorded in the *sijill* during the period. Jamila, who shared some kind of trade venture with her husband but does not seem to be really well off, received a higher dowry than Fatima.

she could refuse cohabitation and sexual relations with her husband, whereas he was obliged to support her and their children. Fatima and Ibrahim's separation (which did not cancel the formal marital agreement) began with Fatima's invoking such *shari'a* sanctions against Ibrahim. She declared in court that Ibrahim had married her and had had intercourse with her as a result of which she had given birth to the twins, but she claimed that he had not paid the dowry nor was he living with her the life of a full marriage *(mu'ashara)*. Because Ibrahim stated he could not pay the dowry, it was decided that he should pay alimony and child support. That they were living separately is not ever mentioned directly: Ibrahim was already living in Acre at the time of the first trial, and it is not clear whether he had been living in Haifa even at the time of their marriage or whether he intended to but changed his mind. In any case, a husband's move to a distant location was a *shari'a* cause allowing the wife to stay behind and demand alimony (Haifa *'am* 7 [1325–1326/ 1907–1908], case 70, 129). Thus, usually when the husband intended to immigrate to a distant place, the judge would give a verdict in the wife's favor, according to *shari'a* criteria for an acceptable distance separating a husband from his wife *(masafat al-qasr)*. The distance between Acre and Haifa would not seem to fall in this category, but there could have been other circumstances causing such a verdict; for example, if the marital agreement contained a special condition that the woman could not be forced by her husband to immigrate to another locality.

After six years of marriage, Jamila continued to claim her immediate dowry, which had yet to be paid, even though she had signed a written divorce agreement waiving payment of the dowry. Her case serves to further the impression, mentioned previously, that demanding payment of the stated immediate dowry at any stage of the marriage was often used by the wife as a tactic to obtain other things, particularly if my assumption is correct that, in customary law, payment of the "immediate" dowry or part of it was sometimes fictitious. There were other trials that began with claims similar to Jamila's in which women who had been married for a number of years and were not (like her) divorced at the time of the trial, demanded payment of the immediate dowry or other marital rights. During these trials, complex patterns of diverse mutual grievances between the couple would surface, and some of these trials ended in divorces initiated by the husbands or in the separation of the couple, whereby the husband was ordered to support his wife and his children and to supply them with a proper house to live in. Such a case strengthens the assumption that women often used their de jure rights of the marital agreement to improve their position in the marriage. Whether these women were eager to obtain a divorce or not, they took care not to endanger their financial rights by initiating one.

To conclude, it therefore appears that women were far from helpless or inept but managed quite well to find their way within the system of rights and obligations imposed by *shariᶜa,* customary law, and the changing circumstances—rights and obligations that differed greatly from those of their husbands. There were women who succeeded in reversing an obviously inferior position, and turning a situation such as nonpayment of the immediate dowry into an advantageous means of pressure.

Thus, despite the methodological problems indicated above, the *sijill* enables us to form a general picture of women's appearance in court and to conclude that women frequently presented claims and used the *shariᶜa* process. Many women appeared in court without being represented by a legal representative *(wakil);* some were represented by their father or their brother or another family member, but most were represented by experienced attorneys *(wukalaᵓ),* identified in the *sijill* as "one of the known pleaders in town", that is, a kind of professional lawyer. The issue of women applying to the court independently or through a representative *(wakil)* is complicated and worthy of further study. For example, to what extent did a woman who appointed a legal representative to appear in court in her place do so because it was more socially accepted for men to appear in court? Choosing a "known pleader," however, may point to other reasons for using a *wakil.* The expertise of such men and their proven ability to achieve better results, as well as the evolution of the custom of using a *wakil* by elite members as a kind of noblesse oblige, probably constituted a much more logical reason than gender prejudice. Besides, women who like Jamila and Fatima had no elite affiliation and appeared on their own in court either as plaintiffs or as defendants showed a fair amount of knowledge of the processes—and possibly the benefits—involved. Even if the protocols with their legal and laconic style distort the overall picture, and even if the expertise was that of the judge, most women showed great skill in taking advantage of this expertise, together with their own keen judgment in appealing to the courts in order to obtain just that result.

Finally, it would appear that the courts or, more precisely, the judges, contributed a great deal to women's ability to realize their rights. In Fatima's case, it is possible that the judge was even favorably predisposed to her side, a point supported by the fact that the judge imposed on Fatima the proof of her husband's financial ability, even though she was not the plaintiff (Ibrahim was), and Fatima's response concerned only the children's age. The judge did so even though according to *shariʿa* judicial procedure, the judge was obliged to put the burden of proof on the plaintiff, unless the defendant presented a counterclaim— a full different version, not just a denial of the plaintiff's version (Majal-lat al-Ahkam, 1298/1881, 2d. ed., 242–43 [arts. 1631–33], 277 [art. 1883]). Asking Fatima and not Ibrahim to provide the witnesses for her husband's financial position clearly favored her. It should be pointed out, however, that such favoritism is absent in most other cases, and even in this case it seems to have been owing to her family connections. In this respect, Jamila's story is more representative; the judge did all he could, within the *shariʿa,* to ensure that Jamila would not leave the courtroom empty-handed. When it became clear that, in *shariʿa* terms, Jamila's husband's version was a counterclaim, the judge made him provide evidence as required by *shariʿa* law. The judge heard four witnesses testify to his version of the divorce, saw the divorce agreement, checked with Jamila that the divorce was in effect, and heard two additional witnesses concerning the child's age. After the judge had examined each detail and found the husband's version irrefutable, he decided to ask for the *mufti's* opinion, a procedure that caused the divorce agreement to be renegotiated. Thus, he enabled Jamila to come away from the trial fairly successfully. It should be noted that he did this through *shariʿa* channels, taking care not to deviate from them.[8]

From the above, it would seem to be quite clear that the *sijill* contains a great deal of valuable information, much of it "between the lines." Thus, special tools and methodology are needed to extract this information carefully. Though of necessity focusing on only a few aspects of the information available, my limited discussion has indicated that women's appearances in the *shariʿa* court in matters of personal status were characterized by a considerable amount of what we might call "legal sophistication," and judges' expertise was a factor in ensuring that women's rights were realized within the bounds of the *shariʿa,* though in no way am I suggesting that the *shariʿa* court system gave preference to women rather than to men, or vice versa. The picture of

---

8. In similar cases in Egypt, the judge himself tended to cancel the relinquishing of child support in a divorce agreement, on the grounds that the woman could not have released her husband from paying her money for their child because, in doing so, she was relinquishing a right that was not hers but her child's (Shaham 1991, 132–35).

gender relations and differences is far more complex. Any examination of the *shari*a court in this respect must be set within the entire social context in which it functioned—and this calls for more extensive and fundamental research. Here my intention has been only to illustrate some of the possibilities offered by the *sijill,* and, if possible, to let the reader savor some of the social flavor one can extract from it.

PART THREE

The Ottoman Household

9

Marriage among Merchant Families in Seventeenth-Century Cairo

Nelly Hanna

A number of historians have made connections between the growth of the modern state and the development of patriarchy in the family, both in Europe and in the Middle East. The need for the state to extend its controls through the family seems to have been a recurrent phenomenon, which historians have noted in sixteenth-and seventeenth-century England, as well as for nineteenth-century Egypt (Stone 1975, 13–58; Tucker 1985; Sonbol forthcoming). This control through the family was done in a number of ways. One of them was by changing or codifying family law; another, by concentrating property rights on male heads of families or on nuclear families, still another, through the educational system, and through state manipulation of religious activity and religious opinion. The end result was that women were often living under more restrictive conditions than they had before. In other words, in the process of state building itself, as the state took over some of the functions families had been doing, the family, and most particularly, women, were deprived of some of their mobility.

This assessment can throw some light on the situation before the nineteenth century. We know that patriarchical family structures existed, but the form that they took is less well known. The Oriental Despot model, developed with regard to the state, has often been applied to the family in the premodern period, either in explicit or implicit terms. This model of family structure presumes that the relations in the household or family were entirely vertical: the head of the household, resembling the ruler, and everyone else, the ruled. He gave the orders, while they obeyed and submitted to his authority passively. Segregation and confinement of women was one method of control because it set up a fixed space within which his control was absolute. In the form that it has been elaborated, this model is hardly applicable when compared to the archival data available for Ottoman Egypt.

That patriarchical structures existed is true; but as archival material shows, in a different form. In this article, I review family structures in the early seventeenth century in Cairo, especially in light of the relation between the state and the family, some two centuries before the emergence of the modern state. It examines household relations in the context of a relatively weak and distant state. If the state strengthened patriarchy, what happened to the family structure at times when state structures were weak and distant? If the nineteenth and twentieth centuries experienced a development of patriarchial structures, what was the case before that? That the patriarchical family system was present is evident, but was it comparable to the Oriental Despot model as has often been implied?

A second perspective that I explore with regard to the household structures has to do with class. In general, it was within the upper social strata that patriarchical authority was held to be the strongest, seclusion being a luxury that only few could afford. A close examination of the archival material indicates that within the merchant class (probably the wealthiest indigenous group), this is an oversimplification of a much more complex situation, which needs some elucidation. The women of the merchant group are prominent in the archival material used, and one discerns in their patterns of behavior certain features that reflect the tendencies of the period.

The patterns of household and family that characterize the period can be placed within the patriarchical structure, but they show the particular forms this structure could take and the different alternative forms it could have. This is manifested by the more or less widened sphere of influence that a certain number of wives could have in their homes and the more restricted spheres of their husbands. This phenomenon can be related to some of the general features of the period. Politically, in the course of the Ottoman period (1517–1798), the state had a weak presence in Egypt. This period had a number of particularities. For the first time in about seven centuries, Egypt was ruled from outside of its borders and Cairo was a provincial capital, after having been an imperial capital in the Mamluk period. In other words, the core of the state and its functions, located in Istanbul, were at a certain distance.

On the other hand, the structure of government in Egypt, as set up by the Ottoman authorities after their conquest of 1517, brings up another aspect. Egypt was governed by a pasha appointed by the sultan. But to ensure that pashas in the provinces did not get too powerful, the appointments were for short terms, a year usually, renewable in some cases to two or three years. For the same reason, other limitations were set up. Notably, two other Ottoman officials were appointed by the Ottoman sultan to head the judiciary institution and the financial bureau, neither of whom took orders from the pasha. Power at the top was therefore divided. Furthermore, the pasha governed through a *diwan* (council), which met once a week and which had to approve decisions he made. For much of the Ottoman period, all of these factors made by the state and its representatives in Egypt were not all powerful or all dominating. Therefore, as far as political structure goes, the parallel between the Oriental Despot and the despotic head of the household is hardly applicable under these circumstances.

A second phenomenon that helped to structure the family in the Ottoman period, not unrelated to the first, is the spread and development of the court system. When the Ottomans conquered Egypt in 1517, one of the first things they did was to adapt the exiting judiciary system to bring it in line with the other Ottoman provinces: by creating new court houses all over the city, in the north, in the city center, the west, and the south of the city. By the time they had done that, there were fifteen court rooms in Cairo. They were thus situated so that no one lived too far away from a court house. In other words, physical accessibility is one of the important features of the judiciary of the period.

Perhaps because Ottoman officials wanted the judiciary system to pay for itself, they not only instituted fees for claimants of different types but also pushed people to use the courts. This is very clear as far as marriage is concerned: Ibn Iyas recounts how they ordered that all marriage contracts had to be done in court, to the great distress of the population, for whom this was evidently something new (Ibn Iyas 1961, 5:451–52). Nothing in Islamic law requires a contract to be written in court, or even to be written at all, the presence of witnesses being sufficient to conclude the contract. Whatever reasons they may have had when they instituted the changes, the consequences were vital for the marriage institution as such and for family structure. With time, the court became an intermediary institution that mediated in family disputes, all the more so as people were very willing to take their cases to court, both men and women. Justice was quick and simple. There were no long delays and no complicated procedures. Moreover, the courts took *'urf* (customs and traditions) into consideration when they judged a case. If religious texts were not specific on a particular matter, ʿurf was applied. It was up to the qadi (judge) to decide when ʿurf was applicable in making his decisions.

A close view of how the courts applied Islamic law in general and with regard to the family in particular shows a number of significant points in the way that law was applied. They seem to have been accommodating on a number of levels. People could notably choose between any of the four schools of law for any case they brought to court. Nor were they tied to stay within one school. A person could decide to rent a shop according to Hanbali law one day and get married according to Hanafi or Maliki law the next. The procedures were simple enough for any person to understand without necessarily having reached any particular level of education—this in additon to the courts' physical accessability in the city.

I will consider the family structures and the way that the courts could play a role in family patterns by looking at the marriage contracts registered in court records. These documents are numerous, and so they contain data on a wide spectrum of the population and reflect the patterns of both the society as a whole and specific social groups.

One of the reasons why these documents are so important for social and family history is because they allow us to formulate certain criteria, other than the veil and the harem, by which to evaluate the position of women in the family, in the household, and in society. These criteria come from within the documents and can be seen as expressions of the concerns, the worries, and the aspirations of the persons who formulated them and as expressions of the arena within which people at that particular time and place could move. They show us, in other words, both the individual and the social dimension, the concerns of the individual and the alternative forms of behavior that society considered acceptable. They are also useful to help us to identify how various social groups related to these questions and the variation in forms that coexisted at a particular time in history.

Marriage Contracts

Marriage contracts registered in the courts gave the name of the bridegroom, sometimes indicating his origin and profession, that of the bride, usually giving her father's profession, and indicating if she was a virgin (bikr) or a woman who had had a previous marriage (marʾa), if she was a minor (qasir) or a major (baligh); then the amount of bridal money exchanged and the way it was to be exchanged. The section of most significance for our purposes then followed, the conditions put by the bride and accepted by the groom. In this section, the bride or her family could add as many clauses as they saw fit that would, in their view, give guarantees to the bride that certain patterns would be followed in her future conjugal life. Implicit in the marriage contract itself was the bride's right to conjugal relations and to maintenance. The clauses went beyond that, either to exert certain restraints on the groom or to guarantee certain liberties to the bride.

The stipulations in marriage contracts were, in fact, varied because they reflected individual concerns. One can nevertheless see that, globally, certain issues were frequently included. One of these was the question of polygamy, or the husband's right to have wives other than the one who was the subject of the contract. This was an issue both of controversy among religious scholars and between the different schools of law. The classical view of the Hanafi school, which was the official school of the Ottomans, did not support clauses in a marriage contract that limited the rights that had been set down by the Qur'an, notably the right to have four wives; likewise, such clauses were not looked upon favorably by the Malikis, but once they were agreed upon, they were binding (Khurashi n.d., 278). For the Hanbalis, on the other hand, the stipulations were part of a contract and should be respected as such because the two parties were willing to include them (Pearl 1979, 83–84; Sha'rani 1318H, 2:94). And yet in the period covered, all the schools of law, when it came to application, followed the teachings of Hanbal and the marriage contracts containing clauses limiting the number of wives a man could have were written up by *qadis* belonging to the four schools. Marriage contracts issued by Hanafi, Maliki, and Shafi'i *qadis* had stipulations regarding the husband's polygamy. What induced this shift may well have been the 'urf that they took into consideration. The changing habits and usages may thus have been behind the modification of these.

Another topic of concern commonly included in a clause in the marriage contracts of this period has to do with lodging. One of the main features of a patriarchical household was precisely the fact that it was headed by a husband and father who had some form of authority over the other family members living with him. In Islamic law, the husband is responsible for lodging, feeding, and clothing his wife. Traditionally, if material conditions permitted, he brought his spouse to live in his family home. Characteristic of the trends of seventeenth-century Cairo are the numerous and varied attempts on the part of wives or their families to form other alternative types of households, in which the authority of the husband is restrained by serious limitations. If a young husband accepted to live with his parents-in-law, or to move into a house his wife owned, he would have to integrate into a pattern that was not of his own creation. The actual wording of the stipulations concerning lodging were varied, and much depended on whether the bride was a young girl getting married for the first time or a woman who owned her own property.

Another kind of stipulation was about the provision of maintenance, or *nafaqa*. This was implicit in the marriage contract: husbands had to support wives and provide them with food, clothing, and lodging. And yet, many contracts had a clause of some kind to the effect that the husband would not leave his wife for any period of time without maintenance. The period was decided on an individual basis; for some, one month, three months, perhaps six months, or a year. After that time was up, if he did not provide maintenance, she had the choice of divorcing him if she wished to bring her case to court. But if maintenance was self evident and implicit, why did so many contracts specifically include a clause about it? The reason was because the four schools of law were divided about the consequences of such a violation of the wife's rights. The Hanafis, in particular, did not see that absence of maintenance gave her the right of divorce, as seems to have been the opinion of the Shafiʿis (Ibn Nugaym n.d., 4:200–202). One sees in questions such as this a divergence between theory and practice, between what some scholars of one of the schools said and practiced and the law as applied in the courts. As far as this particular point on maintenance was concerned, the fact of including it in a clause, agreed upon by two parties, removed it from the theoretical discussion on maintenance and placed it instead in the specific contractual agreement. In this form, it was implemented by the various schools; *qadis* of the Hanafi rite were willing to treat this matter in the context of a contractual agreement in the form of a condition in the marriage contract, rather than as an implicit right. In practice, the courts frequently granted a wife a divorce if her husband was absent and did not provide maintenance. In some cases, specific mention is made of the conditions included in the contract. Thus, in Shawal 1028/ 1618, Aziza bint Ramadan was granted a divorce from Daʿud bin Sulayman because of his absence for sixty days, during which she was left without any financial provision. She based her case on the condition stipulated in her contract, specifying that sixty days was the time limit for her to be left without maintenance (Bab al-ʿAli 1029/1619, 102:105–465).

Other stipulations reflected individual concerns and situations; a husband could agree that his wife's child from another marriage live with them and that he take charge of his/her maintenance; or that the husband buy the wife a slave; or that the wife continue her work as a peddlar; or that the husband should not beat the wife. These clauses varied according to the situation. It is, in fact, in this variety that one can most perceive some of the ways in which the courts were accommodating the needs of the people they were serving. At a certain level, the court had to be prescriptive. At other levels, the interaction between the court and the prevailing conditions is evident. On the other hand, if the clauses of a marriage contract were violated, it was to the court that the wife went, where she was declared divorced by the *qadi*. Therefore, the courts played an intermediary role in the family, to which people had recourse when they had a grievance. In other words, they provided the horizontal relation between family members and an institution outside the house, which could counterbalance the otherwise vertical relations between the head of the household and the rest of the family.

Groups Concerned

A large number of the contracts consulted from the early decades of the seventeenth century contain clauses with regard to lodging, to wives and concubines, to maintenance, or other less common matters. The conditions seem to have had various objectives, of which the most relevant was to keep the wife from being under the complete control of her husband, either by imposing direct limitations on him or by power sharing between the husband and his father-in-law. Thus, the clauses a wife put in the marriage contract kept her from living in that space where the husband had most control (his house), and the authority that he could employ under such conditions curtailed.

Who made use of these clauses? The majority of marriages, about two thirds, followed the usual patterns, and the partners sufficed themselves with the rights and duties that the contract implicitly provided. The last third of the contracts cunsulted had a condition of some kind, and usually two or three of them. The identity of those who did make use of this mechanism is quite enlightening about the kind of patterns various groups of the poulation of Cairo followed.

In theory, anyone could follow these practices as far as the courts were concerned. One does find quite a variety of people named in these contracts, from the most modest families (barbers, cooks, and water carriers), to the members of the artisan class (textile weavers, goldsmiths, and coppersmiths) to the wealthier families (*shuyukh, qadis,* and merchants). In practice, they did not all make equal use of these facilities. The criterion most frequently included in contracts is economic. And the groups most likely to stipulate this criterion in their marriage contracts were the artisans and the merchants.

For a number of reasons, the poor of the city, who, if they did not form the majority of the population certainly formed a great part of it, do not often appear in this kind of document. In spite of the fact that the Ottomans "encouraged" people to register their marriages in court, because fees had to be paid, the poor were the least likely to conform to such encouragement. That is why, although one occasionally finds marriage contracts for family members of a barber, a cook, a porter, or a vegetable seller, the numbers are too small to be representative.

Moreover, the financial and lodging conditions that these people lived in were not likely to encourage husbands to take several wives, or to buy concubines, or to be able to offer much choice as far as lodging was concerned.

At the other end of the spectrum, some members of the military groups, who in the early seventeenth century were in the process of consolidating their power, got married in court; but the number of contracts referring to them is too limited to allow us to have a clear picture of the patterns they followed, perhaps because in relation to the city's population, they were too few to appear over a limited period or perhaps because they did not get married in court. In any case, the private and family life of the military class deserves to be studied more comprehensively.

The groups that do appear in great numbers are the families of artisans, traders, and merchants, who formed the majority of the population, and shaykhs and religious scholars in much smaller numbers. In other words, the marriage contracts, or that third of contracts consulted with some clause or other, was mainly from this group of the population.

And yet, these categories included various levels of wealth and material conditions. Depending on their circumstances and their conditions, clauses could reflect their needs or their restrictions. A woman who peddled goods included a clause to the effect that her husband "will not stop me from pursuing my work." A wealthy merchant getting married was required to provide his wife, as part of the clothing she was seasonally entitled to, in silks, the most luxurious and expensive textiles (al-Bab al-ʿAli 1061/1650, 129:198–746); a *muʿallim,* Daʿud bin Sidhum, jeweller, on marrying a minor, agreed to live with her father, wherever he lived (al-Bab al-ʿAli 1029/1619, 102:342–1448).

Women from Merchant Families

In reading through the numerous marriage contracts in the court registers, one cannot help but notice that there are certain patterns that seem to be peculiar to merchant families. Although many of the conditions in these contracts were basically similar to those in other contracts, as in their restriction on polygamy, they stand apart from others because of the stringency of their conditions and the way in which they were formulated. One could be even more specific and identify among those contracts of brides belonging to a merchant family, those brides who had had previous marriages, that is, women who may have inherited some money from a deceased husband or father and were financially well off. Experience from a previous marriage, in addition to the prestige that having been married seems to have given them, makes their marriage contracts stand out in relation to others of their period. What these documents tell us about this class is valuable because so little is known of the family life of merchants. The documents contradict the generally held view that the physical movements of women from comfortable milieux were very limited, and that they only moved out of the house on two occasions, the first on the day they got married, from their father's home to their husband's home, and the second when they died, from their home to the grave. If this was the practice, how widespread it was and at which periods it was applied are not known. The archival material allows us to understand these statements with a different perspective.

Of course, one could argue that, if the women of merchant families were the ones who had the most stipulations in their contracts, that was because their socioeconomic conditions were most likely to keep them confined to their houses than other social groups. Houses of the upper socioeconomic groups were more likely to be autonomous entities in the sense that they contained commodities and utilities to run everyday life without the inhabitants having to have recourse to public amenities. It was the houses of the wealthy that might have a private bath and thus dispense its inhabitants from going to public baths; wells that dispensed them from going to public fountains; stables that dispensed them from using public transport. All these facilities made it easier for them, whether they were men or women, to live more within the confines of their residences. Therefore, by living in a more confined space, wealthier women could be more under the control of their husbands. Moreover, their husbands were likely to have a large house, buy slaves and concubines, and have more than one wife.

These points are of course true. But they can only be part of the explanation. The clauses protecting women within their own spaces are in fact an important part of the contract. But their conditions went much further than that, including clauses that are not found in other contracts of the same period, restricting their husbands in a way that more modest women did not seem to be doing.

A closer look at some of these contracts, those of Sayyidat al-Nazirin bint al-khawaja Nur al-Din al-Shuja'i; of Umm al-Hana bint al-khawaga Isma'il Abu Taqiyya, *shahbandar al-tujjar;* Laila bint al-khawaja Ahmad Abu Taqiyya; Juwayria bint Hasan bin Salih, *shaykh Suq* al-Nahhasin bin Bayn al-Qasrayn (al-Bab al-'Ali 1004/1595, 82:335–1599; 1016/1606, 90 rep:36–189; 1026/1617, 100:143–1126; 1051/1631, 114:37–92). All of them had in common two points: first, they were from merchant families and, second, they had been married before. To a certain extent, one can explain the stringency of their conditions by their being wealthier or from more prestigious families than their husbands. That is probably true of the Abu Taqiyyas, their brother/father Isma'il, having been *shahbandar al-tujjar* or (head of the merchant guild) from about 1612 to 1624. The prestige of this position would certainly rub off on his daughter and sister, even if their bridegroom were a merchant (for Laila) and a secretary at the Treasury (for Umm al-Hana). But with regard to Sayyidat al-Nazirin, even though her father, Nur al-Din al-Shuja'i was extremely wealthy, her prospective husband was not exactly a pauper, but was in fact both very well known and very wealthy, belonging to the old and prestigious Sufi family of al-Bakri: al-Shaykh Muhammad Ibn Abu'l-Mawahib al-Bakri. The fourth, Juwayriyya, was returning to the man to whom she had been married before, a paper merchant, *(warraq)*. There were therefore some differences in status, but not enough to explain the whole story.

One has the definite impression that experience from earlier marriages played a role in formulating the anxieties and aspirations of these women. Conditions such as those put down by Juwayriyya could only be the result of a previous, alas bitter, experience that had taught her that everything should be spelt out in black and white, and no room should be left for ambiguity. No innocent newly wed could have thought up the details she spelt out in her stipulations. After the usual stipulation about other wives and concubines, she concerned herself with ensuring that her daily life and that her social contacts would not be disrupted. To that effect were included clauses that he would not stop her from: going to the public bath; visiting her lady friends whenever she wished; receiving the visits of her children, companions, relatives, and friends, whenever they wanted and for as long as they wished. Two additional clauses guaranteed that she would be allowed to go to Mecca and that she would be allowed to return from there.

One also senses, at the same time, a certain wisdom that years and experience provided, perhaps an acceptance of what one could not change. As in most marriage contracts with clauses, the question of restricting the husband's possibilities of having other wives appears in all the contracts of the ladies mentioned above, but in varying forms and degrees. Only Laila's contract specifically rejected any other future or past wife. The others imposed limitations without completely annulling the possibities of polygamy. Sayyidat al-Nazirin's clause restricted her husband from getting married, but did not refer to the wife/wives already with him, except to state that she/they were not to live in the same house as her. In other words, one finds the attempt to define a space within which she could function in her own way. The same is probably applicable to Umm al-Hana. The document is clear about his other wives, one living in Giza and the other in close-by Misr (Cairo) and his concubine, who has mothered his child. It was also clear on her conditions, in addition to the usual clause about his not remarrying or obtaining a new concubine. Again, the sense of her own space comes out. His other wives should never live with her in one house, nor are they to move to a house close to her. Umm al-Hana appears quite consciously to be creating a space within which her husband's control was diluted to the last degree. Not only were they to live with her mother and brother but he was specifically enjoined to behave in a way acceptable to them, to her sisters, and to their spouses.

It is probably at the level of restricting the husband's movements that the contracts of the women of merchant families, more specifically Juwayriyya and Umm al-Hana, go somewhat further than many other of their contemporaries. Both of them curtailed the husband's possibility of sleeping outside the house. Umm al-Hana's husband was not allowed to sleep out for more than two consecutive nights—without a good reason or a legally accepted excuse (*'uthr shar'i*)—without express permission from her, her mother, and her brother. Juwayriyya, who liked clarity, put down a flat five consecutive nights as his limit for nights out.

Unusual as these conditions may appear to us, there must have been an implicit social acceptance of these forms of behavior and of social relations inside the house among married couples. Some of the persons involved in the contracts that were cited were notables, some of high repute and respect in society. Their registration in court confirmed the respectability and legality of these undertakings. In other words, one is talking of forms of behavior, which if not entirely orthodox, were socially sanctioned.

Thus, these documents imply a particular kind of pattern of family structure, which probably represents one type of household of the period. The cases cited were not unheard of, even if they went further than most in imposing a certain system. They should be seen as one of many variations that existed in this period. They coexisted side by side with much more patriarchical households, in which the head of the family had a large household, including slaves, servants, concubines, and wives over whom he could exert his authority. The best example one can give for this early period is that of Isma'il Abu Taqiyya, *shahbandar al-tujjar*. He had married four wives, a number of his children were mothered by his concubines, he had a number of other slaves and concubines living in the house. And yet, it is not surprizing to learn that his own sister and his daughter, were among those whose contracts stood out by their numerous clauses. In other words, within the merchant group, even within the same family, more than one family pattern was being followed. The society that emerges is one that intergrated an amazing degree of diversity.

In conclusion, the patterns of household and marriage in Cairo in the early seventeenth century highlight a number of significant points. The family remained essentially patriarchical in structure, but conditions in the seventeenth century had brought about modifications in the contours of that structure. The family structure was influenced by the state's being weak and distant and by the growing role that the courts of Cairo were playing in people's everyday lives. In an age before the modern codification of law, the *qadi* had a wider scope for movement. The courts seem to have been finding ways to accommodate both the changing norms among the various segments of the population and a wide spectrum of diversity. Their role was fundemental as an intermediary institution, providing horizontal relations with the members of a household, or family, to counterbalance the vertical relations that the head of the household, whether husband or father, had with them. The traditional patriarchical patterns were not destroyed in the process; far from it. In fact, they continued to be one of the established forms, probably the dominant one, that was practiced by important segments of the population. But at the same time there was a broadening of the forms of behavior that were acceptable socially and within the family, and for which the courts were finding ways to intergrate them into their system.

10

The Ties That Bound

Women and Households in Eighteenth-Century Egypt

Mary Ann Fay

The Rise of the Household

*I*n the late seventeenth century, the Mamluk system, which the Ottomans never succeeded in eradicating from Egypt, began reconstituting and reasserting itself, ultimately posing a serious challenge to the supremacy of the Ottoman government.[1] After a series of internecine

A version of this paper was presented at the VIth Annual Conference on the Economic and Social History of the Ottoman Empire and Turkey (1326–1960), sponsored by the Institut de Récherches et d'Etudes sur le Monde Arabe et Musulman, Aix-en-Provence, France, in July 1992. Material in this paper also appeared in my doctoral dissertation, *Women and Households: Gender, Power and Culture in Eighteenth-Century Egypt,* which was supervised by Judith Tucker, whose support and guidance I gratefully acknowledge. Research for this paper was conducted in Cairo on a Fulbright-Hays Dissertation Research Grant in 1990–1991. My thanks also to Nelly Hanna and John Willoughby for their constructive comments on an earlier version of this paper.

1. Daniel Crecelius (1981) described the Mamluk system which arose in the last part of the seventeenth century as "a revised Mamluk system" to differentiate it from that of the classic Mamluk sultanate of the medieval period. P. M. Holt (1982) called the system in Egypt during the Ottoman period "neo-Mamluk," noting that it lacked the homogenity of its predescessors. In one of the most recent articles on the Mamluk system of the Ottoman period, Gabriel Piterberg (1990) argued that it is irrelevant whether the system was revised or had continued to exist without interruption after the Ottoman conquest. For Piterberg, the important point is that the system was mamluk because it relied primarily on the recruitment of slaves who were non-Egyptian and primarily Georgian in ethnicity.

struggles among the various Mamluk houses, the Qazdughli *bayt* (household) eventually emerged as the most powerful. ʿAli Bey al-Kabir, the most powerful bey in Egypt between 1760 and 1772, succeeded in eliminating his rivals and consolidating power within the Qazdughli *bayt*. As a result, the Mamluk system changed from one in which the most powerful *amir* (prince, leader) was *primus inter pares* to a quasi-monarchical system with power consolidated in one house.

Also around mid-century, the process began of fusing the military institution founded on the *ojaq*s (Ottoman forces in Egypt) and the Mamluk organization dominated by the beylicate. The result was one system in which service in the *ojaq*s became a career path within the Mamluk system. As André Raymond has said, by the end of the century, almost all the positions in the Ottoman hierarchy were held by members of the mamluk houses (Raymond 1983, 15–89). In 1798, Ibrahim Bey described the ruling class as a unique system in which the beys, *kashifs* (governors), mamluks, officers, and soldiers of the *ojaq*s constituted a socially homogenous and hierarchical group.

The resurgence of the Mamluk system in Egypt challenged the supremacy of the Porte, making its representative in the country, the pasha or the *wali* (governor, prefect), increasingly irrelevant. ʿAli Bey challenged the Porte directly by attempting unsuccessfully to extend his power into Syria. Ibrahim Bey and Murad Bey, although they did not mount a similar challenge, withheld tax payments to the Porte and vied for power with Ismaʿil Bey, who was regarded as the Porte's ally in Egypt. The Porte was able to subdue Ibrahim and Murad with the 1786 expedition of Hasan Pasha to the country. The subordination of the beys to Ottoman authority lasted only as long as Hasan Pasha was in the country, however, and did not survive his recall to Istanbul the following year.

Thus, the story of the Mamluk resurgence is, in fact, that of the rise of the beylicate, whose power was based on the households of the beys. As power was usurped from the Ottoman establishment by the beylicate and as beys like ʿAli Bey al-Kabir and his successors became the de facto rulers of Egypt, the Mamluk house became the foundation of power and the basis for administering the state and exploiting the resources of the country.

The Mamluk household is the key to understanding not only the political system of the eighteenth century but also the position of elite women. This is because the position of these women was linked to their membership in powerful households and, thus, to their status as part of the ruling class. Women's membership in these households was buttressed by their economic rights and property ownership, the importance of marriage and alliances created through extramarital sexual unions to the reproduction of the Mamluk system, and the ability of women to construct patronage networks of their own.[2]

The historian Suzanne F. Wemple (1987) has shown that elite women in Western Europe possessed power or autonomy or both as members of families who exercised power and authority in the absence of a strong, centralized state. This occurred after the fall of the Carolingian Empire in the ninth century and continued until the mid-eleventh century during the period known as the first feudal age. The empire founded by Charlemagne broke up into a collection of small principalities, or seignories, in which authority extended as far as the fuedal lord could enforce his will. Women, with their dowries and their family connections, could make a vital contribution to the advancement of their families. The power that these aristocratic European women exercised was derived in part from their membership in ruling families but was secured by their right to own and inherit property at a time when land was the foundation of power. As Wemple has written:

> Endowed with their own property and rights to inheritance, secure in their marital status, women were equipped to act with power and decision in the fluid society of the first feudal age. . . . Out of the ruins of the Carolingian state, the family emerged as the most stable and effective element in a troubled world. Profiting from the almost unlimited power of their families, women for two centuries were able to play a central political role. Since land had become the only source of power, by exercising their property rights, secured in the Carolingian period, a growing number of women appear in the tenth and eleventh centuries as chatelaines, mistresses of landed property and castles with the attendant rights of justice and military command, proprietors of churches, and participants in both secular and ecclesiastical assemblies (Wemple 1987, 178).

2. We know that women have economic rights granted by the *shari'a* and that women exercized those rights as buyers and sellers of property. See e.g., Jennings (1983), Abraham Marcus (1983), and Tucker (1985). In the specific case of eighteenth-century Egypt, my evidence of property ownership comes from *waqfiyyat* examined in the archives (*daftarkhanah*) of the Ministry of Awqaf, Cairo, in 1990–1991. According to these documents, women endowed about one-quarter of the new *waqfs* (religious endowments) established in the eighteenth century. They endowed a wide variety of urban commercial, residential, and agricultural property, including various kinds of shops and workshops, warehouses, living units in apartment houses; (agency, resthouse), the foundation of Egypt's transit trade; and *rab's* (tenements or apartment buildings for the urban lower class).

The comparison with women in feudal Europe is helpful to our understanding of aristocratic Egyptian women, even though the two cases are not identical. One of the dissimilarities is that land tenure in Egypt did not endow the proprietor with judicial or military authority. But the world of eighteenth-century Egypt is similar to feudal Europe because, in both, households, or families, exercised power in the absence of a centralized state with well-defined institutions and a bureaucracy. In Egypt, such a state, the Ottoman, existed, but it became increasingly unable to exercise its authority, so that real power was wielded by beys like ʿAli Bey al-Kabir, Muhammad Bey Abu Dhahab, and their successors. Also, while the cases of medieval Europe and eighteenth-century Egypt are not identical, the historical evidence from both appears to indicate that upper-class women were much better off than in the succeeding periods of stronger, more centralized states. In both Europe and Egypt, in periods characterized by fragmented sovereignty and powerful households, aristocratic women had higher status, more autonomy, and greater influence than in succeeding periods characterized by the centralization of power and the development of institutions for the administration of the state.[3] Although historians are aware of the importance of the household and even though our overall knowledge of the eighteenth century has increased, we still know very little about the inner workings of the houses and households of the period. What we do not know about the eighteenth-century household can be organized around a series of questions: How do we distinguish between a house, a household, and a family? Who were the members of the household? What was the relationship among the male and female members of the household? And, finally, what was the role and position of women in the household?

Definitions

Should we make distinctions between a house *(bayt)*, a house as a residential structure, and a household? Relying on al-Jabarti, David Ayalon defined *bayt* as a group or faction whose members were linked by both Mamluk and family ties (1977, 291). Thus, *bayt* can be understood in the wider sense, as the Qazdughli *bayt*, for example, and in the

---

3. The evidence for a decline in women's status in the Middle East, including Egypt, is not as well-developed as for European women. Tucker (1985) has argued that the socioeconomic transformation of Egypt in the nineteenth century had a negative impact on peasant and lower-class urban women. Evidence for a similar decline in the position of upper-class women is still lacking.

narrower sense, as a group or faction within the *bayt,* such as the ʿAli-wiyya faction within the Qazdughli *bayt.* Ayalon also pointed out that al-Damurdashi and Nicolas Turc, used the word ʿila (colloquial for ʿaʾila, family) synonomously with *bayt* (Ayalon 1977, 297).

Therefore, *bayt* and ʿila have a fluidity of meaning that is not helpful or useful for an analysis of the Mamluk household. For the purposes of analysis and conceptualization, I suggest we attempt to make distinctions among the various components of the Mamluk system. Let us begin with the overarching entity, the *bayt,* as a sociopolitical concept and the basis upon which the system was organized and administered. Thus, we would describe as a *bayt* the Qasimiyya, the Faqariyya, and the Qazdughli. Within these houses *(buyut),* factions emerged such as the Iwaziyya and the Shanabiyya within the Qasimiyya or the ʿAliwiyya and the Muhammadiyya within the Qazdughli. We can follow al-Ja-barti's lead and refer to these factions or groups within a larger house as ʿashira (clan) or qabila (tribe).

Then, we are left with the most problematic of the concepts, the household. Here, it may be useful to begin with a comparison between the eighteenth-century Mamluk household and the British and French households of the same period. Jean-Louis Flandrin, in his book *Families in Former Times,* researched English and French dictionaries of the early modern period for the meaning of family that he found was synonymous with household. According to Flandrin, from the sixteenth to the eighteenth centuries, the concept of family was divided between the notions of coresidence and kinship, that is, a set of kinsfolk who did not live together as well as an assemblage of coresidents who were not necessarily linked by ties of blood or marriage (1979, 4). For example, Samuel Johnson's 1755 dictionary defined family as those who live in the same house and gave as a synonym, *household. Le Dictionnaire royal françoys et anglois* of Abel Boyer gave as the definition of *famille,* "all those who live in the same house, under the same head" and listed as English equivalents "family" and "household." The French *Dictionnaire de l'Academie* of 1694 defined *famille* as "Toutes les personnes qui vivent dans une même maison, sous un même chef" (Flandrin 1979, 4–5). As Flandrin has written, "It was still the case in the second half of the eighteenth century, both in France and England, and whatever the social milieu concerned, that the members of the family were held to include both the kinsfolk residing in the house and the domestic servants, in so far as they were all subject to the same head of the family" (1979, 5).

This meaning of the word *family* or *famille* emphasizes the notion of coresidence, so that a family or household is said to consist of all those living under the same roof. For British and French historians, one of the primary issues was whether the persons living under one roof considered themselves and were considered by society at large as a family. Flandrin suggests that this was indeed the case. We can perhaps agree that this was also the case in eighteenth-century Egypt because of the seeming interchangeability of the words *bayt* and *ʿila,* as suggested by the chronicles and according to the *Lexicon* of Edward Lane.

What is problematic for the Mamluk system, however, is the notion of coresidence, that is, whether a family or household consists of all those living under the same roof whether related by blood or not. I would argue that this is not an adequate definition of the Mamluk household because it does not include those persons linked to the master of the household by ties of clientage, marriage, or concubinage who were not coresidents with him. For example, al-Jabarti's obituary of Jalila Khatun, concubine of ʿAli Bey al-Kabir and wife of Murad Bey, related that ʿAli Bey built her a house at Azbakiyya (al-Jabarti 1967, 382). Does this mean she was no longer a member of ʿAli Bey's household? In another example, ʿAli Kathkuda Mustahfizan added to his *waqf* the house of his two wives, Zulaykha bint ʿAbd Allah al-Baydaʾ and Nafisa Khatun bint al-Baydaʾ al-Jirjiyya (Waqf no. 2407). Are these women no longer members of their husband's household because they have their own residence? We know that an *amir*'s dwelling had to be large enough to house his *mamluks,* particularly during times of strife, as well as the *amir*'s wife, children, and servants. For exmple, ʿal-Jabarti described the house of ʿAli Bey al-Hindi as vast and large enough to hold the *mamluks* and partisans of the beys who had been killed in a factional struggle.[4] However, an *amir*'s freedslave *(maʿtuq)* might have a residence of his own that he shared with a wife continuing to reside at times with his master *(ustadh)* or to work in his master's service in his residence. Did he cease to be a member of the *amir*'s household?

It appears that a Mamluk household encompassed more than those persons housed under one roof. Lane's definition of *ʿaʾila* is useful here: "a family or household; a man's *ʿaʾila* are the persons whom he feeds, nourishes, or sustains; or the persons who dwell with him, and whose expenses are incumbent on him, as his young man, or slave, his wife, and his young child" (1955, 2201). As a working definition of a household, I

---

4. Al-Jabarti, *ʿAjaʾib* 1:146; and *Merveilles Biographiques et Historiques ou Chroniques du Cheikh Abd el-Rahman el-Djabarti,* 1:157. In subsequent references, the Arabic edition is cited first.

would submit the following: all those linked to the head of the household through slavery, service, marriage, or blood; all those for whom the master has a financial responsibility or who are dependent on him for sustenance, but who do not necessarily reside with him.

In addition, the Mamluk household was hierarchical in structure, and the links between the master and the other members were always vertical. A new household formed from the parent household when a freedman *(ma'tuq)* established his own residence and purchased his own *mamluks*. Thus, the members of a household would include the master, his wife or wives, concubines, children or other relatives, *mamluks,* and freedmen are all linked to him by ties of clientage, and domestic servants.

The Ties That Bound:
Men and Women in the Mamluk Households

As noted above, the foundation of the Mamluk system was the household. It is our key to understanding the politics and society of the eighteenth century as well as the position and role of elite women. The household system was held together by personal ties and alliances both horizontal and vertical. For men, one of the most important of the horizontal links was that of *khushdashiyya,* the tie between comrades in servitude and manumission. The most important vertical link was that between the master and his *mamluks* that was maintained after their manumission (Ayalon 1977, 169). The sources, including the chronicles, travel literature, and the *Description de l'Égypte,* abound in descriptions of the deference and respect due to a master from his mamluks as well as the proper way to behave toward the master.

It is also clear from these sources that the Mamluk system in the eighteenth century was in fact a fictive kinship system in which descent was traced through the male line. For example, the word *akh* (brother) was used as a synonym for *khushdash* (Ayalon 1977, 172). A master/ patron referred to his mamluks as *awlad* (sons; s., *walad*) while his mamluks referred to him as *walid* (father). A man could refer to the *khushdashun* of his patron as his *a'mam* (uncles; s., *amm*) and the patron of his patron as *jadd* (grandfather). Earlier generations were regarded as the forefathers or ancestors *(aslaf)* of the present generation (Ayalon 1977, 285–86).

As *waqf* documents demonstrate, ruling-class men tended to use the institution of *waqf* to strengthen the cohesiveness of their households. One of the differences between the *waqfiyyat* of men and women is that women do not show the same concern for the solidarity of the *bayt* and the household that is exhibited in the men's *waqf*s. Some examples are the *waqf*s of Isma'il Katkhuda (Waqf no. 929); al-Amir Ibrahim al-Sinnari, the freed slave of Murad Bey (Waqf no. 937) and al-Amir 'Ali Katkhuda Mustahfizan (Waqf No. 2404). In each of these *waqf*s, the donor stipulated that any of his freed slaves (*'utaqa'*) who married outsiders *(ajanib)* would be penalized by the disinheriting of their children.

In the *waqf* of Ibrahim al-Sinnari, the stipulation is: "*idha tazaw-waj ahad min al-'utaqa' bi-ajnabi harij 'an al-'utiqa' wa-la dakhl*" (if any of the freed slaves marry a stranger from outside the (group) of freed slaves and not from inside). In his *waqf*, 'Ali Katkhuda Mustahfizan is careful to state that he is referring to both male and female freed slaves: "*kul rajul min 'utaqa' al-waqif al-mushahhar ilayhi tazawwaj bi-ajnabi-yya . . . wa-kul imra'a min ma'tuqat al-waqif . . . ilayhi tazawwaj bi-rajul ajnabi*" (any man among the freed slaves of the renowned donor who marries a foreign women . . . and any woman from among the freed women slaves who marries a foreign man).

Al-Amir 'Ali Katkhuda Mustahfizan makes a similar stipulation but only for his black women slaves who will be disinherited with their children if they marry an *ajnabi* and who, in any case, can inherit only half of what the white slaves, male and female, and black male slaves will receive. It should be noted here that this last stipulation is an unusual one among the eighteenth-century *waqfiyyat* that I read for this study. In every other *waqf* document, the donor is careful to stipulate that for the purposes of inheritance, no distinction should be made between male and female slaves or white and black slaves.

'Ali Katkhuda makes another stipulation in his *waqfiyya* that shows both his deference to his patron and his concern for the continuity of his *bayt*. Upon the death of all the beneficiaries of his *waqf*, 'Ali Katkhuda stipulated that the *waqf* should become part of the *waqf* of Salih Jalibi. Both 'Ali Katkhuda and his wife, Hanifa Qadin bint 'Abd Allah al-Bayda', were the freed slaves of Salih Jalibi. Upon the merger of the two *waqf*s, 'Ali Katkhuda wanted half of the income from his *waqf* to be used to buy slaves and weapons for the Mustahfizan and the Jawishan, with the money divided equally between the two corps. The *waqf* was dated 1178/1764.

Like men, women built their own patron/client networks through the purchase and manumission of slaves. Al-Jabarti's obituary of Jalila Khatun, the concubine *(suriyya)* of 'Ali Bey al-Kabir and the wife of Murad Bey said "most of the women of the *amir*s were among her protégés *(akthar nisa' al-umara' min jawariha)* (al-Jabarti 1967, 382)

The word *jawar* and its variants (e.g., sing. *jariyya*) are only used in connection with women and should be understood as the female equivalent of *mamluk* or *tabi'*, that is, as a slave who is manumitted and becomes a client of his/her patron. Like *mamluk,* the word *tabi'* is used to describe the relationship between men, not between men and women or women and women. Women are *ma'tuqa* or *jariyya.*

The *waqfiyyat* provide additional evidence that women built parallel patronage networks through the purchase and manumission of slaves. All of the women's *waqf*s I read for this study were *ahli,* or family *waqf*s. In their *waqfiyyat,* the donors listed the beneficiaries of the income of the *waqf* after the donor's death. The usual pattern was to designate children, other relatives, including husbands, and freed slaves, thus demonstrating that women did indeed purchase and manumit slaves of their own.

The *waqf* of Khadija Qadin bint 'Abd Allah, freed slave and wife of the Amir Ahmad Katkhuda of the Mustahfizan and the Qazdughli *bayt,* sheds a gread deal of light on the creation of these female networks as well as on the system of alliances as a whole (Waqf no. 1177). In her *waqfiyya,* Khadija stipulated as one of her conditions the following: The *nazir* (administrator) of her husband's *waqf* was empowered to go to Georgia and purchase a slave *(jariyya)* of Georgian nationality *(jirjiyyat al-jins)* who must be mature/adult *(rashida)* and proper in her religion and everyday concerns *(saliha li-dinha wa-dunyaha).* If she is found to be dishonorable, the *nazir* is ordered to sell her and buy another. If, on the other hand, she has the qualities mentioned above, he must manumit her and marry her. Again, if after the marriage, she is found to have a defect or shortcoming *(khalal),* he is ordered to drive her away and purchase another. The price of the slave *(thaman al-jariyya)* is specifically set aside for this purpose. The point of this stipulation is that the woman will become the *nazira* of Khadija's *waqf* after her death. What this remarkable story indicates is the importance of ethnicity and of marriage in the creation of solid bonds among the members of the household. In other words, becoming a member of a house and household was not enough to ensure loyalty and fidelity; the link was stronger if the patron and client shared the same ethnicity and stronger yet if there was the additonal tie of marriage.

The Political Economy of Mamluk Marriages

As we have already seen, the ties between men were often strengthened by the ties of marriage. Masters like Salih Jalibi often arranged marriages between their *mamluks* and their female slaves. Mamluks also married the daughters, sisters, and widows of their masters.

There are numerous examples of marriages between a mamluk and the female slave of the same master in the *waqfiyyat,* where names often constitute a genealogy of the donor. For example, the *waqfiyya* of Mahbuba names her this way: *"Al-Sitt Mahbuba Khatun bint ʿAbd Allah al-Baydaʾ maʿtuqat mawlana al-Amir Ibrahim Bey al-Kabir wa zawjat Ismaʿil Bey Kashif maʿtuq Ibrahim Bey al-Kabir;"* (The Lady Mahbuba Khatun daughter of Allah, the White, freed slave of the esteemed Amir Ibrahim Bey and wife of Ismaʿil Bey the freed slave of Ibrahim Bey) (Waqf no. 3131). Thus, Ibrahim Bey al-Kabir was the master of both Mahbuba and Ismaʿil and undoubtedly arranged the marriage between his two slaves. Another example, in this case of a widow marrying the former *mamluk* of her deceased husband, is Amnatullah bint ʿAbd Allah, the widow of ʿAbd al-Rahman al-Katkhuda, who married Muhammad Jawish, the freedman of her dead husband (Waqf no. 134).

The Mamluk system was a gendered system, that is, to be a *mamluk* meant to be a man. Thus, the question arises of whether women were considered members of the household in a political sense. In my opinion, the answer to that question should be in the affirmative because of the importance of marriages or extramarital sexual unions (concubinage) in strengthening the links between male members of the same household. In addition, elite women owned valuable income-producing property in Cairo and the provinces. Because in the Ottoman period, political power was based on the control of property and its revenues, ruling-class women have to be seen as having some political as well as economic power.

Women as owners of property were often the means by which property was transmitted from one member of a household to another and maintained in one household. When an *amir* died, it was customary for his successor to inherit not only his title but also his widow and the deceased's property. There are numerous examples of this in al-Jabarti, who remarked on the prevalence of this custom among the Qazdughlis particularly: "The mamluks of the Qazdughli *(bayt)* married their widows and established themselves in their houses" (al-Jabarti 1967, 1:114; 2:146). When a widow remarried, she brought to her new marriage not only the property she owned outright but also the property she inherited from her deceased husband and property she might control as the *nazira* of her deceased husband's *waqf.*

One example from Jabarti is of the Amir ʿAli Bey Zulfikar, who was the *mamluk* of Zulfikar Bey. During Zulfikar's lifetime, ʿAli Bey served as his master's treasurer. After Zulfikar's murder, ʿAli Bey inherited his master's rank, *sanjak bey*, and married his widow (al-Jabarti 1967, 2:46, 57). Another example is the intriguing case of Shawikar, the favorite concubine of one of the most powerful and wealthy men of the eighteenth century, ʿUthman Katkhuda al-Qazdughli. Al-Jabarti recounted that one of ʿUthman's followers, Sulayman Jawish, was his testamentary executor. After ʿUthman's death, Sulayman seized the entire estate and married Shawikar (al-Jabarti 1967, 2:57–58, 72–73). Sulayman died in A.H. 1151/1738 and 3–5 years later, Shawikar registered her *waqfiyya* in court, which included a dwelling *(manzil)* that was part of the *waqf* of ʿUthman Katkhuda (Waqf no. 921). At the time, Shawikar was the widow of the Amir Ibrahim Katkhuda Mustahfizan al-Qazdughli. There is no indication in the *waqfiyyat*s of either ʿUthman Katkhuda or Shawikar of how the property came into Shawikar's control. She may have acquired the property through her marriage to Sulayman or as one of the beneficiaries of ʿUthman's *waqf*. In either case, she was able to hold onto it until her own death and preserve it as an inheritance for her heirs. As P. M. Holt has pointed out:

> The tendency toward fragmentation and factionalism is even more marked in the neo-Mamluk households since each Mamluk generation in turn founded new households, which, although part of the parent-clan, were rivals for political power and the spoils of office. It was this above all that delayed the revival of the beylicate in the eighteenth century, and rendered its paramountcy, when once acquired, so unstable and precarious (Holt 1982, 144).

These centrifugal pressures on the Mamluk households, however, produced powerful centripetal forces at the same time. The tendency toward fragmentation was counteracted by consolidating measures such as marriages and sexual unions that strengthened the links between men. In addition, these unions served as a means of transmitting and preserving property within the same household and, even more importantly, of perpetuating the household from one generation to another. Holt and others have overlooked the importance of women and marriage in stabilizing an inherently unstable system and in perpetuating the Mamluk system from one generation to the next.

In the Circassian Mamluk system during the medieval period, freeborn Muslims could not inherit Mamluk status. The sons of the

Circassian sultans and *amirs* could not inherit their fathers's rank and title. In the eighteenth century, as Ayalon has noted, this began to change as the sons of *amirs* began to inherit their ruling-class status from their fathers. In each case, women were crucial elements in the system. Women provide the necessary continuity either through remarriage to their deceased husband's *mamluk* or *tabi*ᶜ or through the physical reproduction of sons and heirs. It seems clear from Jabarti and from the *waqfiyyat* that women were important in providing not only continuity but also legitimacy to the Mamluk system. It was not enough for a man to inherit or seize his master's property and assume his rank and position, he also apparently needed his master's widow to legitimize his actions. Thus, women and marriage served not only as conduits of property but also of power. For these reasons, we should no longer regard women as irrelevant and inconsequential to the reproduction of the Mamluk system, which has been conceptualized in the past as entirely male.

An extreme example of the role women played in the system is the widow of Muhammad Shalibi al-Sabunji,. whose house at Azbakiyya was seized after his death by Ibrahim Katkhuda al-Qazdughli. Ibrahim married Muhammad's widow to the treasurer, Mahmud Agha. When Mahmud died, Ibrahim married her to Husayn Agha, whom he named *kashif* of Mansura (al-Jabarti 1968, 2:116, 150).

In his study of the Mamluk system during the Ottoman period, Ayalon noted the phenomenon of the "open house" or *bayt maftuh*. This was the house belonging to a Mamluk *amir* who was the head of a powerful Mamluk faction that served as the focal point and center of activity for his family and supporters. Ayalon described the *bayt maftuh* as "the headquarters in which assemblies and meetings were held, schemes and conspiracies hatched, and from which orders for action were sent. . . . For the family it was the apple of the eye, for the enemy (or enemies) the main target for destruction" (Ayalon 1977, 293).

Thus, as Susan Staffa has pointed out, an *amir*'s followers, including slaves and freedmen, his family, and his residence, were inseparable.

> We can see that the frequent marriages between mamluks and the
> women of their patron's family did not merely symbolize and rein
> force the male bond, but also provided them with organized estab
> lishments, households to be the *foci* of their own clienteles and
> reinforcing female clienteles that provided another deeper level of
> support in the fabric of society. If a mamluk married the widow of
> his patron to keep the house open, he found a tremendous asset in
> the acquisition of an established power base (Staffa 1987, 80).

Thus, women were caught up willingly or unwillingly in the bloody internecine conflicts that characterized the eighteenth century. For example, in 1725, during a struggle between the Qasimites and the Faqarites, one of the Faqari leaders obtained a decree of exile against three prominent Qasimi women—Hanum, the daughter of Iwaz Bey; the mother of Mustafa Bey, one of the conspirators against the pasha, who was arrested and executed; and one of the concubines of ʿAli Bey (al-Jabarti, 1:163; 1:153.). The order so outraged ʿUthman Jawish al-Qazdughli that he persuaded the pasha to change the order to house arrest. In another incident later in the century as ʿAli Bey al-Kabir was rising to power, the wife of an exiled *amir* took up arms to defend herself and her husband. As al-Jabarti told the story, ʿAli Bey ordered ʿAbd al-Rahman, *agha* of the Mustahfizan, to put to death an officer named Ismaʿil Agha, who had been exiled to Lower Egypt but had returned to Cairo and was living in a house in the Saliba section of the city. Al-Jabarti reported that Ismaʿil was known for his bravery and celebrated for his courage.

> When he saw ʿAbd al-Rahman and his entourage in front of his house, he knew he had come to kill him, and he refused to show himself and closed the door of his house. ʿAbd al-Rahman began to shoot. Ismaʿil Agha had only a musket and a rifle and with him only his wife, a Turk. His wife fired one of the two guns while he used the other. The fight lasted two days. Many of the men of ʿAbd al-Rahman Agha fell, struck by Ismaʿil's bullets. Finally, he ceased firing on his enemies: his powder and his shot were gone. ʿAbd al-Rahman promised him safety. Having faith in this promise he descended the stairs but one of his enemies ambushed him there and ran him through with a saber. All the others then fell on Ismaʿil and decapitated him (al-Jabarti, 2:390; 3:14–15).

Given the importance of women and marriage to the reproduction of the Mamluk system, the question that arises is whether women could refuse marriage or remarriage. The weight of the evidence from al-Jabarti and other sources such as the *waqfiyyat* consulted for this study seem to suggest that women did not have much say in the matter. It should be noted, however, that women's status and power were linked to their membership in a household that would provide a strong incentive to marry and remarry. Crecelius has given one example of a woman who successfully refused an offer of marraige, Salun, one of the widows of ʿAli Bey al-Ghazzawi. Ismaʿil Agha, ʿAli Bey's brother, asked Salun to marry him; but she rejected him and entered another harim. She eventually married Isma'il, but only after the death of his first wife, Fatima, who was the daughter of Salun's former patron (1981,118).

Daily Life in the Harem

Unfortunately for historians of eighteenth-century Egypt, we do not have a woman traveler like Lady Mary Wortley Montagu, who not only was a guest in the *haramliks* (women's quarters) of Istanbul but also recorded her observations and impressions for posterity. As far as we know, Lady Mary was the only European, male or female, to visit the harems of the Middle East in the eighteenth century. Although male travel writers routinely wrote about upper-class women and their harems, they were forbidden to talk with the women or enter their homes, and so their observations could not have been firsthand. Lady Mary, whose view of Turkish women's lives is so different from the Orientalist view of male travel writers, commented on this phenomenon in a letter describing her visit to the baths at Adrianople:

> You will perhaps be surprised at an account so different from what you have been entertained with by the common voyage-writers who are very fond of speaking of what they don't know. It must be under a very particular character or on some extraordinary occasion when a Christian is admitted into the house of a man of quality, and their harems are always forbidden ground. Thus they can only speak of the outside, which makes no great appearance; and the women' s apartments are all built backward, removed from sight, and have no prospect than the garden, which is enclosed with very high walls (Peck 1988, 125–26).

Keeping Lady Mary's words in mind, Chabrol, in his essay in *Description de l'Egypte*, reveals important and interesting information about life in the *haramlik* Chabrol (1822, 361–526). Although filtered through an Orientalist prism, information about upper-class women and their harims from Chabrol or travel writers was based on their own observations—such as seeing women participating in public festivals or visiting the cemeteries on Friday—or from conversations—like Volney's with the wife of a merchant who sold cloth to the women of the harems and reported that Mamluk women were not beautiful (Volney 1799, 95–96).

Some of the information from Chabrol's essay, we know from other sources, such as that male children remain in the *haramlik* until puberty or that the *haramlik* was off-limits to men unrelated to the mistress of the household and that even a male relative could not enter when she was entertaining female friends. According to Chabrol, the only other men allowed access to the *haramlik* were the doctor and the mistress's secretary "which women of high rank ordinarily employed" (1822, 119). The secretary remained in a room next to the woman's apartment and communicated with her through an open door. The doctor was only permitted to see his patient in the presence of her female slaves and the eunuchs, and she never removed her veil.

As noted earlier, women created parallel patronage networks through the purchase and manumission of slaves. Based on Chabrol's information, it appears that personnel and staff in the women's households also paralled that of the men's (1822, 122). For example, the post of treasurer was the most important post and was occupied by the highest-ranking freed slave in both the men's and women's households. Next in rank and importance were the concierge, followed by the inspector of the kitchens, both of whom were freed slaves. A freeborn woman was employed as a steward, or chargée d'affaires. The men with the most access to the women's private apartments were the eunuchs. Indeed, their access was even greater than the master's because he could not enter the *haramlik* when the mistress was entertaining friends. According to Chabrol, the eunuchs occupied an apartment on the ground floor and served as the means of communication between the mistress and master of the household (1822, 122).

Wealthy women had baths in their own homes. Even though they may have gone to the baths to socialize, they also customarily invited a close friend or friends to bathe in their home. Thus, a woman might be away from her home for an afternoon or for several days at a time. Women also left their homes to visit their family and on ritualized occasions, like the birth of a friend's child. Chabrol described such a visit that took place on the seventh day after the birth: All the women who had been slaves of the mother come to visit her. They were received in the principal salon (*qaᶜa*) and served coffee and sorbets. After a quarter of an hour, the mistress appeared. All the women approached her and kissed her hand (1822, 125).

This visit among women appears similar to Savary's description of how men of status and women of the harem received their guests in their separate apartments (1785, 136–39). There was the same deference paid to the master as well as the mistress, the offer of food and drinks, the basin holding rose water for washing after the meal, and the burning of sweet-smelling wood to perfume the room. Among the women, at the end of a meal or as part of a celebration, the ʿalmas (Oriental dancers) were invited to dance, and sometimes the women themselves join the dance. Both Chabrol and Savary noted that the female dancers invited into the homes of upper-class women were of the "first order" of dancers, who were more refined and accomplished than the "second order" of dancers seen on the streets of the city (1822, 120; 1785, 155). Chabrol recognized that the freedom of women to leave their homes made it possible for them to have what he called "intrigues" or extramarital liaisons with the help of their slaves. He said, "They will appear to be going to the bath or on a visit but instead have a rendezvous." According to Chabrol, water carriers *(suqqaʾ)* played a principal role in almost all amorous intrigues, probably as message carriers between the parties (1822, 120).

Like Chabrol, Lady Mary recognized the possibilities that upper-class women had for extramarital affairs. Unlike Chabrol or the male travel writers, however, Lady Mary attributed this to the freedom of upper-class Turkish women. For example, Lady Mary thought veiling gave women sexual opportunities because "tis impossible for the most jealous husband to know his wife when he meets her, and no man dare either touch or follow a woman in the street. . . . This perpetual masquerade gives them entire liberty of following their inclination without danger of discovery" (Peck 1988, 111).

On the other hand, male travel writers considered veiling and the harem as examples of the extreme oppression of upper-class women and did not link the concept of freedom to Oriental women of any class. C. S. Sonnini, for example, described the women of the Mamluks as "perpetually recluse, or going out but seldom, and always with a veil, or, to speak more correctly, with a mask which entirely covers their face. . . . And for whom are so many charms thus carefully preserved: For one man alone; for a tyrant who holds them in captivity" (Sonnini 1972, 164).

Lady Mary, however, explicitly described Turkish women as free. "Upon the whole," she wrote, "I look upon Turkish women as the only free people in the Empire" (Peck 1988, 111). In another letter, she criticized a British travel writer and all his fellow voyage writers who, "lament the miserable confinement of the Turkish ladies who are (perhaps) freer than any ladies in the universe" (Peck 1988, 189). Lady Mary understood that one of the reasons why Turkish women enjoyed so much freedom was because they controlled their own finances.

Both Lady Mary and Chabrol agree that upper-class women did not engage in much purposeful activity and that they spent their time amusing themselves, buying clothes and jewels, and embroidering. Chabrol said that life in the harem was monotonous and that the women spent all their time reclining on soft pillows and attended by their slaves. To this idleness and inactivity, Chabrol attributed the fleshiness, or *embonpoint,* that he said characterized these women and that Turkish men allegedly admired (1822, 189).

In this regard, Lady Mary was being less perceptive than usual, although this may be because she only met women like the Sultana Hafisa on social occasions. But, considering that a harem woman might own considerable income-producing property, might also be the *nazira* of her own or others's *waqf*s, managed a household the size of a small hotel, and directed a corps of household staff and servants, as well as had social obligations in connection to her family and her patronage network, it would seem that *haramlik* women were very active indeed.

Although we are beginning to piece together information that can reveal to us details about the inner workings of the Mamluk households, the relationships between the members of the household still remain largely inaccessible. There are many mundane questions that remain to be answered: Did the mistress and master of the house take their meals together? Did they sleep together in the same room or did they retire to separate rooms in different parts of the house?[5] Moving from the mundane to the emotional, we can ask if Mamluk marriages were not only political unions but affectionate ones as well? And, were the ties between a master or mistress and their slaves and freedmen merely links that served the interests of power or were they also bonds of affection? About the latter, we know that the Mamluk system was a fictive kinship system. It is possible that if a man called his *khushdash,* "*akh*" (brother), or his mamluk, "*walad*" (son), he was expressing not only the hierarchy of the Mamluk system but also the ties of affection normally associated with these relationships. We also know from the *waqfiyyat* that men and women routinely named their male and female freed slaves as beneficiaries of their *waqf* along with their spouses and those to whom they were related by blood, such as their children, brothers, and sisters. We have only a smattering of details about the emotional and affectional component of the links that bound men and women together inside the Mamluk household, however.

5. Chabrol said that men and women did not dine with each other and slept in separate apartments (1822, 126).

In conclusion, the four questions posed at the beginning of this article demonstrate how little we know at the present time about the families and households of Ottoman Egypt. Because births and deaths were not recorded in the Islamic world until modern times, scholars of the Arab provinces during the Ottoman period probably will not be able to duplicate the kind of historical research and writing on marriage and the family that has been done by historians of premodern Europe. But if birth and death records do not exist separately, the *shari'a* court archives give us this information in other ways, through marriage contracts, child custody cases, inheritance records, and judicial inventories of the deceased. In addition, there are also the collections of *fatawi* (formal juridical opinions) and *waqfiyyat*, which contain important details about the families and households of the donors.

For example, the *waqf* documents cited in this article show the importance of ethnicity and marriage in linking the various members of the household to each other. The *waqf*s of ruling-class men show a concern for the solidarity of the *bayt* and the households that women's *waqf*s do not. Women's *waqf*s reveal that female aristocrats constructed parallel patronage networks the same way that men did, through the purchase and manumission of slaves. As for the relations between men and women, it can be argued that women carried weight in the aristocratic household because of the importance of marriage alliances to the Mamluk system, the patronage networks they created, and the property they owned and administered. Although we cannot yet answer the question posed in the title, we can interrogate old sources in new ways to enhance our understanding of the Ottoman family and household.

II

Drawing Boundaries and Defining Spaces

Women and Space in Ottoman Iraq

Dina Rizk Khouri

*I*t has perhaps become a truism to state that space communicates, that it has meaning. What is more contentious, however, is the issue of why and how a particular organization of space has meaning within a cultural and social context. Discussions of women and space have to contend with a number of problematics that touch on social constructions of boundaries and their interaction with gender. The most vexing of these revolves around the role of culture and ideology in ordering space and its use by women. To what extent does culture, broadly conceived as a set of meanings, shape the organization of space? Do certain cultures develop certain ideologies based on a clear distinction between a "core" male versus female experience? Finally, do such ideologies define hierarchies of space within each culture? (Agnew and Duncan 1989; Lawrence and Low 1990; Ardener 1981; Moore 1986; Bourdieu 1991; Giddens 1985).

Most readings on women and space in the Middle East start with the assumption that there is a clear distinction, articulated in an elaborate Islamic ideology on purity, between the public and the private. This distinction informs the injunction on veiling, of segregation of the sexes, the importance of cleanliness (read as nonmenstruating women) during fasting and praying, and the distribution of functions within the physical space of the household. Historians and anthropologists have tended to take two venues: Either they show how everyday practice by women challenges and defines this ideology or they bracket the issue of culture and ideology altogether and focus instead on the role of women in the reproduction of social and economic relations. (This is an oversimplification of quite complex and nuanced arguments (Friedl 1991; Julie Marcus 1992; Seni 1984).

These approaches tend to undermine the power and continuity of the Islamic traditional discourse as articulated by urban Islamic scholars. More often than not, and there are a number of exceptions, these scholars fail to contextualize the political and social meaning of such discourses. Talal Asad is one of the few anthropologists who have attempted to tackle the legacy of Islamic traditional discourse (Asad 1987). He neither brackets it, nor does he regard it as a body of traditions that is perpetually being challenged. Rather, he views these traditions as a living and continuously evolving "authoritative discourse" in a symbiotic relation with the political economies of their societies. According to Asad, the question that needs to be asked is, "How do particular social and economic conditions maintain or undermine given forms of authoritative discourse as systems?" (Asad 1979, 607). It is this question that I shall answer in this study of women and the transformation of space in eighteenth-and nineteenth-century Mosul. First, I will analyze discourses on boundaries in the work of two Mosuli scholars writing within the parameters of the "authoritative discourse," and second, I will compare these with the writings of two early twentieth-century Iraqi modernists. I will show that, although there were contending discourses on boundaries, as for example between certain Sufis and 'ulama' or between the khassa (elite) and the 'amma (general populace, citizens) the "authoritative discourse" had, until the end of the nineteenth century, an elasticity of meaning that allowed for a certain degree of co-option of the infraction by men and women who chose to cross these boundaries. This situation changed in the early twentieth century as two systems of discourses with different histories were juxtaposed. The discussion on boundaries became much less malleable when new cultural elites closely associated with certain modernization ideologies pit themselves against the upholders of the traditional discourse. In both contexts, the discussion on women and boundaries often expressed the concerns and interests of a social class or group within a specific historical moment.

The second part of the paper is based on a different set of documents. The religious endowments and court records of the city of Mosul in the eighteenth and nineteenth centuries allow us a glimpse of the actual division of public and domestic space and women's perceptions of such spaces. Women's concerns in these documents were to communicate their identity to outsiders and to hold their own within the household. In both cases, the constant variable, as we shall see, was class or social group.

Discourses on Boundaries

Mosul, the northern Iraqi city that provides the setting for the work of Yasin and Amin al-ᶜUmari, became part of the Ottoman Empire in the sixteenth century. By the eighteenth century, its politics had become dominated by households headed by the Jalili family. These households assigned themselves the task of reshaping the cultural and spatial landscape of the city (Kemp 1979; Rauf 1976; Khouri 1991). Culturally, they sought the support of the upper echelons of the ᶜulama᾽ by suppressing Shiᶜi practices and creating an educational apparatus and court culture that provided employment for this group. At the same time, they cultivated the economic support of the new Catholic Christian notability and a middle peasantry, thereby creating the potential of friction with established Sunni ᶜulama᾽. Moreover, they proceeded to develop a new spatial hierarchy that paralleled and contested the older one (al-Diwahji 1963). They built commercial and religious complexes away from the most populous and politicized quarter, its saints, and its shops. It is within this context that the work of Yasin and Amin al-ᶜUmari, brothers and scions of a Mosuli family of religious scholars, should be analyzed (Khouri 1991, 1992).

Al-Rawda al-fayha᾽ fi tawarikh al-nisa᾽, by Yasin al-ᶜUmari, is a biographical dictionary of women based on earlier compilations. What gives it specificity is the author's choice of material. Like a number of scholars before him, Yasin al-ᶜUmari opined on the merits and dangers of women. In this he echoed the popular Mosuli conceptions of women as reflected in the vernacular poetry and proverbs. They are temptresses, sometimes ruinous, often necessary for sexual pleasure and reproduction, and can bring men good fortune when they are virtuous (Al-ᶜUmari 1987, 78–80).

It is in his discussion of the issue of *khuruj* (literally exits), that al-ᶜUmari's work demonstrates a surprising ambivalence. He cites several opinions on the issue of veiling and seclusion. He draws distinct boundaries among women based on status and age. Citing a legal scholar, he argues that a free young woman should not expose her face, hands, or legs to an outsider *(ajnabi)*. Then he cites a dissenting opinion by another legist who believed that looking at the face of a foreign woman *(ajnabiyya)* was not prohibited *(haram)*, but it was discouraged in the absence of any need for it. He concludes by giving his opinion on the issue. Men and women should be separated, and women should not leave their houses even to visit the tombs of saints (Yasin al-Umari 1987, 81–82).

Having argued his point, al-ʿUmari proceeds to demonstrate through his discussions of the lives of women how seclusion was imposed on early Muslim women despite their objections. Umm Kulthum, ʿAli's daughter and wife of ʿUmar ibn al-Khattab, objected to being prohibited from going out. She was told by ʿUmar that she should be content being the wife of the Prince of the Believers. ʿAtiqa, wife of Zubair, was prevented from going out to the mosque to pray by her husband. When she objected by quoting the Prophet's saying, "do not prevent women from going to the mosque," Zubair disguised himself and pinched her while on her way to the mosque. ʿAtiqa then confined herself to the house. She is reported to have said that the absence of honorable people made her house look spacious enough for her. *"Kuntu akhruj waʾl-nasu nas, ama idha fasuda al-nas fa-bayti awsaʿu li."*

What is of interest in these arguments and narratives are the ambiguities surrounding the issue of seclusion and women's spaces. The method of argumentation presented is common enough: the citation of two different opinions and the declaration at the end of one's own without clear indication of the reasoning involved. But both opinions carry equal weight to the reader, and it is only the particular scholar who has decided on the issue of veiling and seclusion. The boundaries that are defined unambiguously here are those of status and age. Strictures do not apply to slaves and old women. At the same time, the definition of *ajnabi,* outsider, is quite ambiguous. Does it mean men and women outside one's extended kin, or men and women outside the *mahalle,* (town quarter) and one's own sect? This open-endedness in the definition of boundaries is a reflection, I think, of their being contestable and contested ones.

The narrative of women who resist seclusion reinforces this view. The women cited in the narrative were venerated and emulated women. Umm Kulthum was and still is regarded as a saint in the Islamic world. Eighteenth-century Mosul had a popular mausoleum erected over her alleged grave. Her example carried much weight to scholars of Mosul, who realized that ʿUmar ibn al-Khattab was well known for his temper and his belief in the imposition of strictures on women. When ʿAtiqa attempted to bolster her position by citing a *hadith* (prophetic tradition) of the Prophet, Zubair did not contest that but used subterfuge to ensure her seclusion. One is left wondering why Yasin al-ʿUmari would use this example to demonstrate the virtues of seclusion. The tension in the narrative between the prescription of the Prophet and the lustful desires of men does not seem to point to a definite resolution in favor of seclusion.

What is clear is that the traditional discourse on boundaries for women in eighteenth-century Mosul was by no means unambiguous. This difficulty in setting incontestable boundaries is also evident in the history of a mausoleum given by Yasin's brother, Amin al-ʿUmari (1968, 2:70–72). The mausoleum of the two sons of ʿAli, *imam*s Hamid and Mahmud, was built by the Atabeg princes in the twelfth century as a Shiʿi shrine. The shrine had fallen into disrepair, and the wife of the governor of Mosul had renovated the mausoleum, built a mosque, and endowed it with some books. A teacher of Shafiʿi law was assured a stipend.[1] What had been a decrepit mausoleum frequented by commoners and Sufis, was now a new edifice constructed by the funds of a new ruling elite. Amin al-ʿUmari was well aware of the implications of this transformation. The various anecdotes he offers in his narrative about the mausoleum appear to be a jumble of disconnected incidents in the form of free association. All the anecdotes center around boundaries that are being contested, however. These boundaries were between ʿamma and *khassa*, men and women, Shiʿis and Sunnis, Christians and Muslims.

Amin al-ʿUmari begins his narrative by attacking popular lore about the presence of the two *imam*s in Mosul. Commoners believed that the two sons of ʿAli had jumped in a well and died in order to avoid a tyrannical or unjust person *(zalim)*. Al-ʿUmari disputed this by simply stating that the sons of ʿAli could not have been so foolish. It is the ignorance of commoners that is at the basis of such views. This ignorance does not only cover matters of religion but other matters as well. Commoners believed that such ailments as sore throats were caused by the spirits of unmourned relatives. Al-ʿUmari then attacked the popular practices of commoners, both Shiʿi and Sunni, during the rituals of ʿashura³. At these ceremonies commemorating the death of Hussain in Karbala³, a number of boundaries were contested: women and men mixed freely and were allowed to express strong emotions, and Sunnis participated in what was a Shiʿi ritual. Boundaries were crossed between men and women, Sunnis and Shiʿis, and Christians and Muslims. Mosulis had introduced innovations *(bidaʿ)* because they were celebrating Lent and other Christian saints' days.

The works of both al-ʿUmaris reflect the views of members of the ʿulama³ establishment who were firmly tied to the Ottoman political system and were beneficiaries of the munificence of the current ruling

---

1. See *waqf* of Hamidayn mosque by ʿAisha Khatun, mother of Mahmud Pasha al-Jalili, governor of Mosul, dated 1212/1797 in *sijill waqfiyat muhafazat Ninawa*, Directorate of awqaf, Mosul, Iraq.

elite. Their concern with issues of women's seclusion is a reflection of their antipathy to the lower classes and minorities. Under the tutelage of the Jalilis, some Christian families had attained positions within the local government; and villages with a large Christian population had developed a class of middle peasants. Among this group, the popular belief was that the Jalilis had originally been Christians. This, they believed, explained their support of Christians in the city (Asmar 1844; Bazi 1969; Bahnam 1962).

The rise of Christian notables and middle peasants must have elicited the hostility of established *ʿulamaʾ* families, such as the al-ʿUmaris. Although the celebration of Christian holy days by Muslims might have been a pre-eighteenth-century ritual, it became problematic to the al-ʿUmaris because of the political and social visibility of Christians. Amin al-ʿUmari was quite happy to rescue the two imams from the clutches of the *ʿamma* and Shiʿis. At two places in the narrative he points to the service the Jalili household had rendered to orthodoxy first by building the mosque and then by outlawing the practice of *ʿashuraʾ*.

The al-ʿUmaris were more ambiguous in their views of women's use of public space. Amin al-ʿUmari decries the practices of the Rifaʿi Sufi order, which allowed women into their ritual practices. The presence of women in such circles distracted men from communion with God (al-ʿUmari, MS no. 12602, fols. 3, 8). It was more important that a clear distinction be maintained between commoners and, by extension, women of the lower classes and women of the urban middle classes. For this latter group, seclusion should be maintained.

The attitude of the *ʿulamaʾ* toward aristocratic women was somewhat different. In *Tawarikh an-nisaʾ*, Yasin al-ʿUmari groups women into a moral hierarchy. There were good, evil, and intelligent women. The last list was a short one but interesting because the author does not seem to know what moral judgment to pass on this group of women. As al-ʿUmari's biographies move away from the early Islamic period, there is a noticeable shift in the position of women. Beginning with the Abbasids, aristocratic women become part of the political machinations of the state. The issue of seclusion had been settled by then. Women ruled over extended households, controlled sons, and played a role in the appointment of high government functionaries. There was a clear convergence between household and state (Peirce 1993; Keddie and Baron 1991).

The formation of provincial ruling households, modeled loosely on the Ottoman imperial household, was a common phenomenon in provincial areas of the empire (Schilcher 1988; Meriwether 1981; Hatem 1985; Marsot 1979). Under the Jalilis, political power in Mosul became the prerogative of a number of households dominated by the ruling branch of the family. Within these households, women played an important role in cementing marriage alliances, brokering peace between different elite factions, mobilizing populations for war, and defining public spaces. Their visibility in public life might have inspired al-ᶜUmari to write a biographical dictionary of women.

The al-ᶜUmaris' views on social boundaries were shaped by a combination of the traditional discourse on such boundaries and the social and political realities of the eighteenth century. These boundaries were contested by the different groups; and the desire of the al-ᶜUmaris to impose certain restrictions applied to women, Christians, and commoners. Implicit in their texts is the belief that a different set of restrictions applied to women of different classes.

By the end of the nineteenth century and the beginning of the twentieth, a hybrid form of discourse on women and boundaries emerged in Iraq and the rest of the Middle East. Some of it co-opted parts of the traditional discourse but added new elements. The works of Jamil Sidqi al-Zahawi (1863–1936) and Maᶜruf al-Rasafi (1875–1945) are emblematic of this trend. Both are regarded among the earliest modernizers of Arabic poetry, and they were committed modernists with strong views on the social inequities of the old order. Al-Zahawi was educated as a legal scholar in Istanbul during the Hamidian era. He became closely associated with the ideas of the Ottoman Constitutionalists and was a vocal critic of Abdul Hamid's policies. Al-Rasafi was not grounded in the Islamic legal traditions but joined Zahawi in his support of the Constitutionalists. Like other Arab nationalists of the period, they became hostile to the Young Turk government after 1909 (Nadhmi 1984, 74–106; Lazim 1971, 105–56).

In 1910, while al-Zahawi was a teacher at the Baghdad law school, he published an article in a Cairo journal calling for women to discard the veil. His argument combined elements of the traditional discourse and some new ones. The anonymity that the veil provided to women, he argued, allowed them opportunities to betray their men. The veiling of women's identities made it easier for them to go anywhere they wanted to without being recognized. In addition, the isolation that veiled and secluded women felt lead them to form relationships with their servants *(ghilman)*. Nor was the veil a preserver of honor, as there were unveiled Bedouin women more honorable than veiled urban women.

Elsewhere, al-Zahawi would argue that there were no injunctions in the Qur³an on the veiling of women (Lazim 1971, 184).

Thus far, al-Zahawi had turned the ⁽ulama³s arguments against them. The premise for both groups of scholars was the same; women's sexuality had to be controlled. It was not seclusion and the veil that would allow for such control, however. In fact, the opposite was true. Veiling provided the opportunity for women to have more control over their sexuality. New elements were also included in al-Zahawi's article. The veil was synonymous with ignorance, and it was a travesty that half the human race should be ignorant. Women should be educated in order to function effectively within the family. Veiling and ignorance contributed to unhappiness in marriage. Marriages contracted between a woman's guardian and a prospective husband without her consent created miserable conjugal unions. In these two lines of argument, al-Zahawi developed what would, under the Iraqi monarchy, become a pronounced call for the radical transformation of women's roles in society.

There is a shift in the narrative from the control of women's sexuality in public spaces through veiling to women's role within the family. This was a crucial transformation in the literary discourse on women between the eighteenth and early twentieth centuries. The al-⁽Umaris were concerned with women's crossing the boundaries from "private" to "public" partly because this change would threaten the stability of the social and moral orders. The public was threatening to the morality of the family. Al-Zahawi and later al-Rasafi constructed the idea of motherhood as a sacred calling and component of citizenship of the modern state. In the early years of the monarchy, al-Zahawi and al-Rasafi would call for the eradication of the veil and desegregation of middle-class and elite women in the interest of building good citizens.

Both men constructed very clearly the ideal private domain as a space, a house made up of a nuclear family headed by a father and supported by an educated mother. They called for the opening up of this private domain to the state, which was the force capable of reforming it. Although for the al-⁽Umaris the private domain of the middle-class urbanites was to be shielded from the corrupt moral order of the public and the lower classes, for al-Zahawi and al-Rasafi, the private is identified as the sphere of oppression *(istibdad)* and *(zulm)* that should be penetrated by the public. Al-Rasafi uses the word *istibdad* to describe forced and unhappy marriages, and Zahawi uses the word *zulm* to describe marriages contracted without the consent of the women and without love. The use of the terminology is interesting. Both words were almost always used in reference to political, religious, or administrative (that is, public) oppression (Lazim 1971, 187–90).

Elite women, as portrayed in contemporary historical works and other documents of the period, functioned within extended political households that encompassed kin, servants, slaves, and, at times, outsiders. These households were social organizations that were successful in co-opting members of different classes. Al-Rasafi and al-Zahawi called for the transformation of these households to families. They wrote poetic narratives about oppressed women and groups within the household. Thus, al-Zahawi's narrative poem entitled "Suleima and Dijla" is concerned with the oppression of nonelite women within the extended household. The implicit remedy for such oppression, these poets believed, lay in the breakup of such households (Lazim 1971, 193).

The al-ʿUmaris', al-Zahawi's, and al-Rasafi's views on women and boundaries were, to a large extent, a reflection of the changed political and social order of the eighteenth and early twentieth centuries. They were men who belonged to the intellectual elites of their milieu and were intimately connected to the centers of political power at one point or the other. The al-ʿUmaris' main concerns were with the formation of elite political households in the eighteenth century. The attempts of these elite to form a hegemonic cultural discourse and practice was contested by various sectors within Mosuli society. The ambiguity of the al-ʿUmaris' position toward the crossing of boundaries between sects, genders, and classes was a result of their position within the new order. They were clearly in favor of the ruling elite's repressive policies toward Shiʿi rituals, concerned with the emergence of Christian notables and middle peasants, and anxious that their precarious and dependent position be maintained vis-à-vis the loose practices of commoners. Hence, their hostility to popular Sufi orders and women's freedom of movement became a way of drawing distinctions between them, the *khassa*, and others, the *ʿamma*.

Zahawi's earlier views on women presented a hybrid of old and new. In part, this was the result of his own background. Descendant of a respected *ʿulamaʾ* family who had been allied to the state, trained as an *ʿalim*, and raised in the conservative milieu of Baghdad, his view on women would be radicalized after World War I, as would his views on religion. After the formation of the monarchy, al-Rasafi and al-Zahawi became fervent proponents of the ideology of an intellectual elite that sought to liquidate or limit the power of influential households. This explains, at least in part, their attitude toward the older system of gender and social oppression.

I have chosen these discourses as archetypes of views on women and boundaries. They were by no means uncontested discourses. Throughout the eighteenth and nineteenth centuries, popular Sufi orders and public rituals were means by which women overlooked these restrictions (al-Lawand). Even within the limitations imposed by such strictures, there were women who were able to discard them altogether without creating opposition. For example, two women of the Jalili household participated in certain political events. Nineteenth-century Mosul had a woman scholar who taught men and was one of the proponents of the *salafi* movement. The woman in question had an *ijaza* (certificate) to teach and was a *mufti* (al-Mukhtar 1962, 2:65). Nor were al-Zahawi's and al-Rasafi's views widely accepted among groups of their political persuasion. Thus, the *mufti* of Mosul in the first decade of the twentieth century was pro-Ottoman, anti-British, and an Arab modernist. Yet, he wrote a book entitled, *Al-Jarathim Thalatha, al-ʿUmaraʾ waʾl-ʿUlamaʾ waʾl-Nisaʾ* (The Three Parasites: Princes, Ulama and Women) (al-Mukhtar 1962, 2:50–53).

It is important at this point to turn to an analysis of a different set of documents that deal with the actual division of space in the city and within the houshold in order to gain an understanding of how the discourses on boundaries intersected with different conceptions of space in eighteenth-and nineteenth-century Mosul. These are the *waqf* and religious court documents.

Women and the
Politics of Public and Private Spaces

For the elite women of eighteenth-century Mosul, members of the Jalili household, the investments they made in public building form defined them as members of extended political households. In this respect, their agenda and identities were intimately bound to those of their kin (Rapoport 1989, 6–35; Marcus 1989, 277–328). Like their male kin, they attempted to create new loci of population within the city. Two of these women built mosque/*madrasa* (school) complexes in areas outside the most populous and highly politicized quarters of the city. Thus Rabiʿa, sister of the governor of Mosul, built a mosque and *madrasa* complex adjacent to the quarter of her family's residence, on the edge of Bab al-Iraq quarter, which until the eighteenth century was the center of commercial and political activity in the city. The quarter became the Rabi'a quarter. 'Aisha, mother of another Jalili governor, built a mosque/*madrasa* over a derelict Shi'i mausoleum frequented by commoners both Shi'i and Sunni. It was built in the relatively underpopulated western section of the city in what was named the Mahmudayn quarter.[2]

Elite women's participation in the shaping of public spaces declined in the nineteenth century. There are a number of reasons why. The elimination of the political power of the households did away with the social and political incentive for these women to define themselves to outsiders as members of such households. The overall building drive by Mosuli elite declined in the second half of the nineteenth century.[3] In addition, legal reforms allowed these women to sell shares of their investments to outsiders, that is, to men and women outside the household. Whereas many of the stipulations of the eighteenth century *waqf*s of the Jalilis made it imperative that women marry within the household or that they sell their share to relatives in the event that they marry outside it, there were no such restrictions imposed in the late nineteenth-century endowments.[4]

Despite the fact that elite women shaped Mosuli public spaces, they were rarely identified with a specific space in the court records. They were described as daughters, wives, or mothers of certain heads of households. This identity was more important than their residence in a certain quarter or neighborhood. Like their male kin, their distinctiveness lay in their ability to represent the city as a whole and to transcend a particular locality within it.

Elite women carved their identities within the public spaces of Mosul in very tangible ways. Middle-class women did not communicate their distinctiveness as clearly. Their investments in public spaces were

2. See the *waqf* of the Hamidayn mosque mentioned above. For the Rabi'a *waqf*, see *waqfiyyat* Rab'a Khatun bint Isma'il Pasha, 1181/1767. The mosque was built in the Shihr Suq quarter. The area around the mosque eventually became known as the Rab'iyya quarter.

3. Of the more than forty endowments made by Jalili men and women in the eighteenth and nineteenth centuries, less than a quarter were made in the second half of the nineteenth, and these were mostly small endowments. About half were made by women.

4. See for example *waqfiyyat* Ahmad Pasha al-Jalili, 1233/1817, which stipulates that his female descendants marry within the Jalilis or forfeit their shares to a relative within the household. In addition, widowed Jalili women who married outside the household also lost their share. This is an obvious circumvention of *shari'a*, and it seems that many of these endowments were founded at least in part to circumvent Islamic inheritance laws.

minuscule compared to those of elite women. More often than not, they followed their male kin in their decisions to invest in certain quarters of the city and ceded the *tawliyya* of their endowments to male relatives.[5] Together with their men, they seem to have defined themselves to the court as residents of a quarter. The inviolability of the middle-class household was not as closely guarded as that of the elite, as middle-class women could marry and sell their property to outsiders. Outside the immediate family, identity was communicated through residence in a quarter.[6]

Within the quarter itself, however, markers of social hierarchies were not clearly drawn. *Ulama*' families, such as the al-ʿUmaris, lived alongside lower-class families. The great social divide within the quarter, the difference between the ʿamma and the *khassa,* was the seclusion of women in larger residences. As in the case of elite women, the drawing of boundaries in space, boundaries involving women, became the means by which different groups within Mosul's social hierarchy maintained their distinctiveness.

Communicating one's social standing was of paramount importance in defining gender hierarchies to outsiders. But in private residences, women sought to carve their domains within the household and family. The organization of space within the household was determined by class: it was more hierarchical and separate in elite households, less so in middle-class households, and not at all among the lower classes. Women tended to contest their position within the household in spatial terms; that is, through ownership of parts of the household, sometimes measured in arms lengths.

Gender hierarchies were most clearly defined in elite households. Elite residences were distinguished from middle-class residences by the existence of a third court, that of the *haram,* in addition to the inner and outer courts. Yet, by having a male guard at its entrance, the *haram* was equal in importance within the household to the outer court, traditionally

---

5. For example, Zaynab Khatun, of the wealthy merchant Chalabi family, owned small shares in properties dispersed over the commercial area of the city. She assigned the *tawliyya* to male relatives and bequeathed the rentals of the endowment to male descendants of her daughter. In the eventuality of the extinction of the male line, then the rentals should go the the female line. This is a formula that is very common in endowments instituted by merchant and *ulama*' families. See *waqfiyyat* Zaynab Khatun al-Sayyid Darwish, 1234/1818. See also *waqfiyyat* al-Haj Yahya bin Haj Abdal, 1139/1721.

6. For example, a court case would read, "When Maryam bint Ahmad from the residents of the Suq Saghir quarter died. . . ." See Sijill at Qasamat, 1268–1275/1851–1858, slide 5, case 1, Mahkama *Shariʿa* Records, Musul.

the domain of men, which had its own guard.[7] The presence of such guards seems to point to the crucial role that elite women played in the era dominated by the politics of households. Furthermore, the space of the *haram* was rarely divided among elite women in inheritance records and was never shared by male kin. Thus stricter definition of boundaries within such households meant more power within and outside the house.

For middle-class women, the spaces that remained inviolable domains within the house were named the *bayt*, (literally, the house). The *bayt* was the sleeping quarters of the individual women within the inner court of the house, which often included the kitchen and reception area *(iwan)*. Although the inner court was shared with male and female kin, the *bayt* was rarely divisible and appears to have been the only truly private space of the women and their children.[8] The domain of women within the household vanishes as one goes down the social ladder. For example, in houses costing less than 1,000 qurush, there were no rooms defined as women or men's spaces.[9] There was a *hawsh*, a court, and a subterranean room used for storage and refuge in the hot summer months.

For most urban Mosulis, one's residence constituted a large part of one's wealth. In addition to being a social marker, the residence was regarded as the space in which various members of the family held shares. These shares were often defined spatially. Thus, a document stated that a woman inherited from a husband parts of a house. These parts were: "Within the inner court, from the beginning of the large reception area *(iwan)* to the door of the kitchen excluding the outer court, and from the window of the stable contiguous to the outer court, to the corridor *(riwaq)* that is adjacent to the decrepit outer court."[10]

---

7. See, for example, the *waqf* of Ahmad Pasha al-Jalili, made in 1817 and mentioned above. Elite houses also had baths within the haram, further segregating elite women from middle-class and lower-class women. See also the *waqf* of Rabiʻa Khatun bint Ismaʻil Pasha al-Jalili mentioned above, in which the division of the house starts from the door to the haram to the outside court.

8. Of the ninety-four inheritance court cases I reviewed, approximately half dealt with division or sale of space. I did not come across a single case where the *bayt* was divided up between relatives or even sold seperately. The word *bayt* also denotes a residence *(bayt sukna)*, a tent *(bayt shaʾr)*, or a kitchen *(baytmattbakh)*.

9. A house in mahallat jamiʾ al-Kabir, worth 500 *qurush*, had a courtyard, a cupboard, and a room. Sijillat Qasamat, 1280/1863.

10. Sijillat Qasamat, 1275–1278/1858–1861. This is a complicated case that involved much litigation. The house, located in the district of Shaykh Abi Ali, was eventually divided by a court-appointed architect *(miʿmar)*.

Clearly, for the divisions to be at all meaningful, they must take for granted that the family unit should remain intact. Although entire residences were sold to outsiders, including Christians, very few shares within the house were ever sold to people outside the family. When actual divisions were added to the original structure (usually walls were constructed after two members of the family had a falling out), these were meant to assert one's identity within the household rather than to outsiders. In one case, a woman divided the space to make a new opening that would give her access into the street without having to go through the family's common space.[11] The spaces within the house were designed to define women's place in a hierarchy of age and gender within the household. They gave women a stake in the house and allowed them room to negotiate their position either through the threat of sale to outsiders or through the sale of their shares to members of the family more amenable to their needs. In this manner, private space became a contestable arena in which alliances were forged or broken within the family.

In conclusion, the eighteenth-century discourse on boundaries contained few facts, but truths and falsehoods sometimes juxtaposed within the same narrative. There were opinions and contending protagonists. Consensus was achieved only tenuously. The lines were drawn more clearly in the early twentieth century when Zahawi and Rasafi could marshal facts to support their views. There were the facts of "backwardness," "oppression," and "ignorance"—all grounded in arguments based on concepts of natural rights. Whether one analyzes eighteenth-or early twentieth-century discourses on boundaries, the views of different authors can only be understood within the specific context of their societies. The al-ʿUmarisʾ views built on a centuries-old discourse, an Islamic one; but their choice of material and their narrative reflected the concerns of their class, group, and city. Similarly, both al-Zahawi's and al-Rasafi's views derived from those of Egyptian modernists, such as Muhammad Abduh and Qassim Amin, yet they were firmly grounded in the specificities of the Iraqi situation.

These views on boundaries were ideological discourses, however. When one moves to an analysis of the actual use of space by women, one finds that these discourses converge with reality in certain aspects and diverge in others. In their use of public space and in their attempt

11. Sijillat Qasamat, 1280–1285/1863–1868, slide 23.

to communicate their identities to outsiders, women's paramount concern was to define themselves as members of a class, group, or quarter. But in their use of private spaces, it was more important for these women to assert their identities vis-à-vis hierarchies of age and gender within the household.

PART FOUR

Dhimmi *Communities and Family Law*

I2

Textual Differentiation in the Damascus *Sijill*

Religious Discrimination or Politics of Gender?

Najwa al-Qattan

T he status of *dhimmi*s (non-Muslims) and women in Muslim society are the focus of both Orientalist and feminist historiography of the Middle East. At the same time, these issues have inspired the most fervent apologetics in the field. The purpose of this article is to investigate the question of the relative status of *dhimmi*s and women in Ottoman Damascus through a critical reading of the *sijill* record of the Muslim *shariʿa* courts.[1] While in part intended as an assessment of the *sijill* as source for social history, I also question in this paper both the alleged primacy of sexual distinctions in the social arena and the meaning of, the criteria for, and the methodology behind questions of social status in an Ottoman setting.

The *Sijill* as Text

As the official register of the Muslim court in Damascus, the *sijill* represents a daily record of the legal life of Muslim, Christian, and Jewish men and women. Because of the accessibility of the court, as well as the variety of legal affairs transacted, notarized, and settled in it, the

1. This paper is based on material gathered from 150 volumes of the Damascus *sijill* record covering the period 1775–1865. Research was undertaken at Markaz al-Wathaʾiq al-Tarikhiyya in Damascus and Markaz al-Wathaʾiq wa al-Makhtutat at the University of Jordan in Amman. The Jordanian center's microfilm copies of the Damascus *sijill* do not, for the most part, show pagination. Research funding was provided by the Social Science Research Council.

sijill as a documentary source yields a wealth of information about the socioeconomic and sociolegal life of the population of Damascus.

The *sijill*'s documentary account of social life is, however, neither objective nor comprehensive. By its very nature as the record of an officially sanctioned legal institution, the *sijill*'s documented record is enframed both by the religiolegal discursive organization of Islamic law in its historically concrete context and by the demands that are institutionally imposed on it as a professional practice. Thus, the *sijill* represents a specific kind of text that partially articulates with the dominant religiopolitical context—in this instance that of Damascus as an Ottoman provincial capital—and at the same time, exhibits certain autonomous features whose forms are constrained by the genre of legal documentation and whose contents are the arbitrary and haphazard material of everyday life. Approached as a text, the *sijill*'s language and scribal practices constitute the material for a critical sociolinguistic analysis that, by investigating the court's sanctioned ability to generate and appropriate meaning in specific sociopolitical contexts, evinces and delineates its otherwise hidden logic of social stratification (Goodrich 1987, 142–45).

The textual approach to the *sijill* is particularly useful for investigating the status of *dhimmis* and women. Unlike the *shariᶜa* and the various legal literature connected with it, the *sijill* is not the overt instrument of ideology; at the same time, it differs from most contemporaneous eyewitness accounts because it has a clear connection to the official organs of the state. As a result of its quasi-official status, the *sijill* is both vulnerable and resistant to ideological saturation. Its contesting prerogatives highlight in textual form the often contradictory and ambiguous discourse of a legal institution that is called upon to administer justice and, at one and the same time, to discriminate.

According to the legal material found in the Damascus *sijill,* the daily affairs of the courts were guided by the *shariᶜa*, regardless of the social status, place of residence, gender, or religious affiliation of the individual who sought the court for the purpose of adjudication. Although cognizant of the methodological limitations involved in the use of court documents in order fully to determine the workings of the legal apparatus—and in the case of the Damascus documents, these limitations are exacerbated by the strict formulaic organization of the *sijill* document that precludes knowledge of out-of-court negotiations and of the execution of judgments pronounced therein—the material in the *sijill* indicates that the court was not the arena for the practice of extralegal or illegal discrimination, despite the *shariᶜa*'s theoretical discrimination against *dhimmis* and women. On the contrary, the strict adherence to the letter of the law often provided weaker individuals with legal protection against those who were tempted to use gender or religious affiliation to unfair advantage.[2]

As an institutionalized practice of the court, the *sijill* appears to be an Ottoman invention (Manna[c] 1986, 351–53). As a formalized practice, however, the *sijill* must be placed in the context of the law's ambivalence to written testimony. Because *shari[c]a* theory only allows oral evidence, the legal status of the *sijill* is tenuous. Nevertheless, even before the advent of the Ottoman Empire, the evidentiary use of written testimony had long been accepted in practice. As early as the ninth century, Hanafi jurists produced manuals intended to guide the writing process and to ensure strict adherence to the letter of the law. Because these manuals on the "science of stipulations" *([c]ilm al-shurut)* prescribed standardized forms for all legal documents, *sijill* documents—from marriage contracts to purchase and sale agreements, and from lawsuits to *iqrars* (the creation of legal obligations)—are strikingly formulaic and derivative in structure and repetitive in terminology (Wakin 1972, 4–14, 38; Tyan 1945).

The *sijill* as text partially organizes the random details of everyday socioeconomic life according to the legal categories of relevance and inclusion. It thus streamlines unique social interactions into standard formularies that impart to the *sijill* the appearance of a monotonous linguistic as well as visual landscape lacking color and detail. This leveling process is, however, not absolute. In their focused concern to approximate in written form the kind of security deemed legally acceptable only by oral transmission, the *shurut* specify—among other matters— that individuals must be identified as accurately as possible. The *sijill* thus provides a variety of biographical detail—*nisba* (genealogy), *laqab* (nickname), age, occupation, residence, present whereabouts, and others. Although it is true that the *shurut* authors differ on the best means of identification, all agree that "identity based on a number of objective facts can more readily be the subject of inquiry" (Wakin 1972, 50–51, 78). Carried over into the *sijill*, it is precisely the choice of indicators and the mode of their employment for purposes of identifica-

---

2. For example, when Mustafa, a Christian who had converted to Islam ten days earlier, sued his still Christian mother, Maryam bint Mikhail, for allegedly holding his share of the legacy left by his long-deceased father, strict adherence to the *shari[c]a* rules of evidence vindicated the defendant in spite of her religion and gender. (Damascus *Sijill*, 19 Jumada 1 1198/Mar. 1784, 707 [microfilm no. 217]). Moreover, the readiness with which women and *dhimmis* went to court suggests that it was perceived in a positive light.

tion that, at both the semantic and orthographic levels, break the relent-
less monochromatic appearance (both literally and figuratively) of the
Damascus registers and raises questions concerning the *sijill*'s understanding of what among the variety of social ascriptions constitutes an
"objective (and significant) fact."

The *Sijill* as Discriminating Text

Against this background of formal textual and legal neutrality, the
sijill as text identified *dhimmi* men and women by recourse to a variety
of semantic and orthographic devices that rendered their presence both
linguistically striking and visually conspicuous.

Christian and Jewish men who made their appearance in the *sijill*
were marked by a variety of indicators, including direct religious identification (*al-dhimmi; al-nasrani* [the Christian]; *al-yahudi* [the Jew]), the
use of *dhimmi*-specific titles (*al-mad'u* and *al-khawaja*), the use of *walad*
in place of *ibn* to specify the patronym, and the use of *al-halik* or *al-
mutawaffa* as opposed to the Muslim usage of *al-marhum* to indicate
"the deceased."

The subject of *dhimmi* markers is of a complexity that cannot be
justly managed within the spatial and thematic constraints of this study.
Several points, however, need to be emphasized. During the ninety-
year period under investigation, the Damascus *sijill* employed *dhimmi*-
specific markers with remarkable consistency. *Dhimmi* names were
marked in conspicuous and predictable ways in almost all cases. Second,
the *sijill*'s usages changed over time, but the change was again orderly
and consistent. In the earlier *sijill*s, for example, every single *dhimmi*
man was identified as "*al-dhimmi al-mad'u* (name) *walad al-mad'u*
(name)" and described as *al-halik,* when deceased. Beginning roughly
around 1840, however, *dhimmi* men were referred to as "*al-khawaja*
(name) *ibn al-khawaja* (name)"; the word *al-dhimmi* continued to be
used somewhat erratically, but *al-mutawaffa* replaced *al-halik* altogether. Thus, although the usages changed and need to be historically
charted, the *sijill*'s consistency in using *dhimmi*-specific markers was
such that every single *dhimmi* was marked in one way or another. Finally—and this point cannot be overemphasized—the suggestion that
terms such as *al-khawaja* or *walad* are *dhimmi*-specific, and hence discriminating in both senses of the word, has nothing to do with their
dictionary meanings. On the contrary, assuming with M. M. Bakhtin,
that no word is neutral, and that "[e]ach word tastes of the context and
contexts in which it has lived its socially charged life" (1981, 293), these
terms become subject to a *dhimmi*fication process that is both historical

(diachronic) as well as context-bound (synchronic). Furthermore, it is only on account of their sociohistorical signification that they are suggestive of the sociolegal world that produced them.[3]

What is perhaps the most telling aspect about these practices is the manner in which they articulate religious distinctions. *Dhimmi* identity is juxtaposed against what at first glance appears to be an unmarked identity: nowhere does the *sijill* specifically identify a Muslim man as "so-and-so the Muslim." Furthermore, although almost every *dhimmi* man's name is preceded by *al-madʿu* or *al-khawaja,* the majority of Muslim men bear no title at all.[4] Muslim identity is neither substantively indicated nor ever directly attributed. In contrast to conspicuously flagged *dhimmi* individuals,[5] the great majority of Muslims inhabit the body of the text by virtue of almost total semantic omission and silence.

Because in the articulation of religious distinctions the binary juxtaposition *dhimmi*/Muslim operated through highlighting and omission respectively, the unmarked (Muslim) was put forth as self-evidently neutral. Notwithstanding the apparent neutrality with which variety and difference are rendered, the *sijill* obliquely discriminated by counterposing them to a posited standard.

The use of marking devices within the *sijill* is akin to the operation

3. For example, *al-madʿu,* which literally means "he whose name is," appears in the Tripoli *sijill* of the seventeenth century as well, but is used to refer to Muslim men in the context of *"al-rajul al-madʿu* (name)" (al-Humsi 1986, 231, 343). In its Damascene usage, it carries the connotation of "the so-called"; in the Tripoli *sijill,* it signifies "the man who is called." Similarly, for *al-khawaja,* which in sixteenth-century Jerusalem was used in reference to large-scale merchants, both Muslim and Jewish (Amnon Cohen 1984, 113, 145, 184), but is only used as a *dhimmi* title in Damascus after the middle of the nineteenth century. For a detailed discussion of these practices, see al-Qattan, 1994. On the "pejoration" of words, see Schulz 1990, 134–147.

4. For a detailed discussion of Muslim titles, see Reilly 1987, 165. A survey of randomly selected *sijills* covering the period under review shows that the *sijill* contains a rich variety of rarely used Muslim titles numbering around forty. In addition to the titles that Reilly documents, the scribes indulged in long-winded titles of rhyming prose that at times took up three lines on the page. Although it is true that among the elevated titles and descriptions used, it is usually only one or two that meaningfully indicate status or function and that these were selectively employed, the sheer inventiveness and poetic energy invested in these titles stand in stark contrast to the simple poverty of *dhimmi* titles. For example, *"mufakhkhar al-amajid wa al-aʿyan hawi al-mahamid wa al-ʿurfan al-mutadarij ila rahmati rabihi al-mulla al-ʿallam al-haji . . ."* (Damascus *sijill,* 12 Jumada 1 1195/May 1781, 211 [microfilm no. 225]).

5. Although the *sijill* meticulously differentiated between members of the two faiths, it rarely spelled out the particular church or sect affiliations of the Jews and Christians, except in documents relating to the establishment of charitable *waqfs* in which the poor of a particular community (e.g., *saʿalik al-nasara al-yaʿqubiyya*) were specified as beneficiaries (Damascus *sijill,* 19 dhuʾl-Qaʿda 1221/Jan. 1807, 257:398/704).

of "natural" gendering in language that attributes the preponderance of
the so-called neutral male pronoun to natural language rules—a position
critiqued by feminist sociolinguistics, which questions the apparent neutrality of the preponderance and views it as the product of "cultural
discourses" that posit arbitrary and socially constructed distinctions as
natural and inevitable (Cameron 1985, 68–69).

The projection of "naturalized arbitrariness" (Bourdieu 1988, 164)
is particularly evident in connection with the *sijill*'s flagging of *dhimmi*
identity through orthography; that is, through the consistent misspelling
of a number of names whenever their bearers were *dhimmi* men. For
example, in names such as Yusuf, Musa, and Sulaiman, the scribes of
the court consistently replaced the letter *sin* with the letter *sad*. Because
these same names were "correctly" spelled whenever their bearers were
Muslim men, the orthography of *dhimmi* names illuminates the logic of
the *sijill*'s semantic distinctions: it created not a *dhimmi* variation on,
but a conspicuously faulty version of, shared names. The various seman-
tically constructed oppositions in the *sijill* operated by juxtaposing one
assumed or explicit Muslim linguistic unit against another, which became *dhimmi*-specific by virtue of this very juxtaposition. To maintain
difference through opposition in a field where no clear opposition was
available, the misspelling of names represented the process whereby
the "opposite" had to be generated. Although this distinction-through-
orthography is unique among the linguistic distinctions operating in the
Damascus *sijill* in that it resorted to a process that was at once creative
and corrupting in its relationship to language, it serves to highlight the
most crucial aspect of all the distinctions played out in the text, mainly
their artificiality and arbitrariness (al-Qattan 1994).

The Damascus *sijill* identified *dhimmi* women in ways that paralleled the identification of *dhimmi* men. As far as direct identification was
concerned, the *sijill* employed the same means: variations on *dhimmi*,
"Christian," and "Jewish" were employed throughout; and throughout,
the *sijill* regularly affixed the grammatically correct female endings.
Hence *al-dhimmiyya, al-nasraniyya, al-yahudiyya,* and others, were used
in the same manner as their male counterparts.

As far as titles were concerned, *dhimmi* women received the title
of *al-madʿuwwa,* in contrast to the common Muslim *al-hurma* in almost
every instance in the early period of this study. In addition, the deceased
among *dhimmi* women were also identified as *al-halika* and *al-mutawafiyya* in a manner paralleling usages associated with *dhimmi* men.

Unlike Muslim women whose names were often followed by the
respectful title *al-marʾa al-kamila* (pl. *al-niswa al-kumul*), *dhimmi*

women only received this title by virtue of scribal carelessness. Of the approximately fifty *dhimmi* instances of this usage in the Damascus *sijill,* the majority were crossed out. The scribe, having from force of habit penned the title, often stopped to correct his error, and in the process underscored the exclusively Muslim extent of its usage. As a result, the Damascus *sijill* exhibits a specifically feminine visual marking device. Unlike the visual orthography of male names in which "errors" were deliberately committed, however, the crossing out of *al-kamila* represented deliberate attempts to correct real mistakes.[6]

Two particular documents vividly illustrate the workings of this process: in a document dated October 1846, a recent convert to Islam is described as "al-*hurma* Zeina *al-mutasharifa bi-din al-Islam* bint ʿAbdu, *al-marʾa al-kamila*"; in contrast, another document dated July 1864 referred to a Christian woman as "Fatin bint *al-khawaja* Butrus *al-marʾa al-kamila al-ʿisawiyya.*" Only in the second document was *al-kamila* crossed out.[7]

In addition to *al-hurma* and *al-marʾa al-kamila,* the *sijill* referred to Muslim women by using a number of special titles and epithets such as *qadin, al-sayyida, al-masuna,* which were at times differently combined. Although these titles were not as common as *al-hurma* and *al-marʾa al-kamila,* they were never used to refer to *dhimmi* women.

Christian and Jewish female names present a somewhat more complex picture in the *sijill.* Although there were several *dhimmi*-specific names, such as Helena and Katrin for Christian women, and Rifqa and Maziltub for Jewish women, the most popular names among *dhimmi* women—Maryam, Warda, and Qamar—were also widespread among their Muslim counterparts. These names were not misspelled.

The scarcity of religious names among *dhimmi* women was noted by S. D. Goitein, who speculated that the absence of biblical names

6. See, for example, Damascus *sijill,* Safar 1195, 211 (microfilm no. 209); Damascus, 20 Jumada I 1199, 217 (film 193); Damascus, 21 dhuʾl-Qaʿda 1199, 123:102 (film 222); Damascus, 17 dhuʾ-Hijja 1221, 257:348/610; Damascus, 11 dhuʾ-Qaʿda 1227, 275:230/310; Damascus, 3 Rajab 1236, 298 (film 191); Damascus, 11 dhuʾl-Qaʿda 1248, 326:103 (film 201); Damascus, 12 RabiʿI 1253, 346:165/307; Damascus, 15 dhuʾl-Hijja 1257, 369:9 (film 200) and Damascus, 8 Safar 1281, 556:107/150.

7. Damascus *sijill,* 10 dhuʾl-Qaʿda 1263, 400:152/222 and 8 Safar 1281, 556:159/150. This self-editing illustrates "the problem of erasure" that the act of writing introduces (Goody 1986, 134). Once it is written down, the erroneous *al-kamila* may no longer be regarded as a "slip of the tongue"; the written text gives it a dimension of reality that reflects on and enhances the distinction between *dhimmi* and Muslim women even as the text corrects itself.

among the Jewish women of Egypt and Yemen had its roots in an ancient taboo that radically split the world of women from the "Hebrew book culture of the men." Goitein has also remarked that the most popular names among women—Jewish and Muslim—referred to concepts of ruling, victory, and nobility, an act which he interpreted as a female voice of protest against an oppressive male order (Goitein 1978, 3:314–18). In the Damascus documents, however, a similar protest appears to be oriented against the prejudice that only Muslim women have elevated titles: scattered in the *sijill* is a small number of *dhimmi* women whose given names were *qadin* and Sayyida.

To summarize, the text of the Damascus *sijill* presents an ordering of social categories through an interplay of semantics and orthography that consistently and conspicuously marks *dhimmi* individuals against a linguistically formulaic and visually level background in which Muslim identity is projected as neutral. This Muslim-*dhimmi* distinction infected and overrode all other ascriptions and affiliations, including those relating to gender. This is not to say that religious and gender distinctions were the only ones operative in the *sijill*. Textual markers were used to indicate occupational status as well as rural origin, for example. Nevertheless, the *sijill* as text manifests a clear preoccupation with distinctions that focus primarily on religious affiliation and only secondarily on gender identity.

Dhimmis, Women, and Boundaries

Parallels between the status of *dhimmi*s and women is often found in the general literature on Islam and the Middle East. Bernard Lewis, for example, argues that the disadvantaged position of women and *dhimmi*s is rooted in the *shariᶜa,* and he singles out the role of the Muslim idea of justice that, in assigning non-Muslims a definite place in the social order, occasioned their persecution (Lewis 1984, 8–10, 53). This notion of a carefully maintained social balance—a balance that invites upheaval when upset—is a popular construct in the literature about Islam and women (Sanders 1991, 74–76), and has been on occasion even echoed by non-Muslim observers as well (Mishaqa 1860, 35; 1988, 244).

Parallels between the status of *dhimmi*s and women are not confined to boundaries drawn in the imagined space of ideal social orders and textual discourses. They also become manifest in the concrete regulations that demarcate public space. Until the early nineteenth century, for example, the *dhimmi*s of Damascus were periodically subjected to the discriminatory practice of the *taruq*. Referring to depressions that ran down the middle of intramural streets and functioned as gutters and animal lanes, the *taruq*s were occasionally designated for *dhimmi* use in order to make way for Muslims (Hanna 1985, 251, 272). This *dhimmi*-oriented demarcation of public space has gendered variations that transcend the private/public division that dominates the discussion of space and the *hijab* (veil) in the literature about women. A particularly revealing example is mentioned in Huda Lutfi's analysis of a fourteenth-century text whose author argued that: "A woman should go out only for a necessity. . . . If women walk in the streets, they should walk close to the walls of houses in order to make way for men" (Lutfi 1991, 102–3).

The concrete organization of public space according to both *dhimmi* and gender-oriented categories parallels sartorial regulations that carve up public space, not in geometric ways, but by demarcating differences according to the visual code displayed in attire. Moreover, as visual codes, sartorial regulations have affinities with the orthographic code that conspicuously highlighted *dhimmi* names in the Damascus *sijill*. In addition, because sartorial regulations, like the organization of public space, are designed to humiliate, they also create, concretize, and display difference.

That social (and even cosmic) disorder resides in the transgression of boundaries is, of course, an idea that can be traced back to antiquity. The examples cited above are not intended to argue for a uniquely Muslim architecture of boundary, nor are they meant to show that, in the Damascene order, women and *dhimmi*s were identical victims of urban Muslim male domination. What they do suggest, however, is that the logic of gender distinction is not unique to gender, and that the articulation of difference, which takes place in textual representations, the organization of public space, and the rules of dress, employs identical categories.

Some Methodological Considerations

Given the elasticity with which the logic of distinction operates in the two arenas, it is then not surprising that the usefulness of the feminist methodology for understanding *dhimmi*-specific issues may be extended beyond the sociolinguistic critique discussed above and brought to bear on the analysis of *dhimmi* as a social and political category.

Gender has been presented as the central axis in the articulation of power. Joan Wallach Scott, for example, argues that a critical reading of cultural representations reveals that sexual difference is a primary way of expressing differentiation, creating meaning, and representing power. Although acknowledging that other distinctions served similar purposes, she proposes that gender has played a central role in articulating power in both the Judeo-Christian and Muslim traditions (Scott 1988, 44–45).

Similar critical readings of cultural productions have been, however, repeatedly challenged by those who regard sexual difference not as a social construction but as rooted in the natural order (Scott 1988, 60). The essentially ideological practice of grounding political and social hierarchies in nature—a practice in which religion or science is usually called upon to supply the most powerful arguments—is not, however, unique to gender distinctions. The veridicality of all social distinction—whether religious, sexual, racial or even economic—depends upon the transformation of arbitrary (socially constructed) difference into natural difference. This transformation, and its implications for the social order, need not be acknowledged. To do so would detract from its "givenness."

It is then not surprising that studies focusing on gender and *dhimmi* histories of the Middle East have attempted to explain the givenness of the status of women and non-Muslims via a parallel methodological focus that views the *shariʿa* as the *Urquell* of order. The status of both groups is thus explained by reference to an immutable system whose conceptual-religious categories hardened into impermeable social and political boundaries everywhere. This approach is problematic, as this essay has shown.

A second and related issue may be called the myth-versus-reality debate. Gender historians, for example, cite the difference between the cultural representation of women and the actual organization of gender relations and gendered social activity (Ortner and Whitehead 1981, 10). A similar issue concerns historians of *dhimmi* communities of the Middle East. Unlike gender historians, however, these latter researchers are further hampered by the utopian/dystopian extremes that mythologize *dhimmi* status (Mark R. Cohen 1991). Historians who debate this issue usually counterpose theory and practice, ideology versus the "hard facts" of social life. In both cases, a distinction is made between texts that need to be unmasked and exposed and historical "facts" that speak for themselves.

But facts do not speak for themselves. Neither do they represent concrete images of abstract distinctions distilled in categorical legal systems. Like the texts in which they arrive, facts are embedded in concrete social contexts. The historian pursuing objective realities in transparent texts only stumbles upon social contexts, which, like the language of texts that transmit them, are complex, multidimensional, and subject to stratification. Indeed, suggesting that the very distinction between texts and contexts is problematic, the historian Dominick LaCapra has argued that a text is "a site on which contesting and contested discourses . . . engage one another as sociolinguistic forces" (LaCapra 1982, 49–50; LaCapra 1983, 312).

Because of its semiofficial character and an internal logic that straddles the uncontested ideological projections of meaning as well as the contextual and contestory arena of everyday life, the *sijill* reliably mirrors a broader cultural representation of power. Approached as a complex site, the text of the Damascus *sijill* projects an order that is neither simple nor transparent. Because it is subject to the competing demands of the law, the exactions of written documentation, the prerogatives of an urban political administration, and the practical requirements of everyday life, the *sijill* allows the contestory voices of *dhimmi*s and women to break the monotony of the legal landscape, to articulate textual difference, and to suggest in bold strokes the outline of a stratification system in which religion rather than gender carved out the main cleavages of difference and of power. Nevertheless, this outline stands in need of the delineating and detailed contents of socioeconomic and legal life, which are the material of the *sijill* (and other sources) once it is interrogated as a document instead of a text.

The useful application of gender methodology with reference to *dhimmi* linguistic, social, and political questions presents us with a conundrum: while the substitution of religion for gender underscores the social origins of the latter and the absurdity of viewing it as rooted in the natural order, the elasticity of the methodological categories of the feminist critique indicates that gender is but one of several possible centers around which overlapping fields of social and textual cleavages find definition. In this context, questions of status would benefit from theoretically anchored orientations; that is, from a rigorously applied historical approach that permits the determination of relative status and from the employment of categories that translate meaningfully across distinct social arenas. Such categories, like Bourdieu's notion of capital, would enable the historian to represent the social world as a complex space in which status becomes the function of the individual's access to power—religious, sexual, economic, or cultural "capital"—in a process that is always historical and concrete (Bourdieu, 1991, 229–30).

This call for a return to considerations that transcend *shariᶜa* exegesis and categorical imperatives imposed by feminist agendas and communal politics signifies nothing less—or more for that matter—than a return to an integrated social historiography of the Middle East.

13

Reflections on the Personal Laws of Egyptian Copts

Mohamed Afifi

*A*t the beginning of the Muslim era, Islamic influences began to play an important role in Coptic personal law. That was not an easy matter because there were many barriers and problems that needed to be overcome. Heading these problems was the sharp distinction between the theoretical foundations that form the basis of Muslim and Coptic personal laws. Because marriage is the core of personal laws, it is important to illustrate the clear distinctions separating marriage practices of Egyptian Copts from Egyptian Muslims.

Marriage in Coptic Christianity is a holy sacrament and closely tied to other religious rituals. Coptic marriage is based on the principle of "one body," or the Christian belief in the eternal unity of husband and wife. The apostle Paul compared the unity of Christ and the church to unity through marriage and described both as holy secrets of Christianity (Shenouda III 1985, 43).

From this idea comes the distinctiveness of Christian marriages as a bodily function unbreakable by divorce. Christianity does not accept the contractual theory of marriage that allows one of its parties, whether husband or wife, to break it. It follows that Coptic Christianity does not recognize divorce. The church bases this on Christ's words, delivered at the "Sermon on the Mount": "whoever divorces his wife, except through the weakness of adultery *(zina)*, makes her an adulteress, and whoever marries a divorced woman, is an adulterer *(zani).*"

The Coptic Church does allow divorce for particular and special reasons. Here there is a difference between *talaq* (direct divorce) and *tatliq*. *Talaq* happens in according to the direct wish of one of the married couple. As for *tatliq*, it is an indirect divorce according to the wish of the husband or the wife but through the auspices of the church.

Furthermore, Christianity does not recognize polygamy given the holy nature of marriage. A Christian man can have only one wife, who does not have to share her man with another woman. If we suppose that a Christian man married another woman, then the church considers such a marriage to be *zina* and will recognize only the first wife. Christianity also forbids sexual relations with women slaves, considering it *zina* that destroys the holiness of marriage. Thus, we can see how different are the very principles of marriage in Christianity and Islam. It is also no surprise that historically the Coptic community was continually faced with problems and crises because of the Muslim influences that have trickled into Coptic traditions of "personal law." These problems gained significance particularly as the Copts, once a majority in Egypt, became a minority within a larger Islamic community.

Shariʿa (Islamic law) court records dating from the Ottoman period suggest an important phenomenon regarding Coptic marriages because Copts—and Jews—recorded their marriages in front of Muslim *qadis* (judges). Studying this phenomenon is significant because of its contradiction with the nature of Coptic marriage as a holy sacrament celebrated by a priest in church. There is no indication that Coptic marriages recorded in *shariʿa* courts were first celebrated and registered in church and then recorded in *shariʿa* court records.

The issue is more complex than this, however, particularly because marriages recorded by *shariʿa* courts followed the Islamic *shariʿa*. This is because Islamic *fiqh* (juridical interpretations by Muslim clergy) requires a *qadi* to apply the Islamic *shariʿa* according to his particular *madhhab* (creed or school of law) in all cases taken before him, including those by non-Muslims. That is why some Coptic marriage contracts recorded in *shariʿa* courts indicate that the parties concerned accepted that their marriage be in accordance to Muslim law notwithstanding the fact of their being Copts: "[Marriage was enacted] after the aforementioned wife indicated her acceptance of the laws of Muslims to this [marriage] in accordance to the *kitab* (Qurʾan) and Sunna (prophetic traditions)" (Misr al-Qadima, Sijillat 978/1573, 94:209–1000; al-Bab al-ʿAli, Sijillat, 69:43–208). Thus, Coptic marriage contracts recorded in *shariʿa* courts were in clear violation of Christian rites.

It is difficult to justify the phenomenon of Christian marriage registrations in *shariʿa* courts on the basis that the Islamic *shariʿa* is more functional or precise than the Christian *shariʿa*. There are many legal methods for the organization of marriage in the Christian *shari^ca* that were followed by the Copts (Cairo, Coptic Patriarchy, manuscripts 26 & 55); and even though Christianity is a religion of *tabatul* (piety, asceticism), it encourages marriage. The famous medieval traveler, the Catholic priest Father Gonzalez, provided us with what may be an acceptable explanation to the phenomenon of registering Coptic marriages in *shari^ca* courts. According to him, Copts resorted to the Muslim *qadi* to marry them so that they could divorce later. Gonzales also adds that some Catholic foreigners who lived in Egypt also divorced in front of the *qadi*.

The Islamic *shari^ca* defines marriage as a contract between two parties. As a contract, a marriage gives either side the right to add certain conditions that become binding on the other once he/she has accepted them. Interestingly, we find that special conditions were also added in marriage contracts of Copts recorded in *shari^ca* courts. A typical example is that of an early seventeenth century Coptic husband who agreed to the following conditions included in the marriage contract by his wife:

> if he were to take another wife, whether he contracted the marriage by himself or through his *wakil* (deputy); if he were to leave her for thirty consecutive days or more without any *nafaqa* (financial support) and no legal provider; if he were to beat her excessively in anger, leaving traces on her body . . . [furthermore] if he were to take her away from Egypt and travel to another land without the approval of her family; if she can prove that this or any part of it has happened and agrees to release him from a quarter dinar of her delayed alimony *(sadaq)*, then she would be considered divorced one divorce with which she owned herself (al-Bab al-^cAli, sijillat 1009/1600, 6:43–208).

It should be noted that this is the exact same language used by the courts in regard to conditions set out by wives in Muslim marriages (see Abdal-Rehim 1974: al-Barmashiya 994/1589, 707:113–711).

Thus, some Copts made use of the nature of the marriage contract according the Islamic *shari^ca*, even though they were breaking the very basis of Christian marriage, which completely rejects the principle of marriage as a contract between two parties as contrary to Christian teachings that understand marriage in a legal form and as a sacrament and eternal tie between two parties.

At any rate, Coptic marriages contracted in *shari^ca* courts indicate that most social classes of the Coptic community resorted to this practice.

There are *shariʿa* marriage contracts concerning highly placed Coptic financial officials who constituted the Coptic economic and commercial elite. There are also contracts involving goldsmiths, merchants, and craftsmen—weavers, carpenters, and others (Bab al-Shaʿiriyya, Sijillat 1054/1643, 673:105–307; al-Salihiyya al-Nijmiyya, Sijillat 483:304–1228 and 442:169–620). This matter does not allow us to conclude however, that the Copts actually abandoned their *shariʿa* and *tuqus* (rituals) and adopted the Islamic *shariʿa*. Thus, even though these marriage contracts represented most social classes of the Coptic community, they did not involve all Copts and did not even form most Coptic marriages. Still, they formed a very serious challenge to the church's authority and its control over the Coptic community.

To conclude this point, a very important and sensitive issue needs emphasizing that has to do with mixed marriages between Copts and Muslims, which by their very nature constituted a cause of conflict. Bishop *(usquf)* Isthorus (n.d., 455–56) informs us that one of the sixteenth-century Coptic martyrs was Mar Girgis al-Muzahim, whose father was the Muslim *shaykh* Jamiʿ al-ʿutwi and his mother, a Coptic woman. According to the Muslim *shariʿa,* the child of a Muslim man from a *dhimmi* (non-Muslim) woman is considered a Muslim. Mar Girgis al-Muzahim denied Islam and embraced Christianity, however, Here the different outlook of Islam and Christianity toward his situation became apparent. Muslims considered him a *kafir* (apostate) and the laws of *ridda* (apostasy) were applied to him. As for Copts, they considered him a martyr deserving of the wreaths of *shahada* (martyrdom).

One result of the Copts' turning toward the Islamic *shariʿa* was the creation of new conditions within the Coptic family. For example, Ibrahim ibn ʿAbdallah converted to Islam but his Christian wife, ʿAzza bint Salib, remained married to him. This was possible because the Muslim *shariʿa* allowed the marriage of a Muslim man and a Christian woman. Therefore, the Christian wife of a convert to Islam could remain married to him (Pope Shenouda III 1985, 210; Salama, 210). In contrast, Christianity considered a spouse whose husband/wife became a proselyte to Islam, as having the right to divorce. But because this contradicted the Islamic *shariʿa,* the church's law could be disregarded by those Copts wishing to be divorced.

Shariʿa Divorce among Copts

As mentioned above, divorce was one of the Muslim practices resorted to by Copts during the Ottoman period. Because the Coptic

Church allowed *tatliq* but prohibited *talaq,* those wishing for *talaq* resorted to the Muslim *qadi,* who was responsible to render justice to anyone who asked for it, including minorities. Thus, *shariᶜa* court records contain many divorces between Coptic husbands and wives who wished to divorce their spouses. It should be mentioned, however, that the practice of divorce among Copts was not an innovation of the Ottoman period but could be traced back to hundreds of years before that. Coptic sources trace back to the seventh century A.D., according to Coptic sources (ibn al-Muqafaᶜ, n.d., 132). These sources—as well as Muslim ones—do not give us any specific details, however. In contrast, *shariᶜa* court records dating from the Ottoman period give us archival information of great value regarding this matter. Thus, *shariᶜa* court records show us that all strata of Coptic society practiced divorce in various forms acceptable to the Muslim *shariᶜa*. And so there are recorded cases of "first divorces," "second divorces," and *baᵓin* (permanent, nonrevocable) divorces. Furthermore, certain Copts used their right to "take back" *(radd)* of a divorced wife (Bab al-ᶜAli, Sijillat, 4:54–345; and Qisma ᶜArabiyya, Sijillat, 130:41–64).

Divorce left clear influences on the Coptic family as a whole. Included in the sample used in this essay is one divorce case between cousins, four cases of families with infants, two cases involving pregnant women, a divorce before the marriage is consummated *(dukhla),* a case of a family with a daughter, and ten cases where no children are mentioned. Clearly, divorce caused dislocations within these families in a community that did not make allowances for such events. Because the Muslim *shariᶜa* was applied in these divorces, laws requiring husbands to pay divorce and child alimony, as well as the special alimony for suckling an infant, were part of the divorce decrees given by the *qadi,* and hence were beneficial to women.

One should be cautious not to exaggerate the practice of divorce by Copts or allow it to give the impression that Coptic traditions were being destroyed under the influence of Islam. Such a conclusion is not supported by Egypt's history. At the same time, we should not undermine the significance of these divorce cases; for not only were they widely spread among various tiers of Coptic society for long periods of time but they also contradicted the Coptic *shariᶜa,* and the challenge they paused to the church's authority led it to fight back. Hence, Pope Morcos VIII's decree against "those who commit sins and divorce their wives without cause." (Coptic Patriarchy, Pope Morcos VIII, 345:990113). This shows us the extent to which the Coptic Church was aware of the potential danger to its community from this social phenomenon.

Copts were not the only Christians to be divorced by a *qadi* in a Muslim *shari*^c*a* court. Other religious minorities did also. The records contain many divorce cases among Armenians, one divorce case involving a Venetian husband and a Coptic wife, a divorce between a Roman Orthodox man and a Coptic woman, besides frequent divorces between Jews (al-Bab al-^cAli, 313:76–197; al-Salihiyya al-Nijmiyya, 445:102– 268 and 484:51–269, 270). The impact of Islamic traditions on the Coptic community illusrates how the life of minorities can be effected by that of majorities. This is not to say that self-interest is not an important factor as a stimulus for borrowing traditions from another religious group. There is no question that self-interest was at the base of the Copt's resort to divorce and marriage rules among Muslims; and after all, Copts took from the *shari*^c*a* what suited their needs without accepting the *shari*^c*a* itself. Still, that dynamics of change involving the meeting of different cultural and religious traditions cannot be undermined because of the existence of self-interest, as the following discussion on polygamy shows.

The Struggle Against Polygamy

The impact of Islam on marriage and divorce extended to the very important and serious issue of polygamy, which is unequivocally proscribed by the church. *Shari*^c*a* court records (particularly inheritance records) contain many examples of polygamy committed in particular by highly placed Coptic and Jewish government officials and merchants (Shahr ^cAqari, Dasht, 151:3) most probably in imitation of their Muslim peers.

Perhaps polygamy, more than any other gender issue, left an important impact on the Coptic community during the Ottoman period. As a result of polygamy among Copts, their community was split among those who championed the practice and searched for an ideological basis outside of the Islamic *shari*^c*a* to legitimize it, and those who were absolutly opposed to it. This confrontation caused an innovation among Copts. The archbishop of Dumyat announced to the Coptic community that according to the "old" traditions of the church, Christianity could never have proscribed polygamy. His words caused people to question why the "new" age forbade polygamy if the "old" age had allowed it, and the practitioners of polygamy found intellectual backing in their confrontation with the official position of the church banning polygamy. The result was a critical rift suffered by the church until the seventeenth century. This rift became particularly menacing when the archbishop went on to proclaim his position through sermons that served his point of view. To end the breach, the church first used gentle persuasion to bring him back to the doctrine of the church. When this did not work, the pope excommunicated and dismissed him from the church.

The affair did not end there. Rather, things became more complex as the partisans of polygamy asked the state to dismiss the pope because he forbade polygamy, which they insisted, was allowable by Christianity. Because Islam allowed polygamy, the state supported the partisans of polygamy, particularly because most were high government officials who were closely associated with Egypt's rulers. Thus, the state proceeded to oust Pope Morcos V and sent him into exile to a desert monastery. The partisans of polygamy then chose a priest who approved of the practice and made him the new pope. This event was crucial for Coptic history; there were two popes simultaneously, one chosen by the community of Copts, the other selected by the state.

Thus, polygamy caused a serious rupture within the Coptic community and an actual division within the church that lasted as long as the state supported it. When a new governor was installed in Egypt, and the supporters of polygamy lost their close connections with the administration, the "state" pope was forced out of office. Pope Morcos V's return to the papal chair signaled the end of the most important split experienced by the Coptic Church during the Ottoman period. Needless to say, this rift left painful reminders concerning the unity of the church (Afifi, forthcoming).

One can also attribute diversion (*al-tasari*) with slave women by Copts to Islamic influences. Again, it was among wealthy Copts who imitated their Muslim peers that the custom became most prevalent. The church objected strongly to this practice owing to its contradiction to Christian marriage. Although the Coptic Church considered sexual relations with slaves a form of *zina* (fornication), Islam recognized and organized such relationships. Consequently, the church spent great efforts to fight this custom and stop its expansion among Copts. These efforts were only partially successful; large numbers of Copts continued the custom and did not give due attention to the church's wishes in this matter.

According to one account, when Pope John XV visited the town of Abnub in Upper Egypt, he stayed as a guest in the home of one of its rich Coptic citizens. There he discovered that his host was in *tasari* relations with slave women, and so he reprimanded him publicly, thereby shaming him among his fellow townsmen. Feeling the sting of the pope's public humiliation of him, the rich host laced the pope's food with poison. Soon after leaving the town that day, the pope died (Afifi,

1992), thus becoming a victim and martyr for standing up for Christian teachings and the principles of the Coptic Church.

The Church, the State, and Modern Law

With the beginning of the nineteenth century and the spread of modernization in various aspects of social life, it was natural that the Coptic Church would enter into a phase involving great changes that allowed it to play a larger role in the affairs of the Coptic community. The winds of modernization that were shaking Egypt throughout the nineteenth and the first half of the twentieth century, included a debate over the question of personal laws for both Muslims and Copts. This question was to take different dimensions and have new significance. Perhaps the most important question pertaining to personal status law during the modern period is the Coptic Church's reaffirmation of its prohibition of *talaq* and its narrower limitation of *tatliq* to very special and specific circumstances.

There are many divorce cases of Copts that illustrate the gravity of this issue. In 1915, the wife of a Coptic spendthrift sued to have her husband placed under *"hajr"* (declare legally incompetent) for his wasteful depletion of the family's fortune. To get away from this problem the husband converted to Islam to be able to divorce his wife according to the Islamic *shariᶜa*. Once divorced, the wife had no further right to place a *hajr* over him, and the case could be dismissed. This incident caused a public outcry because the husband's conversion was unquestionably motivated by personal reasons and not by any religious beliefs. In short, his actions were a form of religious opportunism (*al-Sufur,* June 25, 1915).

If certain Copts converted to Islam so as to gain the legal ability to divorce their wives, others found no such need but rather turned to Islamic *shariᶜa* courts demanding divorce as Copts earlier did. The Coptic press was enraged in 1952 by the story of a man who asked the *shariᶜa* court of Fayum to divorce him from his wife, even though their marriage had been celebrated in accordance to the Coptic *shariᶜa*. The Fayum *shariᶜa* court agreed to grant the man his divorce, but the Coptic press launched a vicious attack on the court and described its actions as a deliberate attempt to destroy the Coptic family and to force Copts to convert to Islam. The Coptic press also demanded that the state intervene in this matter to protect the Coptic family from this destruction (*al-Manara al-Misriyya,* Jan. 14, 1952).

This demand for state interference into Coptic personal status laws was not limited to the enemies of divorce. The champions of divorce had earlier asked the state to intervene as their champions against the fundamentalism of the Coptic Church and its prohibition of divorce. In a 1941 report to King Faruq, a Coptic man complained about priests and religious leaders who permitted divorce for those who were able to pay large bribes. As for the poor, their reqeusts for permission to divorce were not even looked at, notwithstanding how valid the grounds upon which they based their petitions. Coptic champions of divorce were angered by such actions, which they claimed were performed not only by priests, but also by the Coptic Majlis al-Milli (sectarian council), whose responsibilities included supervising Coptic personal status laws. These champions demanded the official intervention of the state to enforce the right to divorce for Copts "in accordance to Islamic law." More importantly, the report also proposed that the Majlis al-Milli be terminated and replaced by a new organization similar to the Islamic *shari'a* courts (Qasr 'Abdin, Taqrir Mar. 22, 1941, no. 45).

At the same time, some Coptic journals condemned the supervisory role played by the church in the organization of personal status laws and raised suspicions concerning the treatment of divorce by the church, repeating the stories of bribery and corruption. Some complained in particular of the influential role played by the patriarchate's lawyer, who was authorized to issue fast decisions of divorce in exchange for large sums of money.

The matter did not end with slandering the patriarchate's lawyer, but it touched upon the church's elders. Thus, the journal *al-Manar*, which lead the opposition to the church, reported that a priest divorced a man past the age of seventy from his wife, then proceeded to marry him to a young girl. The divorce decree in this case was never sent to the Majlis al-Milli to be approved, but as the journal reported, the priest kept the casefile hidden with him. The journal considered that such an act by the priest exposed him to prosecution according to Egypt's criminal law and should nullify the second marriage and make any children born of it illegitimate. It also pointed out that the action taken was in itself proof of the weakness of the Majlis al-Milli and the lack of respect for its laws (*al-Manara al-Misriyya* 1952).

As for the state, in 1946 it tried to change the personal status laws for Copts from within a comprehensive plan for a general reorganization of all personal status laws in Egypt, including Coptic ones. Without focusing on the legal content of this new orientation, what is important here is the response of the Coptic community to this matter. Simply put, the royal palace received a flood of telegrams from all over Egypt expressing a steadfast opposition to the proposed reforms. The leaders of the opposition to this reform were from a younger generation of Copts who were to become the future religious and secular leaders of the Coptic community. They included Wahib ʿAttallah, Saʿd ʿAziz, and Sulayman Nisim.

Owing to the sharpness of the language used in the telegrams and their expression of the anger felt by the Copts regarding the state's interference with what they considered to be a communal matter, it is important to discuss some of the specific points of opposition that these missives contained. Generally speaking, opposition to reform of Coptic personal status laws was mainly caused by what was conceived as a threat to the very principles of the Coptic faith and community: "It is an attack on the very basis of faith and a trickling wound to our religious honor that will assist in the destruction of our family structure." To stop the retraction of personal status laws from the hands of the church by the state, the missives describe the reforms as "touching upon the core of our faith and the Church dogma to which our hearts are bound." They also asked the king to interfere against the government to put an end to these new laws: "They entreat the benevolence of His Royal Majesty to work toward preventing the proclamation of this law in deference to the pride and feelings of the Coptic people who are loyal to the throne" (Qasr ʿAbdin, Dec. 20, 1946, no. 545; telegram, Dec. 30, 1946; telegram, Dec. 31, 1946).

These events became ever more urgent owing to the increased number of marriages between Copts and Muslims that occurred because of modernization and secularism. This problem became particularly serious in Upper Egypt, where the relative number of Copts was higher and where religious partisanship is mixed with honor and shame. An example of the crisis that evolved from mixed marriages exemplifies the problem. In the monastery of Deir Mawwas in Upper Egypt, a sixty-year-old Muslim man, a cousin of *shaykh al-ghufaraʾ* (chief of government appointed guards) of that area, married a Christian girl without her family's consent. Her parents wrote to the royal palace in Cairo complaining that their daughter was a *qasir* (minor) and that, to marry her, the man falsified the certificate determining her age so that the law would allow the marriage without consulting her family. Other details included in the complaint inform us that the man took the girl to Assiut, where he forced her to declare her conversion to Islam, after which he married her with the false certificate. He then took her back to his home, thereby causing a veritable crisis in the village. The two sides to the case then exchanged threats and assassination attempts. Although the village Muslims stood

behind the man, the village Christians, of all denominations, supported
the girl's family. At the same time, Christian leaders, of all denominations, took it upon themselves to make the authorities fully aware of the
situation. The leaders of the Catholic Church, American Presbyterian
Church, the American Church of God, the Reformed Church, the Angli-
can Church, and the Evangelical Church, sent a joint telegram to the
royal *diwan* (office) demanding that the king do something about the
incident, which they described as "an offence to Christianity and Christians." As men of the Christian religion with the "responsibility to protect
the integrity of our Christian flock, we voice our utmost outrage, implor-
ing swift intervention before a catastrophe happens."

Socially prominent Copts joined religious dignitaries in expressing
their outrage and concern by sending telegrams explaining their vexa-
tion at having become a community "in a sorry and despised state. Even
though we are citizens in our own country, protected by a constitution
which guarantees the freedom of religion, worship, and equality, we are
really enslaved as though we are still in the age of vassalage and bond-
age" (Qasr ʿAbdin, Iltimasat, no. 545).

We can conclude from this situation how distressed the Copts were
toward the infractions of their personal status law and the state's lack of
action in regard to such a sensitive issue. The incident and the reaction
to it also show how politically vocal the Coptic community could be, even
though such political activism was uncharacteristic of them. Perhaps the
sensitive nature of the subject and the issue of honor in Upper Egypt,
caused the smoldering of Coptic feelings in this case. Most important,
the incident illustrated how consolidated the community had become
with the growing role of the state in its efforts to control and determine
the shape of personal and gender laws. Clearly, this was an encroachment that Copts felt constituted a serious step toward their liquidation
as a separate entity with control over their own communal laws.

It should be stressed, however, that not all mixed marriages were
a cause of anger among Copts or that such marriages were unequivocally
acceptable to Muslims. Sometimes, the marriage of a Muslim man and
a Coptic woman led to protests by Muslim public opinion. In 1949, for
example, there was a great outcry caused by the marriage of a Muslim
man who agreed to have his daughters from a Christian wife baptized in
church. The Muslim public saw this as an insult to Islam, besides its
contradiction to the *shariʿa*. The case was taken to the *shariʿa* court by
citizens who charged the father with the crime of *ridda* and *kufr* (infidelity, atheism). The man was tried, and the court passed the judgment of
ridda on him. The court also decreed that the girls were Muslims and

could not be converted to Christianity. Needless to say, the decision angered the Christian community, who declared the *shariʿa* court decision to be an unfair bias in favor of Islam at the price of Christianity (*al-Manara al-Misriyya*, Aug. 8, 1949).

If this was the case in the "liberal age," the question of the personal status law for Copts was opened one more time during the "revolutionary age" following 1952. Notwithstanding the honeymoon between church and state and the special relationship between Nasser and Pope Kereles, the question of the personal status law raised its head one more time from within the framework of the state's policies that aimed toward controlling all Egyptians through a nationalist discourse that intentionally undermined the role of the religious question in national goals.

From here begins the apprehension Copts have had concerning the organization of personal status laws. In answer to this anxiety, in 1958 Pope Shenouda—who was only a priest at the time—began writing his famous book *The Shariʿa of One Wife,* in which he discusses divorce and polygamy, emphasizing the necessity of respecting Christian teachings and the authority of the church as the organizer of Coptic personal status laws.

During the rule of Anwar Sadat, and as part of the important role played by his wife, Gehan Sadat, in reforming the personal status law, the Coptic question was broached. Sadat's plan aimed at giving a Western touch to personal status laws and thereby granting Egyptian women more rights. Although the state did succeed in these efforts as far as the Muslim community was concerned—at least temporarily—notwithstanding strong opposition by conservative Muslims, the state failed in achieving any success on the Coptic side owing to the intensified Coptic resistance lead by Pope Shenouda, who published an expanded version of his book to which he added a new introduction. The book was an immediate success, six editions of it selling out in a few years. Add to this the fact that the state was worried about the impact of Coptic demands that the rights of minorities be respected, and the impression that such demands might have on the Egyptian government's efforts to present Egypt as a picture of democracy to the eyes of the Western world, a picture that Sadat had been cultivating with great care. Thus, the state did not accomplish much in regard to reforming Coptic personal law. This illustrates how problematic this issue is and how hard it is to establish uniform laws that can deal with Egypt as a whole. And so legal policies in regard to personal status continue to follow sectarian lines, as they have since the Ottoman period. As for a unified code, that is not a likely alternative in the future.

The issue of personal status has been one of the most complex issues for Copts over the centuries. There are many reasons for this, some ideological and religious, such as the different points of view vis-à-vis the "old" ways versus the "new" ways discussed earlier. Other reasons are historical, such as the struggle between the clergy and the secularists over the administration of personal status laws. Still other reasons are sociohistorical, such as the Coptic community's transformation from the majority to a minority within a larger Islamic majority. In this context, the infiltration of Islamic cultural practices had a deep impact on Coptic gender and personal relations. Add to this the political reason because the question of personal status is part of the struggle of church and state, whether state intervention was directed toward the support of leading Coptic secularists against the supervision of the church over personal status concerns or during another stage when the national state intervened to extend and secure its own power over legislation. Thus, personal status as an issue proved to be a basic cause for the lack of trust that has marked the relationship between the Coptic Church and the state.

Add to the reasons given above the element of modernity, especially the association of Copts with Europeans and Westerners in general. The growth of personal freedoms in the Christian West was not paralleled by any such movements among Egypt's Copts. The pressures of westernization on the Coptic community has lead to a greater conservatism among its members and a more zealous upholding of its cultural and family norms. This trend increased with the rise in Islamic fundamentalism. The social, economic, and political causes encouraging the appearance of Islamic fundamentalism played a similar role in the rise of fundamentalism among the Copts. At the same time, the stronger the Islamic brand of fundamentalism, the more defensive and fundamentalist the Copts became in a clear reaction to what they considered a threat to their very existence as a community. This meant that any development in Coptic personal status laws will be very slow in coming; after all any attack on these laws has become synonymous to an attack on the Coptic faith in the eyes of the church.

As the Copts have witnessed the modernization of daily life in Egypt, the question of status has been frozen. Daily events related to personal status in the Coptic community provide evidence to the consistent difficulties that Copts face in the most detailed and intimate aspects of their daily life, without the availability of expedient solutions to them.

As for the church, it too faces great difficulties in trying to balance the issues of modernity and tradition, particularly because its own structure is a fundamentalist one. As for Coptic intellectuals and secularists, who are those best placed to lead Egypt as a whole toward a solution to the clash between the religious and the secular but who have been faced with sectarianism and discrimination directed at them by the Muslim majority, they have found themselves becoming closer to the church and hence have lost their historical role.

In closing, the importance of personal status laws for both Copts and Muslims is an issue that cannot be stressed enough. Looking into it has been delayed long enough, it is in need of review and the application of strong and courageous measures.

PART FIVE

Children and Family Law

14

The Rights of Children and the Responsibilities of Women

Women as Wasis in Ottoman Aleppo, 1770–1840

Margaret L. Meriwether

Over the last fifteen years our knowledge of Middle Eastern women's lives in the past has grown by leaps and bounds. Yet, greater knowledge has only underscored the complexity of the questions we ask about those women. How to interpret the evidence and to understand what it means for the realities of women's lives remains problematic. One difficult, but very critical, interpretative issue is the relative importance of cultural ideals in shaping women's lives. Two important studies, although acknowledging that cultural ideals were often not realized in practice, argue strongly for their importance in shaping the environment in which women lived and therefore the options available to them. Deniz Kandiyoti has called the patrilocally extended household the "key to the reproduction of classic patriarchy . . . there is little doubt that it represented a powerful cultural ideal" (1992, 31). Leila Ahmed has argued that "ideals, even though undercut by economic and functional exigencies, are nevertheless an important and influential component of the systems of meaning determining the psychosocial experiences of both women and men" (1992, 27). Cultural ideals about women were articulated most clearly in Islamic law and were embedded in a concept of the patriarchal and patrilineal family. Although women were guaranteed certain rights and the authority of men was not absolute, male power was given legitimacy by the patriarchal bias of the law and other ideals and institutions that reinforced it.

Yet, the question of just how great an impact these ideals had on women's lives remains. Did the demographic, social, and economic realities of everyday life effectively curtail the power of men and offset the constraints imposed by cultural ideals? Did they therefore leave women room to exercise the rights available to them and have some autonomy and control over their own lives? One key to assessing the relative importance of cultural ideals and social realities is to see how cultural ideals as embedded in the law were put into practice through the interpretation and application of these laws by the courts. Did the judges apply the law in a manner that not only affirmed the rights of women as defined by law but gave some teeth to these rights, or did these rights do little to alter the subordinate position of women within the society? Studies of women and property have shown that the courts upheld women's rights to property and that women's control and management of property was not insignificant in many cases (e.g., Abraham Marcus 1983; Meriwether 1993, 70–72). But Suraiya Faroqhi has shown that although women had access to property through inheritance in seventeenth-century Anatolia, they did not retain control of it; some pressures —economic, familial, or social—were causing them to sell (1981, 217).

The issue of the relative importance of cultural ideals and social realities in shaping women's lives will not be resolved any time soon. It requires more comparative studies of the various dimensions of women's lives over time and in different social contexts. One particularly critical area is women's rights within the family. Women's daily lives were spent within the domestic context and shaped most immediately by relationships to other family members. Therefore, how the courts ruled on matters of inheritance, marriage and divorce, and the guardianship of children had the most profound effect on establishing their sense of themselves and the degree of autonomy and control they could exercise. This essay will look at the relationship between cultural ideals and social realities through the lens of women's relationship to children as it was defined by law and interpreted by the courts. The mother's rights with respect to children reflected cultural ideals about the role of the mother, about children, and about the ties of the child to the family. How these rights were put into practice can shed light on the extent to which ideals were realized or limited.

Approaching the relationship between mothers and children through legal rights and how they were applied addresses only a limited dimension of this complex relationship. Moreover, women's rights to children only became an issue in the event of divorce or the death of the father. When this happened, it changed the nature of the relationship between mother and child and activated the question of women's rights and children's rights. This represented an "abnormal" situation, on one level. It was not, however, an uncommon one because the demographic realities of the early modern period meant that many children lost one or both parents before they reached adulthood. Issues relating to the guardianship of orphaned (used in the sense of fatherless) children showed up frequently in the court records. The court's concern with the legal rights of children and what role was assigned to women in these situations provides a different angle from which to consider the position of women and the way in which the courts and the society viewed women. The most revealing evidence comes from cases in which the father had died and a *wasi* (executor) was appointed on the children's behalf. I will focus specifically on this issue of guardianship in the event of the father's death by considering first how the law defined childhood and the rights of children and then by looking at the role of women in the guardianship of children and its implications for the position of women.

The context for this study is late eighteenth-and early nineteenth-century Aleppo. A large, cosmopolitan, and heterogeneous city, Aleppo served as both a provincial capital and a major international and regional commercial center during the Ottoman period. Its role as political and economic center had conferred on it considerable prosperity. Although much of this wealth was concentrated in the hands of the provincial upper class and past and present officials of the Ottoman state who resided there, Aleppo also had a sizable propertied middle class. At the end of the eighteenth century and in the early decades of the nineteenth century, Aleppo went through a troubled period. Sometimes, serious factional conflict between the Janissaries and *ashraf* (descendants of the Prophet who constituted a political faction during this period) recurred periodically. Dissatisfaction with the imperial government in Istanbul culminated in a major revolt in 1819 that cost many lives and resulted in great destruction of property. A serious earthquake in 1822 meant additional loss of life and destruction of property.[1] Underlying all of this were structural changes in the Ottoman economy that were altering Aleppo's role as a commercial city in significant ways. The uncertainties, instability, and disruption of the times affected families as well and made the issue of orphaned children a particularly pressing one.

1. Aleppo has been the subject of considerable study in recent years. For a general overview, see Abraham Marcus, 1989, esp. chap. 2 on social structure. For political history, see Bodman 1963.

Childhood and the Rights of Children

Twenty-five years after Philippe Aries published *Centuries of Childhood* and sparked a lively debate about the concepts of childhood, treatment of children and affective relationships within the family in medieval and early modern Europe, the history of childhood in Middle Eastern societies historically is only beginning to be written. Some attention has been paid to how attitudes toward children, the understanding of their psychological and physical needs, child-rearing practices, and the relationship between parents and children have changed over the last two centuries (Duben and Behar 1991, 226–30). More systematic study of childhood in both the premodern and the modern period remains to be done, however.

A recent study by Avner Gilʿadi (1992) is an important step in making the study of childhood a more central part of Middle Eastern social history. Gilʿadi has shown that the concern with children and the recognition of childhood as a special period were not new issues in the modern period, and he has drawn our attention to an enormous body of literature on children and childhood in premodern Islamic societies: literary works and theological, medical, and educational writings, including extensive collections of consolation treatises for parents.

These writings on children and childhood are fascinating for what they tell us about the attitudes of Islamic society toward children. How these views of children and childhood reflected and influenced the realities of children's lives is the next step toward a history of childhood in the Middle East. On a basic level, children in Middle Eastern societies experienced the often harsh realities of their contemporaries in other premodern and early modern societies. Infant and child mortality rates were high. The average number of children per family in Aleppo in the early nineteenth century was about three, a reflection of high mortality rates rather than low birth rates.[2] Those children who survived these

---

2. Unfortunately, reliable data on family size do not exist. A reasonable estimate can be determined, however, by calculating the average number of children who were living at the time of a parent's death. Although not all inheritances were registered, enough were to provide a sufficiently large sample to be representative. It is unlikely that other households in Aleppo would have been out of line with these numbers. This figure cannot give us the total number of children born to a couple, but it does give the number of children who were surviving at a particular time. Because the survival rate is more significant here than the birth rate, this is not a problem. Estimates of family size have been made by Judith Tucker for Nablus, using this same calculation. She too shows fairly small families (1991, 243).

dangers would often lose either one or both parents at a relatively young age as the large number of people dying while their children were still minors indicates. It is difficult to measure the impact of these realities on children. There is no reason to doubt that strong emotional attachments between parents and children were the norm.[3] The existence of consolation treatises, to help parents cope with the deaths of children, provide the best circumstantial evidence of ties of affection between many parents and children. Although the consolation treatises emphasized the importance of parents being steadfast in the face of the loss of their child and religious teachings emphasized the need for parents to restrain the emotions felt toward their children, the fact that these treatises were needed and that religious leaders felt compelled to discourage expressions of excessive emotional attachment suggests that emotional bonds between parents and children were very strong (Gilʿadi 1992, 118). For parents to lose a child or for children to lose a parent was a wrenching experience.

Apart from the sense of loss caused by the death of a parent, the degree of disruption and distress for the child undoubtedly depended on the circumstances: whether resources were readily available to provide support for the child, how strong extended family ties were, what kind of households they lived in. For children of well-to-do families, the loss of one or both parents would have changed the lives of children very little beyond the sense of emotional loss. The family's wealth would have provided economic security for the child or children and would have minimized their need to depend on the charity of relatives. Often they either lived in joint or extended family households with grandparents, aunts and uncles, and older siblings or were surrounded by a strong extended family network with relatives living close by, so they continued to live in the same place and among the same people they had always known (e.g., Mahkama Sharʿiyya Archives (MSA) 198:171; 211:74; 219:195). At the other extreme were the children of the poor. With few or no resources, providing even minimal maintenance for a child or children was a problem. If the father had left no money or property to help offset the expenses of child support and if the father's relatives were poor, providing for an extra child or children could be a heavy burden. So could taking a child into the home when space was already tight. The possibility that there would be no money to pay support for the child, that a surviving parent might remarry, or that an orphaned child might have no kin to turn to all meant that children

---

3. Goitein made a similar point in discussing relationships between husbands and wives in medieval Fustat. His comments on this are worth remembering (1978, 165).

could be passed from one reluctant set of guardians to another or be left destitute and homeless (Abraham Marcus 1989, 198, 208; Tucker 1991, 244–47).

The situation for most children probably fell somewhere between these two extremes. One parent would be alive to take care of them and provide a home; other relatives were available if needed; there were sufficient resources to take care of child support payments. The average estate left by a male head of household in early nineteenth century Aleppo was about 3,000 qurush, the bulk of which went to his children. The average number of surviving minor children was 2.4, so that each child would have roughly 1,250 qurush to pay child support during his or her minority.[4] Whether this was sufficient depended again on circumstances. Child support payments were generally low, averaging between five and fifteen misriyyas per day in the early nineteenth century, although they varied depending on class and possibly other factors not apparent in the sources.[5] But if the child was very young when the parent died or if there were other expenses on the estate of the parent, the resources could run out, even for children who were well provided for. For example, Sharif Agha ibn Hamza Agha and his wife Rabiyya bint Yusif died at about the same time, leaving two minor children, for whom Shaykh Sa'id Efendi al-Dayri served as wasi. The children had inherited some real estate as well as other assets. The rent from the real estate covered the costs of child support for the three years of Shaykh Sa'id's guardianship. The debts still owed by the estate and repairs to one of the houses meant that Shaykh Sa'id had to spend some of his own money to provide for the children, however (MSA 152:36 Shawwal). In this case, the children had real estate that could be sold or whose rents could be used to pay back the debt owed to their wasi and were not left penniless or indebted to him, but the case suggests that financial insecurity was possible even for orphans of the propertied middle class. The need to sell real estate to realize cash to pay child support, as often happened, underscores the burden that child support payments could impose.

Although particular circumstances, such as family and class background or demographic chance, were most important in determining how well children fared, state and society, through the legal system,

---

4. This figure was obtained by calculating the average of all the estates of men in six mukhalafat (registers of division of inheritance) that covered the years between 1234–1255/1818–1839. The average number of grown and minor children was also calculated from these same documents.

5. Child support payments were not routinely listed in the documents, but they appear occasionally in a variety of different contexts. I have simply compiled all that were available and looked for patterns. The size for these payments was fairly consistent.

tried to provide safeguards to alleviate some of the problems created by the loss of parents and more generally to protect the rights of children. Detailed provisions for the custody, maintenance, and overall well-being of children were laid out by law, as were requirements that were designed to protect the property of minor children. Because of these legal safeguards, and therefore the need to take transactions involving minors to court for decision or approval by the *qadi,* the court records provide important information on how legal matters affecting children were handled.

Childhood was considered to last until puberty roughly. The court records suggest that for girls this was around the age of eleven or twelve; for boys, around fifteen (MSA 137:127; 107:116; 133:83; 181:149).[6] Among minor children, a distinction was drawn between the young child *(saghir)* and the adolescent *(murahiq),* although the exact age at which one reached adolescence is not clear (MSA 113:142; 119:98). Given the patrilineal and patriarchal nature of Middle Eastern societies (at least in law and theory), children "belonged" to the father's family. The father was responsible for the child's maintenance and education and was considered the child's "natural guardian" *(waliyy)* until the child came of age or, in the case of girls, until they married. Any property belonging to the child was managed by the father. Nevertheless, the mother had certain rights with regard to children. The actual physical care and nurturing of the child until a certain age was the responsibility of the mother. This division of responsibility between parents was reflected in arrangements made for children if the parents were divorced or if one or both parents died. If the parents divorced, the mother took custody *(hidana)* of young children until the age of seven for boys and nine for girls, as long as she was of "good character," lived close enough that the father could see the children, and remained unmarried. The father provided financial support *(nafaqa).*[7] If the mother died while the children were still young, the mother's nearest female relative was awarded custody of young children; if she had no close female relatives, the father's nearest female relative would assume this role. The father continued to provide support and assumed responsibility for any property the child inherited from his mother.

6. The evidence in the court registers corresponds to ages mentioned by Gilʿadi when discussing the stage of childhood as seen in the medieval Islamic sources (1992, 116).

7. Because Hanafi law was the dominant school of law in the Ottoman Empire and was the law school to which most Aleppines belonged, this discussion will reflect Hanafi law. It is based on relevant sections of J.N.D. Anderson 1968; Noel J. Coulson 1969; Fyzee 1955; Schact 1964.

The situation became more complex in the event of the father's death and raised the most pressing questions about the future care of the child or children. His death meant not only the loss of the family's main economic support but also the loss of the children's "natural guardian." Not only custody but also the question of who would assume responsibility for the support for the children and oversight of their property, if property was involved, had to be decided. If the father's father was still alive, he assumed the role of *waliyy*. If he were not still alive, as was usually the case, a *wasi*, who was responsible for management of the property belonging to minor children and their maintenance until such a time as the children came of age, was appointed. Sometimes, the father chose the *wasi* for his children before his death (MSA 202:105). In other cases the *qadi* appointed the *wasi* or confirmed an arrangement made by the family.

The concern with the legal rights of children was seen most clearly in the detailed arrangements for the custody and maintenance of the children. Furthermore, any transactions involving minor children and property had to be approved by the judge. For example, the distribution of inheritances did not have to be registered with the judge, unless there were minors involved. Even the rights of unborn children were considered here. If a woman were pregnant when her husband died, the court noted that she was carrying a child, and the unborn child was alloted a share of his or her father's estate (the assumption was usually made that it would be a boy because the unborn child was assigned a son's share of the father's wealth) (MSA 226:45).

The concern with children's property rights was apparent in other ways as well. Executors were sometimes required to account for how the funds in their care were spent, usually because some question was raised about the handling of this property or because there were insufficient funds to pay child support. Suits against former executors by children who had obtained their majority were not infrequent. These suits usually alleged misappropriation of funds. One such suit was brought by the grandsons of Isma'il Shurayyif, the scion of a wealthy merchant family who had not only added greatly to his inherited wealth during his life but had also been a dominant force in Aleppo politics in the early nineteenth century. Isma'il's sons were dead, and his two grandsons were still minors when he died in 1826. The fortune Isma'il left his grandsons was enormous, including gold, silver, and jewels, various expensive items of furniture and clothing, money and grain collected as rents from *malikanes* in Aleppo and Damascus, and debts owed to the estate. (It did not include extensive real estate holdings in Aleppo, which Isma'il had used to set up a family trust before his death.) When the grandsons came of age, they sued their cousins Muhammad Sa'id and Yusif, who had been serving as their *wasis*, for failing to pay them a large part of their inheritance when they reached their majority. After mediation, the dispute was resolved when the grandsons agreed to delay payment of 70,000 qurush of their inheritance for two and a half years (MSA 223:127). What seems to have happened is that the executors were using the assets of the estate for their own purposes and were unable to pay it out when the time came. Other suits of this kind appear. Muhammad Agha Ghawri took his uncle Ibrahim to court, claiming that his uncle had failed to use 2000 qurush left at the end of Muhammad's minority to pay off a debt still owed by his father's estate. Instead, he had used the money for his own purposes. Moreover, Muhammad demanded that Ibrahim pay rent for the time his uncle had lived in his (Muhammad's) father's house and served that he recover some debts still owed to Muhammad's father's estate by some provincial villages (MSA 108:429). The courts were quick to support the rights of minors to recover money properly due to them. Islamic law and the courts took the legal rights of children seriously. Because of this concern with protecting the vulnerable and ensuring that they received their rights, the court also took seriously who was assigned the responsibility for the care of the children and the management of their property. It is to this issue and the question of the role of women that we now turn.

Women and the Guardianship of Children

As indicated earlier, the dimension of the guardianship of children under consideration here is the question of who was appointed as *wasi* for the child or children and therefore was responsible for child support, the management of property owned by minors, and any other issues concerned with their financial well-being. For purposes of this study, I have used a sample of 492 executors.[8] The sample represents largely

8. This sample was compiled in the following way. Three hundred fifty-five of the cases were taken from six registers that contained *mukhkalafat*. Interspersed with these records were appointments of executors for minor children who were heirs to the estates. These six registers come from late in the period under consideration (1234–1255/1818–1839). Such registers presumably existed for earlier periods, but at the time I did research in the National Archives in Damascus (1978–1979 and 1985), they were not available for earlier decades of the period under study. In addition to using these six registers, I compiled a random sample of executors (89 cases) from property sales from throughout this period. Any time that property was bought or sold by a minor, his or her *wasi* would be named. The remaining cases were taken from court transactions of various kinds involving members of the upper class families of Aleppo.

the Muslim population of the city; a few cases involving Christians and Jews appear, but under normal circumstances matters having to do with minors would be handled by their respective communities. The Muslim population in the sample came from all parts of the city and a range of socioeconomic groups, from the wealthy provincial upper class to the propertied middle class to what might be called the lower middle class who had a few resources.

The analysis of these cases reveals one clear fact: women were appointed as *wasi* more often than men. From this sample of 492 cases, women served *wasi* for minor children in 268 (54%) of them. There is some differentiation by class in these appointments. Among upper-class families, men served as *wasi* more often than women. This would mean that, among nonelite families, women served in this capacity more often than men by a margin of four to three.

Of the 268 women appointed as *wasis,* 205 of them were the mothers of the children involved (75%). In cases where female executors were not the mothers, there was a preference for female relatives from the father's family, as one would expect in a society that emphasized patrilineal ties. Grandmothers and aunts were usually chosen (thirteen and ten cases respectively); on rare occasions, a paternal great aunt or cousin would appear as executor. Maternal relatives were sometimes chosen, however. Maternal grandmothers (six cases) and maternal aunts (four cases) were chosen about half as often as paternal grandmothers and aunts. Sisters, however, were chosen more often than any female relative, except the paternal grandmother (twelve cases). Two stepmothers were also included among the female *wasis.* Why female relatives other than the mother were chosen is not obvious from the evidence. The mother was usually still alive, as was true when Hadra bint Nasir was appointed to serve as *wasi* of her three granddaughters after her son's death, although both of his wives were still alive (MSA 226:25–26). Similarly, Amana bint Husayn Miri served as *wasi* for her brother's minor children, instead of the children's mother, Asma bint ʿAbd al-Wahhab Miri (MSA 110:92). Clearly, however, although other female relatives were sometimes chosen to fill this role, the preferred *wasi* among women was the mother.

Why women were chosen as *wasis* at all, when the law placed responsibilities for the financial support of children and the management of their properpty on male relatives from the father's family, is the intriguing question. Unfortunately, the reasons for the choice of *wasi* were not made explicit, but circumstantial evidence is suggestive. One obvious explanation for why women were assigned this role could be that the father had no surviving male relatives. Over half of the 219 males who were *wasis* were either the paternal uncles (sixty-two cases) or older brothers (fifty-nine cases) of minors. Only occasionally did relatives from the mother's side or more distant male relatives serve as executors. Five were executors for their daughters' children, and twelve for their sisters' children. Nine of the male executors were paternal first cousins; more distant paternal relatives like a grandfather's son or a grandfather's brother's son appeared only rarely. Yet in early modern Aleppo, where small families were the norm, life expectancies even for those who survived the perilous years of early childhood were short, and the male population was relatively mobile, it was probably not unusual for a minor child to be left without close male relatives. If this was the case, there were two choices. One was to appoint a man from outside the family, and this did happen. Forty-four of the 219 males who served as executors in this sample were apparently not related to the children involved. The second choice was to turn to a female relative. In at least some cases, then, women were chosen as *wasi* in a sense by default.

There were, however, many more cases in which paternal uncles or older brothers of the minor children were alive and were passed over as *wasi* in favor of the mother or another female relative. The evidence on this point is incomplete for the sample of executors as a whole because in many cases there is no indication of whether there were male relatives. Where there is evidence that an uncle or great-uncle, as well as the mother, was still alive, the children's mother was as likely to be appointed as *wasi* as the children's uncle or great-uncle. If there was an older brother available, the preference for the mother was even clearer. Most of the men whose inheritances were studied had both grown and minor children at the time of their deaths. Older brothers were sometimes chosen as *wasi* when the mother was still alive; nevertheless, if the choice was between an older brother and the mother, the mother was more likely to be chosen. This may simply have been a matter of age. If the older brothers had themselves only recently reached their majority, they may not have been considered appropriate executors for their younger siblings, although young adults were not necessarily excluded from serving in this role. Nafisa ʿAbd al-Baqi, for example, served as *wasi* to her two siblings not long after she herself had come of age (MSA 226:104). If there was a large age spread among the children, older brothers could clearly be mature enough to be considered appropriate executors. Yet, a clear preference for the mother was shown.

More conclusive evidence comes from the one group of the population for whom we can reconstruct families, the upper class.[9] From a sample of 128 cases involving minor children among this class, women served as *wasi* in sixty-one of them and men in sixty-eight. When women were appointed, the mother was chosen in sixty-six (66%) of the cases; paternal grandmothers (five cases), aunts (three cases), sisters (two cases), a maternal grandmother, and a paternal second cousin made up the other one-third. In almost two-thirds of the cases where a woman was appointed, close male relatives of the children—either an older brother or an uncle—were alive and available, at least in theory, to serve in this capacity. In only three cases were there no male relatives on the father's side to take on this responsibility. Similarly, in two-thirds of the cases where men were executors, the mothers or other close relatives of the children were available. In other words, given a choice between a close female relative (including the mother) and a close male relative, the number of times a male was chosen over a female or vice versa balanced out. There was no clear preference for either male or female.

More important than gender in determining who was appointed as *wasi* seems to have been the closeness of the relationship with the child or children. When the choice lay between close female relatives and more distant male relatives (such as cousins or great-uncles), women were preferred over men. Among upper-class families, there were many times when women were appointed as executors' even though cousins and great-uncles were alive and in a position to take on this responsibility on behalf of the father's family. When more distant male relatives did serve as executors, it was usually because the mother of the child was already dead.

The fact that executors were usually chosen from among close relatives suggests that the boundaries of the effective family were narrowly drawn, even within the upper class. Despite a legal system that vested rights to children in the father's extended family, laws that clearly reflected patriarchally defined cultural ideals, family structure worked to limit sharply the involvement of the extended family in the affairs of the family of husband, wife, and children created by marriage. Ties beyond this family group were often not maintained in a way that allowed these relatives to assume responsibility for the children. The in-

9. Family reconstruction is possible for these families because they were the only group that had family names in this period. Family reconstruction is basic to the methodology in my manuscript, "The Kin Who Count: Family and Society in Ottoman Aleppo," and a full discussion of how this was done is found there.

terests of the children would seem to be best served by remaining with close relatives who had multiple ties with them. It was often women rather than men who were in a position to undertake these responsibilities. The implications of this for the authority and autonomy of women and the strength of agnatic ties and the degree of patriarchal control are very important.

The full significance of the fact that women served as executors for their relationship to children and for their position within the family depends on how active a role the women played in managing the affairs of their minor children. Executors were responsible for any property—cash, goods, and real estate—belonging to the minor child, property usually acquired through inheritance from parents or other relatives. The *wasi* therefore was faced with decisions about how to manage that money and property in order to provide adequate support for the child during his or her minority and to make sure that the money was not squandered. Even when sums of money were small and there was little property to manage, the *wasi* often had to make critical decisions. The single biggest asset of most estates, especially those of the propertied middle class, was real estate, usually the family residence. Not infrequently, real estate had to be sold to provide cash for child support. If the real estate was jointly owned, all the owners had to agree to the sale.[10] In some cases, this would involve not only the immediate family but also cousins, aunts, and uncles. In 1785, the heirs of Hasan Hamawi and his two sons, Taha and Isma'il, sold a house in Zuqaq Arba'in to provide child support for the five minor children of Isma'il and the four minor children of Taha. This sale involved sixteen people, not counting the nine minors (MSA 116:78–79). In 1829, sixteen members of the Jazmati family sold six *qirat*s of a soap factory they owned jointly in Bab Qinnisrin for the maintenance of two minor children. One branch of the Qurnah family was even reduced to selling part of the family compound in Bustan, the *dar al-haram* and the *dar al-haram saghir,* for child support for one child. The house was worth 30,000 qurush. This transaction involved twelve heirs, all descendants of Mustafa Qurnah (MSA 175:33–34). Negotiating an agreement to sell jointly owned property

10. In most of the *mukhalafat* records, real estate was not divided up among heirs at the same time that liquid assets were distributed. This was more likely to be the case when some of the heirs were still minors, although joint ownership was often extended well beyond the time that minors had come of age. Real estate would be divided when one of the heirs requested such a division. This could occur almost immediately after the distribution of other assets, or it could occur many years later, depending on family circumstances.

was not necessarily an easy process. The sale also had to be approved by the *qadi* as being in the best interests of the minor child or children. Executors were also involved in other kinds of economic transactions on the behalf of minors. Purchasing property for children, investing in other kinds of economic ventures, collecting rents and income from endowments, and paying off debts of the estate all fell on the shoulders of the *wasi*.

The women who served as executors, like their male counterparts, were actively involved in managing the assets and making decisions about children's property under their control. Female executors were sometimes involved in suits about the estates for which they were responsible. They were sued by others wanting to collect debts owed by the deceased in some cases; in others, they sued to get money owed to the deceased and therefore now the property of the children. Mahbub bint ʿAbd Allah, as heir to her husband's estate and as *wasi* to her two young sons, had to pay off a debt her husband had owed to ʿAbd al-Rahman Siyyaf. Nafisa bint Hashim Shurabji had to sell real estate belonging to her minor granddaughter to pay off the debt of her deceased son (MSA 121:75; 203:3). Amana bint Husayn Hamawi, on the other hand, sued her husband's brothers to get her and her daughter's (whose *wasi* she was) shares of her husband's estate (MSA 139:57).

Buying property on behalf of minor children was also common. Sometimes, this was clearly property bought as an investment. Fatima bint Mustafa Hariri, as executor to her daughter, Amana bint Mahmud Khanji, bought the usage rights to a shop. Sometimes, property was bought jointly by the executor acting for herself and her minor children together with her grown children. This was the case when Fatima bint Muhammad purchased an orchard and land outside Aleppo and a shop in Banqusa with her two grown daughters and two minor sons.

The money of minors was also used to purchase residential property. In at least one case, the money of minors was used to help buy shares of a house from relatives. Fatima bint Ahmad Shurabji bought three and a half *qirat*s of a house in Bayyada from her brother-in-law, using her own money as well as that of her four minor children and her grown daughter. The house was the residence of the buyers already. It seems that the mother and her children were buying out her brother-in-law after her husband's death, so that they would have a separate residence for their immediate family (MSA 116:304). This case at least suggests the possibility that there were female-headed households.

The position of *wasi* required the active supervision of property and the making of complex economic decisions, and women who served in this position took on these responsibilities. In some cases where women were appointed as *wasi*, there was relatively little property involved; in others, she assumed responsibility for the management of large estates on behalf of minors. The widow of Abu Bakr Tabbakh requested a division of the property inherited by her late husband and his siblings from their father and aunt and still jointly owned by them at the time of his death. Over the next several years, she was involved in a series of property sales with her in-laws to rationalize the distribution of the property, so that her and her children's share of the property was not tied up in partial shares of different pieces of property (MSA 144:109, 188; 148:26–28). Yet, another complex estate was overseen by a woman as *wasi* to minors who had rights to that estate. When ʿAbd Allah Miri died in 1769, he left considerable real estate in Aleppo and the surrounding countryside, some of it valuable commercial property, valued at 65,000 qurush. He also died under a load of debt. His heirs therefore had considerable assets, but careful management of the property was required to pay off the debt without jeopardizing his heirs' patrimony. The person appointed to oversee the interests of his four minor children was his sister Amana, rather than either his wife (who was also his first cousin), one of his grown children, or his cousin ʿAbd al-Wahhab, who was also his brother-in-law. This is particularly interesting because both branches of the Miri family were apparently still sharing the family home in Bab Qinnisrin and because intermarriages were frequent between these branches (MSA 110:54; 111:124–25; 113:286–87). The Miri family represented in many respects the model of the wealthy, upper class, patriarchal family, all occupying the same house, marrying frequently within the family, and maintaining joint ownership of property over several generations (ʿAbd Allah's real estate was not divided among his heirs until 1812; at that point, it was done because some heirs by marriage wanted their share of the property)(MSA 180:205–10). Yet even in this family, a woman was chosen for a role that would ordinarily be assigned to a man, even though a close male relative was alive.

The fact that women were *wasi*s and that they were chosen more often than men to serve in this capacity is a highly suggestive indication of the position of women within the family. As indicated earlier, women's rights with respect to children were limited by law and even these rights could be withdrawn. Yet in serving as executors, women were assuming responsibilities that went beyond what the law assigned to them and in effect took on the role reserved for the father's closest male relative, to whom the child belonged. In appointing or confirming women as executors for minor children, the *qadi*s seemed to be ignoring the patriarchal bias of the law that would assign this position to male members of the father's family. The Islamic courts acknowledged women's ability to carry out these responsibilites. They interpreted and applied the law in a way that at least on the surface strengthened the rights of women with respect to the children. All the evidence also points to the fact that this role was not simply a nominal one and that women were actively involved in managing their children's affairs and making sometimes difficult decisions to try to ensure their financial security.

Children and Women's Authority

The active role played by women in the guardianship of children —one that went beyond assuming custody of young children in the event of divorce or death of the father—has important implications for the definition of motherhood, for the relationship between mothers and children, and for the nature of women's authority within the domestic context. Mothers were responsible for the care and nurturing of young children and for early socialization, and the awarding of custody to mothers of young children was a legal representation of this view of the role of the mother. Strong emotional ties could and usually did grow naturally out of this relationship. At the same time the mother's relationship with the child was inherently insecure because the child "belonged" to the father's family, custody rights were limited to younger children, and even those rights could be taken away under certain conditions. Yet, what the evidence on the appointment of *wasi*s indicates is that the mother's responsibilities in many cases extended far beyond that limited role. She was responsible for the well-being of her children on all levels until adulthood. In light of the concern of the law and the courts with the rights of children, this was a significant extension of the role of the mother. Moreover, it had important consequences for the relationship between mothers and children. The emotional ties between mother and child and the influence over her children, especially sons, were not the only ties. Multiple ties that survived over the years, especially economic ties growing out of the mother's responsibility for managing the child's property during his or her minority, created a more complex relationship between mothers and children.

That women, mostly mothers, were being selected in the majority of cases to manage the property of their minor children and that their handling of the property often involved the need for careful management of resources suggests that women were recognized as capable of this responsibility. That they were being chosen instead of the father's closest male relative was a decision at odds with prevailing cultural ideals that gave control of children to the father's family and that assumed that the father's closest male relative would take on this responsibility. This was not just a de facto arrangement, but one made or at least sanctioned by the courts. In assuming such responsibility women were put in a position to exercise some economic autonomy. Their assumption of this role was perhaps a recognition of the authority within the family these women already possessed, or it conferred influence on them. Whatever the realities—demographic, social, economic—that led the courts to interpret the law in a way that strengthened women's authority in this way, they effectively limited the impact of male dominance to some small degree and limited the role of the patrilineal extended family.

I5

Adults and Minors in Ottoman *Shariʿa* Courts and Modern Law

Amira El Azhary Sonbol

Shariʿa Courts, the Madhahib, and History

*I*n 1525, Egypt's judicial hierarchy was restructured according to the Ottoman legal code for Egypt, which reorganized Egypt's government and judiciary. At the head of the judicial hierarchy was placed a chief justice *(qadi askar)* selected by the *shaykh al-Islam* (the chief religious figure of the empire), whose headquarters were in Istanbul. The chief justice was considered the direct supervisor of thirty-seven Ottoman court justices *(qadis)*, who headed thirty-seven judicial districts, into which Egypt was divided. Each of the thirty-seven judges, in turn, was assisted by numerous deputies *(naʾibs)*, who served in different towns and city quarters (Farahat 1988, 14–15). The administrative structure was career oriented and hierarchical, "organized into several classes and levels within each class" (Laurens 1989, 63). The thirty-seven judicial areas were categorized into a six-tier system based, not on supervisory responsibility, but rather on the political importance and affluence of each judicial area.[1] At the beginning of Ottoman rule, only the *naʾibs*

---

1. According to Abdal-Rehim (1990, 334), a *qadi* was expected to pass through the six tiers from the bottom up before he could become a *qadi* of the top tier—which included Cairo, Bulaq, Misr Al-Qadima, Alexandria, Dumyat, Mansura, Mahala al-Kubra, and Manf al-ʿUlya. Abdal-Rehim's source here is Ahmad al-ʿArishi, who was contemporary to the Napoleonic mission. How valid this hierarchization is for the earlier period, however, needs further investigation. The fact that *qadis* had to move from one tier to the other is challenged by the long periods that certain *qadis* remained in the same courts, as is evidenced by court records.

were Egyptians; but the upper levels of the judiciary were assigned from Istanbul, were usually disciples of the chief justice from whom they derived their authority, and their first language was Turkish. Things changed by the seventeenth century, and more Egyptians became *qadis*. By the time the French arrived in Egypt in 1798, all court judges except for some serving the *Bab al-'Ali* court—the preferred court of the Turkish elite—were Egyptian.

That *shari'a* law formed the framework upon which courts rendered justice in the Ottoman Empire is not a matter of dispute. This situation did not eliminate the existence of significant differences, however, given time, place, and *'urf* (traditions), which are closely connected with the *madhhab* (creed, or school of law) applied.[2] Practically speaking, there was a preference for the application of *'urf* in Egypt during the Ottoman period, whereby the public could chose the *madhhab* to be applied to their cases, and *qadis* and *muftis* (deliverers of formal legal opinion) from those *madhahib* administered *fatawi* (juridical opinions). *Fatawi* could be rendered by chief *qadis* and by *muftis* assigned to their positions by the chief *mufti* in Istanbul, or by the *shaykhs* of the Azhar, which occurred frequently. Thus, whereas Turks always went before the Hanafi judge, we find that the Maghariba (from North Africa) usually took their cases to be judged by the Maliki judge and the Syrians preferred the Hanafi judge.[3]

---

2. These schools are the Shafi'is, followers of Imam al-Shafi'i (d. 204/820), which was followed in Lower Egypt, East Africa, and Arabia; the Maliki, followers of Malik ibn Anas (d. 179/795) and his disciples, which dominated in Upper Egypt and North Africa; the Hanafis, followers of Abu Hanifa al-Nu'man (d. 150/767), which was subscribed to by Turkish people and the Indian subcontinent; and the Hanbali, following Ahmad ibn Hanbal (d. 241/855), which is found today in Saudi Arabia (Goldziher 1981, 49).

3. Baber Johansen discusses the connection between the Hanafi *madhhab* and the development of legal doctrines pertaining to property and rent by the Hanafi jurists during the Mamluk and Ottoman periods (1988, 2). The Hanafi *madhhab*—which allows for fluctuations in the value of contracted goods and property (Shafi'i 1988, vi, 212)—has been the preferred *madhhab* of state administration and capitalists in Islamic history. Interestingly, during the Ottoman period, at times of commercial crisis, people generally preferred the Hanbali *madhhab* for registration of partnerships and rents because of the conservative interpretation given by that *madhhab* to financial transactions. Even during affluent periods, merchants seemed to prefer the Hanbali *madhhab*, followed by the Maliki (Hanna, forthcoming b) when transacting long-term contracts. Hanbalis and Malikis protect against economic fluctuations and speculation. When it came to *awqaf* (religious endowment) contracts, Afifi (1991, 151) notes that there was a clear preference for the Hanbali *madhhab* among lessees because it forbade any increase in rent over the amount stipulated in the contract and determined the rent according to *mathilatiha* (its equal) rather than market price. Furthermore, the Hanbalis allowed the inheritance of leases, but the Hanafis did not. Even Christian Copts preferred to conclude *awqaf* leases according to the Hanbali *madhhab* (Afifi 1991, 152; Dumyat Sijillat 999/1592 30:4–47).

Under Ottoman rule, the Hanafi was the sect espoused by the state and was therefore the official sect of the Egyptian administrative and commercial elite.[4] But in *shari'a* courts, the Maliki and Shafi'i *madhahib* continued to be preferred in Upper and Lower Egypt respectively. The fact that the different *madhahib* were honored by the system shows that there was greater legal and social elasticity than would later be the case following Egypt's legal reforms (beginning 1897) when the Hanafi code was established as the main source of *shari'a* law. It also shows the greater independence enjoyed by court judges before the reforms in determining legal findings.

Furthermore, under Ottoman rule judges had been nominated to their positions by their peers and chosen for their wide-ranging knowledge of islamic *fiqh* (juridical interpretations by Muslim clergy). The Ottomans had educated the upper level of the *qadi* hierarchy at special schools for that purpose and the government in Istanbul had assigned them to their posts throughout the empire for terms usually of from one to three years.[5] Lower-level *qadis* and their deputies serving in the courts throughout Egypt were usually graduates of the Azhar and similar schools, like the Salihiyya al-Nijmiyya, who received an *ijaza* in *fatawi* (certification in rendering legal decisions) from the teachers with whom they studied. At that level, it was not uncommon for an individual to be

4. The fact that the Ottomans sponsored the Hanafi *madhhab* in Egypt has led to the mistaken assumption that Egypt was ruled by the Hanafi code (e.g., Hodgson 1974, 110). Certain historians who recognized the application of different *madhhahib* in Egypt did not however see the significance of this fact (Winter 1992, 112–14). Others did not focus what was taking place in the Ottoman provinces (Gerber 1994). Goldziher (1981, 55) puts it best: "The general tendency that prevails in the development of Islamic jurisprudence holds more interest for us than the particulars on which opinions differ from school to school." Udovitch (1981) illustrates the importance of the differences between the *madhahib* but does not apply that to personal laws. Another important study of Islamic law does discuss in some detail the differences between the *madhahib* (Coulson 1978, 86–102). But in following the tradition of Joseph Schacht, Goldziher, and others, Coulson presents a picture of Islamic jurisprudence as an unchanging system. Baber Johansen (1988) challenges the assumption of an unchanging *shari'a* by showing the historical development of the Hanafi code pertaining to property, rent, and taxation. The works of Udovitch and Baber have helped us understand the nature of change experienced by Islamic law.

5. Thus, the *qadi askar* (or *qadi al-qudat,* i.e., the chief *qadi*), the chief *qadis* of the courts of Cairo, and the *qassams* ('Askari and 'Arabi) were selected from Istanbul and were expected to have been educated at "*qadi* schools", from which they were sent to the various parts of the Ottoman Empire. But the deputies of these *qadis* throughout Egypt as well as those under them were chosen by the *qadis* of the quarters in Cairo, or by the *qadis* of the *aqalim* (provinces).

assigned as *qadi* back in his own village or city quarter. Most Shafiᶜi and Maliki judges were graduates of local schools and can be considered to have been organically linked with the communities in which they served. But after the reforms, judges would have to be educated, certified, employed by the Egyptian central government, and assigned to their respective courts.

In this essay, I focus on legal decisions concerning minors that have been rendered by Egyptian courts since the Ottoman period. Besides being an important topic in itself, the issue of age and how it determines the status of an individual is an important area in Islamic legal theory and has very definite determinations in *shariᶜa* courts. First, the marriage of minors and minor women moving into adulthood will be examined. Second, a comparison will be made between legal practices under Ottoman rule—when great diversity in legal practices existed—and the modern period—when the state adopted legal standardization and set up uniform legal codes to handle minors and guardianship.

In this context, the importance of the Shafiᶜi, Hanafi, and Maliki *madhahib* will be pointed out because of the correlation that existed between the particular *madhhab* and the historical context in which it was practiced. This correlation tells us about the society in which the *madhhab* is practiced and, in particular, the form of patriarchy predominant in it. Thus as archival records illustrate, the preference for the Shafiᶜi *madhhab* in Lower Egypt indicates that the extended family predominated in Lower Egypt, the father being the patriarchal head, followed by the grandfather. Upper Egypt was different, and the preference for the Maliki *madhhab* reflected the male patriarchal order headed by male members of the wider clan, from the father to the "chief." I also illustrate the changes in the application of these *madhahib* during the period researched. Finally, because the Hanafi *madhhab* was not popular in Egypt at the beginning of Ottoman rule, I discuss when, where, and among which classes it began to predominate.

Marriage and Minors under Ottoman Rule

To simplify a rather complex subject, the similarities and differences among *madhahib* in regard to minor girls *(qasir)*, adult virgins *(bikr baliqh)* and women *(thayb)*, will be outlined. Here, I am interested in showing similarities and differences between the *madhahib* as well as between particular *madhhab* and the way its decisions were practiced in court, and how these practices changed over time. Because of the connections between the *madhahib* and the historical context, the changes in long-held practices in any one area of the country indicate changes in historical conditions. By outlining the main laws and shifts in legal decisions, the larger historical process becomes clearer.

Before proceeding, however, a methodological problem needs to be pointed out. Whereas in court records of cities like Cairo and Dumyat, the *madhhab* of the *qadi* officiating is usually mentioned, that is usually not the case in most provincial courts. And because there is great similarity between marriage entries in the provincial archival records, determination of the particular *madhhab* followed is difficult. For any marriage to be legal, it had to include the names of the parties concerned: the bride, bridegroom, their *wakils* (proxys, agents) or *waliyys* (guardians), and the witnesses to the *tawkil* (proxy) and the marriage contract. The contract also had to include a dowry and the conditions under which the marriage was being transacted. Therefore, outwardly there seems to be little difference. Careful analysis of the marriages recorded for any particular town over time and their comparison with the theoretical requirements of each *madhhab* provide information of particular significance to historical transformations. For example, whereas Shafi'is do not recognize a marriage that does not include the word *zawaj* or *nikah* (marriage) and their derivatives, Hanafis accept *alfaz al-majaz* (figurative terms) like *hiba, sadaqa, ja'l, 'awwad,* and *tamlik* (offering, charity, grant, compensation, possession or property) for marriage. Besides indicating the philosophical differences with regard to women and marriage between the two *madhahib,* these terms also help to determine which *madhhab* was used for a particular marriage record.

Another terminological difference is the use of *idhn* (permission) and its derivatives for Shafi'i marriages—and in some towns for Maliki marriages—to indicate a *bikr baligh*'s permission to her *waliyy* if he did not hold a *wilayat al-ijbar* (a father's "right to force" a child to marry) to contract her marriage. As for the Hanafis, the term used is *tawkil* because they consider the *bikr baligh* and the *thayb* as having the right to marry without need of *waliyy*. Finally, although most towns normally contracted marriages according to a particular *madhhab;* but when another *madhhab* was used to transact a marriage, the affiliation of the particular *shaykh* or *qadi* was sometimes identified, thereby identifying the *madhab* used.

Qasirs

A *Wilayat al-ijbar* was applied to minor girls and boys. Guardianship included the authority to marry and divorce minors (Dumyat, Ishhadat A.H. 975/1570, 8:54–28; A.H. 1011–1015/1602–1606, 43:11–26, 48–182, 84–182; A.H. 999/1594, 30:9–30; Isna, Ishhadat,A.H. 1191–1192/1777–1778, 29:20–47; Manfalut, sijillat 1228/1812, 5:47–167; Alexandria, Da'awai A.H. 1273–1281/1856–1864, 1:3–8, 11; 1:14–36).[6] Whereas the father was always the guardian of a minor child (except under very specific circumstances), when the father died, guardianship usually went to the mother[7] (Dishna, Ishhadat 1908, 166:9–20, 10–22, 13–30, 15–33, 15–34, 16–35, 20–74; Dumyat, Ishhadat 999/1592, 30:10–33; 1011–1015/1602–1606, 43:84–182), to the grandfather, an older brother, or an uncle. If there was no other appropriate member of the family, the local *shaykh* or *qadi* became the guardian (Dumyat, Ishhadat A.H. 999/1594, 30:26–66).

A qualified difference existed between the authority of a father and that of other guardians. Whereas both a father and a guardian were responsible for the minor's welfare and controlled any property he/she owned, the *madhahib* agreed that the father had the right of *wilayyat al-ijbar* over minors. Shafi'is and Hanafis extended that right to the grandfather, and some Hanafis extended it to brothers. Malikis extended it to a *kafil* (sponsor, or patron) (al-Giziri 1987, 4:27).

If a father's *wilayat al-ijbar* was not contestable in court, that of other guardians was. In a 1910, a girl from Dayud in Wadi Halfa challenged a marriage contracted by her brother to a man he had met in Alexandria, where he had gone seeking work. Through a *wakil*, the girl argued that she was twelve years old and had reached *bulugh* (puberty), as her physical appearance proved. Even though she was still a minor when the marriage contract was signed, her brother was living in Alexandria at that time, and the distance between Alexandria and Dayud constituted a hardship *(qasr),* which according to the *shari'a,* voided his authority over her as a guardian and her uncle had therefore assumed that role. The court found for her and recognized the invalidity of the marriage (Alexandria, Da'awi 1910, 130:73–49).

---

6. The sample of cases used for this essay involve 600 cases from the archival records of Egypt's provincial courts: Alexandria, Armant, Dishna, Dumyat, Isna, and Manfalut, as well as Ma'ya Saniyya records. The cited references are examples of the usual type of case to be found in the records.

7. Hanafis explain the logic of giving the father and grandfather *wilayyat al-ijbar* this way: the closer the *'asab* (lineage), the greater the love and pity and, hence, care for the child (al-Hisari 1986, 475). Yet although accepting the close relationship between a mother and child, Hanafis consider the mother *naqisa* (deficient) of *'asab* and therefore extend *wilaya* to her only if there is no other male *waliyy* available or if she is assigned as *wasi* by the father or the *qadi*. Even though the *madhahib* did not sanction the mother as a guardian, interestingly this constituted the predominant form of guardianship as evidenced by court records.

It was usual for a married minor to remain with his/her own family until he/she reached *bulugh*. There were cases, however, in which a minor bride went to live with her husband, and the marriage was consummated, but only after the dowry was paid (Dumyat, Ishhadat 983/ 1576, 17:13–34). When a young bride stayed with her family, her husband was expected to pay for her support; and her father usually insisted on being compensated for this support before allowing the consummation of the marriage. Here, the *madhahib* differed. Whereas Hanafis did not allow for the husband's support of a minor bride unless he was getting some "service" or "enjoyment" from her, the Shafiʿis made the husband responsible for his wife's support before the marriage is consummated, and the expenses incurred by her family were treated by the courts as a debt for which the husband was held responsible (Alexandria, Daʿawi 1273–1281/1856–1864, 1:63–139).

When the bride was "of age" and the financial arrangements set out in the marriage contract fulfilled, the marriage was consummated. According to Shafiʿis and Malikis, it was only with consummation that a *thayb* was considered an adult; before marriage, a *bikr baligh* was treated like a minor. For this reason, a marriage contract and the consummation of marriage were two different things; without a *dukhla* (consummation) the marriage was incomplete. There are recorded cases in which the father of the bride simply refused to allow the *dukhla* (Dishna, Sijillat 1273/1856, 1:17–97) or the dowry was renegotiated before the bride's guardian allowed her seclusion [ʿala hukm al-khuluw] with her contracted husband, (Dumyat, Ishhadat 983/1578, 17:61–196). In other words, practically speaking, signing a marriage contract did not automatically entitle the husband to intimate relations or even seclusion with his contracted wife.

Bikr Baligh

Although a *qasir* could not contest the father's *wilayat al-ijbar* unless he was morally or mentally unfit or if he did not support her, an adult *(baligh)* could contest the father and did so successfully. For example, the court called on a woman to obey *(taʿa)* her husband, but she refused. In court, she explained that she did not recognize the marriage because her father forced her into it even though she was no longer a minor at the time she was married. The *qadi* asked the husband if this was true, and he admitted it. The court nullified the marriage and ordered the husband to keep away from her (Cairo, al-Bab al-ʿAli 1035/ 1626, 107:169–701).

Similarly, adult virgins were expected to approve their marriages, but that stipulation again depended on the particular *madhhab*. Whereas the Hanafi, Maliki, Shafi‘i, and Hanbali *madhahib* required *bulugh* for "owning herself" *(malakat nafsiha)*, the Hanafis and Hanbalis required that an adult consent to her marriage, either orally or with her silence. The Shafi‘is and Malikis advised the *waliyy* to confer with the *bikr baligh* before agreeing to her betrothal, but applied *wilayyat al-ijbar* to adult and minor virgins alike. Thus, they considered a previous marriage essential for "owning oneself" because they considered experience necessary for maturity. Once a girl had been married and the marriage consummated, she was then free to transact her future marriages (Dumyat, Ishhadat, 952–991/1546–1584, 1:17–18; 975/1570, 8:51–196; 983/1578, 17:17–49, 34–13, 39–128; 1022/1612, 51:124–331; Alexandria, Da‘awi 1273–1281/1856–1864, 1:63–139).

Unexecuted marriage transactions contracted by a guardian on behalf of a minor child could be challenged if the bride/bridegroom reached *bulugh* but was not willing to go through with the marriage. In a nineteenth-century case from Assiut, a man complained to the *qadi* that eight years earlier he had married his minor son to a minor girl whose father used his *wilayat al-ijbar* to contract the marriage and received the three pounds dowry agreed upon in front of corroborative witnesses. Because both the bride and the bridegroom were still minors, they remained with their respective families. When the bride's father died, she went to live with her grandfather, who transacted a new marriage for her with a new husband. The girl came to court in answer to the *qadi*'s summons, admitted she knew of the earlier marriage contracted by her father, adding that even though she was a *qasir* when her father contracted the first marriage and had since reached *bulugh*, she was willing to stand by her father's agreement. When asked about the second marriage, she indicated that her grandfather had contracted her second marriage without her consent and that she was in hiding from him for fear of what he might do to her. When questioned, the grandfather contradicted her statement, saying that he had only acted as her *wakil* in the marriage, that not only had she consented to marry the second husband (who was present in court) but had willingly received her dowry from him (5 foreign pounds, 2 Egyptian pounds, and 18 riyals). The grandfather then produced corroborative witnesses to the *tawkil* she had given him and to the marriage ceremony—including the *shaykh* who transacted the marriage. Even though the *tazkiya* (references, recommendations) of the grandfather's witnesses seemed unimpeachable, the first marriage was upheld, with the second husband deferring to the first (Assiut, Ahkam 1881, 19:8–18).

This case indicates that, even though the girl was married as a minor by her father, once she reached *bulugh,* she could have refused to follow her father's wishes. In its decision, the Assiut court seemed to be guided by this principle because the grandfather had to present witnesses to his *tawkil* by her. The willingness of the second husband to annul the second marriage probably played a decisive part in clearing a case in which the bride could have potentially been found to be a bigamist.

This incident is significant because, even though it occurred in 1881 in Assiut in Upper Egypt—where the Maliki tradition predominated—the marriage could not have been Maliki. The Maliki rule giving the father *wilayat al-ijbar* over a *bikr baligh* meant that there was no need to question her choice in the matter. The marriage was most likely a Hanafi marriage. As the archives illustrate, increasing numbers of marriages in Assiut were transacted in accordance to the Hanafi *madhhab,* indicating the growing importance of that *madhhab* in Upper Egypt before the Hanafi code was made the main source of *shariʿa* law in 1897. This tells us that during the nineteenth century, Assiut was growing in importance as a government and commercial center. The same can be said for Isna, which is located farther south.[8] There, marriages continued to be contracted according to the Maliki tradition (Isna, Ishhadat 1191–1192/1777, 29:20–47, 48; 1194/1780, 31:28–62), but the number of marriages transacted according to the Hanafi code, requiring the consent of a *bikr baligh* either through a witnessed *tawkil* or rendered to the *qadi* in person, increased significantly from the end of the eighteenth century on (Isna, Ishhadat 1191–1192/1777–1778,

---

8. Abul-Futuh (1992, 229–34) supports this finding in his article on eighteenth-century Isna. He describes the growing presence of "titled" persons, whose names and titles were carefully recorded by the *qadi*s. These included Mamluk amirs residing in Isna as well as merchants from various parts of the Ottoman Empire interested in the Red Sea trade. Furthermore, he ties the marked growth in dowry amounts and the end of the practice of paying dowries in installments to the growing affluence of Isna toward the end of the century. Elsewhere (Sonbol, forthcoming), I argued that payment in installments was detrimental to the wife because if she were to repudiate *(khulʿ)* her husband, she would have to relinquish all her financial rights, including the remaining installments of her advance dowry. That the dowry was being paid to the wife in advance in full, I argue, was an indication of important changes experienced in Isna during that period (Isna, Sijillat, 1193/1779, 31:43–46, 53, 61). The fact that this shift was taking place in other towns of Upper Egypt shows deep social transformations. It should be noted, however, that the practice of paying the dowry in installments continued to predominate in other towns, e.g., Manfalut, until the nineteenth century (Manfalut, Ishhadat, 1238–1239/1822–1823, 5–50, 51). Besides, installments were also traditional in Alexandria until the end of the nineteenth century (Alexandria, Ishhadat, 1273/1856, 1:21, 22, 37, 39, 43).

29:21–44, 45, 46, 29–69; A.H. 1193/1779, 30:26–53, 54; A.H. 1195/ 1780, 31:11–28, 21–43, 33–122).

Other towns in Upper Egypt also show a movement, however slight, toward the application of the Hanafi *madhhab* before the twentieth century (Armant, Sijillat 1290–1291/1873, 42:32–68, 19–145; Dishna, Sijillat 1273/1857, 1:1–13; 1274/1858, 1:1–13; Manfalut, Ishhadat 1228–1229/ 1812–1813, 5:33–118). In Manfalut in a sample year, *bikr baligh*s who were married by other than the father through a *tawkil* from the bride with proven witnesses (Manfalut, Ishhadat 1228–1229/1812–1813, 5:33–121; 5:13–56) included *baligh*s married by an uncle as their *wakil* (5:31–114) or by a brother (5:9–37) with the brides' approval in front of acceptable witnesses. But when it was the father who was marrying a *bikr baligh,* then *wilayat al-ijbar* applied (Manfalut, Ishhadat 1228–1229/1812–1813, 5:3–116, 117, 7–25. 9–34, 13–50, 53, 26–95, 31–115, 33–117, 119, 47–167, 31–115; 5:16–66, 67). This may well illustrate a shift in the law in one respect—that pertaining to guardians other than the father—because most Maliki marriages recorded in Upper Egypt permitted a guardian other than the one holding *wilayat al-ijbar* to marry his ward without her *tawkil.* The power of the father remained the same, however. We can therefore conclude a growing tendency toward a patriarchal order recognizing the powers of the father and undermining the powers of other male members of the clan, that is, moving toward the Hanafi and away from the Maliki *madhhab.*

The Mediterranean port of Dumyat shows similar transformations in legal traditions much earlier than towns in Upper Egypt. There, the number of marriages in which a *bikr baligh* contracted for herself, even if through a *wakil,* grew from the sixteenth century onward. The rarity of these early cases gives the impression that a mistake was made in recording the particular case or that they involved outsiders only. On closer scrutiny, however, it becomes clear that these are Hanafi marriages in which a *bikr baligh* was required to give her consent either indirectly through a witnessed *tawkil* or directly to the *qadi* (Dumyat, Ishhadat 975/1568, 8:90–362; 983/1576, 17:17–50, 18–51; 999/ 1592, 30:6–14, 7–16, 8–25, 10–31, 11–38; 1022/1613, 51:37–105; 43:38–77).

The growth of Hanafi marriages seemed to be the trend among townsmen, particularly the richer merchant classes. The following Hanafi marriage from Dumyat illustrates the transitional move of the town's elite toward the "official" *madhhab.* In this example, an adult virgin was given a dowry of 60 new gold dinars (when the norm was 5 to 6 dinars). In his role as *wakil* for the bride, the father was careful to indicate that this marriage was "without force or coercion" *(min ghayr ikrah wa la ijbar)*, a requirement of the Hanafi *madhhab* for the marriage of adult girls. The social class of the family as well as the shift toward the Hanafi code is indicated by the fact that the marriage was officiated by both the Shafiʿi and the Hanafi chief *qadis* of Dumyat (Dumyat, Ishhadat 999/ 1594, 30:10–31). More Maliki marriages were also being recorded in Dumyat's *shariʿa* court, reflecting immigration from the south of Egypt and the expanding Maghribi community in Dumyat, again an indication of the port's growing importance.

Thayb

Previously married women, victims of repeated rape, *zanias* (adulteresses), and nonvirgins—except for those who lost their virginity accidentally—were all considered *thayb,* and the law treated them accordingly. A divorced or widowed girl who lived for one year with her husband without the marriage being consummated was usually included in this group. A *thayb* could not be forced into another marriage but had to give her consent according to the laws of all four *madhahib* (al-Hisari 1986, 482–83). This consent was often given orally in court through a *tawkil* (Alexandria 1273/1856, 1:14–42) or by a witnessed *tawkil* to whoever represented her (Alexandria 1273/1856, 1:13–15, 18). Even though Hanbalis are considered the most conservative *madhhab,* it is interesting that they require the consent of an adult *bikr* and *thayb,* and that they consider that it is the *thayb* who orders her *waliyy* to marry her (Ibn Taymiya 1992, 103–5).

Wilaya and Kafaʾa

As discussed, notwithstanding the basic similarities between the *madhahib,* there were significant differences in substance and procedures that separated them. The most important difference had to do with *wilaya* (guardianship, patronage) and *kafaʾa* (parity). Thus, the *madhahib* agreed that it was preferable for marriage to be witnessed by a *walyy* from the bride's family; in case of a *qasir,* a *waliyy* was obligatory for a marriage to be legal—except for the Hanbalis, who did not see any need for *wilaya* for a *rashida* (reasonable, sensible). If the bride had no *walyy,* then a *qadi* or *shaykh* assumed the responsibility. The schools, however, did not agree on the substance or meaning of *wilaya.*

Shafi°is

In his *al-Risala,* the Imam al-Shafi°i asks that a woman be betrothed through her *waliyy,* whose approval is needed for an engagement to take place (1988, 208). For a marriage contract to be valid, it must include the *ijab wa qubul* (request and acceptance, welcome) of husband and wife or their agents, the term *al-nikah* or *zawaj* (marriage) or their derivatives (al-Bakri 1991, i, 57), the witnessed consent of both parties or their deputies, and a *waliyy* to "give the bride away." Shafi°i further qualifies the woman's consent as being equal in importance to the man's (1988, 213) and denies the validity of a marriage in which a *thayb*'s consent is given after the marriage because of the strong possibility that she was forced by her *waliyy* (1988, 232).

The practice in Egypt's *shari°a* courts differed somewhat from the above. The lack of a *waliyy* related to the bride did not seem to constitute a problem in registering Shafi°i marriages. In fact, in Dumyat the majority of Shafi°i marriages involving *thaybs* did not mention a *waliyy* (Dumyat, Ishhadat A.H. 999/1594, 30:7–17) or indicate that the bride gave her *idhn* to whoever represented her, for example, her father (Dumyat, Ishhadat A.H. 983/1578, 17:17–50). In many instances, the wife undertook to contract her marriage directly by giving the Shafi°i *qadi* permission to marry her (Dumyat, Ishahadat A.H. 983/1578, 17:23–71, 59–188); and she very often received the dowry in her own hands (Dumyat, Marriages 1299/1882, 12:1, 3, 8, 9, 10, 15, 18). Marriages are also recorded in which the *waliyy* was actually the bridegroom, particularly in the case of remarriages (Dumyat, Ishhadat 975/1570, 8:51–196).

Regarding *kafa°a,* although Shafi°is admonished that girls be married to their *kuf°* (equal), who could provide them with the standard of living to which they were accustomed, they had no problem with the marriage of "unequals": "He could be rich and she poor, or she could be rich and he poor." When both parties were consenting adults, their marriage was valid; and the woman's male elders had no right to break it (1988, 232). Finally, Shafi°is considered the dowry to be a necessary ingredient in a marriage, but did not see the lack of dowry as invalidating the contract (1988, 229).

Hanafis

Even though the Hanafi *madhhab* did not apply *wilayyat al-ijbar* to *bikr balighs* and the Shafi°i *madhhab* did, the Hanafi *madhhab* was more patriarchal and elitist than the Shafi'i when it came to *wilaya* and *kafa'a*, as is clearly reflected in courts records. Thus, even though a *bikr baligh* or *thayb* could not be forced into marriage by anyone according to the Hanafis, *wilaya* still applied for a marriage to be valid. If an adult *bikr* or *thayb* chose to marry herself without a male member of her family acting as *waliyy,* then her dowry had to be equal to that expected of her peers, and the husband had to be her *kuf'*. If either of these conditions were not assured, then her elders had the right to annul the marriage, even against her wishes. In the opposite situation, however, where a father married his daughter to a man who was not her *kuf'*, Hanafis considered the marriage valid and did not allow the bride to contest it. The reasoning used in this instance was that, if a girl married a man not her *kuf'*, then she shamed her father and *'asab* (blood relationship); that is, the matter touched on the father's honor and he had the right to redress it. From the Hanafis point of view, this rule reflected their belief that girls tended to follow their feelings and *shahwa* (sexual desires) and could thus be influenced by men not of their class or stature. As for allowing the father to marry his daughter to a man who was not her *kuf'*, this was explained on the basis that money was not everything, and that sometimes certain other qualities were more appealing in a man and that the father knew best what was good for his daughter (al-Bakri 1991, 1:238, 258–261). Finally, Hanafis approved of a marriage in which the bride gave her consent after the marriage had taken place, even if she was forced into it (al-'Asqalani 1987, 12:473).

Malikis

Malikis were similar to Shafi'is and Hanafis in certain ways, different in others. Like them Malikis allow *wilayat al-ijbar* over a *qasir* and extended this *wilaya* to a *bikr baligh*. But although they accepted that a *thayb baligh* could contract her own marriage, they insisted on the presence of a *waliyy,* even if she was *safiha* (immoral). As for a *thayb qasir,* she had to be married by her *waliyy* (al-'Asqalani 1987, 12:483–87). The Malikis differ significantly from the other two *madhhahib* in regard to the delegation of *wilaya.* Unlike Hanafis and Shafi'is, Malikis allowed not only the *wasi* (trustee) of a guardian (the father, his *wasi,* or the ruler) to act as *waliyy* but extended this right to the *wasi* of the *wasi,* and the *wasi* of the *wasi's wasi,* and so on, even in using *wilayat al-ijbar* the same applied to other guardians without *wilayat al-ijbar;* thus, if an uncle was guardian, he could have his *wasi* perform the marriage. One group of Malikis gave the grandfather and the brother the right of *wilayat al-ijbar* if there was fear for a *bikr*'s virtue (al-⁽Asqalani 1987, 12:486).

There are also clear differences between one town and another regarding the status of the bride. Whereas most Maliki towns differentiated in the treatment of the bride depending on her legal status, certain Maliki courts differentiate little between a *qasir, baligh,* or *thayb.* Thus, marriages recorded in Armant—whose available records are for the nineteenth century only—are unique in their consistent use the term *mujbiruh(a)* (he who has the right to compel her) in reference to the guardian of a *qasir* boy or girl (Armant, Talaq wa ⁽uqud 19th c., 1:12–150, 154, 153) and ⁽*aqid laha* (contracting for her) for both a *bikr baligh* (Armant, Talaq wa ⁽uqud 19th c., 1:12–151, 10–144) and a *thayb* (Armant, Talaq wa ⁽uqud 19th c., 10–145).

The issue of *wilaya* is important among the Malikis. For one thing, they attached a father's *wilaya* to his financial responsibility toward his unmarried children. If a father stopped supporting his daughter, then he had no *wilaya* over her, and another member of her family or the *qadi* became her *waliyy* (Manfalut, Ishhadat 1228–1229/1810–1811, 5:9–31, 13–45; al-⁽Asqalani, 11:486). Furthermore, for a contract to be valid there had to be present a *waliyy* (or his *wakil* or *wasi*) or the person of "consequence and decision" among her people. This means that a clan or tribal elder was also a "guardian" from whom she could be betrothed, who had a say in her marriage, and who could refuse to recognize a marriage that she contracted for herself. Malikis indicated their preference for a *waliyy* of the bride's ⁽*asab* (Manfalut, Ishhadat 1228–1229/ 1812–1813, 5:33–118, 13–47), but the more prestigious the *waliyy*'s position and the higher he was regarded, the better. Having many *waliyy*s on the side of the bride was considered a sign of respect and patronage. In Maliki marriages, only women of no consequence, family, money, beauty, or men to protect them were married without a *walyy* or with a stranger as *waliyy* (al-⁽Asqalani, 12:487). An interesting variation on the matter of *waliyy* in a Maliki marriage is that of a *qasir* brother officiating as the *waliyy* for his sister. Because *rushd* (majority, maturity) was a necessary requirement in a *waliyy,* the brother had to be represented by an adult, usually the *qadi* because no other suitable *waliyy* might be available among the siblings (Isna, Ishhadat 1193/1779, 30:27–54). It should be added that the Malikis insisted on *kafa⁾a* as a requirement for the validity of the marriage, a fact mentioned in Maliki contracts with terms such as "with the dowry of her equals" or "equal to her paternal aunt (⁽*amatiha*) (Isna, Sijillat 1191/1777, 29: 20–46, 47, 48; 1193/1179, 30:27–54).

From the above discussion, we can conclude that, although the Shafi'i *madhhab* as practiced in Egyptian courts recognized the authority of the extended family with the father as head and the mother as the logical authority following him, the Malikis gave much weight to the importance of patriarchal relationships that they interpreted as existing within the extended clan and tribe. For them, it was general male patriarchy that was stressed, at least as the laws were applied. As for the Hanafis, they emphasized the importance of the patriarchal family, stressing the *'asab,* interpreted in the form of a male head, or patriarch, of the family. The father's individual authority and protection over his children extended to his father but exluded the mother of his children, except when no other male related by *'asab* existed.

Guardianship and Modern *Shari'a* Law

A nineteenth-century man wished to marry an adult girl from his town of Hamaqa in Daqahlia province in Lower Egypt. When her family turned him down, he eloped with her and married her through the *wikala* of a stranger to her family. Her family informed the authorities, who investigated the matter and referred it to the judiciary *majlis* of Zaqaziq,[9] whose authority extended to Hamaqa. After investigating, the *majlis* ordered that the girl be returned to her family and the man be thrown into prison. This decision was justified on the basis that the marriage was illegal because it lacked a *waliyy* from male members of the girl's family and that her *wakil* was not related to her. The *majlis* then sent out orders to all *qadi*s that no marriage was to be concluded without the presence of a *waliyy 'asib*. If the bride indicated that she had no *waliyy,* the *qadi* must first ascertain if this was true; if so, then the *qadi* must act as the *waliyy* of the bride and make sure that the bridegroom was her *kuf'* and that a proper dowry was paid. This procedure was required for both *qasir* and *baligh* brides (Alexandria, Da'awai 1273–1281/1856–1864, 1:63–139). The *majlis* based its decision on the fear of the trickery played by some men in ruining the morals of girls by convincing them to go against their parents' wishes.

This case is interesting on various levels. State interference in setting standardized laws to be enforced by the courts in the various

---

9. Part of nineteenth-century legal reforms. First introduced in the 1840s by Muhammad 'Ali Pasha, the *Majlis al-Ahkam* and its branches in various central towns, were developed by Khedive Isma'il between 1870 and 1873. They continued to function until the creation of National Courts in 1884.

parts of Egypt was slowly becoming established by the middle of the nineteenth century, although practice followed much slower. The treatment of this particular precedent-setting case was determined according to a need to control "immorality" in a fast-changing environment. It is telling that the couple eloped to Alexandria, which was growing by leaps and bounds during the nineteenth century. The decision of the Zaqaziq *majlis* leaned toward the Hanafi code because of its insistence on both *kafa²a* and *wilaya* and the annulment of a marriage when not approved by the bride's elders on the basis of *kafa²a*. But the Maliki *madhhab* was also in close agreement with the findings, particularly as they relate to the need for a *waliyy*, a fact that was noted by the *majlis*. This seemed to presage the future handling of family and gender issues, with preference for the Hanafi *madhhab*, supported by the Maliki *madhhab* when needed. The Shafi^{c}i *madhhab*, the most popular in Lower Egypt and certainly the least elitist of the *madhahib*, would not be as important in the formulation of the new laws.

This case was reflected in other cases throughout the twentieth century in which an adult woman could not transact her own marriage against the wishes of her family. The usual excuse used by the courts or the police in separating such couples was *kafa²a, wilaya,* or *mahr*. A typical approach to this matter by religious authorities is reflected in the following dialogue, published in *al-Liwa² al-Islami* under the distinctive title of *Hatha al-Zawaj batil* (This marriage is void). A woman wrote asking the *shaykh*'s opinion about the validity of her ^{c}urfi (common law) marriage, which was transacted in front of two witnesses who were not related to her. The answer was that this was an illegal marriage because "it was missing *shart al-wilaya*" (condition of guardianship), even though she was an adult, previously married woman. The *shaykh* goes on to explain that because the marriage had been consummated, the woman deserved a dowry because of what became permissible from her sexually *(bima istahala min faragiha)*. He concludes that for this marriage to be legal, it had to be registered by a government *ma²thun shar^{c}i* in the presence of the bride's father or other male relative, indicating her family's approval. Otherwise the marriage was null (Aug. 12, 1993, 6).

Kafa²a played as important a role. The 1904 case of Safiyya al-Sadat is perhaps the best known, but is certainly not unique. Her marriage to *shaykh* Ali Yusif was annulled by the *shari^{c}a* court in answer to her father's wishes on the basis of non-*kafa²a*, even though the father had agreed to her betrothal to *shaykh* Yusif and she was married to him in the house of her relatives. Her father did not agree with the marriage; and even though she was in her twenties, he took the matter to court,

where he demanded that she be divorced for lack of *kafaʾa,* a requirement of the *shariʿa.* The court's finding for the father was justified on the
basis that it feared *darar* (harm) because the husband came from a
different background *(biʾa),* whose traditions may amount to mistreatment for an upper-class woman (Baron 1991, 275). This was a far cry
from the case mentioned earlier, in which it was the bride who requested
divorce for being forced into a marriage with a man she considered not
her *kufʾ,* or when the courts supported a woman's right to stay with a
husband of her choice even against her father's wishes (Cairo, Bab al-
ʿAli, 1035/1624, 107:701–169). In another case, a wife sued successfully
for divorce for lack of *kafaʾa* with the man her father forced her to marry
while she was still a minor (Cairo, Bab al-Ali 1042/1631, 115:125–600).

Furthermore, as indicated earlier, *qasirs* who reached majority before their marriage was consummated, that is, they were still *bikr,* could
simply refuse the marriage by indicating this to the *qadi* soon after
reaching *bulugh* or learning of the marriage for the first time. This
practice changes in the twentieth century. It was no longer enough for a
baligh to indicate that she refused the marriage into which she had been
forced by her guardian; instead, she had to present proof that she had
not given her permission to her *wakil* to contract a marriage for her.
This requirement was often difficult to fulfill because most marriage
tawkils were orally given, and the silence of a girl was considered consent (Alexandria, Daʿawi 1910, 130:4–5). In short, the new laws—
backed by a gender discourse that pushed the interpretation of the laws
even further—extended the regulations that pertained to minors under
the different *madhahib* and, under Ottoman rule, were the basis for
shariʿa court decisions involving all females, previously married or not.

At the same time, a mother's custody rights were also curtailed as
part of the standardization of laws. Modern courts continued the earlier
practice of awarding legal guardianship to a mother unless she was of
questionable morality, and were as willing as Ottoman courts to extend
the mother's period of *hadana* (custody) beyond that established by the
shariʿa. The big difference came with Law 25 (statute 20) for the year
1929 (replaced by Law 78 in 1931, and later by Law 100 in 1985).
According to this law, the period of custody was divided into two parts,
hadana and *damm* (collecting, joining). *Hadana* begins from the date of
birth until the age of ten for boys and twelve for girls. A boy can remain
with his mother until age fifteen, and a girl until she is married, but only
in special situations in which none of the legally accepted male relatives
demand *damm* and when it appears that this is best for the children and
on condition that there is no *nafaqa* (support) paid to the mother. As for

damm, it began when the child reached the maximum age for the "woman's" *hadana* and ended legally when the child reached the age of legal maturity, which the law sets at twenty-one, following European practices (Al-Bakri 1991, 2:555).

Hadana belongs to the women of the child's family, who included a hierarchical group beginning with the mother, maternal grandmother or great-great-grandmother, then paternal grandmother, sisters, maternal aunts, paternal aunts, niece of a full-sister, niece of a maternal half-sister, maternal aunts, paternal niece from father's aunt, and so on. The father's family followed, moving in a concentric circle depending on the closeness of the blood relationship, but with a precedence being given to the mother's family. Thus, the maternal grandmother was preferred over the paternal grandmother in the situation in which the mother was not fit or was married to a "stranger."

The period of *damm* is designated for "men" and begins after the period of *hadana,* when it is deemed that the child no longer needs the care of womenfolk—that is, he or she is self-sufficient and does not need someone to teach him such essential practices as toilet-training, eating, cleansing, ablutions, and purification—estimated at seven years of age for boys and nine for girls. Even though *hadana* belonged to the women, as per law 25 of 1929, control of the child remains with the father or male *wasi,* even while he or she stayed with the mother. Besides, if the mother marries another man, then the child is either taken over by another woman in the family or, lacking a "woman," the male relatives enact their right to *hadana,* so that an uncle could be preferable to a mother, based on the belief that the closeness of the 'asab is best for the child. But who is closer than the mother? Even more significant is the method used to determine the right to *damm* beyond the father, who had the primary right. Here, it is the right to inheritance of property that constitutes the basis for custody, except that the grandfather was placed ahead of brothers, and girls do not go to those they could marry, like male cousins (al-Bakri, 1991, 2:556–60). The basis of the law in this case is purely the Hanafi *madhhab.*

Clearly in favor of a strong patriarchal order, the Hanafi code is used by the state to establish its own hegemonic control over gender and family relations. This fact is not lost on either the lawyers or the public; and the law has been challenged many times, but without success. In 1974, a mother demanded that the Maliki code rather than the Hanafi code be applied to her child-custody case because it was more favorable to the rights of mothers and children. In his argument, her lawyer focused on the contradictions between law 78 for 1931, which confirmed *hadana* on the basis of the Hanafi code, and the Egyptian Constitution. According to the Constitution "the *shariᶜa* was a principle source of law for Egypt" and "family is the basis of society [whose] foundation (*qawamiha*) is religion." Therefore, for the state to select a particular *madhhab* and indicate it to be the only source of law was against the dictates of religion and against the Constitution. Furthermore, requiring the courts to apply only one *madhhab* meant closing the door to *ijtihad* (legal interpretation) and the ossification of law (Al-Bakri 1990–1991, 2:620–21). The case was taken to court in April 1976 and was dismissed, the *qadi* finding in favor of the validity of law 78.

The *qadi*'s justification in reaching this ruling is enlightening. According to him, the choice of a particular *madhhab* was the prerogative of the *mushariᶜ* (lawmaker), who had the right to require that the judiciary be obligated to stick to it. Because the *waliyy al-amr* (ruler) has decided on a code, the judiciary have no right to apply another; after all, it is the right of the *mushariᶜ* to decide what is most fitting to the conditions of society and to use the power available to him to consolidate the people under one law, thereby putting an end to differences and making it possible for all to understand a uniform law with which all can deal. Besides, the *qadi* continued, because the law allowed for recourse to other *madhahib* in case the Hanafi school did not provide the required answer, it was a mistake to describe the action of the *mushariᶜ* as constituting closing the door of *ijtihad* (al-Bakri 1990–1991,2:623).

As for the logic behind the Hanafi laws being more appropriate for society, the judge's ruling discussed the differences between Maliki and Hanafi laws: although the Maliki *madhhab* is more favorable to the mother because it allows a son to stay in a mother's *hadana* until he reaches *bulugh* and a daughter until she is married (Abu Hanifa estimated the maximum age of *hadana* at ten for boys and twelve for girls) Malik based his estimations for a girl who is inexperienced and had nowhere to go. Therefore, she could be entrusted to her mother. In contradistinction, Abu Hanifa emphasized the age at which the girl reached puberty or *had al-shahwa* (age of carnal awareness), when she must be protected by men. In the modern world, women leave the house, and there is therefore a greater need for their protection from the evils that can entice women or befall them. Thus, the judge concluded that Abu Hanifa is more fitting for modern society (al-Bakri 1990–1991, ii, 616–628).

In actual fact, what the law accomplished is to give the responsibility of the child to the mother during his/her dependent years, then to transfer the responsibility to the father or another male relative when the child reached the "right" age. If the mother resisted the *damm* of her child to the father or another man, then the child was removed by the force of the state and delivered to whomever had the right of *damm* (al-Bakri 1990–1991, 2:584). The justification given to this act is the need for a son to be disciplined and taught to follow the example of a man and for a girl to be protected from herself and others. What the law does not mention, however, is that at the age of twelve to fifteen when *damm* often began, the child had become an asset and no longer in need of the physical care of the mother. He or she was "independent" and productive, and the labor of such children and the dowry that a girl could bring her guardian cannot be discounted. This is particularly so given the tie between *damm* and inheritance rights, which decide which male relative had precedence to a child. One can conclude that children were looked at as a productive asset, a form of property that was inheritable. It was the state that issued these laws, laying the responsibility for the early care of children on the shoulders of the mother, when children were clearly dependent; but once they have grown and become an asset, they are turned over to a patriarch. Moreover, extending the period of *damm* from puberty to the age of twenty-one also further extended the advantage of guardianship to the male guardian. If the child was an asset (e.g., inherited wealth) the male relative can demand *damm;* and the force of the state would be used to support his right (Alexandria, Daᶜawi wa Ahkam 1910, 130:58–33). If the child was not an asset and the brother or uncle did not want him or her, the law could demand and try to force him to "take the child in"; but practically speaking, this was a moot issue.

As has been discussed, although minor children have always been under the control of a guardian, during the Ottoman period, minors (boys and girls) could be married at any age by their guardians who had the *(wilayat al-ijbar).* A minimum marriage age of sixteen for women and eighteen for men became a requirement by law in 1931 as part of *shariᶜa* court reforms (al-Bakri 1991, 1:152–53). This act was claimed by Muslim feminists and reformers as a great success, which it would have been had the laws ended there. But, the same legal reforms established "majority" at twenty-one, although majority had earlier been gauged according to ᶜ*aql, rushd,* and *bulugh,* usually reached by the age of fifteen and often earlier (Ghazali 1990, 31), determined by *hadd al-tamyiz* (ability to discern), which could begin at the age of seven and which allowed a minor to handle his/her own financial affairs.

Establishing majority at the age of twenty-one meant that the time during which minors remained under the legal authority of guardians who controlled their "movements" was substanially extended (*al-Fatawi al-Islamiyya* 1981, ii, 433). This situation proved problematic when an orphan fell under the guardianship of an uncle or an older brother who stood to gain from controlling his ward's property (Fatawi 1305/1888, 1:4–52). Rich orphaned girls often remained under a guardian's control for life through their marriage to a cousin or someone chosen by the guardian for them.

Interestingly, laws of guardianship introduced in the twentieth century were described as being based on the Hanafi *madhhab,* which the jurists claimed to have been the practice of Egyptians before the reforms. In point of fact, not only did different *madhahib* predominate in different parts of the country before the reform of courts began in the 1880s, but state-selected committees were given the authority to choose the laws they considered to be the most acceptable interpretations of the Hanafi *madhhab,* which they considered to be appropriate laws for their time. They were also allowed to look at the other *madhahib* for interpretations they wished to include that they could not find in the Hanafi *madhhab.* In other words, the *shari^ca* code that was applied by the twentieth-century reformers was a selective one, open to interpretation by the adjudicators and guided by new hegemonic elites coming into being as Egypt's centralized nation-state structures were in the process of development.

Here, it is not a question of which laws were better or whether the condition of children and women was better before or after the reforms. The point is that modern personal-status laws were only a partial interpretation of the *shari^ca* as practiced in previous ages. In reality, these were "new" *shari^ca* laws fitting new conditions. The difference is significant; whereas before the reforms different family laws were applied in different parts of the country and *^curf* played an important role in the determination of such laws, now the state is directly involved in social construction with state power backing it. The result is the establishment of a state-sponsored patriarchal order. This does not mean that the *shari^ca* before the twentieth century was an unchanging one; to the contrary, as illustrated here, the *shari^ca* was in process of flux and changed as to time and place. But although the *shari^ca* both before and after the reforms has been transformed as part of the historical process —with the state playing a minor role before the nineteenth century— since the reforms, the state has become a conscious and intentional molder of gender laws.

PART SIX

Women, Morality, and Violence

16

Confined, Battered, and Repudiated Women in Tunis since the Eighteenth Century

Dalenda Largueche

This research, based on a careful investigation of Tunisian archives, should be placed with "histories of distress," or what can be termed "negative history" involving violence, "capitivity," and repudiation. As is given testimony by Tunisian archives, far from being occasional stories of battered and confined women, the incidents described in this chapter are typical of Muslim society of the *ancien régime,* with its clearly drawn social structures, patriarchal mentality, and institutions. If today the movement toward the emancipation of Tunisian women is growing, conditioned by contemporary and future problems, the weight of the past is still heavy in shaping the many levels of the real and the imagined in the life of women. It is in this sense that knowledge of the history of Tunisian women is to be examined, so that present contradictions will become clear and more tangible and thereby define the road to take.

As guarantors of future generations, of the honor and the social order in this patriarchal system, women have been constrained by a stringently controlled normative conduct. The processes of moral control and discipline that were enforced by the guardians of the patriarchal order, defenders of the *shariʿa,* put the social role of women at the center of the moral discourse, causing any deviation or transgression by women to be seen as a moral danger to society. Thereby, a vast apparatus of control and coercion, legitimated by religion, was put in place.

Resisting throughout different historical phases and with the help of the political and religious institutions, this apparatus has continually

259

been reviewed and deflected from its initial goals. The most fragile element of society is always the most vulnerable at times of conjunctural difficulties and crisis of mutation. The mutations in the life of Tunisian women caused by the crisis of the nineteenth century and colonialism, illustrate well this phenomenon. Next to the regulations set up to control conjugal marriage, reeducation and repression of women take on important dimensions.

Under this *ancien régime* brought about by the nineteenth century, *Dar Juwad*s (House of Noble Persons) multiplied in number. In reality, these were houses of arrest and correction, where rebellious and recalcitrant women were enclosed so as to "bring them around" to the prescribed norms of conduct and morality. As evidenced by the archives, violence encountered by women in the old centers of the city grew, which is in contrast to earlier periods when gender violence was more the norm of rural life and when urban existence appeared to be more "civilized." Another fact, no less telling of an ongoing profound social crisis, concerned extrajudicial and unilateral repudiations, whose increasing proportions during the colonial period constitute an indicator of dislocations in the traditional family. There was certainly great concern for the alienation of women; unfortunately, the methods applied to the handling of the "feminine problem" left distinctive marks on different classes of society.

Archives as a Source of Women's History

My archival research is based on a number of sources, particularly "primary sources" in the shape of different types of archives that present somewhat brutal information based on actual events. Notwithstanding their formalized and fragmentary nature, archival information demonstrates objectivity and gives evidence to hiden aspects of everyday life that other sources, such as travelers' accounts, could only touch on in passing.

Fatawi and *nawazil* documents, *shari*ʿ*a* court records, legal actions and decisions, *khataya* and *da*ʿ*awi* registers, and police reports, are fundamental to the reconstruction of the social history of Tunisian women, particularly in relation to intimate conjugal history and gender relations.

1. *Fatawi* and *Nawazil* registers are documents classified as juridical and religious literature. They concern collections of business brought to the attention of the *faqih*s (legist, theologian) and *qadi*s (judges) who then pronounced an opinion or passed judgment on them. These date from the medieval to the modern period. We still retain the *nawazil al-*

Burzuli, fatawi al-Wancharissi, and *ajiwibat Qasim Azzum.* Even though these *fatawi* and *nawazil* are somewhat stereotyped and normative, they give us unique information and details on the life of women. This juridical literature constitutes the first source allowing us to look for the origins of *Dar Juwad.* With the details gathered from the *ajwiba* (answers) and *nawazil* concerning conjugal conflicts and divorce, we are able to relive *Dar al-Thiqa* (House of Trust), the first stage in the genesis of *Dar Juwad* that has been discussed by nineteenth-century sources.

2. *Shariᶜa* court records contain the proceedings of legal disputes brought to the attention of *shariᶜa* courts and judged by the *qadis.* These records are held in the Archives of the Ministry of Justice. Because personal and civil status are at the center of the information provided by these juridical sources, they cannot be bypassed by social historians, particularly those interested in women's history. In a way, they are the written memoirs of the hidden face of society, that of family disorder. It is regrettable that these registers, as with other legal registers were not preserved before 1874. It was at the initiative of the reformist minister Kheiredin (1874–1876) that conservation and organization of the archives was undertaken in Tunis. The archives cover the whole colonial period, but stop in 1956, when Tunis became independent and when *shariᶜa* courts were cancelled and the different institutions of justice were unified under a system of positive law.

3. Notary records are the most important and best preserved of court archival records next to the *shariᶜa* registers. These documents are consigned in registers, each of which was held by one or two notaries. The *khazinat-al-ᶜudul* notary documents enrich our knowledge of Tunisian society's past. Taken directly from social existence, the information contained in these archives constitute a basic instrument for the historian. If the basis of these documents dates back from the period of Kheiredin, another type can be dated back to the beginning of the nineteenth century. Less important, perhaps, these notary acts conserved at the National Archives, and recently classified and reorganized, are a rich source describing multitudes of situations that were confronted by Tunisian society in both public and private life.

4. The *Khataya* and *Daᶜawi* Registers are part of the Beylik Archives. The *khataya* (fines) register contains the penalties and sanctions enacted by the central government against those who break the law and the political, social, or economic plans of the state. The *diyya* (blood price, compensation) is something of a tax that is paid to the state in cases of homicide or abortion. This *diyya*—which can be qualified as political—is different from the customary, or *sharᶜiyya diyya,* known as

"blood tribute" meant to repair damage experienced by the family of a victim. Given the importance of fiscality, the Beylik Archives present extraordinary scenes of daily existence in Tunis since the end of the seventeenth century. Besides indications regarding the crimilality and violence registered in these social records, the documents give us information regarding abortion and its methods, prenuptial relations, and adultery.

5. Municipal Police Archives cover the records of the urban police *conseil des zaptiés* instituted in Tunis in 1860 during the multitude of administrative reforms and political enterprises of the state. This municipal police was charged, in the framework of social control, to assure the security of citizens and to put down offenses and legal infringements. These archives contain daily reports compiled by agents and signed by their chief to be sent to the superior authorities. These reports inform on all businesses undertaken and decisions reached by the police. It is indeed in these reports that one can draw rich information in a condensed form regarding violence, marital conflicts, and other social phenomena in the city of Tunis during the middle of the nineteenth century.

Shariʿa Basis for the Alienation of Women

There is little need to insist on the predominance of the husband within the family in accordance to Islamic law. We would be thrusting at open doors in insisting on the marital power and the great prerogatives accorded to men in the *shariʿa* prescriptions on marriage. At any rate, it is perhaps important to remember that this superiority of the man over the woman that forms the structural basis of the Muslim family was received from pre-Islamic and Christian traditions, and that it is far from being exclusive to Islamic law.

It is difficult to refute that Islam was born in an agnatic society and that its contribution to consolidation of the marriage tie, consolidation of the family, and improvement of women's condition is far from having been neglected. Certainly, Qurʾanic principles structured matrimonial relations around male hegemonic power but at the same time, did not elaborate on specific or systematic gender relations. The subordination of wife to husband, the right given to the latter to correct the disobedience and recalcitrance of his wife, the large marital prerogatives in the repudiation and dissolution of marriage bonds, are stated in the Qurʾan (Surat al-Nisaʾ) and supported by the Sunna (prophetic tradition and precedent). But the rules were elastic and evasive, and the door remained open for an *ijtihad* (theological interpretation) and a multitude of interpretations. Hence, the many divergences between *madhahib* (schools of law) and the differences of textual interpretations between theologians and jurisconsults as testified by *fatawi* literature.

The birth of Islamic law in regard to marital relationships was, thus, the fruit of adaptation of the doctrine to social realities. Between the normative ideal and daily practice, a profound gap has been hollowed out and great divergences established (Milliot 1953).

The Regulation of Marital Conflicts: Between Arbitration and the Confinement of Women

According to the Qur'an: "If you fear dissension between them, then chose a judge from the family! If they want conciliation, God will reestablish agreement between them, God is omnipresent and knowledgable" (Surat al-Nisa')

The principle of arbitration in solving marital conflict announced by the Qur'an was the basis for the creation of *Dar al-Thiqa, Dar al-Iskan* (House of Settlement), and *Dar al-Amana* (House of Honesty, Integrity), the institutional form for arbitrage. What could be more equitable than to put both sides of the conflict under the surveillance of the *ajwad* (people of confidence) while waiting for a just and edifying judgment. The documents attest to debates and divergences among the *ʿulamaʾ* in regard to that institution, however. Some criticized them as such *bidʿa* (innovations) while others admitted and supported that it conformed to Islamic law. Qasim ʿAzzum, *mufti* of Tunis at the end of the sixteenth century, relates the question in his *ajwiba* (Qasim ʿAzzum: Les ajwiba manuscrit de la B.N., no. 4854) and shows us the polemics that it underwent during the time of the *imam* Suhnun (imam of Ifriqiya during the ninth century, famed for his *Mudawina: recueil de ses fatawi*). Before Qasim ʿAzzum, al-Wancharissi (1983) and al-Buzuli (al-Burzuli, *al-Fatawi*, vols. 1 and 2, manuscript, B.N., no. 4851) inform us in their treatises of the same divergences, but they let us know of another procedure that the *qadi* (judge) resorted to in cases of discord between a married couple: a woman of confidence, *amina* (trustworthy), was placed in the home of the couple to observe their attitudes and their actions. Some theologians condemned this practice as having no basis in either the Qur'an or the Sunna (Attar, T11, 584–85).

If this preventive institution has clear *shariʿa* basis, that of *Dar Juwad,* the house of correction where women were incarcerated, is far from the principle of arbitration that was sanctioned by the Qur'an and is in fact nothing more than a deviation in interpretation from that principle. In this way, we have passed from a preventive institution to a repressive one. The life and real status of women in this patriarchal society led the "masculine spirits" to invent a juridical design, about which we have no text, so as to hold women more firmly to the norms and regulations decided upon.

Women and Corporal Punishment

Although the Qur'an appears uncompromising in regard to the question of wives who are insubordinate to their conjugal duties and even enjoined the husband to use corporeal punishment as is said in Surat al-Nisa': "Those whose indocility you fear, reprimand them, send them to separate beds, batter them." That marital prerogative is mentioned at the third level in regard to the proposed procedures to bring an insubordinate wife to her senses in regard to her marital duties. Moreover, the punishment must be moderate. The Maliki *madhhab,* however, gave the wife the right to legal divorce in case of brutality and poor treatment by the husband, and the Hanafi *madhab* goes as far as to administer discretionary punishment *(ta'zir)* for a guilty husband. As for allowing corporal punishment, causes are clearly outlined. They include refusal of conjugal relations without legitimate reason or abandoning married life without authorization or valid excuses.

Although the right to corporeal chastisement was clearly conditional and controlled by many safeguards, its practice was nevertheless widespread enough to fill innumerable pages of the *khataya* and *da'awi* registers (N.A. Register of Khataya and Da'awi, esp reg. no. 396) and to constitute the design for many complaints brought to the police and the courts. The comment should be made, however, that no divorce has been registered in *shari'a* legal documents in which the plaintiff woman is automatically granted a divorce. Even worse, women complainants with their husbands and under the surveillance of the *ajwad,* were often sent by the judge to *Dar Sukna bi Husna* (the new name of Dar al-Amana, Dar al-Iskan, and Dar al-Thiqa) (House of Repose and Charity) to have their responsibilities defined and to receive a final judgment.

The famous nineteenth-century Tunisian historian/reformer Ahmed Ibn Abi Dhiaf placed corporal punishment within its juridical and religious context. Although admitting to the husband's right to correction, he tried to contain it within the confines of rural areas by comparing corporal punishment to the rough temperament of Bedouins and to the harshness of their lives (Dhiaf 1974, 95–61). Nevertheless as will be shown later, urban women were also prey to corporal punishment.

Repudiation, or the Marital Sword

Contrary to sacred Christian law that envelops matrimonial ties with extreme sacredness, making their dissolution forbidden, Islamic law envisages their rupture by instituting divorce *(talaq)* or repudiation. Divorce and repudiation have been placed at the center of studies of the traditional Muslim family, which is often looked at in terms of instability. Certainly, Islam allowed divorce and gave this right exclusively to the husband except in a few precise cases, but many types of repudiation were envisaged without having the same moral and religious qualifications. Divorce and repudiation have not been discredited or condemned by Islamic authorities, however, even though divorce is considered a *makruh* (forced, compelled), about which the Prophet is to have said, "Of all the things permissable, the most hateful to God is divorce."

It is true that *shariʿa* law established regulations for enacting divorce and that it also envisioned the right to a legal divorce for women under particular conditions. But the reality is far from what the regulations and the doctrines established to temper the marital prerogative in matters of repudiation. These doctrines are not always respected, and the favorable circumstances they accorded women are usually ignored by judges, who almost always systematically send women to *Dar Juwad,* to which our archives give clear testimony.

The Form and Practice of Alienation

Dar Juwayd:
A Place of Reeducation and Repression of Women

"Domestic prisons," as they are often called, these houses of seclusion and correction for disobedient and rebellious wives, were part of the vast apparatus of coercion and control used by the patriarchal system for its proper reproduction and maintainance of its equilibrium. A unique institution in the repression of women, it found its legitimacy in a corruption of the the principle of arbitration stated in the Qurʾan to regulate marital conflicts. Quite distinct from *Dar Sukna bi Husna, Dar Juwad* holds a very particular place in the scale of institutions for the management of marital conflicts. Treating all matters of private life, these institutions were often enveloped in mystery and ambiguity that created their own confusions in our collective memory.

These institutions may be close in their vocation and appellation, but they are distinct when it comes to their role and function. It is certainly not by chance that judges sent so many wives to lodge at *Dar Sukna bi Husna* while committing others to internment and solitary imprisonment at *Dar Juwad.*

The nature of the offenses that provoked internment of women at *Dar Juwad,* the treatment that they endured behind its walls, and the manner in which they lived while imprisoned there are all indications of the objectives of this institution and the role assigned to it in the maintenance of the established order. The names of these institutions are in themselves symbols of protection and of confidence of an "honor" from which a woman cannot detach herself: *Dar* (house, home), *thiqa* (trust), *Juwad* (noble persons), are a multitude of moralistic denominations that represent the will of the patriarchal system, are reserved for women, and represent a form of symbolic punishment that is inscribed in the space and world that were being assigned to them.

Dar Sukna bi Husna:
An Institution of Arbitration
Between Conflicting Married Couples

Far from being reserved from women, this institution concerned the household in question because it involved placing the two sides under observation by a judge of good reputation (*salihin* [the upright] or *umana*ʾ [trustworthy]). In the eye of the *qadi* who ordered it, the purpose of this residence was to delimit the responsibilities between the conflicting parties. It was a sort of probing period, a protective period leading to a well-founded decision, which could also give the marriage a chance to find the necessary harmony by which to restore its familial equilibrium. *Dar Sukna bi Husna* certainly puts us in contact with the marriage home, but where exactly does it place us within that home? All the proceedings that were studied concern the daily life of the family, starting from simple conflicts with the mother-in-law to discord between the married couple concerning difficulties in their daily lives. All the reported cases that finished their daily lives. All the reported cases that finished with an obligated stay by the couple at the *Dar Sukna bi Husna* are classified under the rubric of "poor treatment" or "cohabitation difficulties" (*su*ʾ *mu*ʿashara), excluding the cases that touch on the intimate life of the couple, including sentimental and sexual relations.

If the placing of the married couple under question was generally ordained by the *qadi* in a house prepared for this reason, it was not excluded that the couple could be surveyed by persons of confidence in their own home. The documents consulted even tell us about a choice being given to the woman by the *qadi. Dar al-Thiqa* or *Dar Sukna bi Husna* were often solicited by women plaintiffs.

Our sample of plaintiffs drawn from *fatawi* records of the sixteenth and seventeenth centuries, and *shari'a* registers from the nineteenth and twentieth centuries, allow us to conclude that recourse to this institution was considered, particularly by the women plaintiffs, as a beneficial recourse and a refuge against poor treatment by husbands and a guarantee of a dialogue that was not otherwise forthcoming.

At *Dar al-Iskan* or *Dar Sukna bi Husna,* the *jaida* (noble woman), or *amina,* was directed to keep a close eye on every gesture, action, and word of the wife and report them to her husband. After some time, the latter presented complete testimony to the *qadi,* who confirmed or invalidated the accusations made by one against the other.

Such as it functioned, *Dar Sukna bi Husna* was a judicial institution that assured some judicial guarantees for women. It assured some regulation of conjugal life. The rigor and care to provide the impartiality of the *qadi,* the protection of the family cell, and the *ijtihad* of the jurists, put together, contributed to the setting of this institution.

Dar Juwad: Prison of Broken Hearts

Dar Juwad, which for so long has haunted women and has given them shameful memories, is still alive in the feminine memory as a clearly distinguishable institution from those preceding it. It is mostly as we search through the archives of the nineteenth century that we are able to reconstruct the history of that institution. *Dar Juwad* appears to have been a genuine institution for the treatment of conflicts involved in the intimate side of love and sexual relations between couples. It is in fact a prison for women because of offenses of the heart.

In all the cases surveyed in which the *qadi* passed a judgment to seclude a woman at *Dar Juwad,* the case concerned her refusal of an undesirable husband or her attachment for a suitor not acceptable to her father. Confinement at *Dar Juwad* also took place in cases of repudiation during *'idda,* (the three-month waiting period following divorce before a woman can be remarried).

When the matter concerned touched on the intimate life of the couple, whether the woman was the accused or the plaintive, she was almost always automatically sent to *Dar Juwad.* Generally, the *qadi* ordered the internment of a woman at *Dar Juwad* in answer to the request of the husband or the father. The latter usage was owing to right of restraint recognized by the Maliki *madhhab,* which allows the father to force his daughter to marry the man of his choice.

Most of the affairs treated at *Dar Juwad* were repeat-cases of women challenging the bonds of marriage. Other cases involved problems of customary marriage laws that are not sanctioned by written documents—a feminine attitude that translates into a crisis of passion and effective drama. Incapable in all ways to make their sentiments and desires prevail, women were forced to use subtle and roundabout methods.

Now and then, a woman showed courage by refusing a husband chosen by her father or by becoming attached to a man unacceptable to her father. Others were confined at *Dar Juwad* for having dared ask to be divorced. The reason mattered little: a woman who demanded to be divorced, even for valid reasons, first had to spend time at *Dar Juwad.* Zina bint Hamid ibn Gmara insisted on being divorced, claiming that she had sustained irrevocable repudiation; ᶜAïcha bint ᶜAli al-Judi asked to be divorced because she had discovered that her husband was having intimate relations with her mother. They were both sent to *Dar Juwad* (Registre charaïque 1891, 12:7–14). In short, whether she was the aggressor or the one heartbroken, the woman could in no way reestablish grounds for parity with her husband who had the established order on his side.

How long did internment at a *Dar Juwad* last? The period of reclusion of a woman in that house of reeducation and correction was not determined in advance by the *qadi.* It changed according to the particular case, and that depended on the woman's endurance and her ability to resist. In fact, internment at *Dar Juwad* constituted a real ordeal, given the isolation and the psychological, moral, and physical pressures that women were subjected to. It could have lasted a few days, weeks, or months.

Life at *Dar Juwad* was considerably different from life at *Dar al-Thiqa* or from *Dar Sukna bi Husna,* where the woman, accompanied by her husband, continued to live a normal life while being observed. *Dar Juwad* approached being a prison. The voculabulary used by the *qadi*s and notaries in the cases reviewed are indicative of this fact: *prison, imprisonment, arrest.* The mental association with a prison was also held by men of *sharᶜ.*

How did women endure their imprisonment? And by what rules and regulations were they constrained? We have but little information about the life lived by the women behind the walls of those houses.

Nevertheless, there are certain indirect indications. Thus, we know that on the inside of these houses of arrest, the women were subjected to pressures of all types. Solitude, moral harassment (torment), and arduous domestic chores, were all part of internment. In certain cases, the women lacked vital items like food because it was the husband's duty to supply her needs. Husbands' lack of regard often reached the point where fathers complained to the counsels of the *zaptiés* (National Archives, *Zaptiés* 1898, doc. 56). Wives were sometimes exposed to aggression by the husband within that house and in the presence of *Jaid*s who supervised them, as happened in the case of the wife of Ahmad ibn ʿAli ibn Hassan (*ibid.*, 1898, doc. 58).

What social class did these women belong to? The names and occasionally the geographic origins can enlighten us on this question. City, village, and Bedouin women were all clients of the *ajwad* of the city. Closely tied to the *qadi, Dar Juwad* was more of an urban institution, and being a *jaid* was more of an urban vocation. Whether treatment differed for different classes of women and whether there were *Dar Juwad*s reserved for rich urban women and others reserved for less affluent villagers and Bedouin women, it is not easy to tell from our documents. Nevertheless, *"Jaid"* tells us that *Dar Juwad*s were controlled by urban notability. The *Dar Juwad* of the city of Tunis was situated in a distinct part of the médina of Tunis, between the Rue du Diwan and the Rue du Charaf.[1] These houses were under the control of the *ajwad,* whose names showed an eventual social distinction, such as Mohamed Silim, Mohamed Ghraïri, Mohamed Es-Sallawi, Kbair el Harmel or Hédi-Lejmi.[2] Symbol of good education and correction, the urban notability was the recourse of the *qadi* for the reeducation of recalcitrant women. It was the *qadi* who gave the *jaid* and the *jaida* their authority and hence their legal status.

The institution was privately funded, and the *jaid* demanded the cost of residence of the woman under his authority from the husband or the father. The monthly amount was fixed in advance by the *qadi,* based on the *jaid*'s estimation. Besides this fixed rent for room and services of the *ajwad,* the woman's necessary provisions were delivered by her husband or father in weekly baskets. Taking into account that added to the weekly payments were "presents" from the husband to the *jaid,*

1. *Dar Juwad*s did exist without any doubt in other cities of Tunis.
2. A. N. *Serie Hist. Rap. des Zaptiés.* docs. 57, 95, 99. *Registre charaïques des années* 1897, 1916, 1941. Actes des Aug. 24 and Dec. 26, 1897, Feb. 14, 1914, Dec. 19, 1916, Mar. 11, 1941.

which constituted a form of corruption, and that the *jaida* could "nibble" from the weekly supply baskets, the *Dar Juwad* was a lucrative enterprise for its owners. In fact, it was rather expensive for residents, particularly for women of the lower classes who nevertheless occupied an important place in these houses.

How long did internment last? How was it unraveled and how did it end? There was no time fixed in advance by the *qadi*. Resistance and tenacity could prolong the internment and even give a reprieve for those women with undesirable husbands. But rare were those women who resisted until the death of a husband or a father. Despair often defeated them and forced them to submit to the will of men. The confinement was then cut short; and the forced bonds of those marriages that had been contested were acknowledged, and the very human longing for a lover was quickly repressed. Real chastisement for offenses of love and longing was the job of the *Dar Juwad* and its methods for the correction of disobedient women. In this sense, it was an interval of shame and dishonor.

The Chastisement of the Body Between the Normative Discourse and Reality

A history of the feminine body is a page of the history of civilization taken from its most secret and intimate anthropological dimension. The feminine body in Arab civilization has been charged with all the suitable symbols of what is sacred: *taboo, forbidden, seduction, evil,* and *hellish.* The dualistic theory of the sacred/profane of the feminine body has nourished a rich written and oral literature whose golden pages are engraved in the accounts of *A Thousand and One Nights.* But in daily life and through enduring literary accounts that are fascinating and at the same time repulsive, men are continually nourished by patriarchal values that search above all to domesticate and to tame the female body. If done through violence, it is considered as a labor of purification and redemption. This violence and the forms and degree of intensity it takes within particular contexts is a history of domination about pain and resignation.

To his credit, Ahmed Ibn Abi Dhiaf, the famous reformist figure of nineteenth-century Tunis, devoted an entire tract to the question of the status of women (1968, 49–109). But even he continued to be torn between the rigorous constraints of *shari*ʿa decrees and the demands of politics and change. This last urban scholar was obliged to recognize the right of corporal chastisement to correct women, even while attempting to temper it by excluding brutality and harmful treatment (1968, 7th question).

In his argumentation, he presents a discourse mixing the social with the religious in defense of the traditional values of society. Ibn Abi Dhiaf admits to his method, and explains his endorsement of physical punishment as a last recourse for a husband who should not use it except out of desperation. Moreover, he dismisses its significance on the basis that it is a tradition of Bedouins who are ruthless and exercise it frequently as an issue of honor, but that townspeople and villagers never use this right and consider it shameful and repugnant. He adds his belief that Bedouin women actually pursue corporal punishment and see in it a sign of virility and affection from their husbands (ibid.).

Was there any real correspondence between the normative ideal that charged this discourse and daily life? One cannot but adhere to the idea of staggering between these two levels. But to what extent can one interpret the violence against women that we encounter in historical daily life as a cultural or mental structure productive of regular violence? Behind a peaceful façade marked by reports of domination and dependence admitted and internalized by women, a more complex reality is evidenced by the registers of *Khataya* and *Da'awi* of the eighteenth century and the beginning of the nineteenth century (National Archives, Khataya Register, nos. 13, 120, 142, 189, 274, 396). A sample of sixty cases of violence occurring century from the middle of the eighteenth century until 1824 and covering classes from upper-class townsmen to rural regions and Bedouins (Sahel region), will constitute the basis for our analysis.

Not only did the corporal punishment sustained by women appear to be almost a general phenomenon, but also contrary to the affirmations of Ibn Abi Dhiaf, it is suggestive of a brutal violence that often provoked death, abortions, and grave injury to women. This generalized violence points above all to the rural or tribal world. Ninety-five percent of the cases, which is a heavy majority, originated from rural, village, or tribal areas, as compared to only 5 percent from the cities.

As for the form that generalized brutality and daily violence took among rural, normadic, and sedentary groups, it appears to have been yet another form of the violent life that existed in tribal society. Tribal brutality, impregnated with the violence of material conditions and divisive and incessant conflicts, conditioned the comportment, attitudes, and even character of tribesmen.

About 70 percent of the cases of assault on women studied were followed by death, and about 30 percent of the assaults sustained by pregnant women caused miscarriage. In 55 percent of the cases, it was the husband who exercised the violence. The motives for marital violence were many, ranging from simple anger for the most vapid reasons, to punishment for the crime of adultery. For adultery, the husband could exercise extreme violence, including murder, against his wife with the complete sanction of the juridical cadre and appropriate customs.

Once the crime was committed, the husband was acquitted of his "duties" by the payment of the *diyya* of his unfortunate wife. It is important to point out here that, when adultery was the offense, the murderer-husband was spared; and it was the lover who had to pay the *diyya* of the woman in question (National Archives, *Khataya* and *Daʿawi,* no. 274). Responsibility for the crime was placed on the back of the lover. Honor was by far the most important value in this patriarchal system. When honor was soiled, the crime was legitimate. The predominance of tribal and village violence contrasts with city life, where the situation appears to have been more "humane" for women. Is that a result of the diformed prism of the sources? Always there are sociopolitical conditions in the towns that are different from the countryside. The presence of power, the legal and coercive institutions of the state, and other factors dissuade the "potential generators of violence." Also, towns offered women only a series of undefined enclosed spaces, where they were cloistered and devoted to laboring at home, whereas their sisters from the villages circulated quite freely in fields and paths, with all their risks and perils.

But these "peaceful" towns occurred less and less frequently. The violence of the city, when it was declared, announced not more stability but rather its end. It is in archives dating toward the middle of the nineteenth century that we are struck by the reversal of the situation that had earlier made the town relatively safe for women and turned it into a theater of violence against them. This happened at a time when urban society became partially ruralized by the influx of Maghrebien minorities, Europeans, and hundreds of freed, pauperized slaves who settled in the city of Tunis, causing crisis conditions that overflowed and exceeded Tunis's abilities.

Another sign of the manifestation of violence that was faced by eighteenth-and nineteenth-century women, is the multiplication of complaints by the victims of assault by hateful (holding grudges) and spiteful (malicious) husbands or former husbands. The statistics of the urban police during the year 1864 mention more than 3,600 acts of violence or assault that were more or less serious. I have organized a sample of 360 cases, corresponding to 10 percent of the total.

At the center of the sample, the cases that concern victimized or accused women are of particular interest. Of the 360 cases of violence, 76 involved women who were victims of assault, ranging from light assault to murder and representing 27.5 percent of the total victims of violence. This proportion corresponds to the minimum possible if we consider how often a battered woman hesitated in making a complaint, particularly if the baterrer was related to her or if the assault was of a sexual character. Still, 27.5 percent constitutes a significant number, especially if we were to compare it to the category of women charged with battery, who constitute 4.8 percent, as against 95.2 percent who are men charged with the same crime. Clearly, women are overwhelmingly the battered and men are overwhelmingly the batterers because, for every woman batterer, 6 women are battered; for every man battered, 2 men are batterers.

Who were these victims of violence and why were they battered? In addition to those women who were assaulted by husbands, fathers, or brothers, that is, those reflecting a continuity of violence from within the familial framework, we are confronted with is a new category of violence exercised more and more outside of traditional frameworks of the family. It is the violence that occurred in public areas, where the batterer had no family connection or parental ties to the victim. Among 76 assaulted women, only 10 had family ties to the agressor: 7 women, battered or killed by a husband, 2 by their sons, and 1 by a brother.

This new wave of violence marking the urban landscape gave a new profile to women who became exposed to violence by men in the street. Women of the lower classes (married, widowed, or divorced) who ventured into marketplaces and squares of the city, became potential victims; not to mention "hot" streets on the outskirts (suburbs) or in the lower city that was continually alive with "public women," over whom soldiers, policemen, vagrants, and pimps became violently angry (Largueche 1993, chap. 1).

Women victims of violence, whether assaulted, killed, or violated, on a daily basis in all the corners of the city, distance us from that image of the traditional "peaceful and quiet" city, where women were veiled and cloistered, supported (provided for), and subtly repressed (abused) by townsmen.

By the second half of the nineteen century, the image of Tunisian life described by Ibn Dhiaf had changed except for a small, diminishing part of its small urban citizenry. Tunis had become a city of crimes, murder, and violence; a city in crisis and change. And it was the feminine body, with all its fragility, that symbolized the most dramatic aspects of the city's painful transition.

Unilateral and Extrajudicial Repudiation, or the Obsession of the Women of Yesterday

Our attention has been drawn first to divorce of repudiation because of its arbitrary character and also because of the large number of such divorces registered in *sharicа* court archives. Of the three forms of dissolution of the ties of marriage, the unilateral extrajudicial (out of court) repudiation was the most arbitrary and, hence, the most injurious to women.

Abusive and often no more than a capricious marital act, *talaq* is distinctly distinguished from judiciary divorce, which is decided by the *qadi* in accordance to the demand of the wife[3] and which is to her advantage. It is also distinguishable from conventional divorce, in which the wife is party to a dispute. This study is based on a sample of 120 divorce cases drawn from *sharicа* pronouncements passed between 1878 and 1940. It should be stressed that this sample is no more than an indication of the massive number of acts of repudiation that fill the pages of the registers. The systematic registration of acts of divorce and the precise information that they provide, permit us to quantify the phenomenon and its significance to our understanding of the changes in everyday life and those caused by the conjuncture taking place. As pointed out earlier, I are uniquely interested in the unilateral extralegal repudiation in its three componants: revocable repudiation *(talaq rajci)*, irrevocable repudiation *(talaq bayyin)*, and innovative divorce *(talaq bidcа, talaq al-thalath)*.

The case samples permit us to reach conclusions regarding the important proportion occupied by this type of divorce: 66 out of 120, that is, 55 percent.[4] Revocable divorce *(talaq rajci)* tops the list with 36 cases out of the 66, or 54.5 percent. This "single repudiation" is, for the most part, made in cases without indemnity (compensation). Arbi-

---

3. Islamic law gives women the right to divorce in precise and particular situations. According to the Hanafi *madhhab*, a wife can ask for a divorce in case of a husband's impotence or his renunciation of Islam. According to the Maliki *madhhab*, she can also ask for a divorce if he does not pay her *nafaqa* (alimony, child support) for absence or even for misunderstandings (Milliot 1953).

4. This result is close to that of L. Blili (1985–1986). (Université de Tunis: 1985–1986).

trary divorce, even when it is thought out, this *talaq* sanctions the dissolution of marriage by a simple formula pronounced by the husband.
The wife could suddenly find herself deprived of the rights that are
accorded her by the *shariᶜa:* compensation and maintenance dowry
(food, support, nourishment). Juridical procedures are so slow, costly,
and overall humiliating that woman often renounce their rights just to
get divorced.

The innovative repudiation (*bidᶜa* or *talaq al-thalath*), which is the
most abusive of all, has negligible registration: 15 cases out of 66, that
is, 22.7 percent. Notwithstanding that it is considered unacceptable by
the *shariᶜa* and is also considered a grave *maᶜsiya* (injustice, injury) by
the Hanafi *madhhab* (Bousquet and Berche n.d., 80–82), this type of
talaq is far from being minimal among the repudiations registered during
the period investigated. How many families have been dislocated and
how many women have suffered from this irrevocable repudiation?

What social classes are most touched by these different types of
divorce? The names of the husbands in question and their professions
can sometimes give us an indication about where to place divorce in its
social class (see table 16.1).

From these figures we derive that the rate of divorce is higher
among the lower classes, particularly popular ones. Well-off tiers, the
aristocracy, and nobility appear to have been more protected from divorce during that confusing conjunctural period of transition.

Can one then reach conclusions regarding the fragility of marital
ties among popular classes and to the precarious situation of their
women? (Blili 1986, 364–67). It is probable that those families who
participated in the rural exodus suffered from financial difficulties and
disorder to no small degree. Since the second half of the nineteenth
century, women of the popular classes peopled the roads of the medina
and took a place in its public life (Largueche and Largueche 1993).

In total contrast to that way of life, were the affluent, alliances of
interests in marriage transactions, the aristocratic esprit de corps, and
the forced protection of women, served to work together to uphold the
marital ties among affluent and aristocratic classes. Permanent structural
elements of traditional Muslim society, the social phenomenon of divorce was thus in a tight relationship with the conjuncture in which it
occurred. The marital difficulties and the other adversities faced by
women translate eloquently the profound crisis that caused the disinte-
gration of traditional crafts and trades and the misery in which was born
the laboring classes of colonial Tunisia (Pennec 1964).

Table 16.1

Divorce, by Profession of Husband

Profession of Husband	Number	Percentage
Craftsmen	30	37.50
Artisans and Tradesmen	25	31.22
Military Officers	10	10.50
Laborers and Subalterns	6	7.50
Religious Dignitaries	5	5.25
Civil Servants	4	5.00
Total	80	100.00

Battered women, incarcerated women, repudiated women: the feminine figure is weighed down by misery and suffering in the heavily charged history of Tunisian society. But writing these pages of the history of battered women is to answer to a deep and unconfessed social need. It is also to demystify a past styled as modern and described as positive, that necessarily needs to be stripped of all its oppressive sacraments. We cannot sweep away the tracks and the roads for a new construction of civil society, except by baring the contradictions of a past that continues to weight on the mental structures today.

17

Law and Gender Violence in Ottoman and Modern Egypt

Amira El Azhary Sonbol

*I*n this chapter, I focus on gender violence in Egypt from the Ottoman period to the present. By gender violence I mean physical violence
enacted by men on women and vice versa, and mental violence, particularly as it relates to marital relationships. As examples of these two types
of violence, I will focus on rape as an example of physical violence, and
the institution of *taᶜa* (obedience) to illustrate mental and marital violence. By comparing the laws and handling of rape and *taᶜa* under the
Ottomans with their modern counterparts, I wish to make five interrelated points:

    1. A correlation exists between modern gender laws and the evolu-
tion of a new patriarchal order that was coming into being as part of
the process of nation-state building. Although espousing a discourse of
modernity, the nation-state was at the same time reinforcing male dominance, notwithstanding its mobilization of both men and women into its
service.

    2. The method used in formulating modern *shariᶜa* laws was *talfiq*
(patching), by which bits and pieces of Western laws and the interpretations of various *madhahib* (schools of law) were merged together to com-
pose what became known as "personal status laws" to handle gender and
family relations. Even though what was being set up was a new system,
it was bundled into a "legitimate" Islamic package. The idea of such
legal constructs as separate personal status laws did not receive distinct
status in Egypt before the twentieth century, and their establishment
would prove momentous for women.

277

3. The philosophical basis of personal status laws differed significantly from that applied in Ottoman courts. Thus according to personal status laws, the "natural characteristics differentiating human beings from other species form the basis upon which are based the legal principles regulating man's social existence. [Differentiation is made] according to whether the human being is a male or female; a husband, widower, or divorced; a father, a legitimate son; or whether he is legally competent" (al-Gindi 1987, 5). By conceptualizing the law on the basis of sexual differences that are then justified by human nature arguments, the rest of the patriarchal order falls into place. According to this synthesis, women are less reliable than men, they are moved by their emotions rather than by their minds, they are less able to remember facts, and therefore their judgment is not to be trusted. Because they are more liable to sin by nature, women must be protected and watched over. This does not mean that the Qurʾan or *fiqh* (juridical interpretations by Muslim clergy) does not differentiate between men and women on the basis of gender, on the contrary the Qurʾan is clear about this matter: "We created you from a man and a woman and made you into *shuʾub* (nations) and tribes to become associated one with the other" (Surat al-Hujurat:13). The difference comes in making a "psychological" picture of women the determining factor in modern legal disputes. Notwithstanding the nonacceptance of only women as witnesses in court cases, or that two women were equivalent to one male witness, there is no indication that, in rendering legal decisions, Ottoman courts were using generalized established principles that accepted women as more emotional or irrational. Putting aside possible misogyny on the part of the *qadi* (judge), the intent of the courts was to determine particular disputes and arbitrate marital and personal conflicts rather than to set generalized statements regarding gender relations. Hence, the clear differences in court decisions from one part of Ottoman Egypt to the other depended on the particular *madhhab,* local ʿ*urf* (tradition), and socioeconomic standards.

Modern reformers conceptualized society as an entity to be structured according to plans that fit with the needs of the nation-state. In other words, nation-state building involved the creation of society and culture, modeled after "imagined" superior structures. In such a system, it is the social unit, such as an institution, a class, or a particular gender, that is seen as a recipient of the law. Before the appearance of this type of nation-state structuralism, this was not the philosophy behind the pronouncements of legal judgments. Homogenization and codification were not the central issues in the minds of jurists of the schools of

Hanbal, Shafi'i, Malik, or Abu Hanifa, notwithstanding the centrality of the religious discourse. Rather, they debated laws, taking into consideration particular cases and which traditions pertaining to them were of greater validity. Hence, the differences both between and within the various *shari'a* schools, some of which constituted great differences for their age but appear less so to us today, although others were clearly minor.

4. Structuring and systemization involved dividing Egypt's court system into five different courts during the nineteenth century to suit different vested interests that constituted the ruling elite. Thus occurred the establishment of *shari'a* courts as part of the five-court system set up under colonial tutelage during the last quarter of the nineteenth century. The *shari'a* courts were described as essential to the needs of a Muslim community that demands that the laws continue to be Islamic, and that is probably correct. What is not correct is that these courts continued to practice the exact same Islamic laws that were practiced by Islamic courts during the Ottoman period. In fact, the structure, the codes, and the judges used in the new courts were quite different from those existing previously. The law was going to be essentially Hanafi law, except when it suited the hegemonic order, then Maliki law was used, plus a good dose of Western-inspired laws that were "infused" under the pretext of making the laws fit with modern times. The codes were written down and systematized as is normal with nation-states. This meant that not all the interpretations of these *madhahib*, with their founders, and the commentaries of their disciples and heirs, would be a source-of-law from which a judge can pick and choose given the specific context of the case and the general conditions of the time, which allowed for greater maneuverability depending on the details of the particular case. Instead, a standard formula was set according to which the judge had to rule.

The judges themselves were to be educated in a centralized way. They were assigned certain textbooks, selected and compiled by governmental committees, in which they were examined before being appointed to their positions by a central government under definitive codes of hiring, transfer, promotion, and firing. The discourse of the *qadis* became that of the state.

5. Although family and gender relations were placed under personal status laws for most situations, when it came to sex crimes, including rape, they were placed under criminal law. But rather than apply the *hudud* (canon law cases with unalterable punishments) to rape, judges preferred to follow modern laws that are much more lenient toward rapists. In short, although judges manipulated *fiqh* laws to establish a

shari*a formula that became oppressive to women, women were denied the deterring protection of *fiqh* laws designed to protect the victim and her/his rights. It is only in cases of gang rapes that also involved kidnapping that the death sentence was decreed as punishment for rape. In 1993, the death sentence was extended to include certain cases of rape, following the 1992 rape of a young girl in the middle of the overcrowded Cairo bus station in ʿAtaba during the month of Ramadan. The initial discussion in the press and in Egypt's National Assembly was pointing toward blaming the girl, and a law was actually proposed to blame families of rape victims for allowing their daughters out of their homes in the first place. Had it not been for public ridicule of such suggestions, perhaps the law would have passed and the death sentence would never have been included as punishment for rape. Even so, notwithstanding the tens who witnessed the rape, the case against the rapists was dismissed in 1994 for lack of evidence. Nor has the law ever been used in cases of rape not including kidnapping, notwithstanding the daily reports of rape of both boys and girls, minors and adults. I should add that the "split-personality" of the legal codes was not solved with the cancellation of the *shariʿa* courts in the 1950s because the separation continued in the laws themselves.

Taʿa and Violence

The institution of *taʿa* is intricately involved with marriage, divorce, and alimony. Marriage in Islam is considered a legal and binding contract, in which each party to the marriage is bound by certain obligations in return for certain rights. In signing a marriage contract, a wife promises to serve her husband, bear his children, and be faithful to him in return for his financial support and protection. These conditions are both written and unwritten, but the legal basis of the contract is "service for support." Long discussions of the marriage contract between the various *madhahib* focused mostly on the conditions upon which the husband had the right to withhold his financial support. The *madhahib* differed on these conditions, but all consistently accepted discontinuing the husband's financial obligations toward a hostile and disobedient wife (*nashiz*). According to Malik, a wife who was *nashiz* deserved no *nafaqa* (financial support if married, alimony if divorced); and if she had previous knowledge of her husband's financial condition yet consented to marry him, or remained with him if she was already married to him, then she had no right to *nafaqa*.

Hanafis and Shafiʿis determined that a *nashiz* lost her right to support for the day during which she acted against her husband's right to *ihtibas* (restrain); that is, *nafaqa* was determined on a day-by-day basis, and therefore a wife's previous knowledge of her husband's financial difficulties might mean her willingness to go without support for one day, but that did not deny her the right for support on the other days (al-Dardir n.d., 2:518). Significantly, even though most modern personal status laws are based on the more authoritative Hanafi code, in the case of *nashaz* and *ta*ᶜ*a*, Maliki laws have been preferred for obvious reasons.

Even though all *madhahib* agreed that a husband had the right to divorce, they did not conceptualize the marriage contract as giving a husband an absolute right to his wife. This interpretation was followed by Ottoman courts in regard to *nafaqa, ihtibas,* and *ta*ᶜ*a*. In an eighteenth-century case from Alexandria, the court upheld a divorce in which a wife divorced herself by simply leaving the marriage home and going to the marketplace. It seems that, earlier, the court had ordered her husband to pay her *nafaqa;* and in return, he demanded *ta*ᶜ*a*, requiring her to get his permission before she went to the marketplace. When the wife decided she no longer wished to live with him, she left the house and called out to her neighbors to witness her act by which she was breaking her *ta*ᶜ*a* to him, that is, breaking the marriage contract. As late as 1881, the Alexandria court again upheld the divorce of a woman who not only had divorced herself by breaking her husband's order not to go out, but had proceeded to marry another man after the ᶜ*idda* (three-month waiting period following divorce before a woman can be remarried). (Alexandria, Fatawi A.H. 1305/1888, case 133).

The accessibility of divorce to women is evidenced in *shari*ᶜ*a* court documents. Women found no problem in appealing to the chief *qadi* for divorce, and it was quite common for women to receive a favorable judgment. The most important proof needed was to show that the husband had broken the marriage contract or that the marriage caused the woman harm *(darar)*. Cases of *darar* included fear of physical harm, mistreatment of a wife's family members, lack of financial support, a husbands' frequent absence from home, and sexual dissatisfaction (Misr, Iᶜlamat 1266–1267/1849–1850, 23:237–635; Manfalut, Sijillat, 1228–1229/1812–1813, 5:26–122, 244–651). Whereas when a wife proved a husband's breach of contract she was always granted a divorce, in the case of *darar*, she was granted a divorce or, as was more usual, was separated through *khul*ᶜ (repudiation). In *khul*ᶜ, either the *qadi* granted the *khul*ᶜ or the husband agreed to the divorce in return for cancellation of his financial obligations toward her and sometimes for an extra payment.

Thus during the Ottoman period, the question facing the *qadi* was to determine divorce or *khul*ᶜ and, thereby, also to determine the financial settlement. In short, the husband had no absolute right to his wife, as was to become the case under modern laws, which give women little chance of ending the marriage contract against their husbands' wishes. In a case dating from 1910, the court forced a woman to stay with a husband that she insisted she had never been married to. She had sued in court to demand that he stop harassing and stalking her, but he presented a marriage certificate that she was his wife. The woman insisted that such a marriage had never taken place and that the certificate was a fake. Even though the court recognized that the wife did not accept the court's decision and that she was *kariha* (unwilling, hating), the court gave him rights to her (Alexandria, Qararat Qadaya Dafᶜ 1910, 130:36–24).

The modern treatment of *taᶜa* cases is based on law 25 for 1920, amended in 1929, 1979, and 1985, which states:

> The wife's *taᶜa* is a husband's right while the *nafaqa* is a wife's right. The fact that a husband no longer demands *taᶜa* from his wife, does not prevent her from asking for what is due her. This is agreed upon through ᶜurf. Accordingly, a wife is not considered *nashiz* except if her husband demands that she move to his legal house and she refuses to do so (al-Gindi 1987, 27).

Thus, the wife has the right to demand *nafaqa* from her husband, and the husband has the right to demand *taᶜa* from his wife. This law initially addressed the needs of women who were facing increased abandonment by husbands at a time of great political and social upheaval. The law also gives the husband an absolute right for *taᶜa*, however, whereby a woman is required to surrender herself or be forced by the police to "surrender herself" to her husband, even if he is abusive and she is living under the constant threat of violence and intimidation. And although the husband has the right to demand *taᶜa* from his wife, she cannot sue for divorce even for abandonment until she has gone through long procedures demanded by the court to ascertain her husband's unwillingness to support her. The violence of *taᶜa* as an institution has led to reciprocal acts of violence on the part of some wives toward their husbands (*al-Ahram*, Apr. 29, 1993) and, in many cases, has led wives to commit suicide or remain *"muᶜalaqa"* (hanging) rather than face *taᶜa* (*al-Ahram*, June 22, 1993).

Personal status laws do guarantee a wife's right to sue for divorce if she can prove *darar*. What constitutes *darar,* however, is the question. It is not wife beating because disciplinary punishment is legally acceptable as long as no limbs are broken or no permanent damage is done (Surat al-Nisa' 4:34.). The harm caused to a woman's pride or her fear of further beatings is not taken into consideration by the law. Furthermore, even though the law guarantees that a woman has the right to divorce if the husband proves to be insane, if such insanity was known to her before the marriage, then she cannot use it as the reason for divorce (Alexandria, Da'awi wa Ahkam 1910, 130:1–1). The fact that she cannot prove that she did not know about his madness before the marriage, that his insanity may have increased, or that she realizes that she can no longer live with him does not mean much to the court. On the other hand, the husband has no such problems in getting rid of an unwanted wife.

The interpretation of *darar* is supposed to have been taken from the Maliki *madhhab;* however, it was not taken in full. Whereas the Malikis insist that a wife has the right to ask the court to chastise and punish an abusive husband, that is nowhere to be seen in the modern laws. Furthermore, according to ARTICLE 6 of the 1920 law, *darar* exists when a husband is unjust, abandones his wife for a long time, or any other reason that would not be acceptable to her peers. This means that in determining *darar,* court judges are to use different standards for different classes. Although judges do not expect an upper-class woman to accept physical abuse, they have no problem in accepting such abuse for poorer women. Using Islam's emphasis on parity *(kafa'a)* in marriage, *qadis* have justified their decisions to force women into the *ta'a* of clearly abusive husbands on the pretext that the poorer classes have always been accustomed to foul language and being beaten by their fathers and brothers. Accordingly, women of the lower classes would not be acting properly unless they were treated in the same way by their husbands.[1]

It should be pointed out that even though there is a general impression that *ta'a* is a problem of the lower classes, *isti'naf* (court of second

---

1. Judges who rule that a wife enter into the *ta'a* of an abusive husband often require that the couple continue to live together but demand that they live among "worthy" people who will then judge whether the *darar* is recurrent or real. In cases where the wife proved excessive beating by her husband, the court still required that she live with him but have neighbors who are trustworthy who could protect her and stop his continued mistreatment. If a wife reconciles with her husband, then she can only complain of new incidents of abuse. Earlier incidents, however serious and no matter how much they caused her to fear for her life, cannot be used in court as evidence to prove *darar*.

degree) court records show that professors, doctors, and engineers, were frequently called to *ta'a* by their husbands.

The most controversial issue regarding *darar* was that of second wives. According to ART. 11 of the 1920 law, a husband's taking of a second wife was considered a "special harm," for which his first had the right to sue for divorce. A wife had to prove, however, that she experienced financial, social, or psychological *darar*, which limited her ability to win such cases. But in law 44 (1979), which repeated ART. 6, law 25, a breakthrough was achieved for women with the determination that the very act of taking a second wife was *in itself* a *darrar*, which gave the first wife the right to divorce. This law was something of a "last hurrah" for the new class of *infitah* (open-door economic policy developed by Anwar Sadat) women entrepreneurs of the 1970s, thus the law was changed in 1980 by a male opposition that combined not only male entrepreneurs, but government officials, *Majlis al-Sha'b* delegates, and the *'ulama'* (clergy). The changes reflected worsening economic and social conditions, as well as the appearance of a new *khassa* (elite) formed of political, government, and business combines, who were aggressively involved in a struggle over the resources of the state. Women were not in these combines and were therefore delegated to a secondary role in their husband's lives—a role of ornamentation rather than of partnership and substance. Although second marriages among the middle and lower classes were in a decline, among the rich elite they became fashionable. The 1980 law reflected these transformations, thus it described the act of taking a second wife as a man's absolute right given by God and not open to debate. Therefore, a second wife could never constitute *darar* "in itself"; instead, *darar* depended on the particular harm that befalls a wife and must conform to the *shari'a*.[2] Because the *shari'a* deals only with the acts of individuals and not with their emotions or whims, a

2. Even though the law does not support the right of the wife to demand divorce because her husband married another woman, there seems to be leniency, depending on the particular judge. The *Isti'naf* court confirmed a court decision that a wife had the right to receive a *mut'a* (enjoyment) allowance from a husband who divorced her at her request. The husband had appealed on the pretext that it was the wife and not him who had requested the divorce because he had taken a second wife because the first wife could not bear him any children after fifteen years of marriage. He had complied with her wishes and had given her all her financial rights. The court, however, found that she had experienced *darar* from his second marriage, and therefore awarded her £.E. 10,000 as a *mut'a* allowance. Thus, the court did not question the law that refused divorce on grounds of taking a second wife but recognized taking a second wife as a *darar* entailing compensation (*Akhbar al-Hawadith*, Aug. 12, 1993, 23).

wife's feelings in regard to a husband's taking a second wife cannot be considered *darar*. Therefore, *darar* should be measured according to financial ability and not according to feelings. If it is an issue of love, defenders of the 1980 amendments explained, and a woman did not like to share her husband with another woman, such a problem is not solved by divorce; instead, a "fuel of purity" should be used to put out the fires of a woman's jealousy.

The fact that, in Egypt, the term used for a second wife is *durra,* which stems from the word *darar,* and that during the 1970s Cairo's *Isti'naf* court alone looked into an average of ten *ta'a* cases each day (*Nisf al-Dunya,* Aug. 30, 1992, 39) did not seem to matter to the formulators of the 1980 law.

Violence and Rape

It was quite common for Ottoman courts to look into crimes like rape. Women often went to court demanding that a rapist be punished and pay them restitution. Given the detailed descriptions recorded in court *sijills* (records of archival documents) of the act itself, it seems that a woman did not fear social condemnation for having been raped. The courts looked at rape as usurpation of property, whereby a person's right to dispense of his or her own body was violated and was therefore due compensation. The handling of rape was similar to the handling of loss of limb, eyes, or forced abortion when caused by another.

In rape, like other cases, *shari'a* courts judged according to whether the victim could prove her case. If there were creditable witnesses to the actual act, then no further proof was needed. As was usual for these types of crimes, if there was no witness to the act, then it was the word of the victim against that of his/her accuser. If the latter confessed, then the case was proven; but if the alleged rapist refused to confess, then the matter rested largely on how believable each was and here the moral standing of the parties concerned was all important. Each was expected to produce character witnesses, and the more authoritative, socially prominent, and upright were the witnesses the better. Because the court usually served a limited locality, and the *qadi* lived and sometimes originated from the same locality, the parties to the dispute were often well known to him. If the witnesses were not well known, then they could bring character witnesses to vouch for them. Everyone was listened to and their words recorded.

A good example of those proceedings is the case of a woman who claimed that a man forced his way into her house, threatened her with a knife, and then raped her. She asked for compensation for the loss of her virginity. When asked, the man denied and took the oath that he had not committed such an act. He also produced a group of men to witness against the woman and vouch for his virtue. Two of the men testified that they had been sitting in front of their shop—located opposite to the woman's house—on the alleged day of the rape but had heard and seen nothing of what she described. They also testified that she was an endemic liar and of ill repute. They asked that the woman not be allowed to continue living in their *hara* (popular residential quarter), and so the *qadi* found for the man and forced the woman and her mother to leave town (Bab al-ʿAli, 1031/1623, 103:176–566).

The decision of the court depended to a large extent on whether the victim was a minor or had reached maturity, and if the victim was a girl, whether she was a virgin at the time of the rape. Other considerations had to do with whether a woman was married or not, if she was a slave, the particular profession to which she belonged, and the religion of the two parties concerned. There was also a great difference between one part of Egypt and the other in the handling of rape, the credibility of the victim, and the compensation expected. In more conservative areas, like Manfalut in Upper Egypt, for example, the credibility of the victim was quite high, but it was much less so in Cairo, and Alexandria. One case from Dumyat depended on the witnesses of character of the mistress of the victim, who was a slave. The relatively large number of rape cases recorded in the archives indicate the common practice of women in leaving their homes at various times of the day and night. Certainly, the details of the case show that to be true because most reported cases of rape were alleged to have taken place outside the home. It should be added, however, that in certain of Upper Egypt's towns, like Armant and Qusayr, there are no rape cases mentioned. This does not mean that rape did not take place or that women were shut at home but that such matters were handled individually and outside of court.

Focusing on an issue like rape shows how valuable *shariʿa* court archives are in regard to the great details they provide on common people. They illustrate a society of great social maneuverability with an active civil order. Still, we must use court records with great caution, particularly in regard to the historicity of the various entries. Questions need to be asked about why certain records seem to repeat themselves from one century to the other. For example, in modern courts, doctors are used to prove the existence of physical signs of rape. The same methods were used in the eighteenth century, when *qabilat* (midwives) were used to check if a victim was telling the truth (Bab al-ʿAli, 1152/ 1738, 221:283–429). My research shows that historicity can be determined in several ways. For example, "compensation." During the seventeenth-century, rapists received *hudud* sentences and were expected to pay compensation, the amounts of which were not given in any great detail. Eighteenth-century records, however, itemize the compensations decided upon by the courts for rape as for other crimes. This list included the marriage settlements, *mahr* (dowry), and *muʾakhkhar* (delayed dowry), decided upon in case the victim and rapist were married. Again, there is a great diversity between one part of Egypt and the other regarding the amounts. This diversity continues all the way into the nineteenth century, toward the end of which the state began to issue orders standardizing the *diyya* (blood price, compensation for bodily harm) due for different forms of rape, which were categorized according to age and virginity. Boys and girls were treated similarly, and the term *ightisab* (rape) was used. The compensation was justified on the basis of property being usurped, that is, used without the owner's permission. There did not seem to be a particular concern with the issue of *nasab* (geneology or blood relationship), thus no differentiation was made between the compensation for boys or girls, or what form the rape took. Great changes in the handling of rape have occurred in the twentieth century. For one thing, it is no longer the victim who brings the case to court but the police, who have jurisdiction in this matter. As for compensation, the victim cannot sue for compensation unless the court judges the case and rape is proven. Thus, the police play a powerful role in investigating and judging rape cases.

There are other important differences that are connected with nation-state building. For one thing, standardized laws were set up to handle rape. These were to apply uniformly throughout Egypt, yet, I should add, the limits of state power are indicated by the continuity of certain patterns of diversity; for example, in Armant, cases of rape are still rarely reported. The uniform laws themselves tell us a great deal of the historical context in which they were issued.

Chapter 4 of the Egyptian criminal laws, entitled *Hatk al-ʿird wa ifsad al-akhlaq* (Disgrace and causing moral corruption), refers to rape as having sex with a woman without her prior approval as long as the woman is not the perpetrator's wife (*Qanun al-ʿuqubat hasab ahdath al-taʿdilat* 1988, 172–73). A number of issues are involved in this law. For one thing, the word *rape* only appears once in all of chapter 4. The word *ightisab* has a very clear linguistic and psychological meaning, denoting a violent act of usurping what belongs to another. The term *hatk ʿird* (disgrace) is a much less offensive term because it encompasses anything from an insult to a simple touch, and certainly does not have the same imagery that *ightisab* has. Also, Joining *hatk ʿird* to *ifsad al-akhlaq* (corrupting morals) in one chapter dilutes the brutality of the offense and says much about the view toward women that was held by the writers of this law. *Ifsad al-akhlaq* as a term indicates acceptance, or at least compliance, of an immature person who does not know any better.

The usual prison sentence for committing *hatk ʿird* is three to seven years hard labor. This changes according to the age of the victim, whether the act was forced or not, and the relationship of the victim to the offender. Thus, for older children, if the victim is female and less than sixteen years old, and the offender is a member of her family, a servant, or a guardian, he receives a maximum sentence of hard labor, that is, twenty-one years (ART. 268 of SECTION 4 of the criminal law). If the victim is less than eighteen years old and no force was used, then the offender receives a prison sentence to be determined by the *qadi* (ART. 269 of SEC. 4 of the criminal law). As for younger children, if the child involved is less than seven years old and force is not used, but the offender happens to be a guardian, family member, or servant, then he gets only a temporary sentence (usually fifteen years) hard labor (ART. 269, SEC. 4 of the criminal law).

In 1980, ART. 291 of SEC. 5 of the criminal code, which exonerated a kidnapper who marries his victim, was changed to allow for the death sentence for kidnapping and rape without marriage (ART. 290 of SEC. 5 of the criminal code, changed by law 214). This was in answer to the marked increase in kidnapping and rape cases, particularly those involving women of the upper classes who were kidnapped and raped by working-class men. Presumably, no marriage could come out of such a situation.

There are other differences that illustrate how society has changed and the direction it may be taking. For example, the nature of the crime: In rape cases reported to Ottoman courts, nearly all rapists were older than their victims and acted singly, and the victims were as often young boys or girls as they were adult women. Today, in single rape cases, particularly when the rapist is well known to the victim, such as a family friend or cousin, the rapist is usually older, and often the victim is also killed or an attempt is made on her life (*al-Ahram,* June 30, 1993). There are also clear signs of the existence of frustrated, unemployed, and lost youth. Most reported rape cases today are enacted by gangs of young men who are between sixteen and twenty-four years of age. In the case of gang rape, perhaps owing to the relatively young age of the rapists, rape is usually not accompanied by killing the victim. *Shillas* (groups, gangs) of young men who join together for narcotics, brigandage (*Akhir Sa'a,* July 28, 1993, 49), or entertainment, are often led to find victims and drag them to abandoned places like the desert or tombs (*al-Ahram,* July 18, 1993, 19: case in Cairo; *al-Misri,* Aug. 8, 1993, 11: case from Sandub, Daqahliya), hills, or apartments (*al-Ahram,* Apr. 8, 1993, 14), where they are raped and often kept for some time before their release. Rape could be the only way that a typical member of these *shillas* could "have a woman," so to speak. Such youths have no prospects, no hope of a job, marriage, or even respectability. The fact that the police can do little about these cases, and are often unwilling to do much, except when murder is involved or the case becomes well known, may indicate the limits of the power of the state; but given the relatively easy nature of rape laws, one must hypothesize that rape is simply allowed to happen (*al-Misri,* Aug. 8, 1993, 11).[3] Compared to the swift justice meted out to those who are considered enemies of the state (e.g., a man received ten years hard labor for possession of explosives) or death for trafficking in narcotics, it is disconcerting not to see the same type of attention given to rape. The death sentences passed on those involved in terrorist acts provide the highest percentage of death sentences relative to crime in the last twenty years of Egypt's history (*al-'Arabi,* July 19, 1993, 4). The state has been exceedingly firm when it comes to the Islamicist elements and does not shrink from passing death sentences. We have yet to see the same for the crime of rape.

What do the *'ulama'* have to say about all this? Nothing much, the blame and caution are always placed on the shoulders of the girl. "Be careful," the girl is told. "Do not leave your home without your Islamic garb, and do not look at strange men." Even in the extreme case of a patient being raped by her doctor, the *fatwa* (juridical opinion) of one *shaykh* was that a girl has to be careful where she goes and with whom; and even though the doctor is to blame, she has to carry part of the blame for going to see a male doctor in the first place (*al-Sha'b,* May 7, 1993, 11)!

---

3. In this case, the officer actually refused to move because the regulations do not require him to do anything unless the victim reports the rape herself at the police station. That it was the victim's husband who was reporting the attempted rape and attempt on the life of his son was not good enough for the officer, who asked the husband to get lost and stop wasting the police's time.

18

Women and Society in the Tulip Era, 1718–1730

Madeline C. Zilfi

The "Tulip Era" and Its Historiography

Nev şehirli Ibrahim Pasha served as grand vezir to his father-in-law, the Ottoman sultan Ahmed III (1703–1730), from 1718 to 1730, the period that has come to be called "the Tulip Era." The label is as much a verdict on İbrahim's vezirate as a description of its pastimes. The tulip was the preferred motif and cultivar in the period, and as a short-season flower it aptly symbolizes an era known for its extravagance and swift passing. Nonetheless, the label does not do justice to a regime that undid, even if briefly, more than a century of the empire's self-imposed cultural isolation.

Against a background of free spending, Sultan Ahmed and İbrahim Pasha sponsored innovations—in construction and urban design, arts and letters, fashion and entertainment—based in part on non-Ottoman, often non-Islamic, sources of inspiration. The Tulip Era arguably nurtured more artistic experimentation and sheer volume than any set of decades in the previous hundred years. It was responsible for the first Ottoman-Muslim printing press, established in the 1720s, as well as the first exploratory embassy to Europe. Other embassies widened relations further, while ambassadors from Europe settled in Istanbul in greater numbers and with greater social freedom than ever before.

The cultural opening was not directed only toward Europe. İbrahim Pasha and his wife Fatma Sultan, daughter of the sultan, founded a *medrese* (mosque school) that provided for instruction in the

290

Persian language and Sufism *(tasavvuf)*. Although Persian had been removed from official curricula more than a century before, and Islamic mysticism had rarely been included, the new foundation endorsed their fitness for the empire's religious students. (Aktepe (1960), 156–58) New libraries, including Ahmed III's own grand foundation on the grounds of Topkapi Palace, reflected new intellectual openness. The extensive book collections of İbrahim Pasha and others of the ruling elite, and İbrahim's sponsorship of *ulema* (clergy) debates, had to do with patronage and status politics, but they were also evidence of cultural openings and aspirations. So, too, was İbrahim's willingness to set aside convention to converse with foreign diplomats and, more remarkably, to dine with them. The barriers to egalitarian interaction between Ottoman officials and foreign non-Muslims had not previously been so challenged.

In the fall of 1730, a violent uprising, sparked by the regime's paralysis in the Persian campaigns, put an end to the reign. Sultan Ahmed was deposed in favor of his nephew Mahmud I (1730–1754), and İbrahim and his closest associates were executed. Before the year was over, the rebels had themselves been killed or exiled. Mahmud I on the whole shunned the experimentation that had characterized İbrahim Pasha's vezirate. The Ottoman press limped on, but the Tulip Era was over.

Ottoman historiography identifies İbrahim Pasha's vezirate as the first episode in the enduring debate over the relationship between "Islam" and "the West" and the initiatives behind change in Islamic societies. The Tulip Era is mourned as a lost opportunity, when the Ottomans might have prepared against later Western and Russian encroachment. Instead, it is argued, the leadership wasted itself on frivolity —flowers, games, fashions, flimsy pleasure palaces, and other pursuits that squandered energies and resources. Because of the dismal performance of Islamic lands in later confrontations with the West, this debate has overshadowed a second theme in the historiography—namely, the charges of gross sexual impropriety against the regime. The implications of those charges for the history of women and the question of social change in the period are of concern here.

According to his harshest critics, İbrahim Pasha was not only criminally negligent in matters of state but a defiling panderer who promoted the abasement of Ottoman women (Mustafa Nuri [1877–1909], 3:30). Most accounts of the period employ the vocabulary of waste and profligacy to describe the regime's spending habits. Those who comment on İbrahim's sexual behavior extend such terms to their sexual connotations, referring to İbrahim as a wanton and a dissolute, a profligate in all things (Şemdanizade 1976–1981, 1:3–13, passim; Unat 1943, 28). The shared vocabulary of the Tulip Era's historiographical themes suggests the linkage between İbrahim's failed policies, most notably that between the governing of empire and the governing of women.

Few historians doubt the force of İbrahim's influence over Ahmed III. İbrahim fed Sultan Ahmed's appetites by devising a calendar of "holidays" for the court, and often the populace, to enjoy. Thus diverted from affairs of state, Sultan Ahmed paraded from springtime "tulip illuminations" *(lâle çirağanı)* to winter "helva soirées" *(helva sohbeti)*, all requiring sojourns at different palaces. The completion of a new palace, a frequent occurrence, was cause for more celebrations. Sumptuous banquets *(ziyafet)* became more numerous as officials feted one another to mark the seasons and to fulfill the demands of protocol. Religious holidays were prolonged and more lavishly observed. Ahmed III's fifty-some children, of whom a score or so survived for any length of time (Alderson 1956, table 41), provided additional opportunities for celebration and commemoration, especially because this reign was inclined to celebrate its daughters as well as its sons.

The trappings and even the occasions for merrymaking were not much different from other reigns. Ramadan lights and fireworks, birth, circumcision, and marriage holidays were common to many reigns, but Tulip Era entertainments were more frequent, especially from the 1720s on, and they were spread across the city rather than remaining within the monumental central quarters. Moreover, they were often intended for the wider public, with carnivals and amusement parks especially favored. Thus were populace and sultan diverted, it was said, and the government left in the unworthy hands of İbrahim and his cronies.

Along with the implausible exoneration of Ahmed III in such narratives, the explanation of why İbrahim chose to cater to the sultan's and the public's weaknesses is unconvincing. According to his more strident critics, principally Şemdanizade, echoed with somewhat less vitriol by Cevdet (1891) and Mustafa Nuri (1877–1900), İbrahim's spectacles were deliberate attempts to foster a climate of sexual immorality. "[N]ot content with his own and his followers' pleasure-seeking, [İbrahim] declared that something was needed to divert the people," to blind them to the empire's true circumstances (Şemdanizade 1976–1981, 1:3; Mustafa Nuri 1877–1909, 3:28–30; Cevdet 1891, 1:66). Through the amusement parks he had set up around Istanbul, with "ferris wheels and all manner of swings and merry-go-rounds, and men and women mixing freely together," his personal immorality infected society at its root, through women and the institution of marriage. For "when these women got on and off the swings, swaggering youths embraced them," and as if this were not indecent enough, once the women were on the swings, "laughing and singing all the while," their coats would fly open to reveal their underclothing up to their waistbands. While some of these women came to the parks with their husbands' permission, others, contrary to law and usage, came without such leave, claiming there was "general permission" *(izn-i âm)* (Şemdanizade 1976–1981, 1:3).

Thus it was that women learned to behave badly, we are told, and relations between men and women broke down. Women are said to have forcibly taken spending money from their husbands, and if there was none to take, they sought divorce *(talâk)* on those grounds (Cevdet 1891, 1:63; Şemdanizade 1976–1981, 1:3). Now "it is as though judges in the courts are commissioned to favor women . . . and as though divorce [*tatlik*] is in wives' hands," what with judges humiliating husbands for failing to fulfill their husbandly functions. According to some, because of İbrahim, "there are not five women left in any quarter of the city who can be called virtuous" (Şemdanizade ibid.)

İbrahim is also accused of having developed Sa'dabad ("where felicity abounds") on the Golden Horn, a playground of 120 summer palaces for court favorites, to indulge his carnal appetites (Raşid 1865, 5:443–46; Eldem n.d., 158–59). Although "a number of indecent acts" are reported to have taken place in the course of the Tulip Era's periodic "helva soirées" and "tulip illuminations" (Mustafa Nuri 1877–1909, 3:30), the most wicked of games is charged to the open-air frolics at Sa'dabad. With İbrahim presiding, men competed for the attentions of women in the party "by tossing gold pieces with a flick of the finger at the women's veils" (Şemdanizade 1976–1981, 1:3; Mustafa Nuri 1877–1909, ibid.). The winners, rewarded by İbrahim, were those whose coins landed within the veils. The exact nature of the game's offensiveness is unclear—whether the crude mixing of the sexes, the suggestion of open whoredom in the use of money, or the involvement of the imperial court in such scandals. The fact that slave women were bought and sold publicly every day in Istanbul, and that the imperial court was the major terminus for the traffic in women does not seem to have given critics pause. Sa'dabad was judged responsible for women's degradation.

The chronicles cite few examples—and those of dubious lineage—to support their complaints about the period's impact. Nonetheless, their accounts and contemporary regulations regarding women confirm that well before the "westernizing" reforms of Selim III (1789–1807) and before widespread Western economic involvement in Ottoman Turkey, changes in women's behavior, or the perception of change, were deeply felt. The extent to which Tulip Era policies can be implicated is open to question, but it is a question that deserves exploration.

The Society of the Tulip

During the reign of Ahmed III, women were apparently expanding the range of their appearances in public. Ahmed III's court accelerated change by promoting a more secular public life, centered on leisure, self-indulgence, and the life passages of the dynasty. The regime also encouraged fashionable consumerism through diplomacy, trade policies, and court behavior. And, when women beyond the court experimented with the old strictures, their actions did not bring down the usual repression from the authorities.

There is evidence that economic changes were already underway before 1718 such as to produce new wealth and a certain amount of consumerist experimentation among the middle classes, with or without the "general permission" of government policy. The early eighteenth century was a relatively prosperous time, with more disposable income in the trading sectors particularly. To judge by the spending habits of the imperial entourage alone, merchants and those in the luxury trades who catered to the ruling elite would have been among those enjoying greater prosperity. Those on fixed salaries, many of whom became the rebels of 1730, would have been less well served. However asymmetrical urban economic conditions were in the period, such factors, together with peace on the Western front after 1718 and the presence of numerous foreigners and their families, no longer so ostracized and disdained as before, contributed to the emergence of an Ottoman "fashionable society." It was nascent to be sure, but it possessed a widened social reach and new cosmopolitan elements that had not been possible under earlier regimes.

The regime's building boom promoted the court's role as a model by dramatically increasing the number of imperial domiciles. Ahmed III's court life was ubiquitous and visible. By 1730, palaces, belvederes, pavilions, and seaside villas had sprung up in the choicest locales within ten miles of Topkapı, the principal residence. Palaces became centers of urban subdivisions as imperial architects built up the surrounding property with mosques, roads, marketplaces, and docks.

The rebels who overthrew İbrahim Pasha and Ahmed III made a point of leveling the palaces of Sa'dabad. Although the rebels maintained that the palaces had squandered imperial monies, these new residences were more than consumers of state revenues. Among other things, they symbolized the regime's experimentation with both geographical and social boundaries. As the court pursued new amusements, it redrew the social map of Istanbul. Court society extended not just to the sultan's more numerous residences but to those of his servitors and favorites, as well. These followed the sultan's architectural lead and competed in the new hospitality. In the early 1720s, Ahmed III vacationed in Üsküdar, Kadıköy, Kandilli, Beylerbeyi, Beşiktaş, Eyüp, Alibey Köyü, Kağıthane, Sariyer, Ortaköy, Fındıklı, Kuruçeşme, Karaağaç, Tophane, and Rumeli Hisar, in addition to whiling away the hours at residences within Istanbul itself. Most such visits were the occasion for extravagant parties, usually with rare tulips on view (Raşid 1865 5:160; Asım 1865, 24, 29, 40, 42, 169, 176, 246, 366, 384, 424–27, 456, 480, 529, 569).

Palace society did not simply exchange Topkapı's secretive high walls for new ones. Social occasions were celebrated outdoors as much as in, often outside the residential grounds altogether, in meadows and gardens, as the court sought out flower hobbyists and fresh settings for picnics, sightseeing, music, athletics, and games. Istanbul could scarcely have avoided catching a glimpse of the royal life, even if only in passing. Royal cavalcades were loud, long, and frequent. Such places and pastimes put no food in the mouths of the poor, but they offered social occasions for the larger public. Cavalcades and carnivals were lighthearted, "secular," and relatively free-form, unlike the solemn, exclusivist, set pieces featured in the ceremony of other reigns. The old Ottoman theater of power and piety competed now with a new theater of leisure and consumption.

The period also reset the imperial clock for the new entertainments and notion of leisure. The Ottomans had customarily shut down the city at nightfall by forbidding the use of general street lighting. Ahmed III and İbrahim extended social time for the public through the lavish illumination of mosques. Ottoman mosque illumination of this sort predates Ahmed III by at least a century, but its use had been restricted to major traditional holidays. The Tulip Era created new secular holidays and lengthened old ones through the liberal use of lights. To quash moral and economic opposition, a *ferman* (executive decree or imperial law) of 1723 declared lights to be a "useful innovation" *(bidat-i hasane)* enabling more people to make their way to the mosques for prayers during Ramadan (Asım 1865, 35–36). In 1723, the usual mosques of Sultan Süleyman, Sultan Ahmed, and the Valides in Istanbul and Üsküdar were joined by the other imperial mosques—Aya Sofya, Fatih, Sultan

Beyazid, Sultan Selim, Şehzade, Sultan Mehmed in Eyüp, and Mihrimah in Üsküdar—to broaden the spectacle to new districts. In 1726, more neighborhoods were included when İbrahim Pasha ordered that mosques founded by vezirs should also have "glowing lamps hanging on their minarets, reaching from their balconies to their spires." According to the decrees, lights between dusk and dawn would guide travelers "who customarily set out for the mosques from distant places" (Asım 1865, 372–73). Because virtually every neighborhood possessed its own mosque, the illumination of the most prestigious mosques served social and communal more than theological ends by encouraging people to venture outside their neighborhoods to join in larger, less familiar, gatherings. Religious holidays were being recast in a more secular form, with greater attention to the social dimension of the religious congregation.

Mosques were also illuminated for the growing number of secular celebrations—royal births, circumcisions, betrothals, weddings, military victories, and seasonal galas. The regime was less fearful of the urban populace than other regimes—those of Murad IV (1623–1640) and Osman III (1754–1757) for example—were especially fearsome about the public's mobility and access to information. Although Ahmed III sometimes restricted coffeehouses, street vendors, and migration into Istanbul, the regime appeared to have been relatively unconcerned about limiting the public's knowledge of itself or of the imperial court.

Because of Ahmed III's closeness to his family, the court had a stronger, "companionate," female aspect than had recently been the case. Unlike most of his immediate predecessors, Ahmed III doted on his daughters, celebrating their life passages almost as much as his sons'. He also sought counsel from the female members of his family, especially his sisters and his daughter Fatma. Although one can say much the same about Suleyman the Magnificent (1520–1566) with his wife Hürrem Sultan and daughter Mihrimah, it is the combination of behaviors and tolerances and their influence beyond palace politics *per se* that distinguish the Tulip Era.

All of Istanbul was to some degree affected by the relaxations of the Tulip Era. The population was being permitted to know more about a wider variety of "others" and to have direct experience of them "in public." To the extent that there had previously been public socializing outlets in Istanbul, they were centered on the mosques and, in any case, essentially male. Apart from mosques, shrines, and Sufi *tekke*s (monasteries), the chief venues for social interaction were the home and family, vocation and workplace, market and neighborhood. In the Tulip Era, wine taverns remained off-limits for Muslims; but the monitoring of coffeehouses was eased overall, and new coffeehouses sprang up.

Although coffeehouses were for male customers only, carnivals parks, and meadows attracted women and families as well. A modest "carriage trade" emerged, with many women—royal, native middle-class, and foreign—enjoying the outdoors for the sake of amusement. Using rented or custom-built carts and boats, women achieved notice-able mobility. One has to assume the cooperation of many men; and despite some historians' charges, it is doubtful that women were in a position to force such cooperation. Women's infatuation with carts and boats, though lasting, could be hazardous. Virtually every regime there-after strictly regulated women's travel. In the later period, even with male protectors accompying them, women were vigorously discouraged from taking such outings.

Except for celebrations organized by state officials or the minority communities, entertainments with dancers, puppet shows, and jugglers, for example, were relatively closed affairs, organized by the wealthier classes for their own households and social circles. Such occasions did not break through the household-based insularity of Ottoman society; they did not usually take place in public space, and they were not aimed at an unacquainted "public" audience. In contrast, İbrahim Pasha's parks invited the public to mix with unrelated others in leisure time. Religious and secular holidays provided the pretext for prolonged carni-vals. The end of Ramadan, for example, was celebrated with entertain-ments at At Meydanı, Fatih, and Beyazid in the center of the old city, as well as in Yedi Kule, Bayram Pasha, Eyüp, Kasım Pasha, Tophane, Sa'dabad, Dolmabahçe, Bebek, Göksu, Çubuklu, Beykoz, and Üsküdar, among other suburbs. The commemoration of the Prophet's birth and celebrations of the imperial family were also occasions for far-flung and conspicuous carnivals. Like court outings and mosque illuminations, the sights and sounds of the carnival would have been difficult to ignore.

Urban women of all classes were touched by these innovations, albeit in varying degrees. Women could not participate in public enter-tainments and leisure-time pursuits in the way that men of the same class or means might. Nonetheless, the lights and public fairs, the cult of the outdoors, and the daily passage of imperial cavalcades and boats brought remote neighborhoods into unaccustomed proximity with elite social models. Much of the interaction was only visual, with ordinary city people mere observers of the powerful. But Ahmed III's reign toler-ated the notion of leisure time and pleasures as a general kind of entitle-ment. The public responded by flocking to the parks and entertainments and by organizing sightseeing and picnics of their own. The government always held the charge of idleness in reserve in order to rid the city of undesirables when the need arose. Nonetheless, ordinary people were generally allowed more opportunities to seek their pleasures. Along with the spectacle of the court, there were foreign women to ogle and hear about, just as foreign women did their best to visit and view Ottoman women. Experiments with clothing occurred on both sides, and Europeans moved about more freely during this more receptive reign.[1] Encounters between the two cultures, whether in the empire or in Europe, suggest a mutuality that was lacking in the ritualized interviews that characterized Ottoman-European "social" relations before and after this time.

Although it should not be overstated, a similar element of mutuality characterized the relationship between the Ottoman court and Ottoman society. İbrahim Pasha and others of the regime seem to have recognized that some pastimes of the ruling elite need not be forbidden to the public. In this and other ways, İbrahim Pasha's vezirate possessed a human—and humane—quality that is difficult to detect in other periods. The public was curious about the imperial family, and it was desirable from the point of view of the ruling family in this period that they be so; thus in Ahmed III's time, the population was not prevented, as in so many other reigns, from watching the imperial processions that took the court through the city. The regime's tolerance for nonconformity and the wider range of behaviors it implicitly granted are also evidenced by the near absence of political executions during İbrahim's vezirate. In contrast to most vezirates, when the execution of rivals and ordinary subjects was all too common, İbrahim Pasha ordered barely a handful of executions during his vezirate.

Regulating Virtue

By law and by custom, Muslim women were expected to be chaste, untouched by even the breath of scandal. They were to be "unknown" in the sexual sense by any man except a husband, and "unknown" physically and personally by any man not within the allowable degrees of familial intimacy. Knowing about a woman and carnal knowledge of her were inseparable concepts.

Although the surest guarantor against the "knowledge" of outsiders was segregation, the cloistering harem of separate rooms and layers of servants was possible only for wealthier families. Most women took part in street life, even if only via a basket lowered to vendors or through a

---

1. The well-regarded account of Ottoman women by Lady Mary Wortley Montagu was based on her stay from 1717 to 1718.

window calling to children. Many urban women participated more directly in the urban economy, as weavers of cloth and as owners of property, and many availed themselves of government offices, as court litigants and petitioners, among other things. Older women and the very poor enjoyed greater freedom in public. For all women, the protections of the home extended to the street when they were accompanied by male relatives. The streets, however, were the province of men—native and nonnative, Muslim and non-Muslim—and they were monitored by men, principally native Muslim men. Women were visitors to the street, their presence tolerated only if their mission related to sanctioned obligation—as to faith or family—and so long as their dress and demeanor were appropriate. Men's choices and social access were far from unlimited; they were restricted by their class, vocation, behavior, and religion. Any of those attributes could change during one's lifetime, however, some even at will. Women, on the other hand, were restricted not just by dent of social place or volition; they were, in the first instance, limited on the unalterable grounds of sex.

Women wore "regulation streetwear" to ensure an appearance that was unsuggestive and anonymous. In the eighteenth century, an opaque veil *(yaşmak)* and collared long coat *(ferace)* of a single muted color helped keep the womanliness of the Muslim woman's body indeterminate and her identity unknown. There were a number of differences in outerwear between Muslim women and women of the various non-Muslim communities; each group was assigned particular colors, headgear, and overgarment; and Muslim women were entitled to wear finer cloths. In general, the law did not mandate clear class distinctions for the outdoor clothing worn by women within the same religious community, although there were differences (often indiscernible) in the quality of cloths used.[2] For all practical purposes, however, differences in dress were slight; all women were more or less in the same uniform when outdoors.

Because the moral order insisted on female purity, and because few families could afford the screening that architecture and servants provided, clothing was women's principal cloister. A mobile cloister, it offered the main defense for purity and reputation when women moved outside their homes. To challenge clothing conventions challenged the moral order; and because clothing was easily alterable, clothing required

---

2. In sartorial matters, the law tended to treat women as a group, with the evil deeds of "women" dominating the regulations, and later sections singling out Greek, Armenian, Jewish, or "Frankish" women. Indoor wear was generally not a state concern.

monitoring. In the eighteenth century, monitors were plentiful—family members and neighbors, both male and female, as well as police officials, including the Janissaries and the shore patrols.

In 1726, İbrahim Pasha himself was responsible for a restrictive sartorial decree, according to which "some badly behaved women, intentionally seizing the opportunity [of the government's absence on campaign] to lead people astray on the streets, have invented various innovations in their ornaments and clothing, and have introduced many a shameful fashion, with monstrously shaped headgear in imitation of non-Muslim women." Not only were the new styles the "cause of the Muslim community's being led into perdition," but they had grave economic consequences. Women's insistence on acquiring the latest outfit supposedly impoverished their husbands and, "because of the depressed market for the old style of dress and materials," clothiers as well. To counter the trend, the regulation dictated exact measurements for the outerwear of women who would be virtuous: coats with collars no wider than a finger's width, kerchiefs of no more than three squares of material, and headbands not to exceed a finger's width. Repeat offenders were to be banished. As for the tailors and beltmakers behind "this kind of whorish innovation," they were to be severely rebuked and then have their goods destroyed if they persisted. The regulation directed the *kadi* (judge) and police functionaries of Istanbul to enforce the law with respect to all women, "Muslim and non-Muslim, righteous and sinning," or else face punishment themselves (Altınay 1930, 86–88).

Like many such regulations, this one was unequal to the problem at hand and never much enforced. Given the tolerant stance of the regime the absence of repeat issuances, and İbrahim's famous reluctance to spill blood, the decree seems to have been a special case arising from wartime sensibilities or from the desire to appease moral or guild factions or both. İbrahim's vezirate, so remarkable for the lives it did not sacrifice, was regarded by some commentators as a weakness and the main reason for Istanbul's "disorder."

İbrahim Pasha's vezirate encouraged "looser" behavior on the part of women and men. More women were embracing fashion and individualizing the clothing in which they presented themselves in public. Fashion—that is, individual variation, change for novelty's sake—had always been practiced by men and women inside the home. Men affected the signature styles of their betters, and women wore colors and cuts forbidden as streetwear. Fashion was not absent from outdoor clothing before the Tulip Era, but major changes occurred slowly, as in the nineteenth century with the replacement of the *ferace* by the all-over *çarşaf.* The changing economics of the first quarter of the eighteenth century and the social policies of İbrahim Pasha's vezirate accelerated existing consumerist trends and made others possible. The phenomenon of fashion in outdoor wear, before and after the Tulip Era, indicates that the problem did not begin or end with that period. The phenomenon was chronic, with a life of its own, although its impact to some extent was expanded by social policy. The later sultans tried to enforce sartorial conformity; but far less than in the Tulip Era, they did not control supply, demand, or means.

Some of the most sweeping sumptuary laws were issued by Osman III, whose three-year reign is known for little else, and Mustafa III (1757–1774), who issued another volley of regulations. The chronicles report numerous incidents of hangings, beatings, and drownings, of men and women for sumptuary violations. More than a sultan's moral credentials were at issue; the political stakes behind a regime's moral posture came to require more than an inaugural decree. Sumptuary violations were rife in the later reigns, as the rising bourgeoisie, especially its non-Muslim component, aspired to the marks of status reserved for the ruling elite, had the means by which to exhibit them, and enjoyed a certain amount of protection from European diplomats and from the Ottoman state, which had more and more come to depend upon the overseas trade sector.

İbrahim Pasha's vezirate was in many ways a realistic accommodation to the new facts of Ottoman foreign relations and, less consciously, market forces. For him, peace was a wiser course than war, at least on the Western front, and in any case the world outside the Ottoman Empire had more than war to offer. Though eventually succumbing to inactivity in everything except pleasures, İbrahim and Ahmed III opened the empire to a new peacetime politics. For a brief time, the Abode of Islam-Abode of War *(Darülislam-Darülharb)* polarity was reconsidered; and Europe, no longer the Abode of War, was more fully realized as a cultural locale.

In relaxing the traditional politics of otherness, the Tulip Era did more than provide "a window on the West." The Ottomans had always possessed such a view, but it was narrow and closed at will. During İbrahim Pasha's grand vezirate, the Ottomans charted their own interaction with Western culture, and experimented on their own terms with foreign notions and structures. By the mid-eighteenth century, Europe's economic and military ascendancy would dispel any illusion of Ottoman parity. The Ottomans themselves would be under siege by these very Europeans. In any case, the philosophies of rule of Europe's new imperialism would so devalue other cultures that the Ottomans, even in peacetime, could not again hope for the benign curiosity that had greeted the first Ottoman ambassador when he first arrived in France in 1720.

İbrahim's pastimes and policies also facilitated the breakdown of internal boundaries. The encouragement to open socializing and to market-guided consumption tacitly recognized individual desires and tastes transcending the empire's guidelines for the corporate religious groups it had constructed. The recognition was capricious and limited, but it was a radical, and in many respects necessary, departure from the numbing hypocrisies of other reigns.

İbrahim Pasha bears much responsibility for the Tulip Era's failures. But those who argue that his excesses hardened the population and subsequent regimes against other, beneficial openings to the West have not reckoned with the dynamics of change in Europe itself after mid-century. The openings in İbrahim's day were predicated on dialogue and negotiation between great powers. Such could not be the case later in the century against late-Enlightenment Europe's expansionism, intolerances, and superior power. With regard to the domestic politics of Ottoman morality, it is worth noting that other Ottoman leaders, before and after İbrahim, were hardly more successful as leaders despite their higher moral standing and even when they had not challenged society with the likes of a printing press and a new vision of old enemies.

As for what the Tulip Era can tell us about the situation of women and the nature of social change before the reforms of Selim III and before European domination, there are more questions than there are answers. The issue of whether women in great numbers—not just greater numbers—were defying customs of dress and deportment in the Tulip Era remains unresolved. Whatever the real numbers may be, it is clear that social change disproportionately exposes the actions of marginal people such as women and minorities. And exposed they were in the Tulip Era and thereafter. Also, in societies in which moral order is equated with social conformity, vigilant external policing is indispensable for the maintenance of that order. When, for whatever reason, the accustomed degree of repression is no longer applied, and models for *not* conforming are present, social aberrations occur at an accelerated pace. Such conditions were present during the reign of Ahmed III. Although the more repressive reigns of later eighteenth-century sultans altered those conditions, change continued, driven more by the forces of European diplomacy and economics than by Ottoman policy.

Ottoman Islamic society had traditionally viewed the special restrictions on women and the native religious minorities as vital—and perhaps the most manifest—components of Islamic law in peacetime. Because the implementation of Islamic law was one of the pillars of Ottoman legitimacy, women and the religious minorities were a many-layered imperial concern. In the course of the eighteenth century, the wealth and pretensions of the minorities in time came to draw the greater fire from Ottoman regulators. Unlike contemporaneous Muslim women, minority men came increasingly under the protection of one or another European power, and thus escaped the force of Ottoman law. The growing autonomy of the protected minorities undermined the moral order and dynastic legitimacy. Together with the Ottomans' inability after the eighteenth century to regain their stature as conquerors, this new state of affairs rendered the governing of women all the more critical to Ottoman/Islamic identity.

The question of when and under whose auspices Islamic law and, indeed, Islam, came to be seen as virtually reducible to the control of women has invited historians' interest. Attention has focused less on domestic causation than on the late nineteenth century and the role of European imperialism in identifying the veil and gender segregation with oppressive religion. Nonetheless, the interplay a century earlier among Ottoman/Islamic legal practice, economic differentiation, and dynastic claims offers fertile ground for reassessing the initiative and the chronology underlying the relationship between Islam and women's role.

Glossary of Arabic Terms
Glossary of Turkish Terms
Works Cited
Index

Glossary of Arabic Terms

ʿ**adl:** justice
ahli, waqf ahli: civil, family *waqf*
ʿ**a'ila:** family
ajnabi, f. *ajnabiyya,* pl. *ajanib:* strangers, outsiders
ajwad: people of confidence
akh: brother
ʿ**alim:** clergyman
ʿ**alma**s: oriental dancers
ʿ**amina:** trustworthy
amir: prince, leader
ʿ**amm,** pl. aʿ*mam:* uncle
ʿ**amma:** general populace
aqalim: provinces
ʿ**aql:** maturity of mind
ʿ**asab:** blood relationship
ʿ**ashira:** clan
ashraf: descendants of the Prophet
ʿ**ashura**ʾ**:** yearly celebrations commemorating the martyrdom of Hussein
    (grandson of the Prophet Muhammad) at Karbalaʾ
aslaf: ancestors
awliyaʾ**:** protectors
aʿ**yan:** notables
baligh: boy/girl who has reached legal majority
ballana: woman who went from house to house providing beautification ser-
    vices
bayʿ**a:** oath of allegiance
bayt: household, home
bayt maftuh: open house
al-bayda: common reference to a slavewoman
biʾ**a:** background
bidʿ**a:** innovation
bikr: a virgin girl

bima istahala min faragiha: what became permissible from her sexually
bulugh: puberty
damm: collecting, male custody of children
darar: harm
Dar Juwad: house of noble persons
Dar al-Thiqa: house of trust
Dar al-Iskan: house of peace, settlement
Dar Sukna bi Husna: house of repose and charity
Dar al-Amana: house of honesty, integrity
dhimmi: non-Muslim
diwan: government council, office
diyya: blood price, compensation for bodily harm
dukhla: consummation of a marriage
durra: second wife
fagih: legist, theologian
fasad: corruption
fatwa, pl. **fatawi:** juridical opinion(s)
fiqh: juridical interpretations by the Muslim clergy, Muslim Jurisprudence
firman: executive law
ghilman: male servants
hadana, hidana: raise a child, custody of young children by females
hadd, hudud: Canon law cases with divinely defined punishments
hadd al-tamyiz: ability to discern, judge, differentiate
hadith: prophetic tradition
hajr: declare legally incompetent, put under guardianship
halik: deceased
hamula: Palestinian clan
hara: popular residential quarter
haram: religiously prohibited
haramliks: women's quarters
hawsh: courtyard
hijab: veil, curtain
hurma: previously married woman
ʿidda: three-month waiting period following divorce before a woman can be remarried
idhn: permission
ightisab: rape, forceful usurpation of what belongs to another
ihtibas: restrain
ijab wa qubul: marriage request and acceptance of husband and wife or their agents
ijaza: certificate received after training in a particular religious subject
ijtihad: scripture-based reasoning or interpretation
ʿilla: sickness, disease, weakness, defect
ʿilm al-shurut: science of stipulations
imam: religious personnel

infitah: economic open-door policy instituted by Anwar Sadat in Egypt

iqrar: legal record or obligation

irba: skill, cleverness

istibdad: oppression

istihbab: commendable, well-liked, and desirable acts

istihsan: approval; consent; application of discretion in a juridical decision

isti'naf: court of second degree, court of appeals

iwan: reception area

jadd: grandfather

jahiliyya: period preceding the coming of Islam

jaid, f. *jaida:* nobleman, noblewoman

jariyya, pl. *jawari:* a slave woman

jayb, pl. *juyub:* bosom

jihad: struggle in the way of God

jihaz: trousseau

jilbab, pl. ***jalabib:*** outer garments

jirjiyyat al-jins: of Georgian nationality

kafaᵓa, kufᵓ: compatability between bride and bridegroom

kafil: sponsor, or patron

kafir: apostate

kariha: unwilling, hating

kashif: governor

khalal: defect or shortcoming

khassa: elite

khataya: offenses, crimes

al-khawaja: reference to a merchant during the Ottoman period, a term used for foreigners during the modern period

khulᶜ: divorce by repudiation

khuruj: literally exits

khimar, pl. *khumur:* scarf, scarves

kufr: infidelity, atheism

laqab: title, nickname, family name

maᶜalim: title for a skilled head craftsman

madhhab, pl. *madhahib:* creed or school of law

maᵓdhun, maᵓdhun sharᶜi: government notary public who officiates and records marriages and divorces

madrasa: mosque school

al-madᶜu, f. *al-madᶜuwwa:* name

mahalle: residential quarter

mahkama: judiciary court

mahr: dowry

mahr muqaddam, *mahr muᶜajjal:* part of dowry paid in advance at the time the marriage is contracted

mahr muᵓakhkhar: delayed dowry to be paid at the termination of marriage or death of husband

majlis: council
makruh: forced, compelled
manzil: dwelling, house
mar'a: woman
al-mar'a al-kamila: respectful title for a woman
[fi] ma'rufin: what is right, well-known, beneficial
masafat al-qasr: travel distance separating husband from wife, guardian from his wards, etcetera, which is considered unacceptable by the courts
ma'siyya: injustice, injury, disobedience, sin
mathilatiha: its equal
ma'tuq: freed slave
metwali: director of a *waqf*
millet: term used for religious groups in the Ottoman Empire
minyan: Hebrew term for a religious quorum
miri: state held
mu'alim: a tile of skilled head craftsman
mu'ashara, 'ishra: living together, cohabitation
mu'adhdhin: person who calls for prayers
mufti: top religious legal position
muhajirun, f. **muhajirat:** believing immigrant men, immigrant women
mukhallafat: registers of division of inheritance
al-Mumtahana: She who is examined (title of a Qur'anic *sura*)
murahiq: adolescent
musha': free-hold
mushari': lawmaker
al-mutawaffa, f. **al-mutawafiyya:** deceased
mut'a: enjoyment
nafaqa: financial support, alimony, child support
na'ib: *qadi*'s deputy
naqisa: deficient
nasab: genealogy or blood relationship, descent, pedigree
nashiz: disobedient wife who refuses to comply with a *bayt al-ta'a* order
nasrani: Christian
nazir, nazira: overseer, administrator, superintendent
nikah: marriage
nisba: genealogy
nushuz: status of a wife who is *nashiz*
ojaqa: Ottoman forces in Egypt
qa'a: hall, principal salon
qabila: tribe
qabilat: midwives
qadi: arabic form for the word judge
qanun: secular or executive law
qasir: a minor child
qirat: unit for measuring area of land, 1/24 of a *feddan*.

qiwama: being in charge
qurush: piasters; commonly used coinage
radd: husband's right to "take back" his divorced wife
raᶜaya: populace
riwaq: open gallery, colonnade, corridor
rushd: maturity of mind, be well-guided, majority
sadaq: delayed alimony
saghir: young child
Saᶜid: Upper Egypt
salihin: the upright
shahada: martyrdom
shahbandar al-tujjar: elected head of merchants' guild
shaykhulislam: chief religious position in Ottoman Empire
shariᶜa: Islamic law
shart al-wilaya: condition of guardianship
shaykh, pl. **shuyukh:** elder, Muslim clergyman
shaykh al-ghufaraᵓ: chief of government-appointed guards
shura: political consultation
shurut: stipulations in legal documents
shuᶜub: nations
sijill: files, archival documents, records of *shariᶜa* courts
Sufi: Muslim mystic
suq: market
suq al-Nahhasin: coppersmith market
suqqaᵓ: water carriers
sura: any chapter in the Qurᵓan
taᶜa: obedience
tabarruj: parading, showing-off, strutting-about
tabatul: piety, asceticism
tabiᶜ: escort, servant, attendant
tafriq: separation or divorce
tafsir: interpretation or commentary on the Qurᵓan
talaq: divorce
talaq bain: "conditional" or irrevocable divorce
talaq bidᶜa: innovative divorce
talaq al-thalath: innovative divorce
talaq rajᶜi: revoccable divorce
talfiq: patch or piece laws together
taliqa: divorcée
talqa: single divorce
taqlid: imitation of established legal doctrines
taqwa: devoutness, goodness, virtue
taruq: depressions running along intramural streets that functioned as gutters and animal lanes but were often used for the passage of non-Muslims in the city of Damascus

al-tasari: diversion with slavewomen
tatliq: divorce by judge's or church's decree
tawliyya: responsibility, supervision
taʿzir: discretionary punishment
tazkiya: supporting witnesses, recommending witnesses
thaman: price
tuqus: rituals
ʿud: lute (musical instrument)
ʿulamaʾ: religious scholars, theologians, clergy
uluʾl-amr minkum: those with authority among you
umanaʾ: trustworthy people
ʿumda: village head
umma: Ismalic nation
ʿurf: customs, traditions
ʿurfi: common-law (e.g., marriage)
usquf: bishop
ʿuthr sharʿi: legally accepted excuse
wasi: guardian
wakil: proxy, attorney at law, deputy
walad, pl. **awlad:** son
wali: governor
waliyy, f. **waliyya:** guardian
walid: father
waliyy al-niʿam: the one from whom all blessings flowed
warraq: a paper merchant
wasi: guardian chosen by father for his children or by the court for orphans
waqf, pl. **awqaf:** religious endowment
wasita: intermediary
watan: homeland, nation
wikala: agency, proxy
wilayat al-ijbar: right to force them
yashmak: veil
yahudi: Jew
yazni: commits adultery
zaʿim: patriarch
zalim: unjust person
zaptia: urban police
zawaj: marriage
zina: adultery
zulm: injustice

Glossary of Turkish Terms

Adalet: justice
araba: carts
askeri: military
bedestan: covered market
beytülmal: treasury
bidat-i hasane: In Islamic law, a useful, hence acceptable, innovation
cebren: forcibly
çiftlik: agricultural estate
Darülislam-Darülharb: Abode of Islam—Abode of War
defter, pl. **defterleri:** register(s)
divan-i humayun: Imperial Council
ferace: long coat
ferman: executive or imperial law
fetva: legal decision
hakk: due rights
helva sohbeti: an entertainment featuring conversation and the Turkish
  sweet helvah, made of sesame seeds and honey
hisse: share of property
hücet: court decision
hüküm: executive order, imperial decree
ila: sickness, disease, weakness, defect
izn-i âm: general permission
kadi: Islamic judge
kanun: secular or executive law
kasaba: small town
kayık: boat
khul: divorce by repudiation
lâle çiragani: eighteenth-century Ottoman entertainment featuring the illumination of vast tulip buds
mahalle: town quarter
mahlut: mixing freely together
malikane: tax-farms turned into private property

medrese: Islamic religious college
mehkeme: court of law
mehr: dowry, bride price
mehr-i-müeccel: delayed part of dowry paid at the time the marriage ends by divorce or husband's death
mehr-i muaccel: advanced part of the dowry paid at the time the marriage is contracted
meʾmur: commissioned
mevlid: commemoration of the Prophet's birthday
miri: state land
misafira: a visitor
müfti: authorized religious person, top religious legal position
mülk: freehold, private property
müsaade: favor
mutevelli: director of a *vakf*, trustees of religious endowments
reaya: tax-paying subjects
şeriat: Islamic law
seyr akçesi: spending money
seyhülislam: chief religious position in Ottoman Empire
sicils: archival documents, records of *shariʿa* courts
Şikayet Defterleri: petitions, official complaints requiring government action
sulh: agreement
talâk: divorce
talâk-i bain: irrevocable divorce
tasavvuf: Sufism
tefrik: separation or divorce
tekke: Sufi monastery
ulema: religious scholars, theologians, clergy
vakf: religious endowment
vesi: guardian
vekil: proxy, attorney at law, deputy
yaşmak: veil
ziyafet: sumptuous banquets

Works Cited

Archival Sources

Aleppo. Mahkama Shar'iyya Archives.

Alexandria. National Archives. Shahr 'Aqari.

Amman. University of Jordan. National Archives: Markaz al-Watha'iq wa'l-Makhtutat.

Ankara. Milli Kütüphane. Kadi Sicil. Trabzon.

Baghdad. Baghdad Museum Manuscript collection: Manuscript no. 12602, fols. 3 and 8 (Muhammad Amin al-'Umari, "al-Kashf wa'l-bayan 'an mashay-ikh al-zaman").

Cairo. National Archives:
Dar al-Watha'iq al-'Qawmiyya:
Shari'a court records: Alexandria; Armant; Assiut; Dishna; Dumyat; Isna; Manfalut; Police records, Cairo; Fatawi; Ma'iyya Saniyya records: 'Arabi; Sadir Awamir.
Dar al-Mahfuzat al-'Umumiyya:
Shahr 'Aqari, Dar al-Qada' al-'Ali.
Shari'a court records: Misr; Bab al-'Ali; Bab al-Sha'iriyya; Al-Barmashiyya; Jami' al-Hakim; Mahfaza Dasht; Misr al-Qadima; al-Qisma al-'Arabiyya; al-Salihiyya al-Nijmiyya; Tobon; al-Zahid.
Archives of the Ministry of Awqaf (daftarkhanah).
Archives of 'Abdin Palace, Iltimasat, Taqarir, Telegrams.
Documents of the Coptic Patriarchy in Cairo.

Damascus. National Archives: Markaz al-Watha'iq al-Tarikhiyya.

Haifa. Court Sijill. Jaridat al-Zabt.

Istanbul. Başbakanlik Archives: Şikayet Defterleri.

Jaffa. Hujaj.

Musul. Shari'a court records. Records of Awqaf: Waqfiyyat Rabi'a Khatun bint Isma'il Pasha, waqfiyyat Ahmad Pasha al-Jalili, waqfiyyat Zaynab Khatun al-Sayyid Darwish, waqfiyyat al-Haj Yahya bin Haj Abdal.

Sofia. National Library: "St. Cyril and Methodius." Oriental Department.

Tunis. Archives Nationales. Série Historique: Zaptiés; Fond Actes Notaires, A,
B, C; Fatawi; Khatayya; Da'awi; Nawazil; Archives des Palais de Justice;
Shari'a Court Registers (Registre charaïque).
Qasim Azzum. *Les ajwiba manuscript de la B.N., no.* 4854.
al-Burzuli. *al-Fatawi,* 2 Vols. Manuscript, B.N., no. 4851.

Periodicals

al-Ahram.
Akhbar al-Hawadith.
Akhir Sa'a.
al-'Arabi.
al-Manar.
al-Manara al-Misriyya.
al-Misri.
Nisf al-Dunya.
al-Sha'b.
al-Sufur.

Books, Articles, Dissertations, Papers

'Abd al-Baqi, Muhammad Fuad. N.d. *al-Mu'jam al-mufahras li-alfaz al-quran
al-karim.* Cairo.
Abdal-Rehim, Abdal-Rehim Abdal-Rahman. 1974. *al-Rif al-misri fi al-qarn al-
thamin 'ashar.* Cairo: 'Ain Shams Univ. Press.
———. 1990. *Fusul min tarikh misr al-iqtisadi w'al-ijtima'i fi al-'asr al-'uthmani.*
Cairo: al-Hay'a al-Misriyya al-'Amma li'l-Kitab.
Abdo-Zubi, Nahla. 1987. *Family, Women and Social Change in the Middle
East: The Palestinian Case.* Toronto: Canadian Scholars.
'Abdu, Shaykh Muhammad. 1989. *al-A'mal al-kamila.* Vol. 2. Edited by Mu-
hammad 'Imara. Cairo: al-Hay'a al-Misriyya al-'Amma li'l-Kitab.
Abo El Nasr, Medhat, and Ronald G. Walton. 1988. "Indigenization and Au-
thentization in Terms of Social Work in Egypt." *International Social Work*
31:142–43.
Abou-Zeid, Fawzia al-Ashmawi. 1985. *La femme et L'Égypte moderne dans
l'oeuvre de Naguib Mahfuz.* Paris: Publ. Orientaliste de France.
Abu Zahra, Shaykh Muhammad. 1980. *al-Zawag wa'l-talaq al-madani fi al-
quran.* Cairo.
Abul-Futuh, Muhammad. 1992. "al-Ahwal al-ijtima'iyya fi madinat Isna fi al-
'asr al-'uthmani, dirasat fi sijillat ishhad al-zawaj wa'l-talaq fi al-qarn 12
H." *Majalat kuliyat al-adab* no. 57: *Abhath nadwat tarikh misr al-iqtisadi
wa al-ijtima'i fi al-'asr al-'uthmani 1517–1798.* Cairo: Cairo Univ. Press.
Accad, Evelyne. 1990. *Sexuality and War: Literary Masks of the Middle East.*
New York: New York Univ. Press.
Afifi, Mohamed. 1991. *al-Awqaf wa'l-hayat al-iqtisadiyya fi Misr fi al-'asr al-
'uthmani.* Cairo: al-Hay'a al-Misriyya al-'Amma li'l-Kitab.

————. 1992. *al-Aqbat fi misr fi al-ʿasr al-ʿuthmani.* Cairo.

Agnew, John, and James Duncan, eds. 1989. *The Power of Place.* London: Unwin Hyman.

Ahmed, Leila. 1982. "Western Ethnocentrism: Perceptions of the Harem" in *Feminist Studies* 8, no. 3.

————. 1992. *Women and Gender in Islam.* New Haven: Yale Univ. Press.

Akif, M. 1984. *Osmanli Hukukunda Nikah Akitleri.* JOS, Vol. 4.

Aktepe, M. Münir. 1958. *Patrona İsyanı.* Istanbul.

————. 1960. "Nevşehirli Damad İbrahim Paşa'ya âid İki Vakfiye." *Tarih Dergisi* 11:156–58.

————, ed. 1976–1978. *Findîklîlî Şemdanizade Şüleyman Efendi Târihi Mürit-Tevârih.* 2 vols. Istanbul.

Alderson, A. D. 1956. *The Structure of the Ottoman Dynasty.* Oxford: Oxford Univ. Press.

[Altınay], Ahmet Refik. 1930. *Hicrî On İkinci Asırda Istanbul Hayatı (1100–1200).* Istanbul: Devlet. Matbaası.

————. 1973. *Lâle Devri.* Ankara.

Anderson, J. 1950. "Invalid and Void Marriages in Hanafi Law." *BSOAS,* vol. 13.

Anderson, J. N. D. 1968. "Eclipse of the Patriarchal Family in Contemporary Islamic Law." *Family Law in Asia and Africa,* edited by J. N. D. Anderson, 221–34. New York: Praeger.

————. 1970. *Islamic Law in Africa.* London.

al-ʿAni, Shujaʿ. 1986. *al-Marʾa fi al-qissah al-ʿiraqiyya.* Baghdad: Wizarat al-Thaqafa.

Ardener, Shirley, ed. 1981. *Women and Space: Ground Rules and Social Maps.* New York: St. Martin's.

Asad, Talal. 1987. *Is There an Anthropology of Islam?* Washington: Center for Contemporary Arab Studies.

Asïk, Küçük Çelebizade İsmail. 1865. *Tarih-i Asïm.* Vol. 6 of *Tarih-i Raşid.* Istanbul.

Asmar, Maria Teresa. 1844. *Memoirs of a Babylonian Princess.* Vol. 1. London: Henry Crolburn.

al-ʿAsqalani. 1987. *Fath al-bari bi sharh sahih al-Bukhari.* 12 vols. Cairo: Dar al-Rayan liʾl-Turath.

Auclert, Hubertine. 1900 *Les femmes arabes en Algérie.* Paris: Editions Littéraires.

Ayalon, David. 1977. "Studies in al-Jabarti, Notes on the Transformation of Mamluk Society in Egypt under the Ottomans." In *Studies on the Mamluks of Egypt: 1250–1517.* London: Valorium Reprints.

————. 1991. "Competing Agenda: Feminists, Islam and the State in 19th and 20th Century Egypt." In *Women, Islam and the State,* edited by Deniz Kandiyoti. Philadelphia: Temple Univ. Press.

Badran, Margot, and Miriam Cooke, eds. 1990. *Opening the Gates: A Century of Arab Feminist Writing.* Bloomington: Indiana Univ. Press.

Bahnam, ʿAbd al-Masih. 1962. *Qara Qush fi kaffat al-tarikh.* Baghdad.

————. 1979. "Anthropology and Analysis of Ideology." In *MAN*. 14:606–27.

Bailie, N. B. E. *Majallat al-Ahkam al-ʿAdliyya.* Istanbul: Diwan al-Ahkam al-
ʿAdliyya, Matbaʿat al-Jwaib, 1298/1881, 2d ed. in Arabic, 242–43 (arts.
1631–33), 277 (art. 1823).

Bakhtin, M. M. 1981. *The Dialogic Imagination: Four Essays by M. M. Bakhtin,*
edited by. Michael Holquist. Translated by Carly Emerson and Michael
Holquist. Austin: Univ. of Texas Press.

al-Bakri, Muhammad. 1991. *al-Ahwal al-shakhsiya.* Cairo.

Barakat, Halim. 1984. "The Arab Family and the Challenge of Social Transformation." In *Women and the Family in the Middle East,* edited by Elizabeth Warnock Fernea. Austin: Univ. of Texas Press.

Barclay, Harold B. 1971. "The Nile Valley." In *The Central Middle East,* edited
by Louise E. Sweet. New Haven: HRAF Press.

Bardsley-Sirois, Lois, and Carolyn Fluehr-Lobban. Spring 1990. "Obedience
(Taʿa) in Muslim Marriage: Religious Interpretation and Applied Law in
Egypt." *Journal of Comparative Family Studies* 21/1.

Baron, Beth. 1991. "The Making and Breaking of Marital Bonds in Modern
Egypt." In *Women in Middle East History,* edited by Nikki Keddie and
Beth Baron. Yale Univ. Press.

Baron, Beth, and Nikki Keddie, eds. 1991. *Women in Middle East History.* New
Haven: Yale Univ. Press.

Bassiouni, M. Cherif. 1987. "A Search for Islamic Criminal Justice." *The Islamic
Impulse,* edited by Barbara Freyer Stowasser. London: Croom Helm.

Bazi, Mikhail. 1969. *Baldat Tekeyf: madiha wa hadirha.* Mosul.

Ben Taher, J. 1985. *al-Fasad wa radʿuhu biʾl-bilad al-tunisiyya 1705–1840.*
Tunis.

Berkes, Niyazi. 1964. *The Development of Secularism in Turkey.* Montreal.

Blessing, Julia Ann, and Michael Caspi, eds. 1991. *Weavers of the Song—The
Oral Poetry of Arab Women in Israel and the West Bank.* Washington:
Three Continents.

Blili, L. 1986. *Vie de famille à Tunis à l'époque précoloniale et coloniale.* Tunis:
Université de Tunis.

Bodman, Herbert. 1963. *Political Factions in Aleppo 1760–1826.* Chapel Hill:
Univ. of North Carolina Press.

Bourdieu, Pierre. 1988. *Outline of a Theory of Practice.* Translated by Richard
Nice. Cambridge: Cambridge Univ. Press.

————. 1991. "Identity and Representation: Elements for a Critical Reflection
on the Idea of a Region." In *Language and Symbolic Power,* edited by
John Thompson. Cambridge, Mass.: Harvard Univ. Press.

Bousquet, G. H., and L. Bercher. N.d. *Le statut personnel en droit musulman
hanafite.* Tunis: Publication de L'Institut des Hautes Etudes de Tunis.

Bowlan, Jeanne. 1993. "Prescribing Civility: French Colonialism and Gender in
Algeria, 1919–1939." Paper presented at the 1993 Berkshire Conference
on the History of Women.

Cameron, Deborah. 1985. *Feminism and Linguistic Theory.* London: St. Martin's.

Çelik, Zeynep. 1992. *Displaying the Orient: The Architecture of Islam at Nine-teenth-Century World's Fairs.* Berkeley: Univ. of California Press.

Censer, Jane Turner. 1991. "What Ever Happened to Family History? A Review Article." *CSSH,* Vol. 33.

Cevdet, Ahmed. 1891. *Tarih-i Cevdet.* Istanbul.

Chabrol, M. de. 1822. "Etat Moderne, Essai sur les Moeurs des Habitans Modernes de l'Egypte." In *Description de l'Egypte, Tome Second (IIè partie).* Paris: de l'Imprimerie Royale.

Charnay, Jean-Paul. 1965. *La vie musulmane en Algérie d'après la jurisprudence de la première moitié du XXᵉ siècle.* Paris: Presses Universitaires de France.

Chaudhuri, Nupur, and Margaret, Strobel, eds. 1992. *Western Women and Imperialism: Complicity and Resistance.* Bloomington: Indiana Univ. Press.

Christelow, Alan. 1985. *Muslim Law Courts and the French Colonial State in Algeria.* Princeton: Princeton Univ. Press.

Clancy-Smith, Julia. 1990. "In the Eye of the Beholder: The North African Sufi Orders and the Colonial Production of Knowledge, 1830–1900." *Africana Journal* 15:220–57.

———. 1992. "The 'Passionate Nomad' Reconsidered: A European Woman in L'Algérie Française (Isabelle Eberhardt, 1877–1904)." In *Western Women and Imperialism: Complicity and Resistance,* edited by Nupur Chaudhuri and Margaret Strobel, 61–78. Bloomington: Indiana Univ. Press.

———. 1994. *Rebel and Saint: Muslim Notables, Populist Protest, Colonial Encounters (Algeria and Tunisia, 1800–1904).* Berkeley: Univ. of California Press.

Clancy-Smith, Julia, and Cynthia Gray-Ware Metcalf. 1993. "A Visit to a Tunisian Harem." *Journal of Maghrebi Studies* 1–2, no. 1: 43–49.

Cohen, Amnon. 1984. *Jewish Life under Islam: Jerusalem in the Sixteenth Century.* Cambridge, Mass.: Harvard Univ. Press.

Cohen, Mark R. 1991. March/April 1991. "The Neo-Lachrymose Conception of Jewish-Arab History." *Tikkun* 6, no. 3: 55–60.

Cooke, Miriam. 1988. *War's Other Voices—Women Writers on the Lebanese Civil War.* Cambridge: Cambridge Univ. Press.

Coulsen, Noel C. 1964. *A History of Islamic Law.* Edinburgh: Edinburgh Univ. Press.

Coulson, Noel J. 1969. *Conflicts and Tensions in Islamic Jurisprudence.* Chicago: Univ. of Chicago Press.

Crecelius, Daniel. 1981. *The Roots of Modern Egypt.* Minneapolis: Bibliotheca Islamica.

Daily Routine and Festivities in XVIII c. Rumelia. N.d. Sofia.

al-Dardir. N.d. *al-Sharh al-kabir.* Vol. 2. Cairo.

Daumas, Melchior-Joseph-Eugène. 1845. *Le Sahara algérien.*

———. 1869. *La vie arabe et la société musulmane.*

———. 1912. "La femme arabe." *Revue africaine* 56, no. 284: 1–154.

Dimitrov, S. 1981. *Ottoman Turkish Sources on the History of Dobrudja and North-East*. Sofia.

———, N. Jechev, and V. Tonev. 1988. *History of Dubrudja*. Vol. 2. Sofia.

al-Diwahji, Saʿid. 1963. *Jawamiʿ al-Musul fi mukhtalaf al-ʿusur*. Baghdad.

Duben, Alan, and Cem Behar. 1991. *Istanbul Households: Marriage, Family and Fertility, 1880–1940*. Cambridge: Cambridge Univ. Press.

al-Dulaimi, Sulaiman. 1990. "Social Welfare in the Arab World: The Case of Iraq and Kuwait." Ph.D. diss., Exeter Univ.

Eberhardt, Isabelle. 1978. *The Oblivion Seekers and Other Writings*. Translated by Paul Bowles. San Fransisco: City Lights.

Eldem, Sedad H. N.d. *Saʾdabad*. Ankara?

Esposito, L. John. 1975. "Women's Rights in Islam." *Islamic Studies* 14:99–104.

Farahat, Muhammad Nur. 1988. *al-Oadaʾ al-sharʿi fi misr fi al-ʿasr al-ʿuthmani*. Cairo: al-Hayʾa al-Misriya al-ʿAmma ʾil-Kitab.

Fargués, Philippe. 1994. "Demographic Explosion or Social Upheaval." In *Democracy Without Democrats?* London: I. B. Taurus.

Faroqhi, Suraiya. 1981. *Men of Modest Substance: House Owners and House Property in Seventeenth Century Ankara and Kayseri*. Cambridge: Cambridge Univ. Press.

———. 1984. *Towns and Townsmen of Ottoman Anatolia: Trade, Crafts, and Food Production in an Urban Setting: 1520–1650*. Cambridge: Cambridge Univ. Press.

al-Fatawi al-islamiyya. 1984. Cairo: Dar al-Iftaʾ. vols. 2, 11.

Fernea, Elizabeth, and Basima Bezirgan, eds. 1977. *Middle East Muslim Women Speak*. Austin: Univ. of Texas Press.

Flandrin, Jean Louis. 1979. *Families in Former Times: Kinship, Household and Sexuality*. Translated by Richard Southern. Cambridge: Cambridge Univ. Press.

Fox-Genovese, Elizabeth. 1993. "From Separate Spheres to Dangerous Streets: Postmodernist Feminism and the Problem of Order." *Social Research* 60, no. 2: 234–54.

Friedl, Erika. 1991. "The Dynamics of Women's Sphere of Action in Rural Iran." In *Women in Middle East History*, edited by Nikki Keddie and Beth Baron.

———. 1991. *Women of Deh Koh*. New York: Penguin.

Fyzee, Asef A. 1955. *Outlines of Muhammadan Law*. London: Oxford Univ. Press

———. 1974. *Outlines of Mohammadan Law*. New Delhi.

Gallad, Filib. 1895. *Qamus al-idara waʾl-qadaʾ*. Alexandria: Matbaʿat al-Qamus.

Gallup, Dorothea M. 1973. "The French Image of Algeria: Its Origin, Its Place in Colonial Ideology, Its Effect on Algerian Acculturation." Ph.D. diss., Univ. of California, Los Angeles.

Garnett, L. 1982. *Balkan Home Life*. New York.

Gaudry, Matthéa. 1929. *La femme chaouia de l'Aurès: étude de sociologie berbère*. Paris: P. Geuthner.

Gautier, Emile-Félix. 1931. *Moeurs et coutumes des musulmans*. Paris: Impri-merie Nationale.

Geertz, Clifford. 1968. *Islam Observed*. New Haven: Yale Univ. Press.

———. 1973. *The Interpretation of Cultures*. New York: Basic.

Geiger, H. Kent. 1968. *The Family in the Soviet Union*. Cambridge, Mass.: Harvard Univ. Press.

Gerber, Haim. 1980. "Social and Economic Position of Women in an Ottoman City." *International Journal of Middle East Studies* 12:231–44.

———. 1994. *State, Society, and Law in Islam*. Albany: State Univ. of New York Press.

al-Ghazali, Abu Hamid. 1990. *Adab al-nikah wa kasr al-shahwatayn*. Susa, Tunis: Manshurat Dar al-Ma'arif li'l-Tiba'a wa'l-Nashr.

Giddens, Anthony. 1985. "Time, Space and Regionalization." In *Social Relations and Spatial Structures*, edited by Derek Gregory and John Urry. London: Macmillan.

Gil'adi, Avner. 1992. *Children of Islam*. New York: St. Martin's.

al-Gindi, Ahmad Nasr. 1978. *al-Ahwal al-shakhsiyya*. Cairo.

al-Giziri, 'Abd al-Rahman. 1987. *Kitab al-fiqh 'ala al-madhahib al-arba'a*. 4 vols. Cairo: Dar al-Rayyan li'l-Turath.

Goichon, Amélie Marie. 1927. *La vie féminine au Mzab: étude de sociologie musulmane*. Paris: P. Geuthner.

Goitein, S. D. 1978. *A Mediterranean Society: The Jewish Communities of the Arab World as Portrayed in the Documents of the Cairo Geniza*. Vol. 3, *The Family*. Berkeley: Univ. of California Press.

Goldziher, Ignaz. 1981. *Introduction to Islamic Theology and Law*. Princeton: Princeton Univ. Press.

Gonzales. 1977. *Voyage en Égypte: 1665–1666*. Vol. 1. Cairo.

Goodrich, Peter. 1987. *Legal Discourse: Studies in Linguistics, Rhetoric and Legal Analysis*. London: Macmillan.

Goody, Jack. 1976. *Production and Reproduction*. Cambridge Univ. Press.

———. 1986. *The Logic of Writing and the Organization of Society*. Cambridge: Cambridge Univ. Press.

Gran, Peter. 1991. "Mafhum Gramsci 'an al-muthaqqif al-taqlidi: salihiyatiha li-dirasat misr al-hadit-ha." In *Gramsci*, edited by Hilmi Sha'rawi et al. Damascus: Dar al-Kan'an li'l-dirasat wa'l-nashr.

Hamamy, H. A., Z. S. Al-Hakkak, and S. Taha. "Consanguinity and the Genetic Control of Down Syndrome." *Clinical Genetics* 37/1.

Hanna, 'Abdallah. 1985. *Harakat al-'amma al-dimashqiyya fi al-qarnayn al-thamin wa'l-tasi'-'ashar*. Beirut: Dar Ibn Khaldun.

Hanna, Nelly. Forthcoming. "The Administration of Courts in Ottoman Cairo." In *Administration in Egypt*, edited by Nelly Hanna. Cairo: American Univ. in Cairo Press.

———. Forthcoming. *The Biography of Isma'il Abu Taqiyya Shahbandar al-Tujjar*.

———. Forthcoming. "Marriage and the Family in 17th Century Cairo." In

Proceedings of the Sixth International Conference of Economic and Social History of the Ottoman Empire and Turkey 1326–1960, edited by Daniel Panzac. Aix-en-Provence; IREMAM.

Hatem, Mervat. 1982. "Economic and Political Liberation in Egypt and the Demise of State Feminism." *International Journal of Middle East Studies* 24, pt. 2 (May), 231–51.

————. 1985. "The Politics of Sexuality and Gender in Segregated Patriarchal Systems: The Case of Eighteenth and Nineteenth Century Egypt." *Feminist Studies*, vol. 12.

Hause, Steven C. 1987. *Hubertine Auclert: The French Suffragette*. New Haven: Yale Univ. Press.

al-Hawari, Ahmad Ibrahim. 1976. *al-Batal al-muᶜasir fi al-riwaya al-misriyya*. Baghdad.

Hijab, Nadia. 1988. *Womanpower*. Cambridge: Cambridge Univ. Press.

al-Hisari, Ahmad. 1986. *al-Nikah waʾl-qadaya al-mutaᶜaliqa bihi*. Cairo: Maktabat al-Kuliyya al-Azhariyya.

Hodgson, Marshall. 1974. *The Venture of Islam*. Vol. 3. Chicago: Univ. of Chicago Press.

Holt, P. M. 1982. "The Last Phase of the Neo-Mamluk Regime in Egypt." *L'Egypte au XIXᵉ Siècle*. Paris: Centre National de al Recherche Scientifique.

Humphreys, R. Stephen. 1988. *Islamic History: A Framework for Inquiry*. Minneapolis: Bibliotheca Islamica.

al-Humsi, Nahdi Subhi. 1986. *Tarikh Trablus min khilal wathaʾiq al-mahkama al-sharᶜiyya fi al-nisf al-thani min al-qarn al-sabiᶜ-ᶜashar*. Beirut: Muʾasasat al-Risala.

Ibn Ishaq. 1970. *The Life of Muhammad*. Translated by A. Guillaume. Karachi: Oxford Univ. Press.

Ibn Iyas. 1961. *Badaʾiᶜ al-zuhur*, edited by Muhammad Mustafa. Cairo.

Ibn Nugaym. N.d. *al-Bahr al-raʾiq*. Cairo.

Ibn Saᶜd. 1904. *Kitab al-tabaqat al-kabir*. Vol. 8, edited by Carl Brockelmann. Leiden: Brill.

Ibn Taymiya, Ahmad. 1992. *Majmuᶜ fatawi al-nikah wa ahkamih*, edited by Abu al-Majd Harak. Cairo: al-Dar al-Libnaniyya al-Misriyya.

Ibrahim, Mahmud. 1992. *Merchant Capital and Islam*. Austin: Univ. of Texas Press.

Imber, C. 1991. "Involuntary Annulment of Marriage and Its Solutions in Ottoman Law." Paper presented at the Islamic Conference, Manchester.

Inalcik, Halil. 1988. "Şikayet Hakki: ʾArz-i Mazharlar." *Osmanli Arastirmalari* 7–8:33–54.

Isthorus, Bishop. N.d. *al-Farida al-nafisa fi tarikh al-kanisa*. Vol. 2. Cairo.

al-Jabarti, ᶜAbd al-Rahman. 1967. *ᶜAjaʾib al-athar fi al-tarajim waʾl-akhbar*. Vol. 7. Cairo: Lajnat al-Bayan al-ᶜArabi.

————. 1988. *Merveilles Biographiques et Historiques ou Chroniques du Cheikh Abd el-Rahman el-Djabarti*. Vol. 1. Cairo: Kraus. Original edition, Cairo: Kraus Thomson Organization Limited Edition, 1970.

Jaffe, Eliezer D. 1982. *Child Welfare in Israel*. New York: Praeger.

———. 1983. *Israelis in Institutions*. New York: Gordon and Breach.

al-Janabi, ʿAʾida. 1983. *al-Mutaghayyarat al-ijtimaʿiyya waʾl-thaqafiyya li-zahirat al-talaq*. Baghdad: Wizarat al-Thaqafa.

Jennings, C. Ronald. 1972. "The Judicial Registers (Serʾi Mehkeme Sicilleri) of Kayseri (1590–1630)." Ph.D. diss., Univ. of California at Los Angeles.

———. 1983. "Women in the Early Seventeenth Century Ottoman Judicial Records: The Sharia Court of Anatolian Kayseri." *Journal of the Economic and Social History of the Orient* 28:53–114.

Johansen, Baber. 1988. *The Islamic Law on Land Tax and Rent*. New York: Croom Helm.

Kane, Constance F. 1984. "A Comparative Study of Social Welfare Decentralization in Egypt and Israel." PhD. diss., Brandeis Univ.

Kandiyoti, Deniz. 1991. "Islam and Patriarchy: A Comparative Perspective." In *Women in Middle Eastern History*, edited by Nikki Keddie and Beth Baron.

———, ed. 1991. *Women, Islam and the State*. Philadelphia: Temple Univ. Press.

Keddie, Nikki, and Beth Baron, eds. 1991. *Women in Middle Eastern History*. New Haven: Yale Univ. Press.

Kemp, Percy. 1979. "Mosul and Mosuli Historians in the Jalili Era." Ph.D. diss., Oxford Univ.

Kerr, M, and S. Yassin. 1982. Boulder, Colo.: Westview. *Rich and Poor States in the Middle East*.

Khalidi, Tarif. 1985. *Classical Arab Islam*. Princeton: Darwin.

al-Khamash, Salwa. 1973. *al-Marʾa al-ʿarabiyya waʾl-mujtamaʿ al-taqlidi al-mutakhalif*. Beirut: Dar al-Haqiqa.

Khamis, Muhammad ʿAtiyya, ed. 1978. *al-Harakat al-nisaʾiyya wa-silatuha bi al-istiʿmar*. Cairo: Dar al-Ansar.

Khayyat, Sana. 1990. *Honour and Shame: Women in Modern Iraq*. London: Saqi.

Khouri, Dina Rizk. 1991. "The Introduction of Commercial Agriculture in the Province of Mosul and Its Impact on the Peasantry." In *Commercial Agriculture in the Ottoman Empire*, edited by Faruk Tabak and Caglar Keyder. New York: State Univ. of New York Press.

———. 1991. "The Political Economy of the Wilaya of Mosul, 1700–1850." Ph.D. diss., Georgetown Univ.

———. 1992. "Iraqi Cities in the Early Modern Period." *Arab Historical Review for Ottoman Studies*, nos. 5 and 6.

Khoury, S. A. and D. Massad. 1992. "Consanguineous Marriage in Jordan." *American Journal of Medical Genetics*. Vol. 43/5.

Khurashi. N.d. *Mukhtasar sidi Khalil*. Cairo.

Khuri, Fuad I. 1983. "Classification, Meaning and Usage of Arabic Status and Kinship Terms." *International Journal of the Sociology of the Family*. Vol. 11.

Klat, Myriam, and Adele Khudr. 1986. "Religious Endogamy and Consanguinity in Marriage Patterns in Beirut, Lebanon." *Social Biology* 33, nos. 1–2.

Kuhn, Thomas S. 1970. *The Structure of Scientific Revolutions.* Chicago: Univ. of Chicago Press. Reprint.

LaCapra, Dominick. 1982. "Rethinking Intellectual History and Reading Texts." In *Modern European Intellectual History: Reappraisals and New Perspectives,* edited by Dominick LaCapra and Steven L. Kaplan. Ithaca: Cornell Univ. Press.

———. 1983. *Rethinking Intellectual History: Texts, Contexts, Language.* Ithaca: Cornell Univ. Press.

Lane, Edward William. 1955. *Arabic-English Lexicon* Book I, Part 5. New York: Ungar.

Lapidus, Ira M. 1982. "The Arab Conquests and the Formation of Islamic Society." In *Studies on the First Century of Islamic Society,* edited by G. H. A. Juynboll. Carbondale: Southern Illinois Univ. Press.

Largueche A., and D. Largueche. 1993. "Anthropologie de la prostitution dans la ville arabe." In *Marginales en terre d'islam.* Tunis: CERES.

Laurens, Henry, Charles Gillispie, Jean-Claude Golvin, and Claude Traunecker. 1989. *L'expédition d'Egypte: 1798–1801.* Paris: Armand Colin.

al-Lawand, ʿAbd al-Halim. n.d. *Nadhra fi zajal al-Musul.* Mosul: Jumhuriyya.

Lawrence, Denise, and Seth Low. 1990. "The Built Environment and Spatial Form." *The Annual Review of Anthropology.* Vol. 19.

Lazim, Tawfiq. 1971. *Harakat al-tatawur waʾl-tajdid fi al-shiʿr al-Iraqi al-hadith.* Baghdad.

Leclerc, Adrien. 1901. "De la condition juridique de la femme musulmane en Algérie." *Congrès International de sociologie coloniale* 2, *Mémoires soumis au congrès,* 109–14. Paris: Rousseau.

Leimdorfer, François. 1992. *Discours académique et colonisation: Thèmes de recherche sur l'Algérie pendant la période coloniale.* Paris: Publlisud.

"Lettre d'Ibn Abi Dhiaf sur la femme." 1968. In *Annales de l'Université de Tunis,* no. 5, 49–112.

Levi, Giovanni. 1990. "Family and Kin—A Few Thoughts." *Journal of Family History* 15/4.

Lewis, Bernard. 1984. *The Jews of Islam.* Princeton: Princeton Univ. Press.

Liant, Y. 1965. *Traité de droit musulman comparé.* Paris: Mouton.

Lutfi, Huda. 1991. "Manners and Customs of Fourteenth-Century Cairene Women: Female Anarchy versus Male Shariʿa Order in Muslim Prescriptive Treatises." In *Women in Middle Eastern History: Shifting Boundaries in Sex and Gender,* edited by Nikki Keddie and Beth Baron. New Haven: Yale Univ. Press.

Mahjub, Muhammad ʿAli. 1993. *al-Usra fi al-tashriʿ al-islami waʾl-qawanin alati tahkumha fi Misr.* Cairo.

Majer, Hans Georg. 1984. *Das Osmanische "Registebuch der Beschwerder" (Şikayet Defteri) von jahre 1675.* Vienna: Osterreichische Akademie der Wissenschafter.

Malti-Douglas, Fedwa. 1991. *Woman's Body, Woman's Word.* Princeton: Princeton Univ. Press.

Manna', 'Adel. 1986. "The Sijill as Source for the Study of Palestine During the Ottoman Period, with Special Reference to the French Invasion." In *Palestine in the Late Ottoman Period: Political, Social, and Economic Transformation,* edited by David Kushner. Jerusalem: Yad Izhak Ben-Zvi.

Marcus, Abraham. 1983. "Men, Women and Property: Dealers in Real Estate in Eighteenth Century Aleppo." *Journal of the Economic and Social History of the Orient* 26:137–63.

———. 1986. "Privacy in Eighteenth Century Aleppo: The Limits of a Cultural Ideal." *International Journal of Middle East Studies* 18:165–83.

———. 1989. *The Middle East on the Eve of Modernity: Aleppo in the Eighteenth Century.* New York: Colombia Univ. Press.

Marcus, Julie. 1992. "History, Anthropology and Gender: Turkish Women Past and Present." *Gender and History* 4, no. 2.

Marsot, Afaf Lutfi al-Sayyid. 1979. "The Revolutionary Gentlewomen of Egypt." In *Women in the Muslim World,* edited by Nikki Keddie and Beth Baron. Cambridge, Mass.: Harvard Univ. Press.

———. 1984. *Egypt in the Age of Muhammad Ali.* Cambridge: Cambridge Univ. Press.

———. 1995. *Women and Men in Eighteenth Century Egypt.* Austin: Texas Univ. Press.

Meriwether, Margaret. 1981. "The Notable Families of Aleppo: Networks and Social Structure." Ph.D. diss., Univ. of Pennsylvania.

———. 1993. "Women and Economic Change in Nineteenth Century Syria." In *Arab Women: Old Boundaries, New Frontiers,* edited by Judith Tucker, 65–83. Bloomington: Indiana Univ. Press.

Mernissi, Fatima. 1975. *Beyond the Veil: Male-Female Dynamics in a Modern Muslim Society.* Schenkman.

———. 1987. *Le harem politique.* Paris.

Milliot, Louis. 1910. *Etude sur la condition de la femme musulmane au Maghreb (Maroc, Algérie, Tunisie).* Paris: Rousset.

———. 1953. *Introduction à l'étude du droit musulman.* Paris.

Mishaqa, Mikhail. 1858–1862. NARA. Washington, D.C.; Consular Correspondence Series.

———. 1988. *Murder, Mayhem, Pillage, and Plunder: The History of Lebanon in the 18th and 19th Centuries.* Translated by Wheeler M. Thackston Jr. Albany: State Univ. of New York Press.

Mitchell, Timothy. 1990. *Colonising Egypt.* Cambridge: Cambridge Univ. Press.

Moore, Henrietta. 1986. *Space, Text, and Gender: An Anthropological Study of the Marakwet of Kenya.* Cambridge: Cambridge Univ. Press.

Moses, Claire Goldberg. 1984. *French Feminism in the Nineteenth Century.* Albany: State Univ. of New York Press.

al-Mukhtar, Ahmad Muhammad. 1962. *Tarikh 'ulama' al-Musul.* Vol. 2. Mosul: Jumhuriyya.

Ibn al-Muqafaʿ, Patriarch Sawiris. N.d. *Tarikh al-batarika*. Vol. 1. Cairo: Maʿhad al-Dirasat al-Qibtiyya.

Nadhmi, Wamid. 1984. *al-Judhur al-siyasiyya waʾl-fikriyya waʾl-ijtimaʿiyya lʾil-haraka al-qawmiyya al-arabiyya fi al-Iraq*. Beirut: Markaz dirasat al-wihda al-ʿArabiyya.

el-Nahal, Galal. 1979. *The Judicial Administration of Ottoman Egypt in the Seventeenth Century*. Chicago.

Najjar, Orayb Aref. 1992. *Portraits of Palestinian Women*. Salt Lake City: Univ. of Utah Press.

Nashat, G. 1983. *Women and Revolution: A Historical Overview*. Boulder: Westview.

Nazzal, Laila Ahed. 1986. "The Role of Shame in Societal Transformation among Palestinian Women on the West Bank." Phd. diss., Univ. of Pennsylvania.

Nicholson, J. 1986. *Gender and History*. New York: Columbia Univ. Press.

Nuri Pasha, Mustafa. 1877–1909. *Netayic el-Vukuat*. 4 vols. Istanbul.

Ortner, Sherry B., and Harriet Whitehead, eds. 1981. *Sexual Meanings: The Cultural Construction of Gender and Sexuality*. Cambridge: Cambridge Univ. Press.

Pearl, David. 1979. *A Text on Muslim Personal Law*. London.

Peck, Christopher, ed. 1988. *Embassy to Constantinople: The Travels of Lady Mary Wortly Montaque*. New York: New Amsterdam.

Peirce, Leslie. 1993. *The Imperial Harem*. Oxford: Oxford Univ. Press.

Pennec, P. 1964. *Les transformations des corps de métier de Tunis sous l'effet d'une économie externe de type capitaliste*. Tunis.

Piterberg, Gabriel. 1990. "The Formation of an Ottoman Egyptian Elite in the 18th Century." *International Journal of Middle East Studies* 22.

Pred, Allan. N.d. "The Social Becomes Spatial, the Spatial Becomes Social." In *Social Relations and Spatial Structure*, edited by Derek Gregory and John Urry.

Prochaska, David. 1990. *Making Algeria French: Colonialism in Bône, 1870–1920*. Cambridge: Cambridge Univ. Press.

Qanun al-ʿuqubat hasab ahdath al-taʿdilat. 1988. Cairo: Dar al-Mashriq al-ʿArabi.

al-Qattan, Najwa. 1994. "Discriminating Texts: Orthographic Marking and Social Differentiation in the Court Records of Ottoman Damascus." In *Issues and Perspectives in Arabic Sociolinguistics*, edited by Yasir Suleiman. London: Curzon.

Rahman, Fazlur. 1980. *Major Themes of the Qurʾan*. Minneapolis: Bibliotheca Islamica.

Raşid, Mehmed. 1865. *Tarih-i Raşid*. 6 vols. Istanbul.

Raʾuf, ʿImad Abd al-Salam. 1976. *al-Musul fi al-ahd al-ʿuthmani: fatrat al-hukm al-mahali*. Najaf.

Raymond, André. 1983. "Le Caire sous Les Ottomans (1517–1798)." In *Palais et maisons du Caire, époque Ottomans (XVIᵉ-XVIIIᵉ Siècles)*, edited by Bernard Maury, André Raymond, Jacques Revault, and Mona Zakaryia. Paris: Centre National de la Recherche Scientifique.

Reilly, James. 1987. "Shariʿa Court Registers and Land Tenure Around Nineteenth-Century Damascus." *MESA Bulletin* 21, no.2: 155–69.

Riskin, Shlomo. 1989. *Women and Jewish Divorce*. Hoboken: Ktav.

Rosen, L. 1989. *The Anthropology of Justice*. Cambridge: Cambridge Univ. Press.

Rugh, Andrea B. 1984. *Family in Contemporary Egypt*. Syracuse: Syracuse Univ. Press.

al-Rushdi, ʿAbd al-Hamid. N.d. *al-Zahawi: dirasat wa nusus*.

Sadiq, Maurice. 1989. *Munazaʿat al-ahwal al-shakhsiyya li ghayr al-muslimin*. Cairo.

Safir, Marilyn, and Barbara Swirski. 1991. *Calling the Equality Bluff: Women in Israel*. New York: Pergamon.

Sanders, Paula. 1991. "Gendering the Ungendered Body: Hermaphrodites in Medieval Islamic Law." In *Women in Middle Eastern History: Shifting Boundaries in Sex and Gender*, edited by Nikki Keddie and Beth Baron. New Haven: Yale Univ. Press.

Savary, M. 1785. *Lettres sur l'Egypte*. Paris: Chez Onfroi.

Schacht, Joseph. 1964 and 1970. *An Introduction to Islamic Law*. Oxford: Oxford Univ. Press.

Schilcher, Linda Schatkowski. 1988. "The Lore and Reality of Middle Eastern Patriarchy." *Die Welt Des Islam* 28.

Schulz, Muriel R. 1990. "The Semantic Derogation of Women." In *The Feminist Critique of Language: A Reader*, edited by Deborah Cameron, 134–47. London: Routlege.

Scott, Joan Wallach. 1988. *Gender and the Politics of History*. New York: Columbia Univ. Press.

Şemdanizade, Fındıklılı Süleyman. 1976–1981. *Şemdânî-Zâde Fındıklılı Süleyman Efendi Târihi Mürʾiʾt-Tevârih*. Edited by M. Münir Aktepe. Fakültesi Edebiyat Fakültesi Matbaasi.

Seng, Yvonne. 1991. "The Üsküdar Estates (Tereke) as Records of Everyday Life in an Ottoman Town, 1521–1524." Ph.D. diss., Univ. of Chicago.

Seni, Nora. 1984. "Ville ottomane et représentation du corps féminin." *Les temps modernes*, no. 456–57.

al-Shafiʿi, Imam. 1988. *al-Risala*. Cairo: Markaz al-Ahram ʾil-Tarjama waʾl-Nashr.

———. N.d. *Al-Umm*. Cairo: Kitab al-Shaʿb.

Shaham, R. 1991. *The Muslim Family in Egypt 1900–1955: Continuity and Change*. Ph.D. diss. Jerusalem: The Hebrew University.

el-Sham, Hassan. 1983. "-Brother/Sister Syndrome in Arab Family Life, Socioculture Factors in Arab Psychology: A Critical Review." *International Journal of the Sociology of the Family*, vol. 11.

Shaʿrani. *al-Mizan al-kubra*. Cairo: A.H. 1318.

Shenouda III, Pope. 1985. *Shariʿat al-zawja al-wahida fi al-masihiyya*. 5th ed. Cairo.

Sonbol, Amira. Forthcoming. "Modernity, Standardization and Marriage Contracts in Nineteenth-Century Egypt." In *Proceedings of the Sixth Interna-*

tional Conference of Economic and Social History of the Ottoman Empire and Turkey 1326–1960, edited by Daniel Panzac. Aix-en-Provence: IRE-MAM.

Sonnini, C. S. 1972. Travels in Upper and Lower Egypt. Westmead: Gregg International. Original edition, London: J. Debrett, 1800.

Springborg, Robert. 1982. Family, Power, and Politics in Egypt—Sayed Bey Marei—His Clan, Clients and Cohorts. Philadelphia: Univ. of Pennsylvania Press.

Staffa, Susan Jane. 1987. "Dimensions of Women's Power in Historic Cairo." In Islamic and Middle Eastern Societies: A Festchrift in Honor of Professor Wadie Jwaideh, edited by Robert Olson. Brattleboro, Vt.: Amana.

Stern, Gertrude. 1939. Marriage in Early Islam. London: Royal Asiatic Society.

Stevens, Mary Anne, ed. 1984. The Orientalists: Delacroix to Matisse. New York: National Gallery of Art.

Stoler, Ann. 1989. "Rethinking Colonial Categories: European Communities and the Boundaries of Rule." Comparative Studies in Society and History 31, no. 1: 134–61.

———. 1991. "Carnal Knowledge and Imperial Power: Gender, Race, and Morality in Colonial Asia." In Gender at the Crossroads of Knowledge: Feminist Anthropology in the Postmodern Era, edited by Micaela di Leonardo. Berkeley: Univ. of California Press.

Stone, Lawrence. 1975. "The Rise of the Nuclear Family in Early Modern England: The Patriarchal State." In The Family in History, edited by Charles Rosenberg.

Stowasser, Barbara Freyer. 1994. Women in the Qur'an. Traditions, and Interpretation. New York: Oxford Univ. Press.

Sureyya, Mehmed. 1893–1994. Sijil-i Osmani 3. Cilt: Matba a-i Amire.

al-Thakeb, Fahed. 1983. "Size and Composition of the Arab Family: Census and Survey Data." International Journal of the Sociology of the Family 11, 171–78.

Tillion, Germaine. 1983. Republic of Cousins. London: Saqi.

Tlili, B. 1974. Etudes d'histoire sociale tunisienne du XIXè s. Tunis. L'Université de Tunis.

Tuqan, Fadwa. 1990. A Mountainous Journey: An Autobiography. Saint Paul: Graywolf.

Tucker, Judith. 1983. "Problems in the Historiography of Women in the Middle East: The Case of Egypt." International Journal of Middle East Studies 15(1983): 321–36.

———. 1985. Women in Nineteenth Century Egypt. Cambridge: Cambridge Univ. Press.

———. 1991. "The Ties That Bound: Women and Family in Eighteenth and Nineteenth Century Nablus." In Women in Middle Eastern History: Shifting Boundaries in Sex and Gender, edited by Nikki Keddie and Beth Baron, 233–53. New Haven: Yale Univ. Press.

Tyan, Emile. 1945. *Le Notoriat et le régime de la preuve par écrit dans la pratique du droit musulman.* Lyon: Université de Lyon.

Udovitch, A. L., ed. 1981. *The Islamic Middle East: 700–1900.* Princeton: Darwin.

al-ʿUmari, Muhammad Amin. 1968. *Manhal al-awliyaʾ wa mashrab al-asfiyaʾ min sadat al-Musul al-hadbaʾ,* edited by Saʿid Diwahji. Vol. 2. Mosul.

————."al-Kashf waʾl-bayan ʿan mashayikh al-zaman." Manuscript no. 12602. Iraqi Museum.

al-ʿUmari, Yasin bin Khairallah. 1987. *al-Rawda al-fayhaʾ fi tawarikh al-nisaʾ,* edited by Rajaʾ Mahmud al-Samaraʾi. Beirut.

Unat, Fâik Resit, ed. 1943. *Abdi Tarih-i.* Ankara.

Vatin, Jean-Claude, ed. 1984. *Connaissances du Maghreb: Sciences Sociales et colonisation.* Paris: Editions du CNRS.

Volney, Comte de. 1799. *Voyage en Syrie et en Egypte Pendant les Anées 1783, 1784, 1785.* Paris: Chez Dugour et Durand.

Von Grunebaum, Gustave E. 1962. Reprint. *Medieval Islam.* Chicago: Univ. of Chicago Press.

Wakin, Jeanette A. 1972. *The Function of Documents in Islamic Law: The Chapters on Sales from Tahawiʾs Kitab al-Shurut al-Kabir.* Albany: State Univ. of New York Press.

al-Wancharissi, Ahmad ibn Yahia. 1983. *al-Miʿyar al-murib waʾl-jamaʿ al-mughrib ʿan fatawi ʿalamat Ifriqiya waʾl-Andalus waʾl-Maghrib,* edited by Muhammad Hajji. Beirut: Dar al-Gharb al-Islami.

Wemple, Suzanne F. 1987. "Sanctity and Power: The Dual Pursuit of Early Medieval Women." In *Becoming Visible: Women in European History,* edited by Renate Bridenthal, Claudia Koonz, and Susan Stuard. Boston: Houghton Mifflin.

Wilson, Rev. S. 1895. *Persian Life and Customs.* Chicago: Student Missionary.

Winter, Michael. 1992. *Egyptian Society under Ottoman Rule: 1517–1798.* London: Routledge.

Yazbak, M. 1992. "Haifa at the End of the Ottoman Rule, 1870–1914: Selected Issues in the History of Administration and Society." Ph.D. diss. Hebrew Univ.

Zarinebaf-Shahr, Fariba. 1993. "Recent English-Language Bibliography on Women in the Middle East." In *Women in Islam, From Medieval to Modern Times,* edited by Wiebke Walther. Princeton: Markus Wiener.

Ziadeh, Farhat. 1968. *Lawyers, the Rule of Law and Liberalism in Modern Egypt.* Stanford.

Zilfi, Madeline C. 1993. "Ottoman Dynastic Legitimation in the Eighteenth Century." *Journal of the American Oriental Society* 113/2:184–91.

Zuhur, Sherifa. 1992. *Revealing Veiling: Islamic Gender Ideology in Contemporary Egypt.* Albany: State Univ. of New York Press.

Index